Methodists and Women's Education in Ontario, 1836–1925

Situating the evolution of Methodist education for women in Ontario within the larger social and cultural context, *Methodists and Women's Education in Ontario* describes the often unintended and unforeseen forces unleashed by women's education and the amibivalent and sometimes reactionary education policy created in response to the threat an educated woman posed to society, the church, and the family.

Selles documents nearly a century of Methodist education, from the early seminary movement in Upper Canada, through the establishment of ladies' colleges, to the admission of women to the university. She reconstructs what life was like for women at these institutions and highlights changing ideologies, curricula, and views on women's education, as well as introducing some of the unique personalities who shaped Methodist higher education.

Selles concludes that by attempting to create an ideal Christian woman through education, Methodist educational structures consciously created and imposed a class-based gender ideology.

JOHANNA M. SELLES is a research fellow at Yale Divinity School.

McGill-Queen's Studies in the History of Religion
G.A. Rawlyk, Editor

Volumes in this series have been supported by the Jackman Foundation of Toronto.

1 Small Differences
Irish Catholics and Irish Protestants, 1815–1922
An International Perspective
Donald Harman Akenson

2 Two Worlds
The Protestant Culture of Nineteenth-Century Ontario
William Westfall

3 An Evangelical Mind
Nathanael Burwash and the Methodist Tradition in Canada, 1839–1918
Marguerite Van Die

4 The Dévotes
Women and Church in Seventeenth-Century France
Elizabeth Rapley

5 The Evangelical Century
College and Creed in English Canada from the Great Revival to the Great Depression
Michael Gauvreau

6 The German Peasants' War and Anabaptist Community of Goods
James M. Stayer

7 A World Mission
Canadian Protestantism and the Quest for a New International Order, 1918–1939
Robert Wright

8 Serving the Present Age
Revivalism, Progressivism, and the Methodist Tradition in Canada
Phyllis D. Airhart

9 A Sensitive Independence
Canadian Methodist Women Missionaries in Canada and the Orient, 1881–1925
Rosemary R. Gagan

10 God's Peoples
Covenant and Land in South Africa, Israel, and Ulster
Donald Harman Akenson

11 Creed and Culture
The Place of English-Speaking Catholics in Canadian Society, 1750–1930
Terrence Murphy and Gerald Stortz, editors

12 Piety and Nationalism
Lay Voluntary Associations and the Creation of an Irish-Catholic Community in Toronto, 1850–1895
Brian P. Clarke

13 Amazing Grace
Studies in Evangelicalism in Australia, Britain, Canada, and the United States
George Rawlyk and Mark A. Noll, editors

14 Children of Peace
W. John McIntyre

15 A Solitary Pillar
Montreal's Anglican Church and the Quiet Revolution
John Marshall

16 Padres in No Man's Land
Canadian Chaplains and the Great War
Duff Crerar

17 Christian Ethics and Political Economy in North America
A Critical Analysis of U.S. and Canadian Approaches
P. Travis Kroeker

18 Pilgrims in Lotus Land
Conservative Protestantism in British Columbia, 1917–1981
Robert K. Burkinshaw

19 Through Sunshine and Shadow
The Woman's Christian Temperance Union, Evangelicalism, and Reform in Ontario, 1874–1930
Sharon Cook

20 Church, College, and Clergy
A History of Theological Education at Knox College, Toronto, 1844–1994
Brian J. Fraser

21 The Lord's Dominion
The History of Canadian Methodism
Neil Semple

22 A Full-Orbed Christianity
The Protestant Churches and Social Welfare in Canada, 1900–1940
Nancy Christie and Michael Gauvreau

23 Evangelism and Apostasy
The Evolution and Impact of Evangelicals in Modern Mexico
Kurt Bowen

24 The Chignecto Covenanters
A Regional History of Reformed Presbyterianism in New Brunswick and Nova Scotia, 1827 to 1905
Eldon Hay

25 Methodists and Women's Education in Ontario, 1836–1925
Johanne Selles

26 Puritanism and Historical Controversy
William Lamont

Methodists and Women's Education in Ontario 1836–1925

JOHANNA M. SELLES

McGill-Queen's University Press
Montreal & Kingston • London • Buffalo

ISBN 0-7735-1443-0

Legal deposit fourth quarter 1996
Bibliothèque nationale du Québec

Printed in Canada on acid-free paper

This book has been published with the help of a grant from the Humanities and Social Sciences Federation of Canada, using funds provided by the Social Sciences and Humanities Research Council of Canada.

McGill-Queen's University Press is grateful to the Canada Council for support of its publishing program.

Canadian Cataloguing in Publication Data

Selles, Johanna M. (Johanna Maria), 1952–
Methodists and women's education in Ontario, 1836–1925
(McGill-Queen's studies in the history of religion ; 25)
Includes bibliographical references and index.
ISBN 0-7735-1443-0
1. Methodist women – Education – Ontario – History.
2. Methodist universities and colleges – Ontario – History. I. Title. II. Series.
LC1768.05S44 1996 376'.9713'08827 C96-900395-1

Typeset in Palatino 10/12
by Caractéra inc., Quebec City

To the memory of my parents,
Geraldine R. Akkerman (1921–1988)
and Bert Selles (1915–1993),
and my uncle, Otto S. Akkerman (1922–1993)

Contents

TABLES

Acknowledgments

I wish to acknowledge support from a number of people, without whose help this book would have been an impossible task. The staff of the United Church Archives in Toronto provided not only professional assistance but also friendship and encouragement. I acknowledge the aid of the following individuals: Helen Luchka at Trafalgar Castle School, Whitby; Arie Kortrijk, Albert College, Belleville; Heather Meier, formerly of Alma College, St Thomas; Don McLeod at the Archives of Ontario; Mary Maclean at the Cobourg Public Library; Brian Winter at the Whitby Historical Society; the staff of the Special Collections, Hamilton Public Library; Elizabeth Swain, Special Collections Librarian and University Archivist, Wesleyan University Library, Middletown, Connecticut; Stanley Kozaczka, Director of Library Services, Cazenovia College; Aida Graff, Dean of Women, Victoria University; the staff of the E.J. Pratt Library, Victoria University; and the staff of the University of Toronto Archives. In addition, a number of individuals patiently answered my questions or checked details: Edward Zaragoza, Methodist Library Associate, Drew University, Madison, New Jersey; W.J. Musgrove, Prince Edward County Archives; Mary O'Brien, Syracuse University Archives, Syracuse, New York; and Elizabeth Osborne, Secretary, Benson Building, University of Toronto.

Secondly, I would like to thank people who helped me to clarify my ideas or who provided administrative services, as well as personal support. My adviser, Alison Prentice, was in every sense a mentor, and I am grateful for her guidance. Professor John Moir encouraged me to work on Alma College. Ruth Pierson, Robert Gidney, Wyn Millar, Marjorie Theobald, Elizabeth Smyth, Jo La Pierre, Phyllis Airhart, and Marguerite Van Die were influential in my reaching the final goal. Kate Rousmaniere generously shared her research notes. Friends and colleagues at the Ontario Institute for Studies in Education and the University of Toronto, as well as at Southern Connecticut State University, provided moral support. Yale University Divinity School graciously allowed me to be a research fellow during 1990–92 and 1995–96. The administrative staff of the Department of History and Philosophy of Education at the Ontario Institute for Studies in Education, particularly Margaret Brennan, helped me to finish this work from a distance. The support of the Social Sciences and Humanities Research Council during the year 1990–91 is gratefully acknowledged.

Thirdly, this book was a family project. Regular phone calls and letters from family members provided essential life support, and I thank all the members of the Selles and Roney clans and their spouses for their patience and humour. My deepest thanks are reserved for John Roney, who lived with this project on a daily basis. Renata Roney provides a balance to life, as well as creative inspiration, and I thank her for helping me to understand the love that inspired some individuals throughout the ages to sacrifice for the education of daughters.

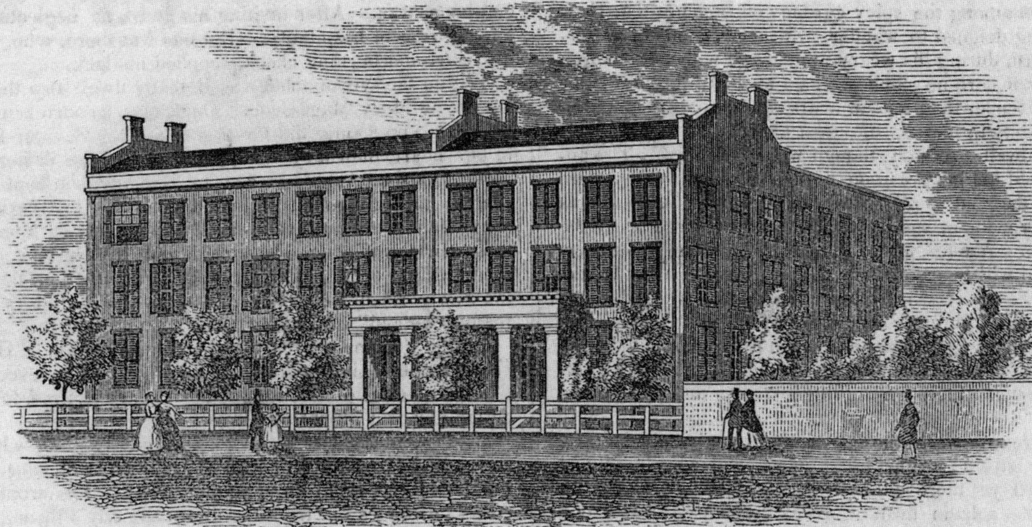

BURLINGTON LADIES' ACADEMY.

We present our Readers, in the present number, with a Cut of the *Burlington Ladies' Academy*. The Building is pleasantly situated on the corner of King and Bay Streets, commanding a fine view of the Bay, and the Picturesque Scenery of the Mountain, Heights, and surrounding country. It is four stories, including basement, and presents two fronts, as represented, 122 and 114 feet. The Dormitories, 48 in number, are sufficiently spacious to accommodate comfortably two occupants each. Besides the Drawing, Library and Philosophical rooms, the former of which is 60 by 24; it contains four School rooms, Music rooms, Painting room, &c., &c , affording ample accommodations for every department of a well organized School. The building is warmed with heated air, a much more safe, convenient, comfortable and healthy method, than by stoves.

Burlington Ladies' Academy (*Source*: *The Calliopean,* courtesy of UCA)

The Wesleyan Ladies' College,

Established HAMILTON, CANADA. A.D. 1861.

DIEU ET MON DROIT

TO THE FRIENDS OF LITERATURE,

Greeting.

Be it known, That Miss Lilly Hardy having completed the prescribed course of study and Sustained Satisfactory Examinations is admitted to the title and degree of Mistress of Liberal Arts and is entitled to our highest Consideration together with all the rights and privileges usually granted to those advanced to the said title and degree here or elsewhere IN TESTIMONY of which we have caused the signatures of the Governor, Principal and Professors with the Corporate Seal of the Institution to be hereunto affixed.

Issued from the College Buildings June A.D. 1887

A. Burns, D.D., LL.D. Principal

George Ross, B.A.

Graham Chambers, B.A.

Professors

A. Burns, D.D., LL.D. Governor

Diploma for Lilly Hardy, who graduated in June 1887 with a mistress of liberal arts degree from the Wesleyan Ladies' College of Hamilton (Courtesy of HPL)

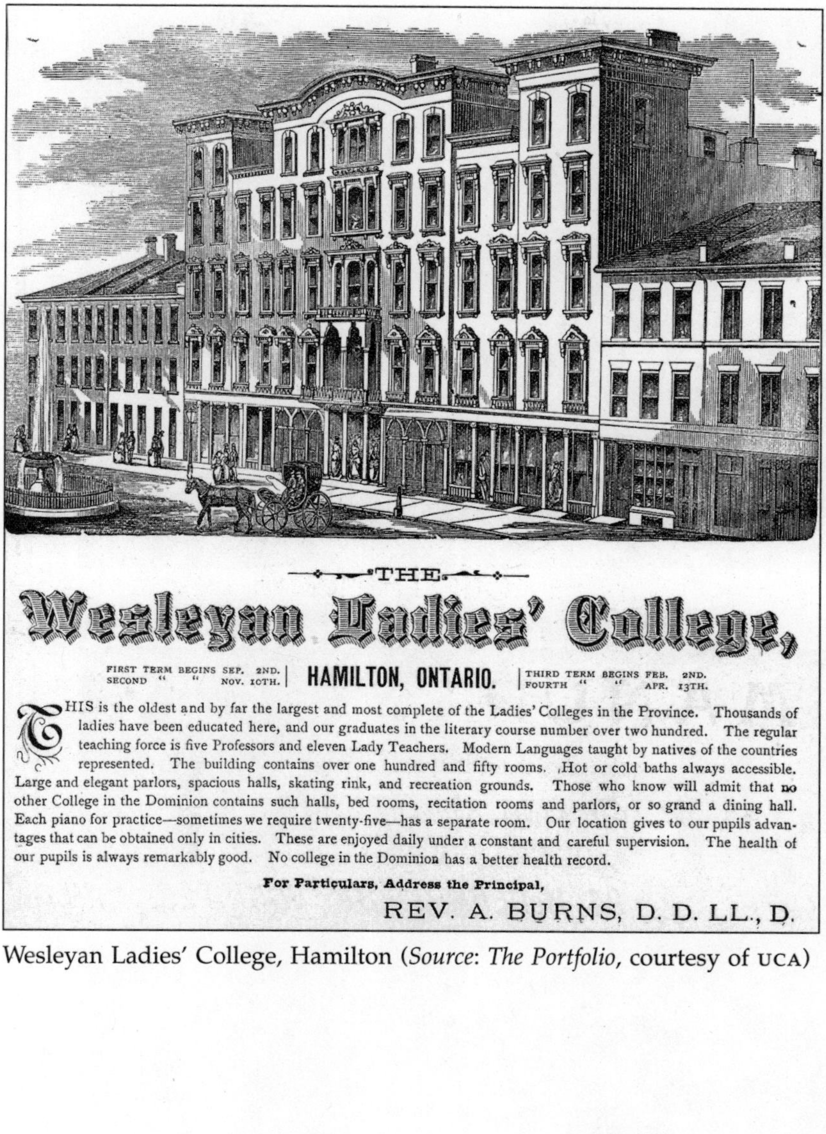

Wesleyan Ladies' College, Hamilton (*Source*: *The Portfolio,* courtesy of UCA)

Two students at the Wesleyan Ladies' College, Hamilton (Courtesy of HPL)

Graduate of the Wesleyan Ladies' College, Hamilton (Courtesy of HPL)

Group of students at the Wesleyan Ladies' College, Hamilton (Courtesy of HPL)

Wesleyan Ladies' College, Class Portrait, 1878. Standing from left to right: Margaret Rutledge, Gussie Harrison, Sophie Hilyard; seated: Emma Rice (daughter of the principal), May Currie, Alice Evans, Ella Howell, Ada Rosebrough; seated on rug: Serena Healy, Jennie Beynon, Annie Pears (Courtesy of UCA)

Wesleyan Ladies College, ca 1886

Women's and Men's Reading Rooms, Birge-Carnegie Library, Victoria University, ca 1910 (Courtesy UCA)

Methodists and Women's Education in Ontario, 1836–1925

Introduction

The emergence in the nineteenth century of a movement favouring women's education has only recently been the subject of scholarly notice.[1] In Britain, Australia, and North America, both Protestant and Catholic champions of women's education built and managed schools for young women. Promoters of women's education in the province now known as Ontario were influenced by this movement. Methodists, Baptists, Presbyterians, and Catholics all established schools in present-day Ontario to meet the needs of Christian young women, who, it was believed, were better served by the private, rather than the public, school system. These students quickly proved their abilities in the arena of higher education. Colleges were built or male universities opened up to create room for enthusiastic women scholars.

The Methodists of Upper Canada started schools for male and female students in a spirit of optimism. Historian A.B. McKillop, in his study of higher education in the province, describes how this optimistic mood was characteristic of mid-Victorian mentality and was based on a belief in the benefits of materialism and in the unlimited expansion of the market economy. Combined with this faith in progress was the ethos of evangelicalism that shaped higher education in nineteenth-century Ontario.[2] Methodist optimism was based not only on the material profits that the rural, but gradually industrializing, society would yield but also on church growth. The denomination experienced a steady increase from the mid-nineteenth to the early twentieth century. In 1871 there were 578,161 Methodists, or 15.6 per cent of the Canadian population, whereas in 1901 there were 916,866 Methodists, or 17.1 per cent of the population.[3] Increased education for the clergy as well as for church members, in addition to an active building program for churches and schools, expressed this optimism. The style and culture of Methodism was changing, and the opening up of higher education for women was one of those changes. Investment in the education of young women paid dividends in a stable family and in church membership. Furthermore, the social position of those who could afford to send daughters to school or offer them as desirable marriage partners was affirmed. Farm families made considerable sacrifices to allow their daughters to attend school, particularly when the daughters were needed for productive labour or for the care of younger children. By contrast, daughters of affluent urban families could easily be spared to attend school. David Tyack and Elizabeth Hansot describe the American high school as "a moratorium between the parental and the conjugal family, a safe and productive way to spend youthful years, free from the dangers of the workplace, and rich in cultural and human associations."[4]

Methodist theology in the mid to late nineteenth century evolved as a result of a variety of transcontinental influences.[5] As historian William Westfall observes, reason was gradually valued over the emotionalism of revivals, and sudden conversion was emphasized less than gradualism and good works. According to Westfall, "the old revivalist had been replaced by the evangelical romantic."[6] Central to the belief system of the romantic was the centrality of the conscience, something that needed growth and discipline to attain its full development.[7] Education played a central role in the evolution of moral conscience. Although conscience was common to both men and women, its ultimate application was defined by specific gender expectations. Furthermore, the gradual transformation of Methodist theology in mid- to late-nineteenth-century Ontario ultimately undermined the transcendent implications of God and assumed that God worked through nature and history – immanence – instead of through miraculous means.[8] Restricting the realm of divine interaction in human history created a greater space for human action and moral responsibility. This change in turn inspired a tremendous drive for moral and social improvement, which opened up many opportunities for educated women. Late-nineteenth-century evangelical theology would further transform the kingdom of God until it was located firmly on earth. As Richard Allen's seminal study of the social gospel argues, adherents of that movement sought to establish the kingdom of God on earth in response to concrete human needs.[9]

Although the gender implications of the social gospel have until recently been ignored by historians, such liberal theology influenced Methodist education for women by increasing the "call" to serve in settlement houses, temperance work, immigrant work, education, and other socially oriented projects. Our understanding of the movement for moral and social reform has been expanded by Mariana Valverde's study of English Canada.[10] She links the motivating principle of mid-nineteenth-century temperance reform to the social-purity movement at the turn of the century. Both movements called for the moral reform of state, civil society, the family, and the individual with the goal of cleansing or purifying society. The similarities between the rhetoric of these movements allowed participants to work in both the Woman's Christian Temperance Union and the social-reform movement.[11]

Although historians tend to focus on one social organization or cause and leave overlapping allegiances to the imagination, several recent studies have shown the fruitfulness of examining the connections between social movements. Nancy Hewitt's investigation of nineteenth-century Rochester, New York, accounts for both class and religious motivation in a variety of social movements.[12] Similarly, the excellent study of the British middle class by Lenore Davidoff and Catharine Hall challenges the utility of public versus private distinctions and analyses in depth the relationship between class, religion, and gender.[13] Historian Anne Firor Scott has examined multiple women's assocations in the United States and has argued that social reform cannot be reduced merely to a desire to control the growing working class. Both the amount of crossover between organizations and the degree of religious commitment must be considered.[14] Central to our understanding of social movements is the role of education in expanding women's vision of their own abilities and in creating space for new professional and volunteer opportunities within the culture.

Although the period covered by this book witnessed radically new and exciting opportunities for women, a note of caution should be introduced lest their achievements be interpreted in triumphalist terms. Women's accomplishments in and by means of education were gained in spite of resistance and resentment by some who opposed change in the prevailing gender ideology. Structural limits were rarely altered or challenged by women themselves, who were culturally bound by norms of propriety. The patriarchy that graciously allowed them to partake at the well of learning also ensured that they would not attain ultimate control over the source. As students and teachers in the field of higher education, Methodist women submitted to decisions made by male principals and boards, and they attempted to turn the pain they endured into a quest for deeper spirituality and perfection. Unlike their modern and post-modern descendants, Methodist women of the nineteenth and early twentieth centuries encountered suffering, including the loneliness and frustration of working within male-dominated educational institutions, as a normative element of earthly life, and they did not expect to be exempt from its bitter hold. This dignified acceptance of unjust structures meant that Methodist education remained in the control of male authority and developed without the valuable input of some of its most experienced leaders, the women teachers and deans.

Not even the most pessimistic participant in the educational movement of the nineteenth century could have anticipated the backlash against feminism and the replacement of the ideal woman as moral guardian by an ideology emphasizing her moral weakness and theological shallowness.[15] From the expulsion of women in quest of academic seriousness from the Upper Canada Academy in 1842 to their gradual exclusion from Bible colleges in the 1940s and 1950s in the United States and Canada, women's educational privileges were vulnerable achievements, subject to revision by theological reinterpretations that ranged from an equal depravity with men to a moral superiority and later to moral inferiority and spiritual shallowness. Methodist rejection of the Calvinist doctrine of predestination placed tremendous responsibility on the individual to experience new birth and to perfect his or her nature. A.B. McKillop traces this revision in theology to the revivalist fervour at Cobourg's Victoria College in the 1840s and 1850s. Women were no longer at Victoria during this period, but similar manifestations of revivals and conversions occurred at the ladies' colleges in Cobourg and the Burlington Ladies' Academy in Hamilton. The "call to seriousness" that McKillop claims characterizes academic life at Victoria was also shared by students in ladies' colleges during these decades. Gradually, they felt the shift in responsibility from the development of their individual consciousness to finding their place in society. Evangelicalism changed from a specific religious disposition "centred in the Christian revelation to a more general (and ultimately more secular) moralism concerned with ethical conduct, with 'culture.'"[16] Middle-class Methodist women sought to find their place in society by applying their education to the realms of home and church, as well as to wage labour in teaching, clerical jobs, and health care.[17] In the late-Victorian and Edwardian period, the "New Woman," armed with an education, was busy making a lifelong career for herself.[18] As historian Patricia Hill notes, the New Woman of the latter 1890s and early 1900s was a doer, even though the realm of her activity was circumscribed by societal expectations for women.[19]

In the 1880s women students were gradually allowed to study at Victoria College, a reversal of the policy that Egerton Ryerson had set in 1842, when the Upper Canada Academy had changed its name to Victoria and its purpose to the education of males only. The pioneer women students at Victoria College in the 1880s demanded privileges that were gradually being extended to women in other colleges of the province at the same time. At the University of Toronto, women had requested access and were allowed to take matriculation examinations by 1877 and to attend classes by 1884.[20] McKillop attributes the new policy, not so much to a transformation of male attitudes, as to a combination of increased provincial school attendance, new vocational opportunities for women, and the persistence of several courageous women.[21] Certainly, women's admission to Victoria in the mid-1880s was less a distinct policy change than an extension of privileges to a hardy minority who were very careful not to intrude on male territory. Educators such as Mary Electa Adams, who became the lady principal of the Wesleyan Ladies' College in Hamilton and a noted educator, and Margaret Addison, who served as dean of women at Victoria College, had clear notions of what could be done for women's education. Their vision included a woman's university or college and residential facilities with rich cultural, religious, intellectual, and social traditions. The powerful example of similar attainments in the United States and Britain increased expectations for supporters of women's higher education in Ontario. The failure of this grand vision must be examined in the light of the many successes that were achieved.

Success stories in Methodist women's higher education include creative developments in the curricula of the ladies' colleges. Anna Sonser argues persuasively that literary studies at the Hamilton Wesleyan Ladies' College were more progressive and creative than those at the University of Toronto in the same period.[22] Although little is known about ladies' college alumnae and their experiences, these alumnae contributed in numerous ways to the social and cultural life of their communities. Their influence can be traced in institutions such as the Hamilton Art Gallery, conservatories of music and music pedagogy, art schools, schools of nursing and home economics, libraries, education, church life, and social services.

Caught between the progressive and the conservative, the practical and the ornamental, ladies' colleges nevertheless provided a vital educational option for hundreds, indeed thousands, of Ontario girls. Continuing financial constraints created a dilemma for the colleges and inhibited some of the pedagogical developments that might otherwise have taken place. Although the Wesleyan Ladies' College eventually closed in 1898, more than two thousand students passed through its doors during the years of its operation. Ladies' colleges such as the Wesleyan provided cultural legitimacy to the notion of women's higher education. Although this education was desirable, less-affluent parents with several children to educate chose the public school alternative. Armed with academic preparation gained in either public secondary schools or ladies' colleges, a slow but steady trickle of women entered the all-male Victoria in the 1880s, until their numbers in the twentieth century equalled and then finally surpassed those of male students.[23]

Methodist education for women responded to a changing society. Ladies' colleges, for example, were established at a time of growing differentiation in class relations in the 1850s and 1860s. The influence of an increasingly visible middle class was felt in other aspects of educational development. Bruce Curtis notes in his study of school inspectors that the rise of bureaucratic administration was driven by the "moral, cultural, and political interests of the rising middle classes."[24] Similarly, the boards of Methodist schools represented the clergy and business élite of their respective towns. Although concern for the youth of the denomination was a clear motivating factor, the establishment of grand schools for women was also a tribute to women's success, status, and permanence as members of the middle class. The lack of financial support that endangered the continuance of the schools was perceived as a threat to both the class standing of its supporters and to the essence of their belief in progress.

In her study of working-class women in nineteenth-century England, Jane Purvis notes that the articulation of a cultural ideal for middle-class young ladies and ladies resulted in a subsequent delineation of the ideal working-class woman. Alison Prentice similarly observes in *The School Promoters* that education not only provided a respectable middle class, but also created a safe and disciplined lower class.[25] The terms "young lady" and "lady" reflected certain feminine ideals. A young lady did not engage in paid work but was assumed to be economically dependent upon a father or other male relative. Her education prepared her for the goal of her life, which was to be a wife and mother. Ladies, the married and mature form of young ladies, became household managers who engaged in unpaid philanthropic work and followed extensive rituals of etiquette and manners. The perfect wife provided emotional support for her husband and children, and the perfect lady was an external symbol of the husband's success.[26] Education played an important role in providing the knowledge that young ladies would need to assume their function as wife and mother. In England as well as in North America, the educated college woman would reject aspects of this ideal as she increasingly chose wage labour, postponed marriage, and challenged limits to her political and social rights. Yet the values that many supporters of women's education hoped to instil in students still included tidiness, industriousness, patience, humility, modesty, obedience, and unselfishness.

The years covered by this study (1836–1925) witnessed tremendous changes in the Methodist denomination. Future Victoria College principal Egerton Ryerson's tours of England in the 1820s to raise money for the Upper Canada Academy stand in stark contrast with the late-nineteenth-century philanthropy of Toronto-based Methodist millionaires such as the Massey, Harris, Flavelle, and Wood families. Although the ultimate goal of Methodist higher education for women was defined by the expectations of marriage and motherhood, it must be remembered that commercial success of immense proportions facilitated the achievement of this middle-class ideal. Michael Bliss's study of Joseph Flavelle provides an excellent analysis of this closely interconnected group of Methodist millionaires, whose business acumen coincided with the development of Canada's resources, utilities, railroads, and trade. The links between economics, religion, and education are evident in the life of Flavelle's associate George Cox, who served as bursar of Victoria College, president of the Ontario Ladies' College in Whitby, and vice-president of the Ontario Prohibition Alliance. He was also president of the Central Canada Loan and Savings Company, the Bank of Commerce, and Canada Life, thereby in 1900 controlling assets totalling approximately seventy million dollars. His wife played an active role as treasurer of the Victoria Women's Residence and Educational Association. Motivation for the support of education was linked to the need for training for new roles in industrial society. Work habits, discipline, and industry were taught through education. For women, manners, taste, and civility would help their husbands achieve financial success.[27]

These Methodist millionaires created the infrastructure for much of Toronto's banking, insurance, retail, and commercial development. Although many of them had only a limited education, they strongly supported educational institutions and brought university graduates into their businesses. Their wives, who primarily defined their identity in relation to their status as married women, not only had the leisure to pursue women's educational organizations, but were able to make substantial donations in support of women's education. Like their husbands, they had little firsthand experience of higher education, but the ideals of the movement captured their imagination. For the first generation of women at Victoria, Methodist women provided important social contacts to students away from home. It was inevitable, however, that the boundaries between philanthropy and power would become blurred. Combined with their limited experience of women's higher education, this unclear division of power would create conflict between the increasingly professionalized role of a woman dean and the women's auxiliary association, which helped to manage the women's residence. Issues of power and control would be fought out between women donors and women educators, as well as between women leaders and the male administration of Victoria College. Money and power was never far from the latent or manifest agenda at Victoria, but the greater priority given to the education of male students and theologues meant that gains for women were severely limited, despite their numbers and achievements. Even in cases where bequests were made for the use of women students, the terms of the endowments were changed, as is evident in the following cases: the Flavelle homestead, donated for the use of women students, which was absorbed by the law school; the Wood residence for women, which became a coeducational student union; and the Lillian Massey School of Household Science, which was eventually absorbed by other departments. None of these bequests for the use of women students created a lasting heritage for them at the University of Toronto.

Methodist education for women shared many of the cultural values that were part of, for instance, Catholic education for women. Assumptions concerning woman's true nature and her capacity to do good affected both the content and the direction of women's education. Once they were successfully involved in higher education, the debate did not end. The hundred years covered by this study demonstrate the recurring and controversial nature of women's education. Secularization allowed for the rise of consumer values in the early twentieth century, which ultimately supported a conservative vision for the middle-class woman. As Carroll Smith-Rosenberg observes, the public world was increasingly closed to the New Women, who, despite the educational advantages they had gained, failed to obtain the real economic and institutional power with which to "wrest hegemony from men and so enforce their vision of a gender-free world."[28]

In the following chapters, I examine the story of women's education under Methodist auspices in order to explore the religious and gender ideology that informed this education. Although Methodist education in the early form of ladies' colleges was clearly intended to prepare women for conservative roles in the church and the family, to what extent did the experience contribute to the development of what Gerda Lerner describes as the "creation of a feminist consciousness?"[29] Advocates of education and opportunities for women did not necessarily articulate a feminist goal, but their efforts may have played a part in the foundation of a feminist world-view. Lerner characterizes Emma Willard, Catharine Beecher, and Mary Lyon in the United States as pragmatic institution builders who proclaimed themselves opposed to women's rights, but nevertheless educated a significant group of community leaders.[30] Education clearly unleashed forces that were often quite unintended and unforeseen by leaders of the Methodist educational movement. Fear of these changes and of an unknown future for women and the family created an ambivalent and often reactionary educational policy. Yet even Methodist schooling could not reverse trends in the culture at large, as forces such as consumerism, secularization, and industrialization shaped the life of middle-class families and individuals. The conscious creation of a class-based gender ideology imposed by means of Methodist educational structures will be examined in the chapters to follow. In Chapter 1, I establish the historiographical context for the study of women's higher education. Chapter 2 examines the Upper Canada Academy in Cobourg and the two female seminaries that opened to meet the needs of female students after the academy closed its doors to women in 1842. How the Methodist Episcopal coeducational model of Albert College affected the content or experience of female education is the focus of chapter 3. To illuminate the competing interests of these institutions, the relations between the Methodist Episcopal Church and the Wesleyan Methodist Church are examined, particularly with respect to the competition between the denominations over educational matters.

Chapter 4 studies the founders, faculty, and students who participated in the early ladies' college movement. The movement, which gained strength between 1860 and 1880, will be situated in relation to the early history of academies and seminaries for women generally. The concept of womanhood as it was defined in the term "female" education in the seminary will be compared to the ideal of "ladies'" education in the college. The gendered nature of the educational message will be explored. In chapter 5 I consider the ideology and curricula of the ladies' colleges as expressed in Alma College, the Ontario Ladies' College, and the Wesleyan Ladies' College. Chapter 6 studies some of the remarkable personalities who contributed to the shape of Methodist higher education, while tracing in closer detail the demise of one of the colleges and the changing character of the other two as they moved into the twentieth century. Chapters 7 and 8 focus on women's experience at the coeducational university Victoria College in Cobourg after 1877 and following its move to Toronto in 1892. The career of Margaret Addison, graduate of Victoria, teacher at a ladies' college, and dean of women at Victoria, will be examined in this section. Her life combines traditional Methodist ideals with a sense that women deserved more direct power over their college lives. The success of the educational experiment at Victoria revived the debate about the propriety of women's education, which was rooted in the early-nineteenth-century seminaries and academies. The threat that an educated woman posed to society, the church, and the family resulted in a reassessment of Methodist educational policy. The resulting ambivalence about the goals of women's education undermined some of the achievements of this education. Despite this ambivalence, women graduates embraced the possibilities that their education opened to them and pursued a variety of professional and familial goals.

This book relies on diverse archival sources in attempting to reconstruct life as it was at the ladies' colleges and the university. The church and secular press, college yearbooks and newspapers, board and senate minutes, photographs, autograph albums, sermons, and diaries were used to re-create this period.[31] Yet the fragments that remain bear witness to the enormous amount of material which has disappeared. Half of Victoria's records on women students has been lost.[32] The need for careful collection and conservation of the papers of women students has often been ignored or has been unrecognized by individuals, families, and institutions. Children whose mothers were ladies' college graduates have often been unaware that this education was a significant achievement, and some have described it as merely a finishing-school experience. Only a few pages constitute the Nellie Greenwood papers in the United Church Archives, and the remainder are still in the possession of the family.[33] The lost portions of the Mary Electa Adams diary have not been found.[34] The Ontario Ladies' College, now Trafalgar Nelson School, stores its historical materials in a cardboard box. Student registers from the college were either lost or are not available to researchers. The Whitby Historical Society archives has collected the bulk of the material that now survives for the OLC. Alma College has closed its archive until further notice, pending legal action concerning the school's future. Individual student records are either unavailable in the case of the Wesleyan Ladies' College and the Ontario Ladies' College or inaccessible in the case of Alma. The Albert College archives contains a large quantity of unaccessioned materials, and the diary of one of its most important lady principals, Ella Gardiner, has not been located. The fragile nature of some of the materials, such as school newspapers and catalogues, demands immediate conservation efforts, or these too will be lost to future researchers.

A second problem compounds the loss or fragile state of existing records. Women's education was often secondary in importance to the focus on male education. Rarely did the women who taught in the ladies' colleges speak publicly about the nature of female education. This task was left to the prominent ministers and businessmen who administered and promoted the colleges. Yet, despite this silence, it is possible to reconstruct much about the women students and teachers and replace the silence with a critical examination of women's education as it was sponsored by the Methodists in nineteenth- and early-twentieth-century Ontario.

1 "The Education of Our Daughters"

Rebecca Hurlburt was born in 1802, and after attending the "ordinary schools" of her neighbourhood, she proceeded to the Upper Canada Academy in Cobourg to "prepare for a life of usefulness." She had been converted at an early age and was known as a "sincere, earnest Christian girl and woman."[1] A portion of her early life had apparently been devoted to teaching in the Ojibway mission schools. The register of women boarders at the Upper Canada Academy listed Hurlburt's residence as Prescott and noted that she had registered in March 1839 and again in September that year.[2] According to her obituary, she would have been thirty-seven years old during the year she was at the school, well above the average age of 16.2 years for the twenty women boarders whose ages were recorded for 1839–40; the next oldest was twenty-four and the youngest twelve. A few years earlier, in 1836, students had paid £22 for board, in addition to £1.5 for tuition in the "higher branches" and £1–2 for extras, such as French, drawing, painting, and music. Available subjects for female students included English grammar, geography, arithmetic, astronomy, belles-lettres, and natural philosophy.[3]

Scant records make it difficult to construct the details of Rebecca Hurlburt's life and of many other girls like her who sought an education in the nineteenth century. How she and her classmates experienced life at the coeducational Upper Canada Academy and how later classes of students fared in separate female academies are among the topics to be explored in this book. The register noted that she took English, "higher branches," and drawing. Students were requested to bring their own sheets and towels to the school.[4] Hurlburt and the other women students would have been supervised by a "preceptress" and taught by a "lady-teacher." The year that she attended the school, she was under the supervision of Maria Boulter.[5] The total number of women students for the year that Hurlburt attended is unclear; however, Nathanael Burwash noted that there were seventy-four women to ninety-six men in 1840 and forty-eight women to ninety-four men in 1841.[6]

One can only speculate on how Rebecca Hurlburt would have reflected on her education before her death in 1890. She might have expressed enthusiasm at the opening of educational possibilities for women at a time when parents had the choice to send their daughters to the coeducational common schools, to hire a tutor, or to overlook formal education altogether. She might have heard many of the debates about women's physical and mental limitations in relation to education, the appropriateness of different subjects, and the propriety of mixing male with female students. Versions of these questions reappeared with the steadfastness of perennials. The performance of women students at Victoria after 1880 may have proved their abilities, but it did not silence critics of women's education. Hurlburt's work among the Ojibways reflects an independance and a personal sense of vocation. Her choice of career followed by additional education was presumably dictated by the opportunities available to her, a pattern that was reversed for most participants in the Methodist education studied here. The opportunities for a waged career and/or rejection of traditional marriage created consternation among observers and critics of women's education. The possible subversion of the middle-class woman's career pattern of wife and mother was only later considered a threat to femininity and to the cause of women's education. Rebecca Hurlburt might also have reflected on the changes within her denomination, the competition between its branches, and the formalization of its forms of worship. She no doubt witnessed the increasing urbanization of Ontario life, the transformation of evangelicalism by an increasing emphasis on a social gospel, and the establishment of a middle class. The questions that the life of a student such as Rebecca Hurlburt present are the focus of this and following chapters.

EDUCATION AND THE METHODIST CHURCH

The history of denominationally sponsored education in nineteenth-century Ontario has been documented in several general and some more-focused histories of education.[7] Although these works generally acknowledge the presence of women in denominational schools, the story of support for, the development of, and the experience of women's education in Protestant circles has been only partially told, and many sources are as yet little known.[8] One reason for this oversight is the fact that historians of higher education traditionally focused on schools that evolved into colleges or universities in the twentieth-century definition, thereby excluding ladies' colleges.[9] As a result, relatively little is known about the school life, curricula, teachers, or supporters of nineteenth-century women's education in Ontario, although there is a growing number of studies dealing with women in the grammar and later secondary schools or in universities across the country.[10]

The connections between education and the denominations that shaped it require reconsideration. An analysis of the relationship between Methodists and the higher education they established has until recently been largely neglected.[11] Yet as Marguerite Van Die has shown in her study of Nathanael Burwash, president and chancellor of Victoria University from 1887 to 1913, theology and education were bound together in his vision of Canadian Methodism's role in shaping education. Furthermore, evangelicalism in its broad Victorian sense, as shared by, Van Die notes, Presbyterians, Congregationalists, and members of the Church of England, posited the importance of "individual salvation through repentance and conversion and the acceptance of a disciplined life that reflected a spiritual transformation."[12] According to historian Michael Gauvreau, the theology that emerged from evangelicalism, itself a product of religious revivals between 1780 and 1860, was not a fixed doctrinal system so much as it was a loose body of beliefs and assumptions concerning God, the individual, and society.[13] Historian David Marshall defines evangelical belief by its constant reference to the fallen state, its emphasis on the need for personal conversion, and the reaffirmation of God's saving grace that characterized evangelical worship. The distinguishing feature of the evangelical faith was "its emphasis on becoming aware of God in the depths of the heart."[14] The doctrine of Christian perfection was another important belief that shaped Methodist life. According to John Wesley, the conversion experience was the crucial beginning of Christian life, but it was insufficient to ensure salvation. Conversion required subsequent growth in Christian understanding, moral sensibility, stewardship, and service to God. Education was an important part of the nurturing that faith required.[15] According to A.B. McKillop, the Methodist rejection of the Calvinist notions of predestination meant that the burden of religious faithfulness fell "directly onto the shoulders – more properly the hearts and consciences – of the individual."[16] Furthermore, the rise of education, specifically Methodist-sponsored education for women, must be understood in the culture of evangelicalism that gave rise to it. Viewed broadly, such a study can reveal relationships between religion, class, culture, and education.

Historians have often uncritically appropriated the whiggishness and evolutionary mentality of the educational movement's better-known heroes, such as Egerton Ryerson, editor of the *Christian Guardian* in 1829, principal of Victoria College in 1842, and eventually superintendent of education for Ontario, who hailed the establishment of Victoria's predecessor, Upper Canada Academy, in 1836 as the beginning of a new era. Optimism abounded at the founding of a Methodist institution whose presence was directly linked to social improvement. "We trust that it is yet destined to add much to the future prosperity of this Province, by sending forth numbers of her native and adopted children, whose intellectual and moral qualifications shall throw a halo around them, and shed an increasing lustre upon all her civil and religious institutions."[17] In a similar vein, institutional histories trace schools from their humble origins through various trials and tribulations to their eventual establishment and expansion.[18] The story of women's education, by contrast, cannot be told without reference to the confusion in cultural attitudes towards women, the debate over their capacity to learn; the ideal form of girls' education; and the nature of women's vocation. There were victories, but they were often small, unintended, or completely marginal to the action on centre stage, namely, the education of young men. Yet within that very marginality the historian can begin to understand the relationships of power and the reproduction of these relationships through the medium of education.[19]

Traditional approaches to the history of education, then, have neglected an important aspect of its development in Ontario. The champions, as well as the enemies, of women's education remain unknown, and the question of educating women and the important relationship of their schooling to the politics and economics of education in the province is still unaddressed. Consequently, the history of higher education in denominational colleges is read as a gradual exchange of privileges among men, mixed with an inevitable degree of secularism, gradually resulting in cooperation between the male-dominated universities and the provincial government.

Denominational education in Ontario for both sexes took place in a constantly shifting geopolitical setting, reflected in the frequent changes to the province's name. First, British North America was the term for what was to become Canada. From 1791 until 1841 the province was known as Upper Canada; from 1841 until 1867 it was called Canada West. In 1791 Upper Canada had a population of about 20,000 (one-half white settlers and one-half Natives). By 1850 Canada West had expanded to a population of over one million white colonists, with only approximately 10,000 Natives. After the early settlement of New France, immigration to British North America had primarily originated in the British Isles, but in the 1780s Loyalists from the Thirteen Colonies who supported Britain and opposed the American Revolution made up the majority of newcomers. Later American settlers, without Loyalist backgrounds, arrived between 1791 and 1812. Finally, from that date to the 1850s ever-increasing waves of migrants arrived from England, Scotland, Ireland, and Wales, propelled by the end of the Napoleonic Wars.[20]

Upper Canada before the War of 1812 was characterized by such occupations as agriculture,[21] trapping, and hunting, supplemented by lumbering. Yet even before the end of the eighteenth century, a social élite of Loyalists, Scottish merchants, and officers from England and Scotland had formed in towns along Lake Ontario. This élite supported the Church of England's right to dominance in the area. American immigrants, because of restriction on landownership resulting from the War of 1812, took a lead in industry and business.[22] By the 1840s and 1850s the economy, with a predominantly agrarian base, now included a growing number of town-based occupations. An alliance formed between the new middle class of merchants and businessmen and the professional gentry in the towns. Churches were built, newspapers proliferated, and schools were organized. The religious composition of Canada West in 1841 was approximately 22 per cent Anglican, 20 per cent Presbyterian, 17 per cent Methodist, and 14 per cent Roman Catholic.[23] Commercial development based on settlement and wheat exports helped to establish Toronto as a commercial centre. Hamilton also benefited in the mid-1800s from the combination of settlement and wheat, as well as from flour exports. The population of Toronto in 1851 reached 30,800 and in Hamilton, 14,000.[24] The increase in commerce witnessed by the development of banks, trade with wholesalers, and growing numbers of stores in the cities presumably affected the population's perception of the need for schooling to train clerks and bookkeepers. When compared to the Anglican colleges, the curriculum of Victoria College by 1842 was more diversified and practical, gradually emphasizing the sciences rather than the classics,[25] perhaps reflecting the need to train young men for the growing commercial centres.

Methodist education for women was also much affected both by this social context and by the denomination's complex and schismatic history. The Methodists of the province were spread throughout the rural areas, but were especially concentrated in the Bay of Quinte region. The Wesleyan Methodists comprised 60 per cent of the total and were generally affiliated with the English Methodists. According to church historian John Webster Grant, they had the highest social standing and the tightest organization in the denomination as a whole.[26] A second group originated with the missionary efforts of the New York Methodist Episcopal Conference in 1791. This work increased the presence of Methodist circuit riders of American origin, who were effective when dealing with American settlers but were suspect in the eyes of Loyalist or British immigrants. The American church created a separate district within the New York Conference in 1794 for the circuits in Canada, and in 1810 the Upper Canada District was incorporated in the new Genesee Conference. Through this institutional connection, American missionaries continued to make their way to Upper Canadian circuits. The work of itinerants bore fruit; by 1810 there were ten circuits in Ontario with 2,600 members.

The war of 1812, however, changed relations between the American church and its Upper Canadian circuits and accentuated the desire among Methodists in the province for independence from both English and American Methodism. A reluctance to tolerate American missionaries was rooted in a increased sense of Canadian identity and a postwar suspicion of anything American. Canadian Methodists thus decided to establish their own "connexion," the Methodist Episcopal Church in Canada. In 1829 it instituted the *Christian Guardian*, a weekly paper under the editorship of Egerton Ryerson, who in 1832 was replaced by James Richardson. Henry Ryan, an elder in Upper Canada between 1810 and 1824, subsequently led a disgruntled group to found the Canadian Wesleyan Methodist Church in 1828.

The American church was incensed by the decision of the British Wesleyan Methodists in 1832 to send missionaries to Upper Canada, a territory that it claimed as its mission field. The decision violated the terms of an 1820 agreement that had assigned Lower Canada to the care of Wesleyan missionaries and Upper Canada to the Genesee Conference. But both the government of Upper Canada and the more anti-American adherents in the province regretted this agreement. For the English Wesleyans and the local ruling compact, the decision to send missionaries was also politically motivated since the missionaries were to suppress anti-government agitation.[27] In 1833 the

English conference and the Methodist Episcopal Church of Canada re-evaluated the situation and decided to join forces to create the Wesleyan Methodist Church in Canada. The agreement included a decision to allow British Wesleyan missionaries into Upper Canada to work primarily with the Natives, but also with those white settlers who had expressed resentment towards American influences. Some Canadian Methodists fought this decision in order to keep the Wesleyans from interfering in what they considered their territory.[28] Clearly, not everyone was satisfied with the 1833 union, and by June 1834 a dissenting Methodist Episcopal Church had been organized. Within a year it had twenty-one preachers and 1,234 members. Smouldering resentment and a fight for control led to a split between the British and Canadian factions of the Wesleyan church in 1840, but they were reunited seven years later. Lay unhappiness in the years of dissent in the 1840s was expressed by a decline in Canadian Wesleyan membership, lost in some cases to the British Wesleyans, the Methodist Episcopal Church, or a third group known as the New Connexion Methodists.[29] In 1854 the Lower Canada District, which had remained connected to the British Conference, was united with the Upper Canada Conference to form the Wesleyan Methodist Church in Canada.[30] In 1874 a partial union occurred between the Methodist New Connexion and the Wesleyans. The Ecumenical Methodist Conference of 1881 urged a more comprehensive union, and three years later the remaining Methodist bodies, with the exception of groups known as the Free Methodists and the Evangelical Association, joined to form the Methodist Church.[31]

The story of the schisms and unions in the Methodist church reflects the various influences and the interference of British and American parent churches in the context of a growing sense among some Upper Canadians of the need for an indigenous church. The attitudes of school promoters towards both the United States and Britain also varied at different times from friendliness to outright hostility, a fact that in turn affected the course of Methodist education. Anti-Americanism, for example, was expressed in a tendency to hire Canadian, as opposed to American, teaching staff or in a desire to eliminate American textbooks from the curriculum. Yet the powerful example of women's education south of the border nevertheless fascinated Upper Canadian educators and provided an important source of teachers and leaders, as well as models for buildings and curricula.

Affiliation with the British Wesleyans in 1833 had resulted in a conservative influence, which subsequently limited the role of women preachers in Upper Canada, at the same time as American

Methodist Episcopal churches were moving towards greater openness and a willingness to entertain the idea of women preachers.[32] Although the Methodist church gave lip service to women's leadership, in reality this leadership had clearly defined limits. Cora Krommenhoek has explored Methodism's attitudes to gender. Ultimately, she argues, the prevailing views were that men should lead and women should follow. This rule governed both family life and women's role in the church, especially since they were not granted equal rights by the General Conference until 1918.[33] Limitations to women's full participation in church affairs were matched by a clearly prescribed ideology of women's role in the home. As Mary Ann MacFarlane observes, the Methodist church used its Sunday school movement to solidify "the church's ideological and material control and influence over Methodist women's lives."[34]

Bitterness between the several branches of Methodism was reinforced by the decision of the courts to award church property to the new Wesleyan church, rather than to the reconstituted Methodist Episcopal Church, leaving the latter with no share in either the property or the new Methodist college at Cobourg. Upper Canada Academy, later Victoria College, was thus destined to be a Wesleyan institution. The Methodist Episcopal Church continued to develop a separate identity when it established its own book room in 1844 and its own paper, the *Canada Christian Advocate*, the following year, and finally turned its attention to the establishment of an Episcopal Methodist institution of learning in 1853. A strong belief among Episcopal Methodists in the principle of voluntarism meant that all government grants had to be declined and the money for education raised from among subscribers.[35] State grants were undesirable because they made institutions dependent on the government and because they were a "dangerous exercise of patronage and often invidious distribution of public funds."[36]

In spite of this independent stance, the Methodist Episcopal Seminary opened its doors in Belleville in 1857, in the midst of a serious financial depression in Canada and the United States. The fierce adherence of the Episcopal Methodist membership to a rejection of any government grants left the school entirely dependent on its supporters, some of whom mortgaged their farms. Chapter 3 will examine how in 1866 the seminary was renamed Albert University and gained the right to grant degrees. By 1870 the school would contain faculties of arts, divinity, engineering, law, and music, in addition to a department of agriculture and a grammar school. From the beginning, the seminary had an adjoining building for female students called Alexandra College. Ladies' college students followed a separate course of study leading to a diploma. A strict physical separation of male and female students was prescribed, with the exception of social gatherings in the reception room for the purpose of developing social graces, which were chaperoned by a teacher. In 1883 Albert College renounced its degree-granting privileges and became a preparatory college linked to Victoria. The affiliation was completed just a year before the Methodist union of 1884.

METHODIST COLLEGES FOR WOMEN

Victoria College and Albert College have been seen as the two major Methodist institutions, and their histories illustrate the complex story of Methodism in Upper Canada. But they were by no means the only colleges founded by Methodists in the province. Nor were they the most important, necessarily, for the education of women. Indeed, when the Upper Canada Academy became Victoria College in 1842, women were excluded. Belief in a totally segregated education for men and women found expression in several all-female institutions. These included two Wesleyan schools run by the Hurlburts and Van Normans in Cobourg and later the Van Normans' Burlington Ladies' Academy, the Wesleyan Ladies' College in Hamilton, and the Ontario Ladies' College in Whitby. The Episcopal Methodist schools included Alexandra Ladies' College in Belleville and Alma College in St Thomas.

An important first step in Methodist-sponsored women's higher education in the province was a meeting of the building committee of the Upper Canada Academy in 1831. The committee resolved to write to the principal of Cazenovia Seminary (later College) in New York State to obtain plans and information about that school.[37] Cazenovia had opened in 1824 as a coeducational school under the auspices of the Genesee Conference of the Methodist Church. At Cobourg a similar coeducational model was adopted, and when the new academy opened in 1836, a preceptress was hired to supervise the female students.[38] The female department was advertised as a separate unit.[39] That the accommodation of women students required some adjustments is evident from the following resolution at a meeting of the management committee in 1837: "That we obviate the inconvenience of the present *out-door* arrangements in regard to the Ladies, the privy on that side be removed to the part of the fence on a line with the n.w. wing of the building – and that a covered path-way to it be formed."[40]

Despite the architectural and curricular adjustments that were made, however, the presence of women at the academy was perceived as an "inconvenience" to the ambitions of those in charge. The change from academy to college "rendered it necessary," according to the *Christian Guardian*, "to discontinue the successful Female department in the Institution."[41] In this case, the name "college" was chosen to indicate a higher level of education. It is difficult to assess the level of a school from its own definition, partly because there was a tendency for it to inflate its offerings. Historians David Tyack and Elisabeth Hansot observe that in the United States, the universe of secondary education consisted of a variety of institutions, reflected in names that included "academy," "classical school," "college," "seminary," and so on.[42] The curricula of each school must be compared in order to make any conclusive statements about the level of education, whatever name the school might be given. It is clear that the mid-century private seminaries and larger academies offered a demanding curriculum combining a solid English education with the "accomplishments."[43]

The adoption of a single-sex, male-only policy at Cobourg immediately resulted in the establishment of two schools for women: the Cobourg Female Academy under Mrs Hurlburt (formerly Maria Boulter of Montreal) and the Cobourg Ladies' Seminary under Mrs Van Norman (formerly Miss Spencer). Although both schools were broadly Wesleyan, their character was associated more with their leadership than with a particular branch of Methodism. Both women were experienced in education, and they were eventually joined in the enterprises by their husbands, who moved from their positions at the new Victoria College.[44] These two seminaries thus continued their links with the community and scholarship at Victoria. They illustrate the phenomenon of husband-and-wife teaching teams, which has been documented by Marjorie Theobald in her discussion of women's studies and the nineteenth-century ladies' college in Australia.[45] Not only did administration by a couple offer the school a combination of talents and subjects to be taught, but it simulated an ideal family atmosphere. As Theobald explains, nineteenth-century educators used the middle-class family as the setting for women's learning, which was thus guided by a father-figure and came under the close moral and physical guardianship of the mother.[46] The father-figure as head of the school was important, but the lady principal or preceptress was a crucial guide for the young girl on her path to womanhood. The contradictions between the images that emerged of the ideal mother and the ideal woman were imposed onto the picture of the ideal teacher.[47] The lady principal maintained a complex balance and enjoyed "a special dispensation of gentility in a society which frowned on women in paid employment, yet insisted that women must be educators of women." The school was also her home, a relationship that veiled her professional self in the family mode of the school. She was therefore a "symbol of moral certainty in the patriarchal social order, a reassuring intermediary in the encounter between knowledge and the female mind."[48]

These early women's seminaries, which were direct descendants of the Upper Canada Academy, were successful but short-lived. This early stage of female seminaries seems to have been largely experimental, and the schools were totally dependent on their founders for survival. They do not seem to have had a management structure that could see them through major changes, such as the departure of the principal. Furthermore, little information is available about the financial status of the schools and whether the Methodist church gave any assistance, other than official sanction.[49] The seminaries were nevertheless considered successful and were associated with a growing sense of the importance of women's education. How, indeed, did the ideal for this education change and develop, and how was this evolution expressed in the formation of grander and more enduring schools founded during the 1860s to the 1880s and in the gradual acceptance of coeducation at Victoria?

The Methodist Episcopal Church established not only Albert College, with its female department, Alexandra College, but also in 1881 opened Alma College for women only in St Thomas. The history of the two colleges illustrates the fact that distinctions between the Episcopal and the Wesleyan Methodists were not always easy to delineate. Albert Carman, a leading figure in the direction of both Albert and Alma colleges and a supporter of women's education, was educated at the Wesleyan Victoria College. The fact that he was later bishop of the Methodist Episcopal Church did not prevent him from becoming a member of the Senate of Victoria College. Because of the many connections between these communities of faith, this book will examine both the Episcopal Methodist schools and those of the Wesleyan Methodists, such as the Wesleyan Ladies' College in Hamilton, the Ontario Ladies' College in Whitby, and, after its admission of women again in the latter part of the century, Victoria University. As R.D. Gidney and W.P.J. Millar have argued, the churches were major participants in advanced education in the first half of the nineteenth century, and the Methodist church was no exception.[50] Denominational rivalry, as Gidney and Millar describe it, eventually led the Methodists, among others, to establish educational institutions that would challenge the claims of the Anglican establishment, exercised through the partially state-supported grammar schools and Upper Canada College, founded in 1830. According to Gauvreau, the Methodist and

Presbyterian churches together promoted institutions of higher learning that eventually "formed the central components of the modern Canadian university system."[51]

But as we have seen, the Methodists for a variety of reasons were concerned not just about young men but also about young women, and thus they founded both coeducational and ladies' colleges administered by male boards representing local church and business élites. Discipline, both mental and moral, through Christian education would create a gendered order that allowed for the continuation of the family and also supported the efforts of the male to secure a place in the rising middle class. The motivation to expand women's education was tied to a sense of order and to the idealization of a sphere for women, which was sanctioned by the teachings of Christian doctrine in the Methodist church. Equally, the models of educational institutions and the architecture that housed them are illustrative of the norms for relations between the sexes, whether in the single-sex female academy or in the coeducational example. It is of interest that Methodists tended to locate their schools in towns rather than in rural areas, a practice in contrast with that of their American counterparts.

The three-tier system of education that now characterizes Ontario was not in place in the years during which ladies' colleges were being established. The confusing history of schooling in the province has been greatly clarified by the historians Gidney and Millar in *Inventing Secondary Education*, which explains how the grammar and common schools were gradually transformed and by the 1870s became, respectively, the secondary and public schools. The secondary level of education was further subdivided into the high school, which was intended to provide the higher common branches, and the collegiate institute, which was envisioned as a classical school with links to the university. There were "overlapping connotations" to the words "college" and "collegiate," which carried associations to residential schools and a superior education, as well as connections to university training.[52]

A gap nevertheless existed between a school's aspirations to offer a superior education and the preparation of the students in attendance. Even at Vassar, an élite women's college in the United States, where the intentions were clearly to offer a college curriculum, the arrival in 1865 of poorly or unevenly prepared students forced the school to offer preparatory work.[53]

In Ontario the shortage of qualified students at the universities was directly related to a low "matriculation" standard, matriculation being the entrance examination required for admission. The lack of coherence between the secondary school and the university until the 1880s contributed to a lack of continuity in studies. The reform of college curricula, such as that of Queen's and Victoria, eliminated the overlap with grammar school curricula. Each of the three levels of the education system had a clearer mandate, which allowed the student to progress in a linear fashion through these tiers. The introduction of Department of Education–approved examinations and inspections helped to regularize levels within the schools but also strengthened the control of the department over curriculum and standards. As the importance of the high schools to the universities increased, "so too did the influence of the minister of education and the high school teachers' association on the admission policies of the denominational universities."[54]

Prior to this increasing standardization and clarification of functions between the public school, high school, and university levels of the educational system, the overlap in functions and the less-than-subtle attempts by Egerton Ryerson and his supporters to exclude girls from classical learning gave the ladies' colleges space to manœuvre. Yet as the provincial department gradually gained more power to standardize education and promote a non-denominational, rather than a sectarian, approach, the climate became more difficult for the ladies' colleges.[55] Furthermore, despite Ryerson's efforts to exclude girls from schools, by 1871 their presence in the secondary schools was no longer contested.[56] The perceived need for separate advanced girls' education, which had originally been a strong motivation to establish ladies' colleges, was increasingly met by the public and high schools, as well as by the collegiate institutes of the province. One could also wonder whether the basic Christian nature of society made the provincial government schools increasingly acceptable to parents, since even if the state schools were non-denominational, they were not yet secular.

During its early years the Upper Canada Academy offered a range of courses from preparatory to higher branches, while it struggled to accommodate the uneven preparation of entering students. After the academy became Victoria College in 1841 and female students were excluded, it functioned in basically the same way until 1884, when an act of the Ontario Legislature changed the corporate name to Victoria University, with government by a Board of Regents, Senate, chancellor, and vice-chancellor. Affiliation with Victoria was eventually granted to the following colleges: Albert College, Belleville; Wesleyan Ladies' College, Hamilton; Ontario Ladies' College, Whitby; Alma Ladies' College, St Thomas; and Columbian Methodist College,

New Westminster, British Columbia. In November 1890 Victoria University was federated with the University of Toronto, and by October 1892 it moved from Cobourg to Toronto. The first chancellor of the university was Samuel Nelles, who served from 1880 to 1887, followed by Nathanael Burwash from 1887 to 1912.

As early as the 1860s the preparatory department at Victoria College, which had accounted for a large proportion of the students, had been discontinued and a special relationship between the college and Cobourg grammar school worked out. Cobourg Collegiate Institute was recognized in the 1870s as a preparatory department of the college by the university senate.[57] Although these arrangements were made for the male students of Victoria, the relationship may inadvertently have worked in favour of those local girls who did not have the benefit of attending one of the ladies' colleges that by the mid-1880s had secured affiliation with Victoria. In 1885 Clara Field and Cassie Munson, described as prize pupils of Principal McHenry at Cobourg Collegiate, were admitted to Victoria College.

Well before this development, during the 1870s, the proximity of Brookhurst, a ladies' college run by Mary Electa Adams, allowed girls from the college to attend lectures at Victoria. Victoria held local examinations for matriculation, which women were allowed to take by 1871, although they did not yet have permission to sit lectures.[58] Mary Crossen, who received an MEL degree granted jointly by Brookhurst and Victoria in 1877, was the first woman to take lectures with male students at Victoria. Details about other pioneer women students at Victoria are provided in chapter 7.[59] Although these early women students did not enjoy the splendour of colleges such as Vassar and Wellesley, their experience was still a positive one. In the words of Nellie C. Greenwood, her years at Victoria College in the 1880s were "a realm of pure delight."[60]

The exact nature of Victoria and details about its female students are difficult to pinpoint during these years. The closure of Brookhurst in 1880 eliminated the possibility of coordinate college status, as well as a residence for women students, and presumably led parents to pressure Victoria College to open privileges more fully than was already the case. The small numbers of students in the early years suggest that instead of a self-conscious adoption of a coeducational policy, the process of admission may have been more in the form of individual favours granted to friends of the college. Augusta Stowe, whose family was close to Samuel Nelles, the chancellor of Victoria, was granted permission to attend classes in 1879.[61] Nellie Greenwood, who was admitted the following year, apparently had a personal connection with Victoria in that one of her grandmothers was a Ryerson.[62] The Senate minutes provide few clues as to how the decision to admit women was viewed. The small number of women students in the years from first admission until the college's move to Toronto in 1892 may have reassured the Senate that this was less of a trend than an exception.

The affiliation agreement of 1884 meant that students from ladies' college were granted two years' advanced standing at Victoria if they had achieved the mistress of liberal arts or mistress of English literature diploma. If the university felt that remedial work was needed, the ladies' college graduate was examined in particular disciplines as a condition of admission. These students were described as "conditioned" in certain areas, a term that also was used in American schools. The arrangement was initially a matter of negotiation by letter between the principal of the respective ladies' college and Victoria. By 1892, however, four of the Methodist colleges, Albert, Alma, Ontario Ladies', and Wesleyan Ladies', sought greater formalization of the process and asked the board of Victoria College to apply to the University of Toronto on their behalf for the appointment of a board of examiners to test their pupils in June each year for junior and senior matriculation in arts, thus regularizing the status of all women students.

The ideology that shaped female education in nineteenth-century Ontario is revealed by examining Methodist schooling. Although it is beyond the scope of this book to compare female with male education in the same period, the contribution of education to the shaping of gender ideals, particularly that of femininity and womanhood, will be studied. Methodist schooling upheld the middle-class ideal of a girl who was fragile, virginal, and in need of training for her role as a woman, which was primarily defined in terms of motherhood. Increasingly, the notion of motherhood required educational preparation, as well as a natural biological unfolding. The development of femininity was closely tied to a middle-class ideal that relieved the woman from wage labour and idealized her function as a primary nurturer of young children. Advanced training, educators argued, had to be thorough and structured in order to counter girls' tendency to sentimentalism and superficiality. The habits of discipline and submission were to serve a woman in her future roles as wife and mother.

Methodist schools offered a structure that supervised virtually every moment of the day, preventing idleness, gossip, and novel-reading from undermining the achievement of mental and spiritual discipline. The ladies' colleges were organized in a manner that simulated the ideal family with a father, who carried most of the power and responsibility, supported by maternal figures, teachers, and governesses, who provided role models of ideal Christian women. The schools endorsed the propriety of a patriarchal system that prepared a young woman for the distribution of power which would determine proper relations with her father, husband, minister, or principal. Men were the primary organizers of the ladies' colleges, and their ambivalence about the actual nature and purpose of women's education resounds throughout the period examined in this study.

Debates about female education centred around the need for special or female studies and the usefulness of traditionally male subjects. The issue of whether women were best educated in single-sex or coeducational settings continually plagued the debate. The assumption that femininity was fragile gave the advocates of special education for women the rationale for single-sex schooling. Although some supporters of women's education had a broader view that allowed wage labour, the ultimate purpose was to prepare a woman for her role in the family as mother and spouse. Women who followed this training seem to have absorbed the values and attitudes in varying degrees, and we will see that some, despite their education, chose a variety of non-traditional occupations and family structures. When women were readmitted to the male university, similar debates about the nature of women's education occurred. Ambivalence about goals and the gendered distribution of power echoed the earlier discussion in the era of ladies' colleges. Methodist education was characterized by both continuity of enthusiasm and ambivalence of purpose, and it is this tension that is a central focus of this study.

2 The Early Seminary Movement in Ontario, 1830–1850

> Many, I doubt not, but feel anxious to see an establishment of the kind, they have sons and daughters, but know not where to send them to a school, liberal in its principles and also in its charges. Many, rather than send their children to the United States, will suffer them to grow up with their minds like the uncultivated wilderness, overspread with thorns and briars.[1]

The early-nineteenth-century consensus that a Methodist institution of higher learning was necessary in Upper Canada included a concern for the education of women. One letter to the editor of the *Christian Guardian* in 1830 asked why the Methodists did not establish an educational institution for the advanced training of both sexes. Despite a reluctance to send children to American schools, these latter institutions exerted a pull, and the influence of American education on the views of parents in Upper Canada was significant.

AMERICAN SCHOOLS AND THE FOUNDING OF THE UPPER CANADA ACADEMY

American Methodist academies and seminaries were established somewhat earlier than their counterparts across the border. Their presence offered a powerful example to Upper Canadians of what could be accomplished. It is difficult to estimate how many parents did in fact send their children to American schools, but there is evidence that a small number did so. At Cazenovia Seminary, a coeducational college in Cazenovia, New York, founded in 1824, some twenty-five or thirty students in the first decade were from Upper Canada.[2] Female students came from Kingston, London, Hallowell (Picton), Cramahe, Presqu'ile, Cobourg, and York (later Toronto). One of the students was Mary Bailey of London, who married the Reverend Thomas Webster in 1834. Webster's views on women's education and equality are discussed in chapter 6.[3] Martha Richardson of Toronto attended Cazenovia in 1835 and was later listed as a teacher; she married Dr William Allen, president of Girard College, Philadelphia. Jesse Hurlburt was a student at Cazenovia in 1835 and was later described as a lawyer and professor in Cobourg. He served as acting principal and science master of the Upper Canada Academy in 1839 for three years and later took on the principalship of his wife's female academy. Canadian women attended other American schools as well. Mary Electa Adams, a privately educated young woman, had came to Upper Canada from Lower Canada with her parents in 1825 when she was two years old. After teaching at the Upper Canada Academy, she was sent in 1840 to study at the Montpelier Academy in Vermont, where her mother had also been a student.

Genesee Wesleyan Seminary (later College) in Lima, New York, was founded in 1832 as a coeducational school under the patronage of the Genesee Conference of the Methodist Episcopal Church. The enrolment of students from Upper Canada seems to have been limited to a handful of female students and approximately ten male students per year.[4] The *Canada Christian Advocate* noted that at the Berea Seminary near Cleveland, founded in 1841, there were some fifteen students from Canada West in 1852 out of approximately one hundred students.[5] Although our information is limited, one can conclude from such enrolments that schools for women, such as the Albany Female Institute, founded in 1828, and the Rutgers Female Institute in New York, founded in 1839, or coeducational schools such as Cazenovia offered Methodist parents a variety of possibilities of higher education for their female children if they were willing to have them educated in the United States. In fact, parents presumably felt that the denominational connection was important enough that they would send their children some distance to another country for this education. Until the Methodists at home could organize a reasonable alternative, a small number of parents thus chose Methodist schools on the other side of the border. The options in the United States were numerous; the Methodist Episcopal Church in the northeastern United States, for example, claimed that in 1853 eight colleges and forty-five academies and seminaries were under its auspices.[6] Susan Houston and Alison Prentice have defined the early academies, seminaries, and colleges of Upper Canada as variations of the same themes. The major distinguishing features were their concern to provide something more than the common branches, the possibility that they might employ more than one teacher, and the possibility of financial aid from the church, the state, or an educational corporation.[7]

A wide variety of subjects were available to the students in the American academies, seminaries, and colleges. At Genesee College the female department offered students painting, mapping, embroidery, needlework, and music. The calendar adds that "young ladies pursuing the Languages or Mathematicks, will receive Instruction in these branches from the Professors."[8] In addition to the accomplishments curriculum, instruction was thus available to women in some of the branches taught in other departments. By 1834 the female department of Genesee College had expanded its own course offerings to include bookkeeping, natural theology, and intellectual philosophy, as well as Latin, French, and Italian. Although courses in Hebrew, Greek, and Spanish were limited to male students, Latin was included in the female department. Lest the list intimidate parents of prospective pupils, the calendar added that the department's aim was to offer a course of study that would "strengthen and unfold the mind, and prepare it for practical usefulness, those branches of polite and ornamental education, which are the chief embellishments of the sex."[9] The school could accommodate one hundred male and female students, and the rest boarded in houses in the village. The rules included a separation of male students from any part of the building or yard "assigned exclusively to the female students."[10]

The curriculum at Genesee College offered a form of higher education. The students from Upper Canada who attended must have had sufficient schooling to be admitted to this level of study. Several types of schooling were available in Upper Canada for parents who wanted to prepare their daughters for such higher education. As Houston and Prentice have observed, schooling at this time was remarkable for its variety: from private tutoring to private venture schools to schools catering to special groups and Sunday schools, in addition to the common schools and district grammar schools that were subsidized in part by the state.[11] Mary Electa Adams and her four siblings were taught at home by their parents before she travelled to Vermont to study.

From the maze of Upper Canadian schools, it is difficult to distinguish the ones that could claim to go beyond the preparatory level to actually offering something that could be defined as "higher education." Seminaries and academies, which began to appear in Upper

Canada in the 1830s, were supported by a variety of means and educated a wide age range of pupils.[12] The purpose of these schools was certainly to give a "higher" level of education to their students than that associated with the common schools.[13] Yet the specific course offerings depended somewhat on the size of the school and the competence of its teachers.

Why were the North American Wesleyan and Episcopal Methodist denominations so active in educational matters? John Reid notes that on the east coast the Baptists and Methodists both had "strong traditions of evangelical zeal that suggested the value of a disciplined education as an antidote to idleness or frivolity in either women or men."[14] Yet even though the original vision for educational institutions was inspired by religious zeal, it is important to balance this idea with the stated mission of schools such as the Upper Canada Academy to provide non-sectarian education. The purpose of the school was not to proselytize or propagate Methodism per se, but to teach in and create an environment that was broadly Christian. To what extent this was an independent vision, as opposed to a reaction to the educational mission of other denominations active in Upper Canada, is hard to say. Donald Masters agrees with Gidney and Millar that to some extent the efforts of Anglicans to establish and control church colleges and the provincial university stimulated the other churches into similar activity, and the motivation behind the establishment of Upper Canada Academy was the determination of Methodists that their young people should *not* be trained in a college controlled by Anglicans.[15] The Methodists blamed the retarded progress of education in Upper Canada on the monopoly that John Strachan and the Anglicans had attempted to exercise over higher education, and they felt justified in establishing an academy that would correct this situation. The Methodist academy was also intended as a school for the middle classes, in contrast with Upper Canada College, which was patronized by sons of the élite. Unlike UCC, which educated the children of the gentry and government officials, the academy at Cobourg would ideally address the needs of a larger body of the population, even though, in reality, few could afford it. According to Egerton Ryerson, the middle classes in Canada constituted "the great body of the population and it is from amongst these that so many of the youth are sent to seminaries of Learning in the United States. I am able to state on good authority that, nearly every one of these Youth would be immediately brought back to Upper Canada, and sent to the [proposed] institution."[16]

According to Ryerson, the purposes of the institution were to educate students in terms similar to schools in New York State, with strict attention to morals. The school would provide free professional training for common-school masters, "poor young men of religious character and promising talents who have an ardent thirst for knowledge."[17] Finally, it would also educate the most promising of converted Native youth to be teachers.[18] The professional aspect of the school was an important part of its mission. By offering such practical training, Ryerson hoped to divert students from travelling to the United States, as had been the precedent. Because there was no institution of the kind in Upper Canada, he argued, more than sixty young people were currently attending similar schools in the United States, and nearly two hundred Canadian Methodists had been educated there.[19] It should be noted that Ryerson's advocacy of the academy made little or no reference to the need to educate women, and one can assume that he did not believe that this was an important mission of the proposed school.

The question of professions was closely tied to expectations concerning the prospective class base of the school.[20] The Anglican schools were intended to educate a social élite consisting of doctors, lawyers, and clergy, whereas the Methodists proposed to train farmers, businessmen, teachers, and mistresses of households, as well as the more traditional professionals.[21] Methodists women's education was clearly intended to prepare the wives of the rising middle class. Upper Canadian politics also had an impact on the development of the Upper Canada Academy. There was certainly a strong connection between Reform opposition to the Family Compact in Upper Canada and the establishment of the academy, which represented not only Egerton Ryerson but the Reform impulse politically.[22] While some aspects of American culture and ideology were perceived as politically threatening, even among Reformers and especially after the Rebellion of 1837–38, Ryerson and the other founders of the academy were among many who simultaneously admired American education and ultimately associated improved education with greater wealth for Upper Canadians and their province.[23]

THE ACADEMY AND THE METHODIST CHURCH

The Upper Canada Academy was founded as a literary institution with a clear non-sectarian policy.[24] The details of hiring staff and providing living space for the faculty of the new college were negotiated by the building committee. Teachers were allowed board or tuition for their children in addition to their regular salaries, which ranged from £65 to £100 per year.[25] Membership in the Canadian

Methodist church had grown from 9,156 in 1829 to 14,999 in 1831, and this increase, combined with an initially positive response to canvassing, created a climate of optimism concerning the future of the academy.

Two factors tempered this optimism, however. First, a commercial depression in 1832 made it difficult for individuals to meet the instalments they had pledged to the academy. Second, the union of the Conference with the Wesleyans in 1833 had apparently offended a large section of the Methodist public, who believed that the local preachers and lay members should have been consulted in their quarterly meetings before the union and before the subsequent name change from Methodist Episcopal to Wesleyan Methodist took effect. C.B. Sissons describes how Elder Case was replaced as superintendent of the church by an English president, who no doubt raised a few pioneer eyebrows with his appearance on his first Sunday in Hamilton in an outfit that included black silk stockings and silver shoe buckles. The extremist reform elements interpreted a government grant of £900 as evidence that "the Ryersons had persuaded the Conference to sell itself to the enemy."[26] The academy was financed both by Ryerson's fund-raising tours in Britain and by subscriptions from individuals within the conferences.[27] He spread his appeal for funds far and wide and approached the British Wesleyans as well as other wealthy individuals, such as a Quaker in Birmingham named Joseph Sturge.[28] The future academy claimed that it would help to educate the Natives, a purpose that garnered both sympathy and financial assistance from the British Society of Friends.[29]

The school was also justified with reference to its location and healthy environment. Education of an appropriate kind, it was claimed, would secure good government and constitutional liberty since "an educated people are always a loyal people to good government."[30] Such education was, therefore, associated with order, as opposed to the disorder of revolutionary movements: "an ignorant population are equally fit and liable to be the slaves of despots, and the dupes of demagogues; sometime like the unsettled ocean, they can be thrown in uncontrollable agitation by every wind that blows."[31] More than merely anti-revolutionary, education was the handmaiden of religion because it was the "will of God that Christians should be *well instructed*."[32] The relationship to religion did not mean, however, that the academy was to be considered a theological training school for the ministry, although it was intended to establish an atmosphere of academic seriousness similar to that required for the education of ministers. Since it was to be a non-sectarian school for liberal studies, it could not be associated with such a narrow denominational focus. The early advertisements made clear, therefore, that the school was *not* "contemplated to educate young men for the ministry."[33] Not until early in the 1870s was a chair of theology established, endowed by Edward Jackson of Hamilton. Nathanael Burwash became a full-time lecturer in theology and the first appointee to the Jackson chair.[34]

By this time a number of changes had affected the nature of worship within the Methodist denomination, increasing the demand for a more formal and educated ministry than the early revivals and itinerant preaching had required. William Westfall describes how these changes in the church emphasized values such as moderation, gradualism, and the central role of a well-established church in the life of the individual.[35] They also had an effect on the education of girls and confirmed the church's responsibility to continue to develop educational opportunities for young women. The key to the educational mission was found in the church's changing views on the relationship between the converted and the world. As Westfall indicates, in the early nineteenth century the sanctified were to live apart from the world, but by mid-century the marriage between holiness and usefulness required a Methodist to be active in religious causes in the world, such as missions, temperance, Sunday schools, and sabbatarianism.[36] These causes, overwhelmingly upheld by women of the church, reinforced the need for education in order that they be equipped for the church's work. The desire to educate women was not in opposition to their function in the family, since the schools constantly stressed that this was a woman's primary responsibility, but her role as mother was extended to the family of God as she reached out to those in need. The universalizing of religious concern and the emphasis on good works resulted in a church that "was presented as the very embodiment of the spirit of God, a part of the Kingdom of God on earth."[37] Similarly, towards the end of the century, graduates at a Presbyterian ladies' college in Brantford, Ontario, would be exhorted to "make full proof of [their] attainments in consecrated labor for God" and to use whatever talents they possessed "for the advancement of His Kingdom, whose subjects you are."[38]

FEMALE STUDENTS AT THE ACADEMY

For the first six years of its existence, female students took classes at the Upper Canada Academy. During this time they were supervised by a preceptress, whose identity changed almost annually. The first preceptress, Mrs Smith, found the salary unsatisfactory and she was dismissed.[39] Maria Boulter succeeded her; in 1837–38 Boulter in turn was replaced by Mary Electa Adams. In 1841 Miss Barnes became preceptress of the academy, assisted by Sarah Jane Beatty.

After the first two years, the Upper Canada Academy began to look to the United States for teachers and offered Jesse Hurlburt a position at the school. He was a Canadian who, as we have seen, had been educated at Cazenovia; he also attended Wesleyan University in Middletown, Connecticut. The Upper Canada Academy introduced the studies of chemistry, physics, and Hebrew, all of which Hurlburt was able to teach. After the first principal, Matthew Richey, returned to the pastorate in 1839, Hurlburt became the acting principal.[40] Richey continued to serve as an absentee principal for three years while he held a ministerial post in Toronto. During the fifth and sixth years of the academy's operation, Ryerson was officially principal, but his connection was loose at first, and Hurlburt continued as acting principal. The June conference of 1840 officially confirmed the appointment of Ryerson as principal, but he apparently did not intend to take control immediately, having just completed his final year as editor of the *Christian Guardian*.[41] Not until the academy was officially recognized as a college in 1841 did Ryerson become more completely identified with its interests.[42] He was formally installed as president of Victoria College in June 1842.

The academy inadvertently became the setting for a romance between Maria Boulter and Jesse Hurlburt that led to their marriage in 1840. This union caused a few problems at the academy, since the principal and preceptress were reported as not taking their seats in the dining hall and by their absence contributing to a "want of proper restraint being kept over the students."[43] Another teacher during these early years was Daniel Van Norman, a Canadian who had been educated at Cazenovia College, Hamilton College, also in New York State, and Wesleyan University in Connecticut. He was hired as mathematical master, but gradually took over classics.[44] William Kingston, at the age of twenty, left his job at a common school near Dundas to take charge of the elementary department at the academy. He had received his education at Cazenovia College and at Girard College, Philadelphia. Kingston taught at Victoria from 1838 to 1872 with the exception of three years between 1847 and 1850. In his history of Victoria, Burwash claimed that the trio of Hurlburt, Van Norman, and Kingston brought progressive ideas to the Methodist college in Cobourg since they had been exposed to American educational methods.[45] Sissons agreed with this assessment and claimed that the American influence could be seen in their positive attitude towards the education of girls, whereas Ryerson, with more of a

British educational orientation, did not believe that young women had a place in the college. New ideas, such as pedagogies initiated by Pestalozzi, had not yet found their way into British or many other Old World schools, but these methods were being welcomed in New England and through the new professors such as Hurlburt and Van Norman were brought to the Upper Canada Academy.[46]

Although the school was in one sense coeducational, a tremendous effort was in fact expended to keep the sexes separate. A "proper restraint" governed all the relations between the sexes. Separate seating was the rule at meals in the dining-room and at the services, which were held at morning and evening in the chapel. Class instruction was also largely separate.[47] The female department at the Upper Canada Academy received instruction in science, mathematics, and languages from the professors of the college and in composition, music, and art from the female preceptress or her assistant. Miss Barnes was commended in 1841 for the effectiveness of her teaching of the writing class, and since her attention was occupied with the higher branches, the committee of management recommended that Sarah Jane Beatty be hired as an assistant, allowing Barnes more time for the instruction of her class.[48] Barnes in her capacity as preceptress was paid £60 10s. per annum and Beatty was paid £50. Male students received instruction in the following subjects not available in the female department: algebra, geometry, calculus, physical astronomy, declamation, Latin, Greek, and Hebrew. The female department offered subjects such as music, drawing, painting, composition, and French that were not available to male students, as well as descriptive astronomy, geology, and conchology.[49] An advertisement for the summer session in 1841 claimed that the playground for young ladies was screened from the public, and within the enclosure was a garden for students interested in horticulture.[50]

The physical separation of the sexes required at times a great deal of coordination, as a letter from the faculty to Principal Ryerson indicated: "it is necessary that [the young men] should go to Chapel and return in a body *before* the young ladies, in order to prevent all intercourse with them."[51] The female students gradually became more visible at public occasions, such as the examinations, however. Original compositions were read by students, and oral examinations were conducted in grammar, geography, astronomy, and French. In addition, students exhibited works of art and performed music. The *Christian Guardian* published tables of merit with the students' names, which the editors of the *Guardian* believed was a more effective method of giving public distinction to successful students than the system of rewards that was generally pursued.[52] The publication of tables of merit was, according to Sissons, a result of the American influences brought to the college by Hurlburt, Van Norman, and Kingston.[53]

These tables of merit are symbolic representations of the situation of female students within the academy. One table from 1842 shows the test results of twenty-eight male students, followed by a separate table with sixteen female students. Males were tested out of a possible total of twenty-three subjects, the females on sixteen possible subjects. Male students were examined in Greek, Latin, and Hebrew, whereas the females were not even allowed to study those languages. The public nature of the examinations was nevertheless an extraordinary step in recognizing and celebrating the achievements of female students. There were limits, however. According to Sissons, great pains were taken to maintain the modesty that "shrinks from permanent exhibition," and the girls actually read their compositions in the academy instead of on the public platform. Perhaps for some, a genuine public reading by young women was too great a step towards coeducation, which might have been seen as a threat to the academic seriousness of the institution and its more important mission to educate males.

Few details remain about those early female students at the Upper Canada Academy. Augusta Richey, daughter of the school's first principal, Matthew Richey, attended. Miss M.A. Bennet was a student who eventually married Sidney Smith, QC, of Cobourg. Mary Field, another student in the first class, became Mrs Hamilton and was a sister-in-law to William Kerr, who eventually became vice-chancellor of Victoria. Two sisters, Nancy Philina Carpenter and Katherine Mahala Carpenter, were daughters of Austin Carpenter, a leading citizen of Cobourg. Nancy married the Reverend John English, and Katherine became Mrs Evans of New York. Another student was Esther Helm (later Mrs Zeland of Chicago), daughter of John Helm of Cobourg, who had a foundry business. Esther Mallory, a daughter of Caleb Mallory, a settler living near Cobourg, married Dr Charles Cameron.

In the year 1837–38 the list of female students included the Misses Hurlburt, McCarty, Aroline Hinman, Caroline McPhail (Toronto), Might (Port Hope), Van Norman, Jemima Williams (Belleville), Mary Brock (Hamilton), Jane Ann Wright (London), Ellen Arnold (Brockville), Jane Beatty (New York City), Mary Beatty (Toronto), Elizabeth Bloor (Toronto), Sully Cow (Rice Lake), Charlotte Houghton (Brockville), Amelia Houghton, Emma Croscombe (Quebec), Jane Pope, Ann June Brown (Port Hope), Jackson, Susan Archibald (Osnaburgh, New York), Harriet Boice, Alice Luchton (West India), Mary Ryerson

(Toronto), Mary Ann Hall (New York), Eliza Scofield (Beverly), Ann Smith (Toronto), and Caroline Sumner (Oakville). The ages of these students ranged from one who was very young (a native girl, Sully Cow, eight years old) to nineteen, although the records are incomplete.[54] During the school year 1838–39, three students, the Misses Archibald, Williams, and Bloor had returned for another year. New students who entered in the fall included Clarissa Evans (St Clair), Ann Southurn (St Clair), Harriet and Elizabeth Burr (Yonge Street), Whiting, Penealply Lewes (Saltfleet), Hester Malrey (Hamilton), Jennet Fingland (Hamilton), Emma Wallace (Brantford), and Augusta Bunnell (Brantford). The youngest student, Ann Southurn, who was only thirteen, departed after a few weeks at the school. Between January and May of 1839 a new group of students joined the class. These included Mrs Th. Hurlburt (Equising), Jane Ann Crawford (Toronto), Thiby Ann Allison (Carrying Place), Mary Dickson (Cornwall), Ann Temblyn (Hope), Anna Cholt (Port Hope), Sarah Wilmott (Nelson), Rebecca Hurlburt, Lydia Powers (Coleburn), Mary Ann Cosford (Newmarket), Mary Tyson (Holland Landing), and Eliza Jane Thompson (Indiana).[55]

Reports from the college indicate that the female department flourished. Jesse Hurlburt wrote to Ryerson in 1840 that more young ladies than ever before were expected, and all the rooms were already engaged.[56] Indeed, the popularity of the female department meant that it could not be discontinued as quickly as some might have wished when the decision was made to educate boys only. In the fall of 1841, twenty-four girls were registered, in the summer term of 1842 there were nine girls, and in the fall that year there were still twenty female students. "On account of previous engagements, and the want of any other place as a Ladies' Seminary, it was deemed impracticable to discontinue the female department in the Institution during the present winter: but it has been separated by the establishment of a distinct boarding hall, and only occupies at present a portion of the College buildings."[57] The question of boarding halls may have been part of the problem for Ryerson in having female students at the college. Alison Prentice notes that he gradually became opposed to the idea of boarding halls. He himself claimed in 1850 that the boarding hall at the Upper Canada Academy nearly caused the financial ruin of the school and injured the morals of numbers of pupils. He believed that such halls weakened the domestic feelings and could not approximate his ideal of family life, which he associated with privacy.[58] This sentiment may have led Ryerson to visualize the new college as one both without boarders and without female students.

When the Upper Canada Academy attained the status of a college, with "prospects large and promising," the change apparently "rendered it necessary to discontinue the successful Female department in the Institution."[59] As a somewhat enigmatic letter to Ryerson indicated in 1841, Hurlburt expressed the desire that the female academy be seen by the public as dissociated with the college. "You will doubtless speak of the female department as being entirely disconnected with the college if you refer to it at all. A mere passing notice might suffice to inform the community that it had no connection with the college, farther than being under the direction of the college officers. As its connection in any way with the college is an anomaly, we should endeavor to guard against the prejudice of the community."[60] A meeting of the board of Victoria College resolved to ascertain the practicality of building a second institution for young women. The absence in the province of an academy for females that was "sufficiently comprehensive in its design" was seen as an important reason to initiate such a school. There were excellent seminaries available, and the board welcomed more, but there was still a need for a school that was "ample, superior, and well sustained in its departments." A new school for females would counter a "showy" training by providing a "sound, useful, respectable education" and would be financed by the sale of £5 shares.[61] Parents who had initially supported the Upper Canada Academy for the education of their daughters were now asked to give more money to establish a new academy. Similarly, Episcopal Methodist parents who had donated to the original Upper Canada Academy had once again to find funds for a separate institution when the school was given to the Wesleyans.

The proposal in 1841 suggested Hamilton as a good location for the institution, which could be called the Adelaide Academy after the first-born daughter of the Queen, Princess Adelaide Victoria Louise. The name of the Adelaide Academy would be linked to Victoria College by means of this reference to the royal family, and the two institutions would be associated with recollections as lovely and welcome in the Canadian Methodist church as they were "British in their character and influence."[62] It is interesting to note that this proposal, which was signed by the chairman of the Victoria College board, Anson Green, would not only remove the female department from the school building in Cobourg, but place it a considerable geographic distance from Victoria College. As will be seen, the first objective succeeded, but the second initially did not.

The question remains, why did the restructuring of Victoria College demand the exodus of female students from the building? Irrespective of whether Ryerson's model of an ideal university derived from

British or American sources or a mix of the two, it is apparent that the seriousness and professionalism that characterized a university education were not deemed possible in a coeducational model. For Ryerson, the model of neither, for example, Wesleyan University in Middletown, Connecticut, nor Oxford University in England allowed women to study for BA degrees. Wesleyan did not admit women until 1871, and in 1884 Oxford admitted women to degree examinations, but not yet to degrees.[63] The objective of establishing a university at this time seemed to require the removal of the women students. By the 1870s Methodists were more inclined to educate men and women together. As David Potts observes, out of more than two dozen Methodist colleges and universities in the United States in that decade, all but four were coeducational.[64]

The seminary model with a single sex housed in one building remained the appropriate setting for female education. At the same time, for all its seriousness of purpose, the educational level of courses offered by Victoria College once female students were removed was characterized by a mix of college and preparatory courses because differing preparation continued to require a large amount of flexibility to meet the students' needs.[65]

THE NATURE OF FEMALE EDUCATION

The link with female education at Cobourg was not easily broken. In May 1842 Mrs Van Norman established the Cobourg Ladies' Seminary, and Mrs Hurlburt opened the Cobourg Female Academy in September the same year. Van Norman was joined in her school by Miss Barnes, former preceptress in the female department of Upper Canada Academy, while Mrs Hurlburt was helped by her assistant and sister, Miss R. Boulter, and by Mary Electa Adams, Miss L. Hurlburt, who had studied at the academy, and "a French lady." Three male lecturers, all clergymen, covered other course offerings.[66] The use of the clergy and male professors to lecture in subject areas for which there were presumably no women teachers seems to have been quite customary and unquestioned. The Hurlburt academy was located within seventy to eighty rods (350 to 400 metres) of Victoria College, which gave the students easy access to special lectures at the college.[67] Similarly, the Van Norman school advertised that its students would have the privilege of attending various lectures delivered at Victoria College.[68] A meeting of the financial committee of Victoria resolved in January 1845 that Van Norman be allowed to attend the lectures on chemistry and physiology at the college with the young ladies of the seminary for £5 per term.[69]

Both Mrs Van Norman and Mrs Hurlburt were joined in their educational enterprises by their husbands, who eventually resigned their teaching positions at Victoria College. During the early years of the Upper Canada Academy, Hurlburt and Van Norman had assisted in lecturing to its female department. The two families did not collaborate in setting up one large school together, but rather pursued their own separate ways, probably because of differences in educational attainments or outlook. In the case of Hurlburt, his resignation from Victoria may have been a welcome relief, since there had been tensions at the school about his work, and during his tenure as acting principal, the faculty had criticized his leadership. A long letter in 1841 to Ryerson from Van Norman and Kingston complained about Hurlburt's incompetence in not being able to write an article fit for a public journal or give a reasonable speech that would not embarrass the school.[70]

About Van Norman's reasons for leaving Victoria, no information is available, but his considerable enthusiasm for the new venture is apparent in the records. In an 1845 letter to Egerton Ryerson, he proudly described the school as "overflowing during the present session – near 70 in all 20 who are boarders."[71] An arrangement was made in May 1845 whereby lectures in chemistry and physiology were given at the Van Norman school by Dr Beatty, possibly replacing the arrangements that allowed the girls to attend lectures in these subjects at Victoria for a fee. Van Norman was so enthusiastic about the lectures given by Beatty that he offered to provide a testimony to the board with regard to his ability to fill the chair of natural science, a position that Beatty obtained in 1849 when he became a professor of natural philosophy and chemistry at Victoria College.[72] In his 1845 letter, Van Norman also referred, however, to a school building that he was having erected in Hamilton with accommodation for eighty boarders; the opening was scheduled for the next fall. Evidently there were now reasons to move the ladies' seminary away from Cobourg.

Lingering ties to the college were also evident in the case of Professor Hurlburt, about whom the board passed the following resolution in 1842: "to address a note to the Rev. Professor Hurlburt reminding him of the resolution passed at the meeting of the College Board ... 'That no Professor shall be employed in the Institution after the close of the Ensuing session who has any connection with another School.'"[73] Perhaps Hurlburt had hoped to continue teaching in both institutions.

Negotiations over the financial situation of a brother and sister also reveal continued contacts and relations between the college and the female academies. William Kingston wrote to Ryerson concerning a Miss Carter who was living with his family and receiving instruction at the Van Norman school and private lessons from Van Norman and himself. The charges for this service required some negotiation, "lest any members of the Board should urge that, as her brother is able to defray her expenses for board and tuition now, he could also pay the amount of his tuition bills to the Institution, I would just say, that he has done some work for me, & it is quite as easy for me to pay him in this way [by instructing his sister] as in any other, indeed much easier."[74]

Neither female school seems to have lacked for students, and there is no evidence of outright competition between the two. In the *Christian Guardian* of 1842, the schools were given equal coverage. A visiting committee composed of Ryerson, Kingston, and other Methodist clergymen visited both schools and supervised their work. Sissons states that Ryerson and Kingston made "obvious if not entirely successful attempts to hold their favour in balance."[75] Fees for both female seminaries were similar, with a £5 charge for board and £1 tuition charge for common English and £1 50s. for each of higher English and a series of extras, including French, embroidery, drawing, and music.[76] Mrs Hurlburt's academy was described as situated in a very healthy part of town, and Cobourg continued to be advertised as one of the healthiest places in the country.[77]

There were important motivational continuities between the female seminary in Cobourg and the parent school. The term "moral and literary character," which had previously described education at Upper Canada Academy, continued to be applied to education at the separate ladies' academy.[78] The CFA was arranged in four departments, which had a permanent staff of five, with two visiting lecturers who were Methodist clergymen and Professor Hurlburt. Mrs Hurlburt was preceptress and teacher of the fourth department in French, music, and ornamental branches. Other staff included Mary Electa Adams, teacher of the third department and assistant in drawing and painting; Miss L. Hurlburt, second department; another unidentified woman teacher who taught the first department; a French woman for French, piano, and guitar; the Reverend T. Alexander, lecturer in ecclesiastical history and evidences; the Reverend Joseph Harris, lecturer in history and philosophy; and J. Hurlburt, lecturer in chemistry and natural philosophy. The four departments were adapted to the "progressive growth of the mind" from the rudiments in reading, writing, and arithmetic to the highest level of botany, natural theology, evidences, philosophy, and literature.[79] The selection of courses was advertised as broader than that usually available to female students.[80] The range of subjects was also expanded by allowing the students the "privilege" of attending all the special lectures delivered at Victoria College, as well as having their own guest lectures once a week on various "useful and interesting subjects."[81]

The system of instruction at the Van Normans' Cobourg Ladies' Seminary was divided into two courses called the "useful" and the "ornamental," and these two streams embraced all the "Literary, Scientific, and Ornamental branches adapted to Young Ladies."[82] Graduates of the two streams received either the first- or second-degree diploma. Additional courses available to students included Spanish, Italian, German, Greek, and Latin, as well as bookkeeping and mathematics. The additional language options were a clear departure from the Upper Canada Academy, where female students were instructed only in French. Students from the seminary submitted essays to a public exhibition in the Methodist chapel in 1844. One observer stated that Mrs Van Norman's young ladies wrote essays that indicated "an even more marked regard for revealed truths than the productions of the College."[83] In 1845 there were ninety-two students at the Van Norman seminary, and forty-four of those students came from Cobourg. Two sisters, Nancy Philina Carpenter and Katherine Mahala Carpenter, who had studied at the Upper Canada Academy in 1836, apparently graduated with a diploma from the Cobourg Ladies' Seminary. The faculty in 1845 included Mr and Mrs Van Norman; Lieutenant Benjamin Hayter, French language; Jane Van Norman, first teacher of English branches; Sarah Ann Van Norman, second teacher of English; Ann McIntosh, piano and guitar; and Maria Zwick, teacher of writing and piano.[84] The school was advertised as "parental" in its governance, the experience of which, it was anticipated, would not only guarantee happiness, but also prepare students for the "relations of social and domestic life."[85] The principal was clearly the authority figure to the students entrusted to his care, and they were expected to submit to his control. The school, which had originally been described as Mrs Van Norman's, had clearly developed a new management structure when her husband joined the enterprise.

The principal offered daily one-hour lessons in classics. The circular of 1845 mentioned that two students had availed themselves of this Latin instruction, which was seen as contributing to mental discipline as well as serving as a step towards the acquisition of French and modern languages and the better understanding of English. A clearer statement of the role of Latin in developing mental discipline is evident in the prospectus from the Van Norman Institute in New York, the school that Van Norman established in 1857. He felt that the language was more effective in developing reasoning powers than mathematics. Latin also facilitated the learning of modern languages.[86]

A description of the pedagogy favoured in the New York school further supported the goal of mental discipline. Students were encouraged to understand facts and principles and to do so thoroughly, in order that "the mind will be more successfully developed, and the pupil be able to reduce to future use all she acquires."[87] Physical exercise in the form of calisthenics was intended to balance out the "unfavorable influence of confinement to study" and also promote gracefulness and general good health. Clubs at the Van Norman Institute included the Calliopean Society, presumably a literary group, which supported the establishment of a library at the school. Reading was closely supervised because there was a strong fear of the evil effects of novel-reading, which tended to develop an unhealthy sentimentality in impressionable young girls. It was important to create a "distaste for fiction and romance by cultivating … a taste for the higher walks of literature."[88]

The non-sectarian principle that had been part of the founding rules of the Upper Canada Academy also characterized the Van Normans' later seminaries. The New York school's intention to provide a broad Christian education was clearly stated in the circular, but "while every proper effort is employed to prepare the pupils, not only for the walks of life, but for the companionship of Angels, the tenets, *peculiar* to the several evangelical bodies, are never mentioned."[89] Students attended the church chosen by their parents or guardians. Nevertheless, the increase in revivals during the 1840s, observed at Victoria College, was matched by a similar spirit at the Cobourg Ladies' Seminary.[90] Van Norman reported to the Conference in 1845 that no session had passed without conversions and that as many as twenty-four of the pupils were converted while "inmates" of the seminary.

Van Norman entertained grand visions for the future of female education. He planned to devote himself to the establishment of an institution that would give to the females of the country everything necessary to obtain an education "suited to the influential and responsible sphere in which they are destined to move in society."[91] Female education, according to him, was even more influential for the progressive improvement and well-being of society than male education. This potential influence of females justified the development of facilities in some degree equal to those enjoyed by male seminaries and colleges. Not only did female students deserve adequate facilities, but the teaching of females, according to Van Norman, required even more skill and prudence than the intellectual and moral training of males. Teaching females obliged one to contend with stronger prejudices and exercise more watchfulness and tenderness. This argument, based on the greater need for female education and the special pedagogy required to carry it out, would be often repeated in the official rhetoric justifying Methodist-sponsored education for women in the years to follow.

Houston and Prentice discuss the nature of female pedagogy in the provincial school system in the middle decades of the nineteenth century. In *Schooling and Scholars* they observe that "instruction for girls had always differed somewhat from that for boys, but bigger schools and an enlarged curriculum accentuated the gender gap."[92] Certainly, the choice of subjects available to boys or girls in the academies and seminaries showed some variation by gender. The size of the school was an important factor in the diversity of curriculum available to girls. In Upper Canada, as in colonial Australia, the prestigious private seminaries and larger academies offered a sound English education with accomplishments. In Upper Canada, then, at least some girls participated in this demanding curriculum, which was somewhat different from that "offered to boys destined for the professions or business."[93] Still, the unifying factor in the pedagogy of this period, despite the different purposes assumed for the education of boys and girls, was what McKillop describes as the "implicit agenda, the tacit alliance between the rhetoric of moral worth and the dynamics of economic advance."[94] In following this agenda, the evangelical revival sought to provide its own group with broad avenues of political, economic, and moral endeavour. The role of women in the consolidation of this economic and religious position in society required strict training in various forms of discipline through the liberal arts and in ornamentals through art and music.

This period witnessed an elaboration of what female education should or should not be. The 1845 circular for the Van Normans' Cobourg Ladies' Seminary concluded with a brief discussion of the five characteristics of female education, namely, that it should be moral, religious, intellectual, social, and practical. Moral education involved the suppression of self-interest and the elevation of a sense of duty. Religious education was broadly defined as the perception of the "Eternal all-comprehending Mind." The intellectual cornerstone of education consisted in building up the force of thought and the ability of analysis. Finally, female education needed to be social in order to "unfold and purify the affections, which spring up instinctively in the human breast" and bind the individual to family, friends, and neighbours, as well as to suffering, which is ever present.[95] Yet female education also needed to be practical in order to fit the pupil for action in her own sphere in life.

How did the rhetoric of male education differ from that of female education, and how did this difference justify women's removal to separate ladies' academies and seminaries, while men moved into a college environment? Ryerson's inaugural address at the opening of Victoria College in 1841 illustrates the difference in emphasis between the two.[96] Three themes emerged from this address, which underlined the vocational, the patriotic, and the mental discipline aspects of an education. Man, argued Ryerson, was made for physical, mental, and moral action. The realm of action, which was understood to be public and was the context of male education, certainly separated it from the female sphere.

Although the goals of female education addressed the physical, mental, and moral facilities, the existence of a public role, or of a female realm of action outside the household, received little attention. Education for women prepared them for action in pursuit of the kingdom of God, which initially meant in the mothering of a nuclear family, but gradually expanded to include service to the church and society. This service was assumed to remain pure and transcendent, partly because it was not supposed to be tinged by wage labour. Victoria College offered male students a preparatory department and a collegiate course; the former prepared them for ordinary business duties and the latter for professional pursuits, such as teaching, the ministry, and government. The thrust of education was tied through a vocational theme to a patriotic objective. Men were called to "higher" employments by religion and the state. Women were meant to support their attainments in these fields.

The development of an English department at Victoria was a necessary innovation, according to Ryerson, in order to instruct students in the proper use of language in the "pulpit, in the legislature, at the bar, in the different kinds of history, in philosophical discussion in grave and light essay, in poetry of all varieties, and in conversation and in epistolary writing."[97] Students who had spent only a year or two in this department and were unable to complete the entire collegiate course would still benefit because there was a wide field of "noble and patriotic exertion" available to them in a life of private and public usefulness. Ryerson's use of the terms "public" and "private" in relation to the worlds that men inhabited remind one that caution must be exercised when describing the male world as public and the female world as only private.

The collegiate department at Victoria in fact offered many of the same subjects that women at the Cobourg seminary studied, such as ancient languages, mathematics, and moral science, as well as rhetoric, belles-lettres, and theology. At the same time, a purpose of the collegiate education was considered to be preparation, not only for private life and the traditional professions, but also for newer ones such as navigation, surveying, and civil and military engineering. Mental discipline acquired through mathematics was useful not only for personal betterment, but also for application to practical pursuits. A recurrent image in Ryerson's address was the increase of power by means of increased rationality and knowledge of the Creator through moral science, as well as through the acquisition of effective speech. Rhetoric developed a power more enviable and formidable than a sword, a power that controlled the very springs of human action. It is interesting to note that in the 1860s at Vassar, women were still being discouraged from oratory and debate, activities considered "incongruous" for women students. They were encouraged rather to read aloud, recite from the poets, and participate in *tableaux vivants* and conversation.[98] At Oberlin College women could not read aloud at commencement until 1858 and could not orate without a text until 1874.[99] Ryerson concluded his Victoria inaugural with the hope that the school would educate hundreds of youth; they would be "ornaments of the pulpit, the senate and the bar who shall advance the literature, science, and arts of their country, and largely contribute to its elevation, prosperity, and happiness!"[100] In the end, the emphasis was clearly on the educated man's public role. Female education, however, shaped the sensibilities of young ladies and prepared them for their essential roles as wife and mother in the Christian family.

THE BURLINGTON LADIES' ACADEMY AND OTHER SCHOOLS

The success of the Van Normans' Cobourg Ladies' Seminary was a factor in its removal in 1845 to Hamilton, where it could be housed in a better and larger building. According to a circular, the principal had long regarded Hamilton as the most desirable location for a literary institute, and owing to difficulties connected with the erection of a suitable building in Cobourg, he had decided to move the school to Hamilton. From a small beginning of 20 students in Cobourg, the Van Normans established the Burlington Ladies' Academy in Hamilton, which had grown to 197 students by 1849. The building was a large four-storey brick structure that included a basement. The BLA was located at the corner of Bay and King streets, with spacious grounds around the building.[101] The Van Normans chose to rename the school, calling it an academy rather than a seminary, perhaps reflecting a desire to be associated with a move to a higher level of education or the embracing of a broader scope. Although the school did not receive funds directly from the church, the 1847 calendar stated that all Wesleyan ministers in the province could be asked for a reference.[102]

Ian Davey's study of the BLA has shown that in 1849, of the 197 students, 84 were listed as residents of Hamilton and the remainder were from the southern part of Canada West, upstate New York, and Montreal. The pupils ranged in age from eight to twenty-three, with the majority (78 per cent) over twelve years of age and 44.4 per cent over sixteen years. Methodists made up the largest group of students, but there were representatives of other major Protestant denominations. The occupations of the students' fathers in 1849 indicated that they were divided between entrepreneurs (29.4 per cent) and professionals (17.6 per cent), on the one hand, and skilled artisans on the other (44.1 per cent); widows formed the final category (8.9 per cent). Davey notes that some of the artisans must have sacrificed financially to have their daughters attend the academy, since the cost of tuition in the common English branches for a day student at the BLA was four times the amount charged by the public common schools.[103] Students at the BLA therefore were not from upper-class origins if they are judged on the basis of their fathers' occupations.[104]

A survey of the *Calliopean*, the student paper of the BLA, reveals a surprising amount of feminist sentiment. One article argued that since a mother's calling was the education of her children in manners and morals, it was necessary that she be well educated. Although she did not need to be a Madame de Staël or a Hannah More, the mother was to be "something more than a slave to her husband's convenience; something more than a canary-bird, to sing and shine for his amusement."[105] Another contributor stated that woman needed to be made aware of her situation in order to be converted from mental bondage to a life of honour and usefulness. The author was adamant that woman had not received her due, and any seeming improvement in her condition would not stand up to close scrutiny. Civilization had left her in total bondage. From infancy to maturity, claimed the writer, everything conspired to divert woman from a path of usefulness, and her aspirations were limited to "the toilette, domestic affairs, and the smiles of man." A lady's education only compounded these problems by surrounding her with prejudice and flattery.

Woman needed to wake from her stupor and "exercise her own energies and talents for her own emancipation."[106]

Unfortunately, little information is available about the students' own experience of life at the academy. One of the few sources is the autobiography of temperance leader Letitia Youmans, born Letitia Creighton. When the young Letitia heard that women were to be excluded from the Upper Canada Academy, she felt that her hopes for an education were dashed. But one morning her father announced that he had attended the examinations at the Van Norman seminary and he had been favourably impressed with the proficiency of the students. He decided that Letitia should attend the school. She left home in the fall with a new pine chest filled with her clothes. She was assigned to study grammar, geography, arithmetic, and English composition, in addition to reading, writing, and spelling. In the first three subjects, Creighton felt that she was breaking new ground, whereas for her classmates the material was a review of what they already knew. While other students played, she had to study to master mathematical rules and grammatical tenses. One morning she woke up at the five o'clock bell and worked with extra diligence until seven. She knocked on the door of her teacher, whose room adjoined hers, and asked to be excused from breakfast in order to work further on her mathematics. When the year ended, she chose the topic of "Perseverance" for her closing essay. The audience included Dr Ryerson, as well as faculty from Victoria College and citizens of Cobourg.

Letitia Creighton taught in a country school for the summer until it was decided that she should return to the Cobourg Ladies' Seminary. In order to keep the costs down, she and another student shared a room near the school and lived on fuel and provisions provided by their parents. When the school moved to Hamilton, Van Norman persuaded Creighton's parents to let her go to the academy to finish her education. To ease the financial burden of this plan, he promised the young woman employment in the school when she completed her diploma. Letitia concentrated on the first course, or the common English branches, which included botany, physiology, natural philosophy, chemistry, meteorology, natural history, astronomy, rhetoric, English classics, geometry, moral philosophy, geology, evidences, and French. She describes taking examinations in mental and moral philosophy, Paley's *Evidences of Christianity*, and geology. The second course, called the ornamental, was something for which she claimed she had no time to spare, nor "did my inclination run particularly in that direction."[107]

After her graduation from the BLA in the spring of 1847, Creighton became ill and returned to her home for the summer. At the end of the summer vacation she went back to the academy and became the first English teacher. She described the position as bearing great responsibility since she had to listen to recitations from nine AM to four PM with one hour for lunch, and in addition she visited the pupils in her section of the dormitory on a daily basis.

Another teacher's point of view is given by the principal's sister, Jane Van Norman, who had a very ambivalent attitude towards the school and her experience there after ten years of teaching in it. She poured out her frustrations in letters to her future husband, A. Dunham Emory. Jane Van Norman wrote that her brother was inclined to be irritable, but she seemed to blame this characteristic on Mrs Van Norman: "that you would have heard the scolding I got today from my dear brother, I bore it very patiently. Poor fellow, he is becoming very irritable but I forgive him and pity him. I would as a friend advise you never to marry a fretful woman, for of all things, I think an unamicable fretful female is to be dreaded. Our school is daily increasing in number; may it increase tenfold in usefulness."[108] The teachers at the school did not always work in a harmonious atmosphere, as is evident in a letter from Emory to his fiancée. He expressed his sorrow at hearing of the unpleasant feelings among the teachers and stated that it was lamentable that professing Christians allowed their feelings to carry them to such an extreme.[109]

Jane Van Norman's writings provide some insight into the principalship of Daniel Van Norman, which relied on a persuasive style of leadership. She was reluctantly appointed editress of the *Calliopean*,[110] the school literary magazine; as she wrote, "I wished to decline the appointment, but brother would not allow me."[111] In another letter she described an incident in which her brother asked her if she had prepared her editorial for the paper; she had replied in the negative, and her brother "seemed much disappointed and said, *well*, I shall have nothing to do with, nor give myself any uneasiness about it."[112] Jane Van Norman decided to set herself bravely to the task, but as soon as the first number appeared, she planned to resign in order to have time to paint and sing.

From the same source one can obtain a rare glimpse of the spirituality that occasionally burst forth in the school.

> The ladies have kept up their prayer meetings during the day, & as a proof that God is with us owning & blessing our labours, several have found that peace & joy in believing. Among whom are Misses Dressor, Harriet Van Norman & others you know not.

They have a prayer mtg. this evening after leaving the conversational meeting. I expect I shall get a scolding for not being there. We had a prayer meeting this morning at six o'clock. The work is still progressing. I pray from my very soul that it may advance until the halls of Burlington Academy will echo with the praises of God, & every soul will feel the forgiving & sanctifying influences of the grace of God.[113]

The connection between this spirituality and the sense of vocation a teacher demanded of herself was illustrated by Van Norman when she discussed her leaving the academy to marry. "I have not yet spoken to brother on the subject and know not when I shall. You see you have spoiled me for a teacher in the Burlington for no one whose whole heart is not in her vocation is fit for it. To tell you the whole truth, I have not, I feel discharged faithfully my every duty during the last session. Still I think I have done as well as the other teachers, but they are no criterion to be judged by. There is one thing in it, I will not be missed as much."[114] Letitia Youmans's account of the school also confirms the spirituality that characterized daily life. She stated that while not sectarian in its teaching, it was "truly evangelical in its influence." There were conversions nearly every session.[115]

Daniel Van Norman's frequent call for female education as a preparation for woman's proper sphere is somewhat ironic when viewed from his personal situation. Apparently he did not feel that his own wife was capable of bringing up their son. The power of a mother clearly had limits when a husband, the father, chose to exercise his vastly superior power. Jane Van Norman wrote that her brother had asked her whether she would take his son after he "quit nursing" and bring him up properly. Apparently, Mrs Van Norman, an American who had not been happy in Canada and considered Canadians a "rough, unrefined and uneducated lot," defended her right to train her own son.[116] But her husband assured Jane that if she would take him, he was hers. That Jane found her brother's request arrogant and presumptuous is evident in her letter to her future husband, which claimed, "Oh! If my husband had not sufficient confidence in me to entrust his children to my teaching!"[117] The situation at the school had exhausted her patience, and she felt that she deserved a chance to begin her own life. "If I were to dwell upon the subject I should soon render myself unfit for the proper discharge of duty. I could think, here I am, shut up & have been for the last ten years & expect in the Spring to get married & no time for anything like suitable preparation, I think I might have at least 3 months to spend in preparation after spending so much of my time for the benefit of the

School, and such like thoughts sometimes cross my mind, but I have to bid them begone."[118]

It was possibly soon after the resignation of his sister that Daniel Van Norman accepted an appointment to a school in New York. An institution built so solidly on the personality and reputation, as well as the financial ownership, of one man could not easily survive a transfer in leadership. Little of Van Norman's personal feelings at the end of this era of involvement in Canadian education for females is revealed in his letter to the editor of the *Christian Guardian*, although he acknowledged that the pinnacle of his hopes for founding a permanent institution for the education of girls had not been reached. But he conceded that he felt comforted in the good that had been accomplished.

According to Van Norman, much of the prejudice towards educating females had been removed. Furthermore, a spirit of inquiry on the subject had been awakened, so that in "almost every neighbourhood, town and city throughout the country, centres of moral influence have been planted." The books that had been carefully collected by students for the Calliopean Library, each one requiring the approval of the principal, were all subsequently donated to the Mechanics' Institute and the Mercantile Library Association of Hamilton. The bookcases were given to the Hamilton Ladies' Benevolent Society for their orphan asylum.[119] After the move to New York, Mrs Van Norman continued her involvement in female education by participating in the Women's Educational Association, begun in 1852, a group whose founding members included Mrs Sigourney, an author, Mrs Hale, editor of *Godey's Ladies' Book*, Catharine Beecher, and Harriet Beecher Stowe.[120] In the meantime, Van Norman himself took over the principalship of the Rutgers Female Institute in 1851, founded his own Van Norman Institute in 1857, and also co-authored a textbook on French.[121] He served as secretary of the American and Foreign Christian Union and was a founder of the American Chapel in Paris.[122]

The Hurlburts meanwhile had moved their school from Cobourg to Toronto and renamed it the Adelaide Academy, thus reviving the name suggested earlier for a girls' counterpart to a Methodist academy for boys.[123] In 1853 they moved again, this time to Hamilton, where they continued their enterprise until approximately 1858. They were perhaps put out of business by the opening of a new Methodist school, the Wesleyan Ladies' College, in the vicinity.[124]

The only other female school with Methodist connections dating from the 1840s was the Picton Ladies' Academy, organized by Daniel McMullen in 1848. McMullen had been born in Nova Scotia in 1799 and was converted in 1820 while working as a carpenter. He served as an itinerant preacher from 1825 to 1836 but when his health suffered he settled on a farm in Prince Edward County. He moved to Picton and opened a ladies' academy and for part of the time a school for boys. The ladies' academy boasted the leadership of Mary Electa Adams, by this time beginning to be known for her great talents in women's education, and a Miss E. Austin, who was in charge of the higher English branches. A report by the committee of the academy boasted in 1848 that Mary Electa Adams was a lady of long experience in teaching in one of the best female institutions in the country, and "considering her abilities and her experience, and the manifest improvement in several departments of the Academy since she assumed the charge of it, the Committee have no hesitancy in expressing their unqualified confidence in her abilities and management."[125] Miss E. Jones taught music in the ladies' academy, and Miss G. Playter headed the elementary department. By 1850 the school had an enrolment of sixty-eight girls in the female academy and forty-seven boys in the male and cost approximately £30 per year for tuition and board.[126] Students were expected to furnish their own beds, bedding, and towels and were charged 40 shillings extra per term in the winter for fuel and candles. Each term of eleven weeks cost £5 for board and laundry. The sexes were kept apart in separate buildings, and the male and female pupils met only at meal times. Extras in the female department cost 15 shillings for French, £2 for music, which included the use of a piano, £1 10s. for oil painting, 17 shillings for drawing, and 7 shillings for needlework and embroidery. In the male department, extras included Latin, Greek, French, algebra, and mathematics.[127] A report in the *Canadian Methodist Magazine* concluded that the academies were too far in advance of the times to be remunerative and were a financial loss to McMullen. In 1851 he rented the buildings to others and moved to a farm.

THE LEGACY OF THE EARLY GIRLS' SCHOOLS

Despite the set-backs and shifts that had occurred during these decades, the 1830s to the 1850s saw important attempts at formalizing higher education for young women. At first, girls were under the wing of the corporate coeducational school structure. A major shift involved the creation of academies that were publicly approved but privately funded and under the management of individuals rather than a board. The management of schools by couples left the female schools vulnerable to changes in leadership, however successful the attempt might have been during the tenure of the individuals involved. Nevertheless, these early schools left a vital legacy. The continued presence of male faculty and principals conveyed a strong message of male authority and of the proper order of gender relations. The structure of the schools with a male principal and a lady principal under his authority emulated the ideal family structure, and the principals acted as surrogate parents for impressionable young women away from home. Submission to the male principal was seen, by extension, as excellent training for the wifely duties that were assumed to be the purpose of female education. The ideal setting for women's learning was the middle-class family household, which also assumed the authority of the father and the moral and physical guidance of the mother.[128]

Similar schools in the United States, such as the Rutgers Female Institute, were referred to by one educator in the 1850s as "nurseries" for the American women's colleges of the future. No conflict was expected between the small private schools and the women's colleges because the functions of the two were anticipated to be quite different; that is, the former would offer college preparatory work as opposed to college-level work once the women's colleges were in place.[129] There were eventually consultations between those working in seminary and college education for women. The Women's Educational Association provided a forum for those interested in the issue. In the United States also, correspondence between principals of female seminaries and ladies' colleges allowed for an exchange of ideas. Dr Charles West, who was president of the Rutgers Female Institute in New York prior to Van Norman's assumption of the post, corresponded with Matthew Vassar about his plans to establish a women's college, plans that eventually came to fruition in 1861.[130]

Education in Canada West during this period was broad, liberal, and non-sectarian, and it attempted to compensate for the uneven and often inadequate preparation of pupils. But "serious" education did take place. Graduates of the female academy occasionally obtained employment in the same or another school, and gradually the province's supply of educated school mistresses increased. Women such as Mary Electa Adams, Miss Proctor, Sarah Jane Beatty, Rebecca Hurlburt, who taught in Ojibway mission schools, and E. Carter, who started a seminary in Markham after studying at the Upper Canada Academy and the Cobourg Ladies' Seminary,[131] received some or all of their training in these early Methodist ladies' schools. For the majority, however, the purpose of education was not vocational in the material sense of becoming a teacher so much as a preparation for the vocation of serving God in the kingdom of the family. The Episcopal Methodist press underlined this role as follows: "To arrive at a just conclusion as to what female education should be, we have only to consider what station young women are educated to fill – *they are to be the mothers and teachers of our race.*"[132] Daniel Van Norman's assumption that he had the right to override the mother's preferences and to make the ultimate decisions over family life reveals that women were educated to be mothers and teachers under careful male supervision. Women's authority over their sphere of action remained dependent on their meeting criteria set by men who knew best. The model of the family, which was advertised as the ideal way to govern a school, was therefore seen as an entirely appropriate training ground for the young woman who would play an important role in her own family. Although the young student was surrounded by women teachers with maternal influence, the ultimate authority was vested in the male principal. Both in the family and in the educational system, the distribution of power was based on a patriarchal model. As educational opportunities for women expanded in the following decades, the notion of God's kingdom would also expand and tie education to a wider definition of service beyond the familial one so clearly articulated in these early decades of female higher education.

3 A Return to the Coeducational Model: Albert College and Alexandra Ladies' College

Thus I have about the most pleasant and cheerful room of the building for private use, as my view is upon a widely extended country to the East … while my recitation room is commodious and airy, being second only to the English classroom for males in size; yet as it is in the Female section of the Institution, the probability is that there will be difficulties of management incident to it.[1]

In the face of the growing control by Wesleyans over education, members of the Episcopal Methodist denomination felt a need to start a school of their own. The rivalry between the two major branches of Methodism in Canada West, the Episcopal and Wesleyan Methodist churches, was therefore a major factor in the decision to establish an Episcopal Methodist school. As we have seen, this rivalry had roots in both Britain and the United States. The *Canada Christian Advocate*, the journal representing the Episcopal Methodist group, reported in 1852 that its church was bound to provide for the mental and moral training of tens of thousands under its influence; to meet this need, the journal recommended the building of a literary institution.[2] Part of the mission of the proposed academy was to upgrade education for the ministry. The *Advocate* also claimed that improved common and grammar schools did not negate the need for a seminary of learning that would offer both a commercial and a classical education, "with the addition of a female department."[3] Furthermore, the size of the geographic area that the church attempted to serve justified the creation of schools in different parts of Canada West.

Belleville, for example, would serve the eastern part of the province, whereas Alma College in St Thomas would be created in 1881 in response to a felt need for an Episcopal Methodist women's college in the southwestern part of Ontario. Similar schools were thus justified in more than one locale. The acquisition of a college by a town was, moreover, a considerable source of pride for its inhabitants. In this chapter the Methodist Episcopal Church's relation to education as a voluntary enterprise in a coeducational setting will be discussed. Coeducation was the subject of debates not only in Methodist schools in Canada, but also in the public and private schools of Britain and the United States. Episcopal Methodist schooling offers the contrast of the coeducational model, but it also demonstrates the fact that the denomination adhered to a strict voluntarism, in contrast to the accommodation with the state which the Wesleyans tended towards. Affiliations and federations with the provincial university and with the Methodist university would eventually test the extreme voluntarism of the early years of Albert College's establishment.

EPISCOPAL METHODIST EDUCATION

Why did the Episcopal Methodists feel a need to found their own school? As we have seen, the Methodist Episcopal Church, which began with Loyalists who had moved to Upper Canada after the American Revolution, in 1834 split from the newly formed Wesleyan Methodist Church in Canada.[4] Because the courts recognized the claims of the Wesleyan church, the continuing Methodist Episcopal Church was excluded from a share in such properties as the Upper Canada Academy in Cobourg. The establishment of an Episcopal Methodist identity moved by steps: after holding its first conference in 1836 and establishing a book room in 1844, the church by 1848 began to organize around the educational question.[5] Membership numbered 8,000 in 1848 and 9,500 five years later. This increase likely led to a sense of optimism in the continued growth of the denomination and the need to prepare for the education of its young people.

Belleville had served as the site of the first conference in 1836 and was an appropriate location for the proposed school. In a calendar from 1866 it was described as a town of about 7,000 inhabitants, situated on the Grand Trunk Railway and "the liveliest port on the beautiful Bay of Quinte."[6] The location of the school in a town, rather than an isolated or rural setting, followed a tendency that seems to have been more particular to Canadian than to American schools.

Although the Episcopal Methodist denomination was concerned with emphasizing Canadian loyalties and with shaping the school as a Canadian institution, ties to the American Methodist church and educational institutions were not easily avoided. When Albert College experienced a shortage of teachers, it had to solicit American instructors and even an American principal in the case of Principal Jabez Jacques, who led the college from 1875 to 1884.

The Bay of Quinte Conference supported the project and in 1853 appointed the Reverend J.H. Johnson as an agent to collect funds. The moral support of the General Conference was important for the survival of the school. In the United States, the stamp of official approval by the conference allowed a school the privilege of going "before the Methodists of the Conference as a Methodist institution, and, on this basis, of soliciting funds and appealing for patronage and support; and not infrequently it received the permission of the Conference to use the pulpits to appeal for such support."[7] A similar process of appeal was used by the Belleville Seminary, as Albert College was first known, as it tried to raise contributions from among the Church membership and the broader community.

The Belleville Seminary was instituted and supported by a tradition that was fiercely independent and voluntarist, thereby necessitating a broad base of support from individual contribution. The issue of state support also surfaced in academies in the United States. The pro-American tendencies of the Methodist Episcopal Church may have increased awareness of this principle. The Episcopal Methodists reacted not only to the existence of Wesleyan Methodist schools but also to Anglican domination in education. From the vantage point of the Episcopal Methodists, the attempt by the Anglican archdeacon of York (Toronto), John Strachan, to found a state university under Anglican control, had been an ominous threat to religious freedom. His charter for King's College, obtained in 1827, led to years of controversy that blocked the opening of the college until 1843. The delay helped the Methodists and the Presbyterians to organize and establish their own colleges. In reaction to the threat of control by the Anglicans, the Methodists stressed the non-sectarian nature of the teaching in their schools. But this emphasis did not satisfy the Episcopal Methodists.[8] John Moir notes that the differences between the Wesleyan and Episcopal Methodists were such that the latter did not consider sending students to the Wesleyan Methodist Upper Canada Academy.[9]

Questions of relations between state and denominational control of education, as well as subsequent university federation, seem to have been debated without direct reference to female education. Yet these very issues were integral to the climate within which female seminaries and ladies' colleges operated. The future success or failure of Methodist-sponsored female education was ultimately determined by the relationships of the leaders of Methodist education to the province and to the provincial university, relationships that were established during this period. As Moir indicates, the pattern of higher education established between 1850 and 1867 was a "patchwork of sectarian colleges, denominational universities, and ... the nationalized, secularized University of Toronto."[10]

THE BELLEVILLE SEMINARY

The early years of Albert College were marked by struggles and growing pains, but it must be remembered that Victoria College also faced extremely trying times. Burwash, in his history of Victoria, notes that enrolment at the college dropped from 149 in 1849 to 39 students and three professors in the winter of 1851. Methodists were urged to consider a grant from the provincial Legislature, as well as donations, subscriptions, and scholarships. Beginning in the 1850s, the government gave the denominational colleges an annual grant of £500, which was later increased to £750. Victoria College had been eager to work out an agreement with the Legislature and the provincial university that would help it fulfil its immediate goals as a Methodist college, but would also guarantee its long-term survival. The endowment controlled by the university was a crucial factor in cooperation, but this was an option that was not open to Albert College, given the stance of the Methodist Episcopal Church that state funding constituted corruption.

Since the church opposed government grants of any sort, it depended on agents to travel the circuits to solicit contributions for the educational fund. A lot was purchased in Belleville and a contractor agreed upon. Contributions did not keep pace with costs, however, and soon the *Canada Christian Advocate* was urging members to send subscriptions to relieve the building committee from its embarrassment.[11] Controversy erupted when the government offered the school a grant to accompany the bill of incorporation in 1855. The education committee of the Belleville Seminary quickly drafted a resolution to express its disapproval of any government grants for the seminary, and when the school opened in July 1857, with Johnson as principal, it had received no state subsidy.[12]

Unfortunately, a financial depression that year, which affected both sides of the border, coincided with the opening of the school, further worsening the financial picture. The crisis did not, however, inhibit the spirit of revivalism in the school and enthusiasm for its continued existence. In 1858 male and female students gathered nightly in the principal's study to pray for the outpouring of the Spirit. The number of students increased until Principal Johnson moved them to the chapel, where professors took turns in preaching and conducting meetings, "which are attended with such signal manifestations of the divine presence."[13]

The curriculum was originally divided into two departments, primary and advanced. The primary department taught reading, penmanship, spelling, geography, arithmetic and history. The advanced department included bookkeeping, algebra, geometry, natural philosophy, chemistry, geology, mineralogy, astronomy, botany, zoology, Latin, Greek, mental and moral philosophy, and natural theology. In addition to these two departments the school offered "extras" such as French, German, Italian, Spanish, music, embroidery, drawing, and painting.[14] Waldo Smith observed that in fact the curriculum offered more subjects "in ladylike gentility than were really wanted" since only two students took drawing and none took embroidery in the late 1850s.[15] The tuition was $5 per term for the primary department and $8 for the advanced department, while extras could add at from $3 to $14 to the basic tuition, and board was $2 per week. The male students were supervised by a moral governor, whereas the "young ladies" were the responsibility of the preceptress. Female students were allowed to attend any classes offered at the institution.

Finances were not the only contentious issue at the new college. Problems concerning discipline and a campaign to discredit Principal Johnson undermined support for the college. After some vicious infighting, Albert Carman, a graduate of Victoria College, became the new principal in 1858. He was the son of Philip Carman and Emeline Shaver, whose families were United Empire Loyalists. Albert Carman had been born in the village of Iroquois in Dundas County in 1833 and had been educated at the Matilda Common School and the Dundas County Grammar School before attending Victoria. His father was an Episcopal Methodist, and despite the church's lack of social prestige, he preferred to remain such. Philip Carman did not want to influence his son's choice of denomination, but he wrote him in 1854 that "he could not conceal his wish that his son remain within the Episcopal fold."[16] A few months later Albert followed his father's advice and joined the Methodist Episcopal Church. He graduated from Victoria in 1855 and completed a master's degree five years later. After serving as head master of the Dundas County Grammar School from 1854 to 1857, he was professor of mathematics at the Belleville Seminary for a year. Between 1858 and 1874 he would be principal of the seminary, president of Albert College, and then chancellor of Albert University, going on in 1874 to become bishop of the

Methodist Episcopal Church in Canada and later general superintendant of the newly united Methodist Church. In 1860 he married Mary Sisk, who was a member of the first honour class at the Belleville Seminary in 1858.[17] Carman acquired, in 1858, the leadership of an institution with a declining enrolment, a deficit budget, and a community split by internal fights. Time would show him to be equal to the massive task of rebuilding.

The early years of the school were marked by struggles between individuals who had widely differing ideas on its governance and who often placed personal opinion ahead of the best interests of the institution. The board, for example, used the distribution of scarce finances to secure support from faculty who shared their views. In 1858 Carman reported that he had received $110, which was presumably only a part of his salary for the entire year; $65 of it was seized with the help of Johnson before it reached the treasurer, and he extracted $15 "to pay a debt when palpable disgrace was imminent."[18] Another irregularity involved the music department. The school suddenly had two music teachers because one, who had previously been let go, was reinstated by the board. Apparently this teacher owed money to one of the board members, and he decided that she should continue to be employed until he could recover his loan. Decisions such as these, made for in the interests of the individual, rather than for the benefit of the school, required a strong leader to handle.

Carman took a stand with the board in 1858 and agreed to stay only if certain conditions were met, such as the firing of this music teacher and the hiring of other needed assistants.[19] Such internal problems had an adverse effect on enrolment, yet Carman remained hopeful that the student body would increase and the debt be dissolved through aggressive action by the church. If the school could not be set on its feet, several wealthy Wesleyans had offered to buy the property "and convert it into a Female Seminary as the complement of Victoria College."[20] Carman wrote to his father that he praised the Lord for "so energetic and successful a Church as the Wesleyan Methodist," and he wished it more success and prosperity. He believed, however, that the Episcopal Methodists had their work to do and "our part of the Lord's vineyard to cultivate." Defeat by the Wesleyans was unthinkable; Carman was a long way from admitting failure, and he believed that "if we allow our Institutions to languish and die, we are morally delinquent."[21] Uncertainty concerning the future of the school was nevertheless deep. Carman privately hesitated about having his brother Robert and sister Metty come to the college in 1858, advising his father that their attendance would be risky. Still, the enrolment needed a boost. One factor the new principal believed would help the school was the fact that a number of students came from a distance; "the more we have the more difficult it will be for those men [the dissident members of the board] to succeed in closing up."[22]

A letter to the *Canada Christian Advocate* in 1859 expressed confidence that the denomination would support the school. But the writer urged that no time be lost because enemies were predicting the institution's demise, with the result that the "Seminary will pass into the hands of the more *favored* Methodists ... who will not scruple to seek for and receive Government patronage, as has been and is the case with 'Victoria College.'"[23] The threat of failure and subsequent surrender to the more affluent and established Wesleyans was no doubt a powerful incentive for the Episcopal Methodists to make their school succeed.

Despite the apparent pro-American proclivities of its founders, Belleville Seminary grew out of a strong sense of a Canadian identity. In the minds of its Episcopal Methodist supporters, the school stood as a symbol of independence from both British and American influence. In Principal Johnson's inaugural address in 1857, for example, he called for the building of a nationality for Canada and looked forward to the country's future greatness. A Canadian education, he argued, meant an education suited to the needs of the Canadian people, in preparation for their future roles in developing the country. Not only did the sciences, classics, and mathematics deserve attention, but also those branches generally considered inferior that prepared students for practical work. The education given at Belleville would be commercial as well as classical and ornamental as well as solid. One error committed in other countries, which Johnson felt should be avoided in Belleville, was the tendency of educating daughters while neglecting their minds and educating sons while neglecting their bodies. A balanced education attended to the physical, intellectual, and moral needs of the individual, whether male or female. Mental discipline acquired through intellectual branches would train the mind, fitting it for a life of usefulness. The implication was that although these aspects were common to male and female education, clearly the ultimate ends of their education would be gender-specific.

Despite such strong commitment to the education of both sexes, the early years of the school continued to be marked by financial adversity. The principle of voluntarism was put to the test in the winter of 1858 when the treasurer of the seminary "drew a grant of eight hundred dollars from the government."[24] The announcement of this grant by the *Globe* damaged the school and caused a withdrawal of support by many Episcopal Methodists. The General Conference of July 1858 took charge of the school, appointed a new board, and organized a campaign to raise money from the various local conferences. By the spring of 1861 the student registration had dropped to fifty students, and Carman's father was sending shipments of food to help them through. Students also often supported themselves at the school by their labour, such as sawing wood, or by paying fees in commodities instead of in cash.[25]

ALBERT COLLEGE

Affiliation with the University of Toronto in 1860 helped to lend the school, eventually renamed Albert College, new credibility. The continual financial crises no doubt influenced the college's decision to seek accommodation with the provincial university. In response to Albert Carman's initial query about how affiliation would affect the structure of the college, Judge Robert Burns, then chancellor of the university, was reassuring. Coeducation was evidently the issue, but Carman was told that coeducation at Belleville would not prevent the school from enjoying the benefits of affiliation with the university. Burns added the following condition: "Of course you would only send us the Students of the male sex inasmuch as the university only receives and confers degrees upon such."[26] The affiliation and the college's eventual status as Albert University in 1866 were steps towards a more secure establishment: enrolment increased in 1868 to 190 men and 72 women, and 99 of these students were in residence.[27]

Albert College functioned as a genuinely coeducational institution at a time when this practice was largely untried in higher education in Ontario. It would be another decade before women students would be allowed even to take Victoria's matriculation examinations. The Methodists in the United States seemed to have generally preferred a coeducational model, or at least a female department, beginning at the secondary level. In addition, schools such as Cazenovia College in New York were coeducational at the higher level. It seems clear, however, that whether education was organized along single-sex or coeducational lines, schools were intended to create a clear gender division based on a heterosexual, middle-class understanding of the roles of men and women.

An impression of daily life at Albert College is revealed in letters written by Albert Carman's sister Metty to her parents during her studies in Belleville. She described her room at the college, which she shared with two room-mates. "Our room is nicely carpeted & pretty well fitted up, with furniture and luggage – we have a nice little stove – A nice sofa, a table, bedstead & a nice large looking glass, so that, I am quite comfortable. Albert has charge of my bedding."[28] Metty claimed that her handkerchiefs had been "pilfered" by other students, causing one of her room-mates to put a lock on their door. Other students regarded Carman's sister with circumspection, and she feared that she would not become well acquainted with them because they were so shy with her. Her presence caused a silence to fall. "If I meet them upon the stairs, going to or from their rooms, It is pardon me, excuse me, at every step, one would think me the preceptress herself – they all shun me so much – & perhaps it is better so, they are in the habit of appearing downtown in borrowed plumes, & I do not care about lending mine."[29]

Although her brother had a great deal of influence over Metty's stay at the college, she rarely saw him, partly because his rooms were located on the same floor as a mischievous group of students. On one occasion the male students threw a large stone at his door and split the panelling. Another group of male students left the building without permission and went to town unknowingly followed by Albert Carman and J.H. Johnson, who then went back to the school to await the students' return. During a meeting of the board, several male students put a bedstead on the roof of the school. Despite these pranks, Carman seemed to have a certain tolerance for the inevitable mischief generated by the male students, as he demonstrated to his father in the following observation: "Boys will have their sport, and eighty of them together will prosecute some mischief – I believe that I am loved by many and respected by all the students."[30] The mischief expected from the ladies seems to have been of quite a different sort, and their behaviour was closely prescribed. An attempt by the board to change the rules regulating students in 1858 was interpreted by Carman as an assault on the government of the school and a declaration of a lack of confidence in the faculty. Members of the board had apparently attempted to liberalize restrictions governing the ladies' going to town and communication between the sexes.[31]

Carman corresponded regularly with his parents and reported on his siblings' progress at the school. He generally oversaw their choice of subjects; for instance, he planned that Metty would take a limited number of subjects, about four, so that she would be "thorough." His choices for her included music, algebra, and French, subjects for which she had expressed some preference. His longer-range plans for her studies were to "incite her to pursue some other branches, as Philosophy, Rhetoric, & if you and Mother have preferences I wish you would make them known." Carman also expressed his hope that during her stay at school, Metty would not experience any deterioration in her religious experience but that her faith would grow and her "joy become full."[32] Part of his program for his sister was to engage her as a teacher for a Sunday school class in town, since she would "find it as delightful a task to instruct children in the way to Jesus here as elsewhere."[33] Metty taught the class, but since it required her to go to town three times on Sunday, she found it very tiring. Her health, Carman reported, was fine, but she had some trouble with her algebra.

Metty apparently attended the school from approximately January 1858 until December of that year. When she left in December, Albert Carman wrote to his father that she had done so with the same eagerness that she had attended the school. He hoped that she had learned that every sphere of life had its difficulties. He also wished that if she was unable to return to school because she was required at home, that she would realize that "true happiness can be derived from increasing the comforts and multiplying the enjoyments of a humble home." If Metty was allowed to return to school, Carman felt that she would benefit from studies in mental philosophy since she had done enough mathematics "for a girl."[34] Metty does not appear on the list of graduates, and it seems that she was unable to return to the school the next semester. Her sister Ada attended in the fall of 1859 but did not graduate.

Robert Carman graduated around 1867 with a bachelor of arts degree and later did graduate work in natural science at Harvard.[35] Albert Carman's early progress reports on his brother were mixed. Robert had initially pursued his studies with diligence, although he did have some trouble getting up in the morning. By the end of December 1859, Carman was less enthusiastic about his brother's behaviour at the school and claimed that Robert had become careless in his study habits and less than exemplary in his conduct. Nevertheless, Carman urged his father to let Robert stay at the school if he could be spared at home.

Responsibilities at home frequently interrupted a student's education. For example, it was the illnesses of Carman's mother and sister in 1858 that led Philip Carman to ask his son to send Metty home to help. Carman urged his father to leave her at school until the formal end of term lest her premature leaving unsettle the minds of other students and cause them also to leave before the end of term.[36] Student life could also be interrupted by the illness of the student, as in the case of Ada Carman. After a doctor had treated Ada by bleeding her, Carman wrote to his father that he had been absent at the time and had not anticipated this treatment; he reported that he "was displeased when I heard of the course he took: particularly when I remembered your antipathy to the practice."[37] Even though Ada could not seem to endure "very close application to study," Albert Carman felt that the school experience agreed with her. He believed that she would be keen to return after the term had ended, but he thought that on the other hand, "it might be better to save her means for other purposes."[38]

Records indicate that, despite the growth in enrolment, Albert College continued to be in financial trouble throughout the 1860s. A deficit for one year in 1862 of over fifteen hundred dollars required some rethinking of the school's needs. One measure, which was suggested for immediate discussion, was to give the female students the opportunity to earn diplomas. "A course of Study for girls with a diploma for its completion might greatly increase the attractions and efficiency of the School."[39] The proportion of female to male students at the school was 61 female to 82 male in 1861, making the presence of female students a significant and welcome addition to revenues from tuition and board. The economic factor was, in this case, an important motivation for the maintenance of coeducation at the school. The catalogue of the school lists a total of 726 students attending between the years 1857 and 1866, of which 296 were girls and 430 boys; the girls were thus about 40 per cent of the total number who attended in that period.[40]

Relations between teachers and the administration were occasionally marked by some awkwardness. Carman, for example, wrote a series of letters in 1861 to J.J. Passmore concerning the employment of the latter's sister as preceptress of the ladies' college. Apparently in the opinion of officers, teachers, and committee, Miss Passmore was "not at all well adapted" to the place she held, and Carman suggested that she resign at the end of the term.[41] There was a great concern over the delicacy of the matter and over giving the appearance that Miss Passmore was leaving on her own account. Her poor performance at the school had left Carman with the impression that she was a "mere child," fighting with her charges like a little girl or getting angry with her pupils and not speaking to them for days. Her strategies for dealing with students resulted in their "losing all their respect." Furthermore, she did not seem to have the "first idea of order as to the arrangement of her work" and demonstrated an inability to set regular practice hours for her music students.[42] Her qualifications were also unsatisfactory. Her real competence was in fact in painting, and in subjects such as music, English, and French, she was actually less qualified than her students. Not only did she avoid the subjects in which she had no competence, but to Carman's chagrin, she boasted to the students of her non-acquaintance with these fields. She apparently had charge of students who were between eighteen and twenty-four years of age, some of whom had been studying music at the school for three or four years. Miss Passmore had given Carman "more trouble in disciplining young ladies than any other Preceptress."[43] The crowning insult to his ideal of how a preceptress should behave was revealed by a petition that he intercepted, written by the students to Miss Passmore and asking her not to make use of their names in relation to an incident where an individual had tied her up in her room.[44] The records contain no further reference to her, and one can presume that Miss Passmore was replaced promptly at the end of term.

Correspondence between Carman and various American schoolteachers suggests that it was somewhat difficult to find women teachers for the school. He was thus led to correspond with authorities in the United States, a practice he had previously deplored. One source of American teachers was the American School Institute of New York, which claimed to transact all kinds of educational business, especially locating teachers.[45] Carman's correspondence also indicates that there was some competition for the best teachers and the most desirable positions, as word spread between institutions about those considered most qualified. Anna Green, for example, was employed at Belleville as preceptress and music teacher, but was also pursued by Cazenovia College for a similar job there.[46] When another applicant heard that Green would not be returning to Belleville, she immediately sent a letter to Carman, applying for the job and referring to her previous experience as preceptress of the Genesee Wesleyan Seminary at Lima.[47] Similar letters of application indicate the variety of institutions from which women had graduated or where they had taught. Clara Brown, another applicant for the job as preceptress, offered references from Lowville Academy, New York, and Wooster Female Academy in New Haven.[48] Eliza Gardner was another American applicant for the position of preceptress; she had graduated from the Gouverneur Academy and then worked as the head of the ladies' department of the Lancerville Academy. The applicants seemed generally willing to teach a wide range of subjects, including Latin, French, German, and higher mathematics, in addition to such accomplishments as painting and music.

Correspondence from parents and students indicates that sending daughters to Belleville often meant economic sacrifice. One father requested an estimate of expected costs for his eldest daughter to attend the school from November 1863 to April 1864, and "perhaps longer if I can accomplish it." He was interested in knowing what branches would be taught to her, "including Musick and drawing with whatever else that might be useful to her that is taught in the Institution."[49] Financial questions also inspired a letter from a prospective student who was enrolled at the Wesleyan Ladies' College in Hamilton, but who was considering a transfer. She wrote, "I like this school very much, and should not think of leaving it only that the expenses are so very great."[50] The Carman family was by no means the only one affected by financial and family circumstances that could restrict or cut short the academic life of students. E.A. Hurd wrote about her school career in 1864, "When I went down to Belleville College there was every prospect of continuing a year if not longer, but pa was taken ill ... it required all that was left in our possessions to pay the funeral expenditures."[51] This student, who signed her letter, "your unworthy sister in Christ," described her intention to continue at a local school where there was a good teacher, and then after a short time of "close application I shall be able to take charge of a small school." She begged Carman's patience concerning the repayment of her debt since both her brothers-in-law were ministers, and "a ministerial life is very promising of those riches which endureth for ever, but *not of this worlds goods*."[52]

The college lost the leadership of Albert Carman in 1874, when he was elected bishop of the Methodist Episcopal Church at the age of forty-two. He was replaced by the Reverend Jabez R. Jacques from the American Methodist Episcopal Church,[53] who with his wife brought to Albert College a wealth of experience in a variety of American institutions. He had immigrated from England to the United States and had served as vice-president of Hodding College in Abingdon, Illinois, and as professor of languages and vice-president of the Wesleyan University of Bloomington, Illinois. When he met his future wife, he was principal of the Troupburg Academy.[54] Mrs Jacques had also had extensive experience in education. She graduated from the Genesee Wesleyan Seminary in 1854 and was elected preceptress of Troupburg Academy. After a year in that position she married the principal. The couple moved on to become the principal and preceptress of the Mansfield Classical Academy. The illness of their first-born led to the child's subsequent blindness. This event, combined with the burning down of the Mansfield academy, resulted in Mrs Jacques's withdrawal from education. She served as a pastor's wife in Elmira and Rochester, where she taught a Bible class. In 1863 Jabez Jacques retired as pastor because of illness, and they made Rochester their home. Mrs Jacques apparently resumed her career in education, because it was while she was preceptress of the Rochester Collegiate Institute in 1865, that Dr Jacques was elected to the Wesleyan University in Illinois. During her ten years in Illinois, Mrs Jacques worked with the Women's Temperance League, a prayer group for women, and the Women's Educational Society, and helped to open a residence for women students at Wesleyan. When they eventually moved to Belleville, she served as preceptress for four years and worked with the Woman's Christian Temperance Union of Belleville and the Women's Christian Association. Her death in 1880 must have been a significant loss for both Albert College and the surrounding community.

ALEXANDRA COLLEGE AND WOMEN'S EDUCATION

The establishment of Alexandra Ladies' College at Belleville in 1869 did not represent a major change in the educational policy that had been in place, namely, offering ladies separate courses, as well as access to the undergraduate program of Albert College.[55] An entrance examination, called the novitiate, was given at the new college and was followed by a three-year course of study. The origin of this term is unknown, but it may have reflected a desire to separate the female exams from the male, in the same way that the term "preceptress" separated female from male professors.

Diplomas, which included the mistress of liberal arts and mistress of modern literature degrees and a diploma in music, were offered to students. Certificates of honour were given to those who achieved first-class honours in any department. By 1871 the college offered several options for board, including room and board in the college ($2 per week), board with "respectable families in the neighbourhood"(from $2 to $2.50 per week), and rooms in the college in which the students could board themselves ($.60 per week). Presumably this last alternative meant that students would do their own housekeeping and provisioning. For young people accustomed to regular tasks on the farm and unaccustomed to the assistance of servants, it would have been a reasonable option. According to the Albert College calendar, this option appealed to many parents because it kept the costs of education low, and it was not an unpleasant choice for those whose homes were within twenty miles of the college.[56] The proximity to home seemed to have taken precedence over denominational affiliation for four Wesleyan girls who attended in 1865, since all four were from Belleville.[57] The list of graduates in the calendar indicates that many students may have attended but not qualified for graduation. Between 1865 and 1871 graduate degrees included four mistresses of liberal arts (MLA), three mistresses in modern literature (MML), and four diplomas in music. The MLA was a respectable degree for a woman, but one that was not considered equal to a BA for a man. "We have not ourselves supposed that the Law of the land would put it upon a par with our B.A. ... though in some cases it may imply a very high degree of Scholarship."[58] Carman believed that the government should recognize the work of "thorough Ladies' Schools and Colleges, as I believe you will admit ours to be."[59]

By the 1870s, divergent opinions existed concerning the degree of seriousness that ladies' education merited. On the one hand, the accomplishments were believed to be the most appropriate focus for their instruction. "As a woman's life is often a life of feeling rather than of action, and if society, while it limits her sphere of action, frequently calls upon her to express her feelings, we should not deny her the high, the recreative, the healthy outlet, for emotion which music supplies. A good play on the piano has not unfrequently taken the place of a good cry upstairs."[60] For some, however, the need for musical training offered the additional advantage that it could be used as a skill for survival. The *Canada Christian Advocate* acknowledged that for many young ladies, the motive for the study of music was not pleasure, but rather so that, in case of need, "they may be able to provide for themselves by teaching."[61]

The debate concerning the structure and purpose of girls' education, as well as the correctness of coeducation, found expression in the church press. One writer, having attended the commencement exercises at Alexandra, remarked with approval on the presence of ladies in college classes on equal terms with the young men, a practice he believed was overdue in other colleges, since "nothing is gained by denying the ladies these privileges, and nothing is lost by their admission to them."[62] Another writer of the same persuasion claimed that the law of the country was in an anomalous position when "no legal value is attached to a lady's degree, which may require years of study, while the highest positions are open to gentlemen that have passed to their Degrees. We ought to have a change in this matter."[63]

An outspoken advocate of women's education was the editor of the *Advocate* Thomas Webster, who defended, whenever possible, the right of women to have equal educational privileges to men. The argument against women's entrance into colleges and universities, which was based on a belief that they had a limited mental capacity, was, according to Webster, a "relic of barbarous and semi-barbarous times" that, although it had been purged from minds in Europe and America, still lingered on the "borders of civilization in all lands."[64]

Canadian colleges and universities needed to be thrown open to young ladies to allow them "to compete with their brothers" for degrees in arts. Webster countered the claim that this type of education would not be useful for women by stating that if a collegiate education was good for men, it would also, on the same principle, be good for women. The proper place to begin the movement was Albert College, and he urged that it be the first publicly to acknowledge the "intellectual equality of the sexes."[65] Coeducation began with God's plan in the family and was continued by education in the public schools. There was no danger in "our daughters knowing too much," and there was also no need to legislate against their intelligence.[66]

The argument gained some momentum at an alumni dinner in 1874, when a Professor Dawson argued that the ladies' degrees indicated an advanced scholarship and needed to be recognized by law. Perhaps, he conceded, some ladies' colleges were not doing thorough work, but in institutions such as Alexandra, where ladies attended the same lectures as the gentlemen and took the same examinations, there was no reason why their degrees should not carry the same weight. His conclusion was that the college should "Give ladies Degrees, and give them the same validity as others, is our Doctrine and give them Degrees, not simply on a man's University course of Latin, Greek and Hebrew, but on such subjects as are adapted to them and will thoroughly educate them."[67] Although Dawson was an advocate of women's education, he clearly believed that specially adapted courses for women students were required. Webster's view was more radical in that he advocated fully equal courses for male and female students. Clearly, coeducation was open to a variety of interpretations, but the majority seemed to agree with Dawson that women's special nature required special educational adaptation. This view, as will be seen, persisted into the twentieth century. Even when students studied exactly the same courses, there was still an expectation that the goals of male versus female education were very different. Change at Albert College proceeded slowly, however, and the curricula and status of women's diplomas remained fairly consistent. The awarding of a BA degree to Miss E.A. Marden of Albert College in 1883 appears to have been a rare exception, and there is no information available to clarify whether she was examined in Latin, Greek, and Hebrew.[68]

In a letter to the editor of the *Globe*, probably written in the 1880s, Carman acknowledged that facilities for the higher education of women had improved, not because women were expected to figure in professional life, but because "mind to be mind must be cultivated."[69] Despite this progress, he felt that education for women in

Canada was still running behind the times, especially when one acknowledged developments at the University of London. Why, questioned Carman, could Albert University not institute university privileges for women, since female students already had the advantages of attending classes with male university students? He suggested two possibilities: either ladies' diplomas should be fully recognized in order that they could be a "passport to positions and honour" or the women should be allowed to take the same course as the men, write the same examinations, and receive fully equivalent degrees. The present structure of course options at Albert allowed female students a choice between Latin and German or Latin and Music, but always required French. Female students who took Latin had a special advantage and full opportunity to attend all college lectures in natural science, physics, mathematics, and history.[70]

ALBERT COLLEGE AFTER 1884

If Albert University was on the verge of offering BA degrees to women, changes in the organization of Methodist education and the provincial university closed this door. By 1884, Methodist union restructured the relationship of Methodist colleges, with the result that Albert surrendered its degree-granting powers. It became a secondary school, and most advanced work in arts and theology was transferred to Victoria University. In 1890 Victoria affiliated with the University of Toronto. Six years later the Albert College calendar announced that the MLA diploma from Alexandra gave students a full first-year standing at the provincial university, which was somewhat lower than schools such as the Ontario Ladies' College, from which graduates received two years' credit for their degrees. Albert experienced a change in leadership with Dr Jacques's retirement in the 1880s and the appointment of Professor Dyer as the new principal. Another addition to the faculty was Miss Ella Gardiner, a BA graduate (1884) from the University of Toronto.[71] These two individuals led the school into the twentieth century.

Having surrendered its university status, the college nevertheless sought to emphasize the professional and practical element in its old advanced programs. The calendar of 1885 showed that Albert offered junior or senior matriculation in art, civil engineering, law, medicine, and theology. In addition, there was a "collegiate" course, a teacher's course, a musical program, ornamental penmanship, fine arts, a mines and agriculture course, and the ladies' college course.[72] The commercial department, which had opened in 1877 and listed graduates starting in 1879, became the Belleville Business College in 1884.

Business students were allowed to board at Albert College and use its library. The business college was thus a department of Albert, and its catalogue named Dr Jacques as its president and a Mr G. Swayze as its headmaster. Business college students were advised that the school was located in the healthiest part of the city.[73] Indeed, the grandeur of the ladies' department, or Alexandra College, where female business students would live, claimed the business college catalogue, was now equal to other colleges of its class in Ontario. It was adorned with brilliant oil paintings, "tasty frescoeing, carpeting, and new furniture."[74] Parents wishing a commercial course for their daughters could therefore have them board at Alexandra, which was "certainly much better than having to seek board and lodgings in promiscuous boarding houses."[75] According to the catalogue, parents had frequently remarked that they would rather send their sons and daughters to an institution situated as the college was "than to have them go to schools kept in the centre of the business portion of cities, in rooms situated over stores, etc."[76] The business college claimed that it offered the same advantages to ladies as to men, being convinced that ladies were just as capable of completing the course and finding positions as their male competitors. Renovations continued at Albert with the creation of a new storey out of the attic in 1889. In the 1890s, with the assistance of a bequest from the Massey family, a new wing was added that housed classrooms, art rooms, a laboratory, and a museum. In January 1896 a gymnasium was built, and both male and female students had the use of the gym at regular assigned hours.

The school's senate in 1891–92 included two women, Ella Gardiner and Emma Clarke. Female students in attendance in 1891 were largely drawn from Belleville and the vicinity. Interestingly, male students derived from a wider variety of locations, including British Columbia, southwestern Ontario, central Ontario, Toronto, Quebec and New Hampshire.[77] According to Waldo Smith, Albert students came from homes with modest incomes; it was an exception to have a student attend from a wealthy background. By 1897–98 the school had awarded to women students thirty MLA and three MML diplomas and six diplomas in the collegiate course, senior matriculation. The small number of collegiate course graduates may have been an indication that parents with scarce resources chose to send their female children to the local secondary school, where they could either finish their studies or prepare for university entrance.

From 1885 until 1928, the college benefited from the leadership of Ella Gardiner, who had been hired to teach modern languages.[78] She was an extremely religious woman whose influence on students must have been considerable. Smith described her as an "educational pioneer" as well as a "devout woman facing her daily work without the sustaining daily affection of family or partner, turning to the inner experience of divine companionship."[79] Gardiner's diary has evidently been lost, but according to Smith, in it in 1890 she confided her spiritual concerns: "I have been teaching in this college for nearly five years. During that time I have been teaching nearly six hundred students. God grant that some good may come to them! I have not neglected my duties as a teacher of Latin, English, French and German but Have I done anything directly or indirectly for Christ?"[80]

One of Gardiner's particular interests was the Student Missionary Society at the college. The mission movement there had originated in June 1876 when a group of women at the college organized the Woman's Missionary Society of the Methodist Episcopal Church. In 1887 a mission band was formed, and one member of the band, Minnie Wilson, went to Shanghai, China. The list of missionaries who received their education at Alexandra College is impressive. It includes Kate Curtis, music graduate in 1884, who served as a deaconess in New York and later went to India to teach music at a mission college in the Himalayas. Annie Lake (Mrs Bird) was a missionary in Africa. Marion Lambly went to Japan in 1894 to act as teacher and evangelist in the Tokyo Girls' School. Rose Swayze, senior matriculant in 1890, taught in the Native mission at Norway House in Manitoba. Mary Doyle attended the college in 1892–93 and taught at a mission college in South Africa. Her sister, Martha Doyle, matriculated in 1897 and studied medicine at Trinity Medical School in anticipation of mission service.[81]

Three student societies at Albert were conducted exclusively by women. These were the Polymnian, which was devoted to the cultivation of literary and musical taste, the YWCA, and the Mission Band. Other student societies included the Athletic Association, the Philomathian Society for Elocution and Rhetoric, the Intercollegiate Missionary Association, and the YMCA. The Albert College *Times* was administered by a board, which in 1896–97 was composed of six males and four females. No secret societies were allowed to meet anywhere on the college grounds.[82] Male and female students were closely supervised, but gradually there was some relaxation of the strict separation. In the dining-room, for example, coeducation meant a chance to teach social graces, as boys were seated across from girls and required to serve the girls first. The girls originally went for a walk twice a day in twos with a female teacher at the beginning and end of the chain. Later, promenades became an acceptable form of dancing and an opportunity for the sexes to meet.[83]

ASSESSING ALBERT COLLEGE'S SUCCESS

Despite a shaky start because of financial and administrative challenges, Albert College maintained a credible educational program into the twentieth century. Several factors contributed to its survival, including the strong leadership of principals such as Albert Carman and J.R. Jacques. The coeducational program with Alexandra College gave parents an option to educate their daughters and provided the school with a steady population base. Coeducation in this system demanded a strictly supervised social space and some sharing of classroom subjects. But the appropriateness of an academic program for a female student was nevertheless decided by her father or, in Metty Carman's case, by her brother and father. For many families, it was likely an achievement if daughters had some learning before they returned to the farm and family. An element of realism tempered the college's desire to provide competitive facilities with similar colleges but yet keep the education within the financial reach of the school's constituency, which was derived initially from local and farm families. The practical necessity of the coeducational policy was underlined in 1926–34 when Albert College became a male-only institution. Enrolment dropped to forty students in 1933, and the college experienced severe financial distress.[84]

Within the Episcopal Methodist denomination, there were strong supporters of women's education. Advocates such as Thomas Webster devoted a great deal of energy to the cause. Webster, whose ideas will be examined in greater detail in chapter 6, repeatedly pointed out the inequality of the college's education for women, which was masked by the illusion of equal opportunity. As long as women's degrees were different in name and in content from the men's, they would continue to be ranked as second-class. For Webster, this inequality needed to be replaced by a complete equality of education. His wish was not realized in the nineteenth century, for Albert, like many of the ladies' colleges, preserved the ladies' diploma into the twentieth century.

Part of that diploma was the accomplishments curriculum. Accomplishments for female students persisted, although in many cases in schools such as Alexandra, the students could not afford the extras. Nevertheless, the image of the girl playing the piano in perfect passivity, as Marjorie Theobald has indicated, continued to function as an ideal vision of womanhood.[85] Resigned to a life of feeling rather than action, the girl required an emotive outlet, which music could safely provide. The accomplishments curriculum has been rescued by scholars such as Theobald from the disdain with which it has been regarded by many historians. She considers the curriculum an invisible college of female studies and a gender-diffentiated form of the humanities. Although the accomplishments were considered an acceptable use of women's intellect in a man's society, the diplomas gave graduates opportunities for wage labour. Webster's call for equality of educational significance for both male and female studies, on the other hand, was a threat to the order and balance that had been achieved in these early seminaries and academies.

Albert College's unique attainment in functioning as a university from 1866 until 1884 is generally overlooked. It would be remiss to describe the college as an uncomplicated success story, particularly considering the personal suffering experienced by the leadership, which is evident in Albert Carman's correspondence and in the writings of Principal W.P. Dyer. The near failure of the seminary during Carman's leadership caused him a great deal of worry. By contrast, the popularity of the college in 1903 was evident in a record enrolment of 340 students, consisting of 184 female students and 156 males. Both the large enrolment and the cares caused by student sickness during the school year, which included pneumonia, mumps, and scarlatina, led Dyer to confide in Carman: "Both Mrs Dyer and myself are completely worn out. I have been now for several days just on the verge of Nervous Prostration, and do my work only with the greatest difficulty. I cannot go on without dropping in my steps. I write to you as a boy would write to his father."[86] An additional worry for Dyer was the question of the approval of the school by the provincial Department of Education. The department sent inspectors into the private schools to see whether their facilities and programs would allow them to be rated as "approved high schools."[87] Albert College was not the only Methodist school to face this problem in the twentieth century, as will be seen in subsequent chapters. Yet this was one more issue that would test the adaptability of the school and its leadership.

4 The Ladies' College Movement, 1858–1898: Founders, Faculty, and Students

It is simply frightful to contemplate the amount of human life wasted by compelling women to pursue accomplishments for which they have no taste or capacity, through long years of dreary dullness. Let the ladies' colleges lay down as fundamental and necessary introduction to all their graduating courses, a certain uniform and thorough education in the common branches of study.[1]

By mid-century, female education in Ontario sponsored by the Methodists had undergone several changes since its early manifestation in the coeducational, albeit strictly segregated, Upper Canada Academy. In his study of schools in Hamilton, Ian Davey notes that by 1861 a relative balance between attendance for boys and girls was achieved, and a decade later there were more school-age girls than boys in state schools.[2] Historian Robert Gidney notes that only after school reform in the mid-century did the private schools become associated with an expensive rejection of the state system.[3] In their study of grammar schools in the nineteenth century, Gidney and Millar observe that the choice of grammar school over private or boarding school was largely determined by family size. Families with several children to educate chose the local grammar school as a way to conserve resources. Attendance patterns in the grammar schools of the 1860s show that girls were more likely to attend for shorter periods over the year, as well as being more likely to have shorter school careers.[4]

Private schooling for girls was formed very much in response to trends in the public schools. The fact that the impetus for state-school reform derived from the Methodist chief superintendant of education, Egerton Ryerson, should be kept in mind. Ryerson had been responsible for the exclusion of women students from the Upper Canada Academy in 1842. He continued to believe in and to attempt to promote the separate education of males and females throughout the 1860s. Despite his efforts to exclude them, by the mid-sixties, "girls constituted 40 to 50 per cent of grammar school enrollments."[5] School reform in the late 1860s and the 1870s made way for the demise of the grammar schools and the rise of the secondary schools, which were clearly coeducational institutions.

Developments in state-sponsored education were closely tied to the aspirations of Methodists to provide an alternative. Questions concerning the schooling of girls and the propriety of coeducation were important elements in rationalizing the need for denominational education. The growing presence of Catholic schools further challenged Protestant advocates of education to join in the educational market-place. Ladies' seminaries or academies were founded at Cobourg, Picton, Dundas, Toronto, and Hamilton during the years from 1842 to approximately 1862. These seminaries were single-sex schools usually headed by a male principal assisted by a lady principal or preceptress. As we have seen, the authority structure mirrored the patriarchal family. Eventually the ladies' seminaries gained the official approval of the Methodist Church and helped to articulate and reinforce a Methodist ideal of an educated woman.

Certain continuities existed between these seminaries and the grander ladies' colleges that emerged later. The early ladies' academies and seminaries helped to educate teachers who would later assist in the more elegant ladies' colleges. Teaching provided one of the few employment opportunities for women at this time. Furthermore, the idea of educating females gained acceptance as Methodists acknowledged that such schools were good and necessary, particularly since they were perceived as providing preparation for women in their role as wives and mothers. Finally, the program of studies, which had its roots in the early academies, was adapted to the ladies' colleges, giving women a liberal arts curriculum, as well as accomplishments, physical education, and ultimately diplomas that could provide opportunities for wage labour.[6]

The ideal of female education went through subtle transformations from its appearance at the Upper Canada Academy in 1836 and the seminaries that resulted from the closure of the academy to women in 1842 to its expression in the ladies' college movement of the 1860s to 1880s. While Albert College experimented with the coeducational model, the separate approach was developed at the Wesleyan Ladies'

College in Hamilton, the Ontario Ladies' College in Whitby, and Alma College in St Thomas. The early female seminaries had developed the ideal of a liberal arts education in a mode similar to, but somewhat different from, that offered by their male counterparts. Nevertheless, Greek, Latin, mathematics, and the sciences gradually found their way into the female curriculum, in addition to the more traditionally female and ornamental subjects. The clergymen who headed the colleges were trained in philosphical and theological traditions, which they in turn brought to the ladies' college curriculum. William Paley's natural theology, for example, found its place in the program. This development was not surprising because, as McKillop has shown, educators in Canada combined the English ideal of a liberal education with Scottish common sense as elaborated by Thomas Reid and Dugald Stewart. The idea that moral truths could be understood by appealing to common sense was combined with Paley's natural theology, which allowed proof of God's existence to be found in the world of nature. This combination of common sense and natural theology gave rise to a "devotional frame of mind."[7] It was a world-view most appropriate to the Victorian ladies' college student as she was encouraged to gain an appreciation of life around her in a reverential attitude of piety and devotion. Graduates were expected to face the world, not with critical inquiry, but with silent acceptance of their calling to the family and church. Yet principals such as the Reverend Alexander Burns of the Wesleyan Ladies' College gave his students enthusiatic lectures in political theory in the early 1890s. It would seem that propriety in the curriculum was interpreted broadly when it allowed for the expression of the personal interests of clergymen. The feminist implications of this education were apparently not lost on some students, as an examination of the student newspaper shows.

The ladies' colleges offered two aspects that differed from the earlier female seminaries: first, the ideal of educating ladies in more elegant environments and, second, the notion of vocational preparation. The organization of education into larger and more physically impressive and purposeful ladies' colleges was initiated with a great conviction that such colleges were necessary and with optimism that people and the churches would support these ventures. The larger schools had the advantage of being able to offer a more diverse faculty, with better facilities and more options. The optimism that propelled these colleges into existence was sanctioned by the notion that God's will for "ladies" was being carried out. This belief gave the movement tremendous impetus, but one that became somewhat more difficult to maintain in the face of the harsh financial realities.

Ultimately, economic depressions in Ontario in the 1850s, 1870s, and 1890s,[8] changing class composition, the rise of the state secondary schools, and the financial advantages of coeducation would threaten the future of the ladies' colleges.

THE WESLEYAN LADIES' COLLEGE IN HAMILTON

The demise of the proprietary schools run by the Hurlburts and Van Normans meant that Wesleyans in the province had no specific school that addressed the needs of female education. Parents who desired this type of education for their daughters could send them either to Mount Allison Ladies' Academy in Sackville, New Brunswick,[9] or to the United States.[10] The other possibility in Upper Canada was the Wesleyan Female College of Dundas (or Dundas Female College), which was a very small institution with only forty students in 1859 and as few as eighteen in 1861. Under the care of the Wesleyan Methodist Church, the school employed approximately five teachers and offered preparatory studies as well as collegiate courses in mathematics, logic, rhetoric, classical languages, philosophy, modern languages, natural sciences, music, and fine arts. Girls who completed the course were promised testimonials that were promoted as being equal to an AB from a boy's college.[11] The school offered additional subjects and "accomplishments"; among them were Latin, Greek, Italian, piano, drawing, and painting. Special provision was made for students who hoped to teach, including help in obtaining positions.[12]

Information about the school is scarce, and the details about its demise are somewhat murky. In 1859 it was incorporated by the provincial Legislature. The Reverend Robert McGonegal, who left the next year, was replaced as head by Mary Electa Adams. Her most recent position had been preceptress at Mount Allison, and she was now "well-known in the United States, and New Brunswick, and also in Canada, as a most accomplished and efficient Preceptress, having had charge of some of the best institutions."[13] In 1840, when she was seventeen, Adams had travelled to the Montpelier Academy in Vermont, where she studied classics and advanced mathematics. A year later she returned to study at the Cobourg Female Academy, graduating with a mistress of liberal arts degree. Adams remained at the school as a staff member and moved with the Hurlburts to Toronto when they established their new school, the Adelaide Academy. She continued advanced studies while teaching at the academy. Her next position was principal of the Picton Ladies' Academy, followed by a teaching post at the Albion Seminary in Michigan. In 1854 she returned to British North America to teach in the women's department of Mount Allison Academy in Sackville. Adams and her sister Augusta managed in their three years there to establish a curriculum that "favored the academic over the ornamental."[14] She resigned from her position at Mount Allison to care for her sick mother in Dundas. Augusta was also on staff at the Dundas school. According to one source, the Dundas Female College struggled to compete with the Wesleyan Ladies' College, which was started in Hamilton in 1861, but by 1866 the Dundas school decided to combine with the Hamilton one.[15] Steadily declining enrolments and financial constraints no doubt made the prospect of closing or amalgamating attractive. Marion Royce surmises that the position of principal at the college in Hamilton, once the Dundas school began to decline, must have been a tempting prospect for Adams.[16] She entered the position with more experience and preparation in the area of women's education than the organizers of the other ladies' colleges, and she would hold the position until she resigned in 1868.[17]

The Reverend Samuel Rice, who was stationed in Hamilton from 1857 to 1862, had foreseen the possibility of a larger school than the one in Dundas, to be housed in the downtown Anglo-American Hotel. He had worked in the field of education at Mount Allison and as moral and domestic governor at Victoria in Cobourg from 1854 to 1857. He was appointed governor and chaplain of the Wesleyan Ladies' College in 1863, and two years later he began teaching natural theology, mental philosophy, and evidences of Christianity. From 1868 until 1879 he would serve as principal of the college. He was elected general superintendant of the Methodist Church in 1883.[18] Because of a depression in the 1850s, the hotel could be purchased for $24,000, even though it was valued at $100,000.[19] Adjoining grounds were also obtained to provide ample room for "retired play and exercise grounds."[20] Rice rallied the support of upstanding Hamilton Methodists to make the investment. These men comprised the first stockholders; they included Edward Jackson, who had served on the Dundas Female College board, Joseph Lister, Dr J.W. Rosebrugh, Archibald Macallum, principal of the Central School in Hamilton, Edward Gurney, D. Moore, George Roach, and Dr C. McQuesten.[21] To raise the money, a joint-stock corporation was formed based on a proprietary principle. The capital stock consisted of $50,000 divided into five hundred shares of $100 each. The board was composed of two-thirds laymen and one-third ministers, a measure that was intended to secure the "religious and Methodistic character of the school."[22] At least eight out of ten of the laymen were to be proprietors and members of the Wesleyan Methodist Church in Canada.

This corporate structure was developed to raise the large amount of capital necessary for such a grand scheme, as well as to establish an organization more lasting than previous private schools had been.

The non-sectarian policy that had been established at the Upper Canada Academy was continued at the Wesleyan Ladies' College. This meant that the institution was proclaimed as Christian in its orientation, but despite the hope that the school would be "Methodistic," it would in fact be respectful and supportive of the individual traditions that the students represented.[23] Although the non-sectarian policy caused some initial grumblings, the success of the school eventually overcame these objections. The composition of the student body in 1861 reflected the non-sectarian principle. Although Methodists were most numerous at 54.5 per cent, Anglicans comprised 15.2 per cent of all students, Presbyterians 24.2 per cent, Congregationals 3.0 per cent, and others 3.0 per cent.[24] Students were encouraged to attend the church chosen by their parent or guardian, and the Wesleyan Methodist students marched together in procession to the Centenary Church, sitting in designated pews.[25]

Descriptions of the hotel-school indicate that it must have been extraordinary indeed. Some changes were made to adapt the building for school purposes, such as the transformation of a billiard room into a classroom, whereas other features – the original dining-room, for example – remained intact. The upper floor contained rooms for students and staff, with a drawing-room in the west wing. A boundary was placed around the school by means of a high wall. The college had a capacity of one hundred and fifty bedrooms in addition to magnificent parlours and bathrooms.[26] The catalogue of 1866–67 described the rooms as large, "with glass ventilators connecting them with unusually lofty and spacious halls." Each sitting-room was apparently carpeted and furnished. The large drawing-room, twenty-five by sixty feet, looked out on a fountain. The dining hall was "airy, light, and furnished in fresco, with panelled walls and emblematic designs."[27] Other facilities were a marching shed for inclement weather and a skating-rink.

Apparently the grandeur of the hotel also had its shortcomings, as Mary Electa Adams recorded: "Hotel parlours, however elaborately furnished, do not make satisfactory class-rooms." When she made her first tour of the building, she asked Dr Rice how the rooms were to be heated, to which he replied, "I don't know."[28] A grand setting, however, combined with healthy surroundings and strict supervision, characterized the ladies' colleges of this period. The use of a single building to house students and staff served to keep the students "physically in place."[29] Like some of its American seminary counterparts, the Wesleyan Ladies' College structured each moment of the day into purposeful activity. The college was viewed as a family, and this family, housed as it was in a gracious home, could be carefully supervised by teachers and staff.[30]

The location of the college was a source of pride; the calendar pointed out that students had "city advantages" and easy access to concerts and churches. Hamilton, it was noted, was also unsurpassed for the healthfulness and beauty of its location.[31] This location must have demanded a great amount of watchfulness and supervision of the students, as their opportunities to meet males also increased. Other Ontario schools, such as Alma College, established by the Methodist Episcopal denomination in St Thomas, and Ontario Ladies' College in Whitby, were very proud of their small-town, more rural locations. The urban location of the WLC also contrasted sharply with that of many American private schools and colleges, which, as we have seen, more frequently sought out smaller towns and rural sites.[32]

The college was incorporated in May 1861, and the opening ceremonies took place in October the same year. The *Christian Guardian* noted that the Hamilton college filled a long-standing gap in female education: "For years there had been a very earnest enquiry on the part of a large class of our people for a place of education, first in its intellectual advantages and secure in its moral influences. When the crash of 1856–7 came, it appeared as though it would take a score of years to recover such an amount of independence as would give the hope that an institution for female education could be secured."[33] At the opening of the college, the Reverend Dr Joseph Stinson expressed confidence that it was the mission of such institutions to provide, not what had been designated "blue stockings," but "help meets." He was convinced that "the young ladies who were educated in, and left this college, would be a blessing to the circles they may be called upon to adorn."[34] At the same occasion, Egerton Ryerson, first principal of Victoria College and now superintendant of schools for Upper Canada, described the opening of the college as a sign of the "progress" that marked a new age, by which the present generation would exceed the previous one in intellectual acquirements, so "that the son, the daughter will be better, more accomplished men and women than their fathers or their mothers."[35]

After such a glorious beginning, an almost inevitable disappointment set in. The Wesleyan Ladies' College did not initially flourish, and a letter to the *Christian Guardian* by its governor, Samuel Rice, questioned why so few were interested in enjoying the benefits of the school. "The patronage since the commencement has varied from sixty-five to thirty-five. It has been felt by the directory that by some means the ministers do not feel interested in the success of the College. They reason further that forty Wesleyan pupils from a membership of 53,000 is a strange contrast."[36] The stockholders might have expected some return on their investment, but the school was not meant primarily as a money-making enterprise.[37] The revenues gained from attendance were, by 1865, not sufficient to meet the expenses, a fact that was "painfully discouraging" to the directors, "several of whom have assumed heavy responsibilities for its establishment and continuance."[38]

There was a certain amount of rivalry between the Wesleyan Ladies' College and Albert College, but it was the speech at the closing exercises of the WLC in 1867 by the Reverend Dr Wellington Jeffers, editor of the *Christian Guardian*, that really brought down the fury of the *Canada Christian Advocate*. Jeffers had claimed that the WLC was the only female college in the province. How, the *Advocate* asked, could he make such a claim, when a successful Episcopal Methodist college existed in Belleville? The *Guardian* replied, with a certain degree of sarcasm, on 10 July that it was not aware that the act conferring university powers on Albert had given such powers to the female department of the school or that its female professors were members of the senate.

One observer from the *Advocate* had claimed in 1863 that the graduation exercises he had seen at the WLC were inferior to those at Alexandra College; "some of the instrumental music [was] well-executed, but the vocal performances were perfectly outrageous." The reports in the local paper, influenced heavily by Wesleyan Methodists, were so biased in favour of the WLC, in contrast, that the paper praised the singing of one professor for whom "nothing but courtesy" prevented him from being taken off the platform.[39] Despite these evidences of awareness of each other's activities and the occasional verbal disputes when one college believed that it had been slighted, on the whole the ladies' colleges coexisted peacefully in the province.

Costs at the Wesleyan Ladies' College originally ranged from $6.75 per term for the preparatory department to $12.75 for the collegiate course, to which various fees for extras were added. Tuition charges had changed only slightly by 1881; the calendar commented that the rates were "barely sufficient to maintain the Institution in its growing efficiency." The college's managers claimed that they could charge lower rates than other colleges because they carried no oppressive debts. Their purpose was not "to compete with those who are traversing the country advertising cheap boarding houses under the name of Colleges, but to aid in the higher education of women, by bringing advanced facilities within easy reach of all at very reasonable rates."[40] In 1887 the tuition rates remained constant, but the calendar reminded patrons that "cheap education is often like cheap cloth or cheap butter and equally valuable."[41] The college was still managing to keep the costs at the same level in 1891, although new courses with a more commercial orientation had been added, including bookkeeping, shorthand, and typewriting. The choice of "extras" was further expanded to include harmony ($15), violin ($15–20), guitar or harp, and a special class in perspective and model drawing.[42]

THE ONTARIO LADIES' COLLEGE IN WHITBY

The building that would house the Ontario Ladies' College in Whitby had originally been erected for his own use by Nelson Reynolds.[43] He was born in 1814, the son of an Episcopal Methodist bishop. Educated at Upper Canada College and Cazenovia Seminary, he commissioned his "castle" to be built by Toronto architect Joseph Sheard. It cost $70,000 and was constructed in an Elizabethan style. In 1872 Reynolds, under financial pressures, had begun to consider selling his house, and on the strength of this possibility, on 24 December a group of a hundred Whitby residents met to discuss the establishment of a "female seminary" in the town. The Reverend Joseph Sanderson, minister of the Methodist Tabernacle, argued that the "central" area of Ontario now needed a second women's college. A second organizational meeting was held in February 1874, attended by influential Wesleyan Methodists from Belleville, Bowmanville, Darlington, Pickering, Cannington, and Whitby. Samuel Rice of the WLC came and explained to the assembled crowd the financial basis of the Hamilton college.[44] A provisional board of directors was appointed, headed by Sanderson, and stock subscriptions worth $15,000 were offered to the town.[45] The board anticipated buying Reynolds's home for $35,000.

In the meantime, the Toronto Conference of the Methodist Church examined the plans for the college and recommended that it be a "connexial institution," which meant it would receive patronage from the church but no direct financial support. Visitors appointed to oversee the school and report on it to the conference included Samuel Nelles of Victoria College, E.H. Dewart of the *Christian Guardian*, and W.H. Withrow of the *Canadian Methodist Magazine*, all clergyman. In 1875 the by-laws of the college were changed, and the number of directors was increased from nine to twenty-one, seven of whom were to be ministers named by the Toronto Conference.[46] The college was under the principalship of the Reverend Dr John James Hare, and Joseph Sanderson served as governor.

Parents of prospective students were advised that they were sending their daughters to study and that they should not yield to their "fancied requirements in dress."[47] Daughters would feel the change from indulgent homes to the "regular and impartial routine of College life." In order to help them to adapt to this new routine, parents were encouraged to prevent the students from going home too frequently, as it would be an interruption to their study and to the maintenance of the "order and regularity necessary to success in mental culture."[48] Discipline and a regulated life for girls were offered in opposition to laziness and self-indulgence in the home.

The college was opened in September 1874 by the governor-general, Lord Dufferin. Judge Burnham addressed the crowd gathered for the festivities and explained that the college was a place that would offer to young women "thoroughly sound practical education, and where, while being instructed in what are considered the higher branches and accomplishments, they could also be taught simple but refined manners, and trained to domestic habits, and their minds imbued with religious principles, and thus be prepared to discharge usefully the great duties of life."[49] The college, like both Alma and the WLC, claimed to be managed on "strictly Christian, but unsectarian principles."[50] It was housed in a handsome and finished building; "the internal arrangements are complete in every respect, no pains or expense having been spared to provide for the comfort or pleasure of the pupils attending. The rooms are furnished in the best manner possible from the kitchen to the parlour."[51]

The building, boasted the calendar, was the finest ever appropriated to college purposes. All aspects, including the windows, the doors, the classrooms, and the dormitories, were "so elegantly constructed that appreciative young ladies must experience inspiration and delight."[52] The grounds included facilities for "croquet and other innocent pursuits" as well as a gymnasium and a skating-rink. They encompassed ten acres, with the possibility of "shady walks beneath ornamental and fruit trees,"[53] and Whitby was described as a "pleasant and healthy town."[54] The combined beauty of the building and the grounds had the effect that, "instead of the severe restraint and wearisome dullness, too common to school life, there is here the freedom of a cheerful home, with judicious oversight, and in happy combination with regular hours of study."[55]

The domestic arrangements were under the direction of a steward and matron, who would ensure that the students had a varied, nutritious, and acceptable diet. In this regard, boxes of cake and pastries from home would prove injurious, and parents were advised against sending them. A hearty exercise program would counter the effects of such food, and the girls were encouraged to take part in walking, riding, and gymnastics under the supervision of Major Dearnally of the Queen's Life Guards. Students desiring riding lessons were advised to bring a riding skirt of black lustre, medium length, and a saddle.

Academic departments followed the scheme that was in place at the other ladies' colleges, with preparatory, academic, and collegiate divisions. Tuition in the respective departments was from $4.00, $6.00, or $8.00 per term. The costs were increased by any extras, such as modern languages, which added $4 per term, painting $8.00, and music $8.00 to $15.00. The yearly cost of boarding in the academic department was $158 and in the collegiate department $166.

A rare glimpse of school life is provided by a student's letter to a friend. Written in November 1878 by a young woman we know only as Minnie to a friend called Jenny, it appears to be an account of Minnie's first months at OLC. Her early impressions of life at the college were marked by a tremendous loneliness "on account of coming to a strange place, and amongst strangers but I like it a great deal better now as I am getting accustomed to the rules of the college which are very numerous."[56] Minnie liked her room and her companions, and she stated that they had had only two entertainments so far, but would soon have them every two weeks. The entertainments comprised singing, reading, and music by the students and the reading of compositions; this last caused her to write to her friend, "just imagine us having to stand up and read our compos before the whole College."[57] The most recent entertainment had left quite an impression because Mrs Sanderson, the wife of a faculty member, had invited some young fellows who had finished their intermediate examinations at Whitby, and the students knew nothing of their coming until they strolled in. Some of the students threw kisses at the boys when the teachers were not looking. On the occasion of Hallowe'en the students went to the chapel and played games. The teachers were there too and were "as full of fun as any the rest."[58]

Principal Hare taught natural science and higher mathematics. Mr Sanderson instructed in the English language classics and in mental and moral philosophy. The remainder of the faculty consisted of Miss Wilson in the senior English classics, Miss Jarvis (gold medallist of 1877), who taught the junior classes, Misses Crowle and Kerr in art and music, Mr Torrington and Miss Brown, who also taught art, and

Mlle Buchanan and Mlle Guillet, who taught modern languages.[59] By 1879 the science course had been expanded to equal the first year of the regular university course.[60]

The directors had made plans by 1877 for an expansion to the main building designed to accommodate 50 additional boarders, as well as a new residence for the governor.[61] The new wing was called Ryerson Hall and contained an auditorium capable of seating 500 persons. On the second and third storeys were twenty-four rooms for pupils. Dr Ryerson was present at the opening of the new addition, and his comments underlined his belief in the importance of separate education for adolescent females and males. By 1878 there were 110 students in attendance at the college, with 88 boarders and 22 day students. In the same year, elocution was added as a course of study. In 1879 the *Sunbeam*, a student newspaper, was started,[62] and by the following year a college alumnae society had been organized.

Mary Electa Adams, formerly of the Wesleyan Ladies' College, became lady principal, or governess, in 1881. After she had resigned her principalship of the WLC, Adams had travelled in Italy for two years with her sister Augusta. They had returned to Cobourg and in 1872 opened the Brookhurst Academy for female students close to Victoria College. Adams was forced to close the school after eight years, and she took a teaching position at the Ontario Ladies' College in 1880.[63] In addition to her responsibilities as governess, she taught belles-lettres, Italian, art criticism, and manners and morals. Her duties also included receiving students when they first arrived, assigning them rooms and room-mates, guiding the formation of their personal habits, "and exercising a general, maternal supervision over their moral interests."[64] Adams accepted the position at the OLC with some heaviness of heart, having closed Brookhurst and faced the disappointment of her dream to turn that school into a type of Girton College affiliated with Victoria. Her long experience in a variety of schools had left her "weary of trying to drag great Institutions out of debt," schools with the additional complication: "how many boards of stockholders for Ladies' Colleges know what they need?"[65]

On her arrival at the OLC, Adams found to her disgust that, without consulting her, Principal Hare had introduced a paragraph in the college's circular stating that her duties would be performed under his supervision. She claimed that she would not accept a subordinate position and if there had been a misunderstanding she pronounced herself quite ready to retire. Although at the time, Hare promised to withdraw the offending paragraph and ensured Adams the same "independence of action as he claimed for himself," the chain of command was to cause an endless amount of friction. After a career of teaching in ladies' schools, Adams had acquired a reputation upon which the OLC was eager to capitalize. Indeed, she had heard from her niece that many of the students were sent to the college on her account, because "their mothers, or aunts or friends, having known us – my sister & me in Hamilton or elsewhere."[66]

Adams minded not so much the sharing of power as the weak governance that Hare effected. "I am dissatisfied with the weak and uncertain government, I feel the whole burden of it thrown upon myself, while another stands responsible before the public."[67] Not only did she find Hare to be lacking organizational power, but the directors also were inexperienced. Both were subject to "most exaggerated fits of depressions and exaltation alternately according as there is a flush of letters applying or a disappointment" in the numbers expected.[68] In one conflict between the school steward and Principal Hare, Adams observed that Hare "alone has the ear of the Directors – I am in entire isolation & the real facts of the relations between himself and the steward are unknown except as he imparts them."[69] Her diary was one of the few places where she could express her frustration at the poor management of the school, and she tried to develop a spiritual maturity to help her to cope with the situation. A similar evaluation of Hare's leadership comes from Margaret Addison, later dean of women at Victoria, who taught at OLC from 1889 to 1891. In a letter to her brother, Addison commented, "Dr Hare is such a queer man. He never seems to have any definite mind of his own on any subject or at least in college matters of any importance, but talks like a spoiled little boy when he wants his own way."[70]

Students at the OLC in 1885 took honours in three groups and headed the list in the junior matriculation examinations for the University of Toronto.[71] Dr Haanel, examiner for a class in mineralogy, commented that students at the school passed on the same conditions as male undergraduates at Victoria University. The success of students in the university-level exams led the *Saturday Globe* to comment enthusiastically in 1889, "There is a grand field in Canada for a ladies' university, and the present condition and past work of the OLC indicates that with a little encouragement it would soon put on the dignified air of a university and be the pride of the Dominion."[72] Diplomas in elocution were issued in 1887 and in commercial art by 1888. Adams organized a branch of the Women's Missionary Society at the school in 1889,[73] and two years later she initiated the Victorian Society, which was intended to encourage the development of the library.[74] By 1891 a committee composed of George Cox, the Reverend Mr Potts, and Drs Burwash and Hare was directed to confer with the

Senate of the University of Toronto concerning university affiliation. The course of study was expanded in 1891 to cover first- and second-year university work with honours, "thus qualifying pupils to become specialists in our high schools and collegiate institutes."[75] The school advertised the professional programs to attract students interested in obtaining qualifications for teaching.[76]

The 1880s witnessed the growth and firm establishment of the college; enrolment peaked at 175 students in 1887. Adams did her utmost to nourish a congenial atmosphere at the school. One student during this time wrote: "We have to go down to the drawing room this afternoon. We have one every Saturday from three to four and Miss Adams reads to us while we do fancy work. Miss Adams has a reception every Friday night."[77] However, another student's comments in a letter home raise the question of how good things really were at the college.

> I get up at half past five and then practice from six to seven, then study from seven to eight – then breakfast & school till half past one. I generally paint or draw in the afternoon & then study & practice again in the evening. Next week I am going to have an early breakfast and then practice from eight to nine. I think it will be much better than from six to seven in the winter. I hope you will send me as many of the things as you can get in the box for I am hungry nearly all the time. I suppose the board is as good as at other schools but it is really not good. The other day the meat was so rare & tough that the teacher had to send for the servant to cut it. I could not touch it & we never have butter for dinner so I had to eat dry bread & potatoes & a little bit of rice pudding without sugar or milk.[78]

For some, the opening up of educational possibilities was not greeted with unrestrained enthusiasm. At the closing exercises in 1895, for example, Samuel Dwight Chown, general secretary of the Methodist Church's department of temperance and moral reform and later the co-superintendent of the Methodist Church of Canada, warned graduates in his baccalaureate sermon of the dangers of the New Woman movement.[79] In a similar vein, Alexander Burns of the Wesleyan Ladies' College spoke at the OLC commencement exercises in 1899 and commented that he did not agree with the current system of education because it looked as if the aim was to be able to fill an examination paper. He "did not plead for less work for the young ladies but for more suitable preferring music to mineralogy, and art to astronomy."[80] The development of a critical intellect or even increased control over their lives was not intended to result from this type of education. In fact, leaders of the ladies' college movement were expressing some fear about the consequences of educating women.

Mary Electa Adams who was an important advocate of such education, carefully preserved the propriety of women's education by making her charges doing fancy-work while she read aloud. The need for education was generally accepted by the Methodist community, but the content and structure of that education carried clear gender messages preserving the femininity of the young ladies. Carol Dyhouse observes that in nineteenth-century England, needlework taught girls cleanliness, obedience, caution, and concentration, as well as other virtues.[81] The virtues associated with needlework were necessary for the womanly role, which would also include other domestically oriented skills such as cookery. Eventually these skills would be organized into a science, but even in their early form, the arts of fancy-work were essential milestones in the development of a respectable lady.

In an address to the students in 1899, a Miss Masson, on the other hand, celebrated the educational opportunities and possibilities open to women. She urged them to take their education seriously and to acquire the ability to "become co-partners in the affairs of the home, the community, the world." Education was intended to lead women to financial and mental independence, as opposed to marriages made thoughtlessly.[82] According to Masson, the "struggle for existence is a mighty teacher, and the once small voice of woman's appeal for higher education and fuller equipment has become as a trumpet tone, at whose sound the college doors turn slowly on their hinges, and at last stand open wide."[83]

ALMA COLLEGE IN ST THOMAS

It was Bishop Albert Carman, among others, who promoted the idea of an Episcopal Methodist college for young ladies in western Ontario. He had long been involved in educational matters, as we have seen. In 1876 an organizational meeting was held to discuss the possibility of starting a ladies' college in St Thomas, a town that boasted a network of rail transport and a healthy environment. The meeting included a representation of St Thomas's religious and business leaders, such as Judge D. Hughes, Archibald McLachlin, county registrar, Sheriff Colin Munroe, Mayor Drake, Captain James Sisk, Colin McDougall, MP, John Smith, merchant and former mayor, J. Farly, banker, John Arker, businessman, and Dr A. Griffith, minister of the Central Methodist Church.[84] The purpose of the proposed college was to afford young ladies a "liberal course of instruction and all that tends to make their lives useful and happy, and their tastes elevated and refined."[85] The college was intended to be non-sectarian. The committee proposed that the town grant the school $5,000 dollars and that it be built for no less that $20,000. The committee also recommended that the ladies' college be affiliated with Albert University for degree-granting purposes.

The movement was underway, and a lot was purchased for $2,600. A college agent had been appointed to travel the circuits and solicit subscriptions to the college, and by 1877 he had canvassed twelve circuits and secured subscriptions for $3,650.[86] The board was confident that funds would be acquired for sustaining the building, and they held a ceremony at which the cornerstone was laid by Adam Crooks, the minister of education for the province, assisted by Miss McLachlin of St Thomas, daughter of Archibald McLachlin, a board member. The day selected for the ceremony was the birthday of Queen Victoria, who "as a Woman reigns over the mighty British Empire, and our dominion forming a part of that Empire, it was deemed most appropriate befitting to Evidence our regard, and honour, to her Person and Rule, that this ceremony should take place, on this day, especially, as the College is for the Education of Women."[87] At the ceremony, Miss McLachlin placed a number of articles within the cornerstone, including a copy of the appropriately titled *Woman Man's Equal* by Thomas Webster, long-time editor of the *Canada Christian Advocate*.[88]

The details of equipping and building the college provided the board with a host of worries. The executive had to decide on the furnishings, design, and functioning of the college, down to the most minute details: "That the Water Closets should be placed in an addition to the building in rear, with Entrance thereto from the landings of the main staircase, protected by double doors, and such other precautions as may be found necessary, to secure the comfort and health of the inmates."[89] The charter, which had been secured in 1877, stated that the occasion might arise when the school would be enlarged into one for boys also, but this situation never occurred. The board also wanted extended financial powers to allow it to negotiate loans and mortgages, and such powers were granted by the Ontario Legislature in 1880. They were necessary because the subscriptions were not being paid and the board had insufficient funds to cover the building costs.

The design of the campus had been chosen from twenty submissions by architects, of whom James Balfour was the winning competitor. The main building was one hundred feet in length, seventy-three feet wide, and five story high, with fifty rooms able to accommodate a hundred students. The contractor chosen to build the main building was Henry Lindop of St Thomas, at a proposed cost of $25,064. The expenses of steam heating, ventilation, plumbing, and gas lighting, as well as fencing and landscaping the grounds, soon brought the cost up to $50,000. By the end of the three years of building, the final cost was closer to $60,000. Bishop Carman remained undeterred, however, believing that the college was "bound to rise above all the clouds of financial difficulties to where perpetual sunshine shall settle upon it."[90] To meet the shortfall, the town was urged to contribute $5,000 towards the building, and the Conference prevailed upon the young women of the church to raise $1,000. The Niagara Conference also recommended that 250 shares worth $100 each be sold.

Before the school opened in 1881, the principal-elect, Benjamin Fish Austin, and the board promoted the school by means of advertisements in newspapers in Ontario, Montreal, Detroit, and New York, as well as in other colleges, libraries, and churches. The prospectus claimed that St Thomas was situated in the midst of splendid country, and although large enough to be served by a network of railways to make it accessible from all directions, it was also small enough to be "comparatively free from the vices and snares incident to overgrown cities."[91] The pitch for St Thomas as a school location thus appealed to different sentiments from similar advertisements for the WLC, which tended to highlight its urban and cultural location. St Thomas was described as prosperous, industrious, and healthy, with the advantages of fresh produce and a moderate climate.

Despite the financial clouds, the building opened with great fanfare on 13 October 1881. The administrative structure of the college vested authority in the principal, who was expected to supervise all aspects of its internal affairs, both in academic and in managerial matters, and also to direct the spiritual welfare of the students in his role as pastor of the entire college.[92] At Alma the next level of authority was divided between a preceptress and a governess. The preceptress both taught and shared responsibility with the principal for the direction of studies, whereas the governess took charge of the health, manners, morals, personal habits, and domestic relations of the students, "acting towards them at all times as a kind and considerate matron."[93] Aside from this division of labour, all staff were expected to "aid in the cultivation of manners and in securing the domestic comfort and good order of the Institution."[94] The practical details of school life were under the direction of the steward and stewardess, who managed the table and the domestic and business details and ensured good health, cleanliness, good order, and the cultivation of good manners – all of this with the "strictest Economy."[95]

Teachers were appointed who represented a variety of educational backgrounds. The Reverend Robert Ironsides Warner had graduated from Albert College with a BA and held an MA from Victoria College. Among the lady teachers were Maggie Baker from the New England Conservatory in Boston, Emma Sisk, a graduate of Alexandra College with a diploma in music, E. Gibbard, Amelia Brotherhood, and Margaret Capsey. The principal had been directed to advertise in the Ontario newspapers for lady teachers holding either first-class provincial or normal school certificates who had five years of experience.[96]

The first year of operation showed a loss of $824, and it was noted that the tuition fees did not cover the teachers' salaries by nearly $300. The acquisition of an $800 debt after the first year of operation was evidence, according to the secretary of the board, of "intolerable mismanagement – but mismanagement which perhaps can only be corrected by experience."[97] The secretary mentioned in a postscript that the report to the Conference did not show the exact result of the year because in his mind it was better "that it should not."[98] There was obviously a tenuous balance between making the financial needs of the college known and creating the image of a successful enterprise that people would want to support. The need for public relations in these matters was also indicative of the ambiguous relationship between the church and the college. The college was to some extent a responsibility of the church, especially since the bishop was its chief advocate and the link between it and the larger church structure. Carman's position ensured that the situation of the school received publicity and a measure of sympathy.[99]

Enrolment in the first year was sixty-three students (thity-six resident), and of this total, eleven were registered in preparatory work, five in academic, and the remainder in special classes in music or art.[100] By contrast with the Wesleyan Ladies' College, a large proportion of students were enrolled in music and art, rather than the collegiate option. Costs for the programs for resident pupils taking a preparatory course were $38 per quarter, for academic $42, and for collegiate $45. By 1886 the college was full, and the board proposed the building of an additional wing. The plans that were drawn up by the original architect, Balfour, provided a music hall for five hundred, bedrooms for five students, four new classrooms, and an art studio with skylights.[101] The cornerstone of the new McLachlin Hall was laid in 1888, and the building was formally opened in October by the minister of education for Ontario, George Ross. The expansion of the building was matched by a corresponding expansion in the debt to $50,000.[102]

The actions of the united General Conference of 1883 had several effects on Alma College. The board found its available pool of resources limited because Alma was now competing for funds, not only with Albert and Alexandra colleges, but also with the WLC in Hamilton and the OLC in Whitby. Furthermore, ministers of the Methodist Episcopal Church were required to submit large amounts to their superannuation fund to allow them to enter the union on equal footing with Wesleyan ministers. Many of these men were unable to do so and either retired or moved to the United States. The failure to collect money from these circuits and ministers had a detrimental effect on Alma College's finances. Without endowments and with tuition not covering expenses and the cost of paying agents to collect subscriptions, the college was in a precarious position. Any revenues were dispensed to pay interest on the heavy loans that the college had incurred during the building process.[103] After union, the practice of canvassing the Methodist Conference for funds stopped, and the board itself assumed greater responsibility for the financial relief of the college.[104]

Increased competition for students and funds resulted from the proliferation of ladies' colleges, and the board, well aware of the competition from other schools, recognized that Alma could not afford to tarnish its image. A special report was commissioned in the late 1880s investigating the reasons why the college was not attracting more students or support. The report concluded: "So far as I can understand the failure of patronage has arisen mainly from competition and the stringency of the times and possibly to some extent from external causes. When Alma opened in 1881 there were fewer schools in competition. The two conservatories of music, Moulton College, Havergal College, and the Presbyterian Ladies' College, Toronto, have all come into competition since 1881."[105] According to the historians of Ontario secondary education, R.D. Gidney and W.P.J. Millar, the multiplication of girl's boarding and day schools in the seventies and eighties demonstrated that some parents continued to prefer segregated schooling.[106]

A rumour that Alma College attracted a "lower class" of students was reported to be one detrimental factor. Yet at the same time, the fees charged by Alma meant that the college could not compete with convent schools, which charged only $160 per year. The author of a special report on the financial problems of the college quoted the sisters of Loretto, who claimed that 50 per cent of their students were Protestant, a fact that could be explained by the cheaper cost of a Catholic education.[107] Alison Prentice observes that Roman Catholic schools were considered inferior by many Protestants: "it is clear from mid-nineteenth century discussions of the whole separate school question that respectable religion, education, and status all went together, and that all three were only to be obtained in respectable schools, which to many Protestants and certainly to Egerton Ryerson did not include the separate schools of the Roman Catholic minority."[108] According to historian Elizabeth Smyth, at the St Joseph Academy in Toronto between 1861 and 1870 there were a total of 161 boarders, of whom 146 were Roman Catholic and 15 non-Catholic. In 1871–80 there were 215 Catholic boarders, compared to 64 non-Catholics; in 1881–90 there were 272 Catholic boarders and 86 non-Catholics. Costs at the St Joseph Academy in 1866 were $16 annually for a day student, plus $28 per year for extras such as piano or $20 for art.[109] At the Ontario Ladies' College in the 1870s, the tuition was $4–8 per term, music was an additional $8–15, and boarding cost $158 per year. The fees were therefore comparable, with a similar scale of charges for extras.

Although the expansion of Alma was a tremendous drain on the college's financial resources, the new facilities were a drawing card in obtaining a larger student body for the school. The calendar of 1889 boasted the magnificence of the college.

> The principal feature in the design is the main tower and spire which together stand 136 feet above the level of the ground outside. Through it is the public college entrance. The doorway is supported on either side by a cluster of cut stone gothic pillars supporting a rich entablature, and presents a fine, generous, and inviting appearance ... Inside is the vestibule, from which a second flight of some half-dozen steps leads into the central court ... Across the corridor from the central court above described is the grand stair-case, winding its successive flights through four stories, and lit by stained glass windows from the south front.[110]

At the northeast corner was a public entrance and vestibule leading to the office of the principal, and in the west tower was the entrance to the principal's private apartments. McLachlin Hall added a "most imposing appearance," which offered an interior handsomely finished in oiled ash, spacious corridors, high ceilings, and independent ventilation in each room. Furnishings were "elegant and modern ... in keeping with the internal and external appearance of the buildings, and are not surpassed by those of any similar institution in the land."[111] The college grounds had been carefully landscaped since the early days of the school and included six acres of land with a wooded ravine, affording "convenient and pretty subjects for landscape sketches."[112]

The planned elegance of the grounds and building contrasted with the attempt by the board of management to impose a harsh economy on all aspects of college life. Thus coal tar instead of coal was used for heating, fees for modern language classes were increased, and a less expensive female teacher was hired for art in lieu of the more costly Professor F.M. Bell-Smith.[113] Economy also extended into the recommendation for painted floors and rugs in the dormitories instead of carpeting, as well as a restraint on generosity at social events.[114] Despite these measures, the financial picture would worsen before it finally began to improve in the 1890s. Part of that improvement resulted from the assistance of the town in resolving the college's financial indebtedness, and part was due to endowments, such as one from Hart Massey, which helped reduce the amount that the college owed.

THE CHARACTER OF LADIES' COLLEGES IN ONTARIO

The Wesleyan Methodists during the 1860s to 1870s had founded two single-sex colleges, and the Methodist Episcopal Church instituted Alma College in 1881. These colleges had several features in common. They were clearly intended as female schools, little serious consideration having been given to allowing boys to study at the schools. In the case of Alma, the possibility was initially discussed but never formally pursued. This consensus on the necessity of single-sex education seems to have been almost taken for granted. By contrast, in the United States, at both the secondary and the college level, the Methodist Church was supporting female education that tended to be coeducational. In 1862 there were forty-four Methodist schools in existence in the United States, but only nine of these were exclusively for women, and women comprised a large proportion of the enrolment in the others. Cazenovia Seminary admitted women from the beginning on equal terms with male students. In the coeducational schools they sat in the same classrooms with men, although social intercourse was forbidden.[115] Despite the fact that in the United States, Methodists tended towards coeducational instruction, there were, of course, exceptions. In the case of the ladies' colleges discussed in this chapter – Wesleyan, Alma, and Ontario Ladies' colleges – the institutions' founders intended to make the schools single-sex from the beginning.

Another feature that these colleges shared was that they were educational enterprises for which most board members were not fully prepared financially. Board members were Methodists who were important in the church or individuals involved in local business, and a tremendous amount of faith and idealism guided the early years of the colleges. At an organizational meeting of the OLC in 1874, Dr Rice of the WLC gave the audience his summary of the expenses involved in running such as college, but the Whitby audience was not deterred. They believed that some of the expenses at the Hamilton school, such as $1,200 for roof repairs and $2,000 for insurance, would not apply at Whitby since the repairs would be "almost nothing, so perfect and durable are the buildings."[116] The boards did not count on the financial hardships generated by depressions in Ontario nor on parents preferring the cheaper alternative, the public secondary schools. The blossoming of numerous private schools within Methodism, as well as those sponsored by the Presbyterians, Anglicans, Catholics, and private individuals, increased competition for resources. Finally, endowments were infrequent, and since the income generated by tuition barely covered the operating costs, the schools were unable to eliminate debts incurred by over-optimistic building schemes and expansions. Quality could not, however, be compromised, and therefore both the facilities and the programs were improved and updated as much as possible. The need to provide additional dormitory rooms at both OLC and Alma seems to indicate a demand for residential schools for girls. The boards felt that if they could serve larger populations of students, more income would be generated by tuition.

All three ladies' colleges were bound by various ties to Victoria College. Burns of the WLC had an honorary doctorate from Victoria, as did B.F. Austin of Alma College. Both had received their BA degrees from Victoria College, but Burns had also graduated with an STD degree from Indiana State University in 1870 and had received an honorary LLD from Victoria in 1878. John James Hare, the first principal of the OLC, was also a Victoria graduate; he had gained his BA in 1873 and his MA in 1879. The colleges tended to hire Canadian teachers, often with ties to Victoria. Of the principals, Burns was the most conversant with educational values in the United States, since he had spent more than a decade there between 1865 and 1878.

The role of the principal at the ladies' college was to direct the institution and to promote its interests publicly before the church at the Conference and in public addresses at convocations and baccalaureate sermons. To a large extent this public role was carried out through statements in the church and secular press. The work of the principal was situated in two realms, the material and the spiritual. He was charged with the management, efficiency, and academic thoroughness of the institution, as well as with the spiritual welfare of the students and the entire college.[117]

The role of the principal's wife was much less recognized as valuable or worthy of public note, but it deserves to be taken into account. She held an important supportive position that resembled that of a minister's wife. Her behaviour was expected to be socially appropriate and her labour was voluntary. Certainly it does not appear that these women were encouraged to express opinions on the affairs of the college. A principal's wife, however, served as a preceptress on occasion, particularly when the colleges were experiencing financial hardships, and her services were implied in the principal's salary. Wives were also important role models, teachers of etiquette, and social coordinators within the colleges. Mrs Burns was active in the Women's Missionary Society, which met in the Wesleyan Ladies' College building, for example. In 1891 Mrs Hare was listed as the vice-president of the Victorian Society at the OLC, and the following year she taught etiquette to the students after the retirement of Mary Electa Adams. She was referred to in the calendar of 1894 as lady principal.[118] At social events, such as the annual conversazione, the principal's wife served as chaperon. At Alma College, Mrs Warner, the wife of the school's second principal, was thanked at an annual meeting in 1900 for her untiring and unselfish service.[119] Involvement in alumnae organizations provided another area of service, as, for example, when Mrs Warner was appointed in 1905 as the president of the St Thomas branch of Alma Daughters. It is interesting to note in an 1882 report to the board that both Mrs Austin and Mrs Warner had taken some courses at Alma College and they had received a rebate on their tuition.[120]

Although it is difficult to arrive at substantial conclusions without access to individual pupil's school records, it appears that many students attended the ladies' colleges school either with interruptions or for a short time. Financial factors, as well as family responsibilities, inhibited them from completing programs. In addition, the need to educate siblings put pressure on parents to offer as many of their children as possible a chance to attend school for a period of time, rather than to focus on a completed course or degree as the end-product. Ian Davey notes that school attendance at the common schools of Canada West in the 1850s varied with the seasons and with the urban or rural location of the school. In rural areas, poor crop yields meant that fewer children went to school, whereas in times of good harvest, increased attendance was evident. Girls' attendance at school was also mediated by the necessity to care for younger siblings.[121]

The colleges urged parents to leave their daughters in school until the end of the semester and to give adequate notice before they dropped out of a program in an attempt to curb a casual attitude about the school year. Changes in the program aimed at keeping students in school were considered by, for example, Principal Austin of Alma. He wrote to Albert Carman, a member of the board, about a proposal to change the collegiate course, making Latin, history, geography, and English compulsory and offering choices between mathematics and natural sciences on the one hand and French and German on the other. Austin wrote, "As matters stand it takes about four years for a Young lady who has entered H. school to graduate which is longer that we can keep the average candidate."[122] One program was to be called the modern language course and the other the natural science course.

The tendency to leave school without finishing a program must be balanced against the apparent seriousness with which some students pursued diplomas in art, elocution, and music, all of which offered opportunities for wage labour. Also, there were students who excelled at the ladies' colleges and either continued their studies at another school or university or began careers teaching at other colleges or nursing schools. For these students the education, discipline, and graces taught at the ladies' college were clearly essential preparation for lifelong vocations. Although some students managed to use these educational opportunities as stepping stones to employment, the fact remains that both the education and the occupations were strongly gendered and required the development of culturally appropriate feminine behaviour.

The next two chapters will examine in greater detail the daily life, curriculum, and ideology of the ladies' colleges in order to establish how the curriculum was gendered and how students perceived that message. The continuities in education offered at the ladies' colleges can be traced to the early seminaries in Cobourg, but at the same time, the three women's schools developed different emphases, and the size of the staff allowed for a more diverse curriculum than the early academies and seminaries had been able to provide. The schools also fostered the careers of educators with diverse views on women's education. Between the lines of individual life stories and the school catalogues, one glimpses a sense of uncertainty and ambivalence among Methodists. The celebration of women's accomplishments was tempered by a frequently expressed fear of the consequences of their education. In the following chapters, the nature of this ambivalence and its effects on the direction of women's education will be discussed.

5 School Experience at the Ladies' Colleges: Early Ideology and Curricula

If the education of one or the other must be neglected, wisdom would demand that the education of women should be held of first importance. The mother is more with the children than the father, and if well informed herself can do very much to educate the children even before they attain school age.[1]

The ladies' college movement within Ontario Methodism began with the establishment of Alexandra College at Albert College and reached its peak during the years that the Wesleyan Ladies' College of Hamilton, the Ontario Ladies' College in Whitby, and Alma College of St Thomas were instituted by the Episcopal and Wesleyan Methodist churches. The schools were administered by a board of directors, representing Methodist leaders, laymen, and local business élites. Financial success in the community did not always provide these men with the necessary skills for educational administration. At the Wesleyan Ladies' College, the Hamilton members of the board in 1871 comprised two merchants, one manufacturer, two tinsmiths, two gentlemen, one importer, one minister, one physician, and one principal.[2] After the glorious beginnings of all these schools, the reality of scarce resources and expensive outlays put a great deal of pressure on their governing boards to find resources. Building, renovating, and outfitting the schools were only the beginning, because their maintenance, salaries, food, and equipment continued to keep them in a deficit position.[3] Income from students' fees rarely covered these costs. Moreover, during the first decades of the ladies' college movement, the question of the ideal form of female education continued to be discussed. To some extent this ideal was a theoretical concept that would soon be revised by financial realities.

Ladies' colleges were established at the same time as the state was reorganizing education at the provincial level. Gidney and Millar observe that Ontario high schools "gradually obtained a quasi-monopoly on secondary education and the credentialling process that education involved."[4] The publicly funded high school had a financial advantage in that it provided free education. In addition, the private sector offered little to distinguish it from public institutions. The matriculation examination, which became the entrance requirement for university, had the potential to give rise to a system, independent from the public schools, that might have strengthened the autonomy of the ladies' colleges, but in fact, the examinations standardized secondary education.[5] Methodist school promoters were not only affected by developments in state education, but were also quite aware of the establishment of other private schools. The presence of Catholic girls' schools was used to demonstrate the growing influence of Catholicism and the need for Protestants to become more militant in their support of ladies' colleges.[6]

The ideal form of schooling was a continual topic of discussion, linked to changing notions of the family. As Alison Prentice argues, some Upper Canada educators felt that schools ought to imitate the family. But the ideal family had by the mid-century changed from a large patriarchal one to a small private family, a change that Prentice links to developments in the pre-industrial economy. The family's role was not only to protect the child from the harshness of the world, but also to prepare her for it. By mid-century, supporters of boarding-schools and colleges believed that these institutions provided a trustworthy substitute for the Christian family. New ideals of family and educational environment were actively designed, argues Prentice, to serve a rising urban middle class.[7] The ladies' colleges served both day and boarding students, but there was a tremendous amount of concern for providing an atmosphere that resembled the ideal family. Students would learn by exposure to the model college parents what their future role would be. That this role would be tied to the creation of a middle-class household in an industrializing economy is clear. Order and uniformity ruled college life, as young women learned the practical habits that would help them to run a household and provide emotional support for working men. Yet within this college realm, women would also find the link to greater opportunities. As Caroll Smith-Rosenberg argues, "women, who had little status or power in the larger world of male concerns, possessed status and power in the lives of other women." Organizations such as ladies' college alumnae and church and social clubs offered women this sense of power.[8]

THE WESLEYAN LADIES' COLLEGE

The Wesleyan Ladies' College of Hamilton had been established as a "seminary of learning of a collegiate character for the education of female youth, based upon Christian principles."[9] The course of study covered departments ranging from primary through preparatory to academic and collegiate. The collegiate course was ambitious; it offered Latin, French, mathematics, philosophy, science, and evidences of Christianity.[10] The prescribed collegiate course could be supplemented by the study of other modern languages, such as Italian, Spanish, and German, as well as by Greek and Hebrew. Certain further substitutions could be made. A high degree of attainment in music or drawing, for example, could replace one of the modern languages in the collegiate course. By the 1890s, the WLC was *emphasizing* the fact that the Latin taught was at the collegiate level.[11] This language was especially important by this time since it was necessary for admission to men's universities and represented the male model of advanced schooling.

Although Latin had been available previously at the Burlington Ladies' Academy, there the rationale had been only that it provided a means of mental discipline which facilitated the learning of French and other modern languages.[12] As we have seen in an earlier chapter, the 1860 catalogue for the Van Norman school in New York gave a different rationale for learning Latin. The central place of both English and Latin, it claimed, was to encourage well-defined language and thought. Because a woman "presides at the fountain of life, and is the first teacher of language," she has a great need to understand the science and art of speaking.[13] Latin also was thought to bring together all the faculties of the mind, developing the reasoning capacity. Van Norman believed that the study of language was inherent in the female mind.

Like Van Norman's American school, the WLC encouraged an academic curriculum that would develop mental discipline, disdaining courses that were for mere show or pretence. The seriousness with which the curriculum was regarded is evident in the following introduction to the English program: "We deprecate the feeling, all too prevalent in some quarters, that in a lady's education music, painting, and kindred accomplishments should constitute the essence and chief attraction, often to the depreciation of a good English education and the mental culture that results therefrom."[14] The program was similar to the university curriculum yet allowed for creative developments absent from male curricula. Teaching at the WLC contained both conservative and progressive forces, particularly in English. The traditional areas of penmanship and composition are found side by side with literary criticism. According to Anna Sonser, the Arnoldian ideal of sensitive appreciation and of culture as a vehicle for guidance and training fit the Victorian women's role of "imbuing the lives of their husbands and children with spiritual and refining influences."[15]

Nevertheless, all students were given training in vocal music, and beyond the general training, students could pursue private music lessons. In addition to musical training, the "accomplishments" curriculum in the early years of the school consisted of creating wax fruit and flowers, drawing, and painting. The latter subjects were treated in depth, beginning with a study of the laws of perspective and proceeding from elementary pencilling from models to original sketching and working with oils, watercolours, or pastels. Several resources enhanced the academic status of the school, such as the library and a cabinet of geological and botanical specimens. The library boasted five hundred volumes and a comfortable reading room. The cabinet of geological specimens included more than a thousand items and an assortment of fossils, largely contributed by Professor Wright. The school was furnished with educational technology: globes, topographical maps, a microscope, and chemistry equipment.

The administration kept a merit roll, which consisted of a record of standings, both literary and moral, that could be transmitted on request to parents and guardians. The students were not, however, individually ranked. Diplomas available to them included mistress of liberal arts or mistress of English literature, as well as certificates for examinations passed in a partial course. A prerequisite for obtaining a certificate or diploma was a good moral standing, which in turn was dependent on the student's observance of the principles of the school. Government of the school was "firm without being arbitrary" and was based on confidence in the pupils and the desire to teach them self-control, obedience to principles, and a "conscientious regard for the right."[16] These often-mentioned principles, which were illustrative of the behaviour considered normative for young ladies, included truthfulness in opposition to "pretence in anything." Other prized virtues were patriotism, love of home, devotion to parents, simplicity, and "avoidance of heartlessness and display."[17] Self-control was apparently an important aspect of training at the college, but it entailed control of the emotions and sentiment, not of wildly deviant behaviour.

By contrast, the rules for the all-male Dundas Wesleyan Institute required its pupils to be punctual, cleanly, and gentlemanly. Students there were forbidden to damage the rooms, trees, or shrubbery, to visit saloons or taverns, to contract debts at stores in town, to converse with the servants, to take lamps out of brackets, to throw anything from the windows, or to use profane or foul language.[18] A local history confirms the necessity of these regulations by describing the fights the school boys had with the local town boys and the structural damage the students inflicted on the school building.[19] Clearly, the behaviours expected from male and female students were very different. A certain amount of devilment was tolerated in the progress from boyhood to manhood. The quest for feminine perfection, on the other hand, allowed fewer indiscretions and tolerated only minor misbehaviour. In 1847 at the Upper Canada Academy, Burwash notes that the school exerted a military discipline over the students, who ranged in age from ten to twenty. Few students in those years escaped "black marks," and there were frequent suspensions and even expulsions. One student described explosions of home-made bombs made of ink bottles filled with powder and riotous feasts in the students' rooms on stolen turkeys and ale. It is illustrative of the toleration of boys' misdeeds that Burwash notes such mischief could be found in the history of all schools.[20] Had such acts taken place in a ladies' college, one could be assured that the building would have been closed.

Students at WLC had access to "*select* society" without its late hours and "general dissipation." The purpose of this exposure, combined with the college's other benefits, such as its general Christian character, was to "produce a rich, deep and graceful character, generous and sympathetic, with self-reliant independence of thought, and freedom from weak sentimentalism."[21] Novel reading contributed to female sentimentality. The school closely guided the student to read only the classics and poetry.[22] By 1881 the following clause was added to the WLC calendar: "No young lady will be allowed to retain her connection with the school, whose example tends to encourage indolence and insubordination, or whose influence in other respects is injurious."[23] Clearly, the family atmosphere, with its emphasis on moral example, would not tolerate deviant behaviour.

The principles for students' behaviour were accompanied by a strictly prescribed daily schedule. Study hours, for example, were from 6 to 7 AM, recitation and class from 9 to 12, with a recess, and class from 2 to 4 PM, with evening study from 7 to 9. The hours had changed somewhat by 1881, so that students spent from 9 to 1 PM in recitation and other class work, with no classes in the afternoon, and study hours were from 6:30 AM to 7:30, from 4 to 5:30 PM, and from 7 to 9:30 PM.[24] Day students were also required to spend two hours per evening studying at home. To conform to this routine, the number of interruptions was kept to a minimum. Shopping, for example, was only allowed once a month in the company of a teacher. Visitors were permitted on Friday afternoon and on Saturday until 3:30 PM.

Religious instruction was a central feature of school life. It was absent from the weekday curriculum, but students were given a Bible class by the governor of the school every Sunday afternoon. Bible study was thus separate from the academic curriculum, but still made a part of the general school life. In addition, family worship and religious exercises opened and closed the school day. Earnest efforts would be made, claimed the calendar, to "produce a strong conviction of the paramount importance of personal religion."[25] Students were encouraged to attend the church of their parents' or guardians' choice. The spiritual dimension of life in the college was lauded by the *Christian Guardian* in 1862. "It will be gratifying to our Brethren in the ministry and people generally, to learn that a very considerable number of the young ladies in attendance have recently professed their conversion to God; and indeed, so general has been the religious influence prevailing, that but few in the college remain unsubdued by its gracious and heavenly power."[26] The non-sectarian emphasis of the school was illustrated by the presence at the commencement in 1889 of Rabbi Birkenthal, who spoke on Bible study. Birkenthal congratulated himself that a rabbi could stand on the platform in a Christian church and address a Christian audience, an event that he interpreted as "the greatest evidence of progress the world has yet seen."[27]

At a college commencement in 1892, the valedictorian commented on the positive effect the college had had on her religious ideals and thanked the principal, Dr Burns, "especially for having broadened and liberalized her religious view. Before she began her college course, she used to regard every person as wicked who did not conform to her religious creed. Now she could not understand her old prejudices; she had learned to regard the spirit of the creeds as more essential than any form of creed, however valuable as an aid to faith."[28] Burns commented at the graduation the following year that none of the objectionable features of denominationalism existed in connection with the college and even though it was a Methodist institution, the student body contained more Baptists and Presbyterians than Methodists.[29] He pointed to the fact that the school had never received "a dollar from Church, State or individual" and that in fact it generated $40,000 to $50,000 worth of revenue for the city.[30]

As early as 1865 the faculty was large. It included five teachers in the collegiate department, one in academic, one in preparatory, two in modern languages, one in fine arts, and two in music with three assistants. The total number of women faculty members then was eleven, as opposed to three men, all of whom were clergymen.[31] By 1874 the teaching staff comprised six teachers in the collegiate department, four in the academic, and four in the preparatory department, in addition to two in modern languages, one in fine arts, and five in music.[32] There were now five men, compared with seventeen women, for a total of twenty-three. In 1890 the school had twenty faculty, of whom nine were male and eleven female.[33] Ladies' colleges provided viable employment for women, and they in turn were a cheap source of labour for these schools. Teaching during this period was still the principal waged career open to educated women.

One of the few descriptions of life inside the college can be found in Arthur P. Coleman's diary.[34] At the age of fifteen, he and his brother were sent to stay with their aunts, Mary Electa Adams, principal, and Augusta Adams, mathematics teacher at the college. Both aunts took an active interest in the education and upbringing of their nephews. Coleman described how they took their meals in the hall with all the young ladies and how the day was structured: "Very cold this morning. I am beginning to get accustomed to college life. Every morning a bell rings at half past five. We then arise and dress. Then we read for a short time until aunt Augusta comes in and reads a chapter in the bible with us. Then we go down to breakfast at 7. During the day we read study play croquet or walk about the city or mountain."[35] This description, written in 1867, preceded the aunts' departure in 1870 to travel in Italy. On their return from Italy and a short trip to New England to visit friends, the Adams sisters moved to Cobourg and the Coleman brothers followed them there, undertaking to do gardening work in return for room and board with their aunts. While the boys studied at Victoria College, Mary and Augusta Adams worked to make a success of their own ladies' school, Brookhurst. In addition, Arthur assisted Mary with copy-writing a projected book related to her travels in Italy. By 1874 he noted, "I have became Lucius' successor as bookseller and stationer to this establishment. I am drawing master, errand boy, man of all work, guide, philosopher, and friend, etc. to Brookhurst."[36] A small, familial establishment, Brookhurst would never compare with the splendours of the WLC.

At the WLC, extracurricular activities increased the college's visibility and tied it to the community. By 1880, student publications such as the *Portfolio* contained advertisements by Hamilton merchants.

Social events at the college, moreover, were highlights of the Hamilton social calendar. These included recitals, guest speakers, convocations, and conversaziones, which the *Hamilton Spectator* covered in glowing detail. Descriptions of extracurricular activities balance the impression otherwise produced that the school housed a docile group of sheltered upper-class girls. Student life in fact exposed young women to the community, current events, and a discussion of educational developments at other colleges. For many girls the contours of their college life must have been much broader than the daily life of their mothers or of life at home in the family circle. Alice Chown, author of the radical autobiographical volume *The Stairway*, studied at the Wesleyan Ladies' College, presumably in the early 1880s, after attending a Kingston high school between 1878 and 1880. She had been born in 1866 to a Kingston Methodist family of professionals that included doctors, lawyers, and clergymen, such as her uncle, S.D. Chown, the general superintendent of the Methodist Church. In 1887 she entered Queen's University in Kingston and subsequently wrote numerous articles and worked as a journalist with the Toronto *Daily Star*.[37] After the death of her mother in 1906, Chown travelled to England, Chicago, and New York, where she was exposed to a variety of radical ideas. She attempted to apply her ideas to labour, dress reform, and a campaign to revolutionize philanthropy.[38] Chown was also a founding member of the Women's Peace Party.[39] One cannot determine where her radical ideas ultimately came from, but it is possible that some seeds were sown during her years at the all-female Wesleyan Ladies' College.

The literary offerings on the pages of the *Portfolio* reveal something of the subjectivities of ladies' college students. To what extent did the college contribute to what Gerda Lerner calls "the creation of a feminist consciousness?"[40] Lucy Lister, college student and daughter of a wealthy Hamilton merchant, in 1888 urged students to consider the model of noble women who found their life work outside of the home sphere, such as Frances Power Cobbe, Harriet Martineau, Hannah More, Clara Barton, Florence Nightingale, Harriet Beecher Stowe, and Elizabeth Fry. The author felt that women could exert moral influence not only in the home but also in society. She believed that the redemption of the world by Christ's sacrifice helped to elevate woman "to her rightful place as co-equal with man."[41] Woman would work on, not envying man his greater strength or freedom, but employed in her own secluded sphere. Clearly, this student was calling for as many opportunities as possible for women within a Christian feminist framework that did not challenge the acceptable hierarchy of gender relations.

Another student, Nettie Burkholder, argued in the same issue of the *Portfolio* that a woman who had taken a college course could not become a butterfly of fashion. Women could continue to develop their minds or work for the elevation of humanity. A woman who placed herself before the public was like "the peach robbed of its down, the blushing beauty is gone forever."[42] Yet this peach needed to be self-supporting, since men were scarce or sometimes failed their obligations. Acceptable options for women seeking to earn money included teaching and business. In 1890 Burkholder reiterated her point about the need for training for wage labour. She deplored the low wages paid to millions of self-supporting women in the garment industry in the United States. In her list of alternative careers for which she felt women were suited, Burkholder included detectives, business, farming, sheep raising, medicine, teaching and school inspection, the WCTU, and missionary societies.[43] By 1895 the *Portfolio* carried an article supporting women's right to practice law and reassuring readers that the practice of law does not "unsex all women engaged therein."[44] The question of a legal career was no doubt connected to the influence of Principal Burns, who lectured students on political economy. An earlier editorial had commented that the writer hoped that the king would give his Canadian subjects free trade (something which Burns supported).[45]

ALMA COLLEGE

The curriculum at Alma College was in many ways similar to that of the Wesleyan Ladies' College. Departments allowed a wide range of ages as well as types of preparation, so that the student's needs could be accommodated. Course offerings at Alma expanded until in 1884 students had the choice of three main departments, which were similar to the Wesleyan Ladies' College: preparatory, academic, and collegiate. But in addition, courses were offered by the conservatory of music, the art academy, the school of fancy-work, and the commercial department, all of which were contained within the institution.

Financial problems lent some urgency to the discussion of Alma's status as a school. Board meetings grappled with the problem of how the college would fit into the larger school structure of the province. In June 1889 the board recommended that the senate reconstruct the curriculum to bring it into harmony with the high schools and collegiate institutes "so far as practicable."[46] Entrance into the collegiate course was dependent on passing examinations in the same subjects as were required for high school entrance; the academic course contained the same subjects and options as the departmental regulations for third-class public school teachers' certificates; and the collegiate course reflected the subjects and options of the second-class certificate. Thus, by 1887, "collegiate" course meant a secondary school course, not a college one. By October 1889 the *Christian Guardian* could report that the college work had been brought in line with the public school requirements for second- and third-class certificates and that provision had been made for a full course for first-class certificates and university matriculation work.

The board in 1882 had suggested that the executive committee take the necessary steps to secure university affiliation for Alma College. The college continued to explore its relationship to the university and to the secondary school. Diplomas attained by graduates in 1895 included mistress of English literature, mistress of liberal arts, and those from the specialized departments listed above. The availability of diplomas in elocution, commerce, and domestic science reflected a practical orientation. An article entitled "Music as a Bread Winner for Girls" emphasized the earning potential of, for example, a music graduate. "The income of the girl who can teach the piano and, perhaps, the violin, or singing, will always be greater than that of her less fortunate sister in the factory or counting-room."[47]

One music graduate of Alma College, Mary Capsey, became head of the piano department at the Huntsville Female Seminary in Alabama and later at Garrard Ladies' College in Lancaster, Kentucky. In 1889 she married the Reverend A. Solandt of St Thomas and followed him to churches in Vermont, Illinois, Iowa, Nebraska, and Kansas until her death in 1915. Florence Edna Freek graduated from Alma College in vocal and instrumental music in 1901. She took a one-year course at London Normal School and taught for a year in the public schools of St Thomas. After studying music for two years in New York, she taught for a subsequent two years at Alma. She then moved to Regina and was a soloist in the Methodist church there. Freek, who became better known by her married name, Sharon, also contributed to the musical column in the *Toronto World* newspaper and was eventually a musical and dramatic critic at the *Regina Standard*.[48]

The early introduction of domestic economics distinguished Alma from other Methodist schools. The domestic science department promoted connections with professional nurses, since it was believed that nurses who studied the subject were more successful in helping patients convalesce. But there were other professional possibilities for students who chose this course. One graduate of the program, Nellie McCally, continued studies at the Lillian Massey School of Household Science in Toronto. Another graduate, Louise Spiers, taught domestic science under the auspices of the Brantford YWCA. Isabel Murray, a graduate of the program in 1902, continued her studies in the Normal School course in household science in Toronto, which undoubtedly led to further professional possibilities.

Academic work was combined with a regimen of physical activity that included at least one daily walk and calisthenic. In addition to academic subjects and physical activity, students were encouraged to participate in extracurricular clubs organized on the basis of activities considered appropriate for young women. By 1899 the college calendar listed the following groups: the Alumnae Association, the Almafilian Literary Society, the Tennis Club, reading circles such as Sorosis, and the Alma College Missionary Society. As the last named group suggests, religious and moral development was a central goal of the school's program. The college advertised that it was non-sectarian, but still distinctively and positively Christian in its character and teachings. As in other colleges, students attended the church chosen by their parents or guardians and were accompanied by a chaperon. In contrast with the WLC, which offered Bible study only on Sundays, at Alma, study of the Bible was integrated into the curriculum.[49] All students had to follow a Bible course during their program. The goal was to provide a complete environment for students, and this environment was shaped by manners and morals. "Good manners are founded on good morals, and our wish and effort is to utilize every occasion and means for inculcating a knowledge of polite forms. Our true ideal is the perfect culture – that of brain, soul and social being."[50]

The moral aspect was enforced by a system of discipline and a clearly defined code of behaviour. Girls were given demerit points for infractions: misconduct in church, unexplained absence from class, receiving a caller without permission, and pranks, such as concealing the college bell. Drunkenness, profanity, or the destruction of school property do not enter the discussion and apparently did not occur. Room doors had to be left open during study hours. On Saturdays, between four and six, students could receive visitors, but "it is forbidden that students walk or ride in public without attendance by some adult and responsible member of the family."[51] Restrictions on behaviour extended to all the details of daily life. Students were allowed, for example, to write only one letter per week to anyone outside their immediate families and were permitted to cut their hair only with their parents' consent. Two students lost all their social privileges for the term because they threw snowballs at a visitor to the college.[52]

Although Alma College asserted that it was non-sectarian, it made no claims to being free of racial prejudice. In 1891 Professor Warner moved at a council meeting that the presence of "Negro" students might prove prejudicial to the financial interest of the school and might "imperil the usefulness of the school for the purposes contemplated in its foundations."[53] International black students were, however, already at the college in the mid-1880s. Presumably, the presence of black students destined to return to the Caribbean fit into the college's mission, whereas the acceptance of Canadian-born "Negro" students presented a very different, and to Warner, unacceptable image to the constituency of the school. The *Christian Guardian* in 1884 announced that rooms at Alma were engaged for two young blacks from the Bahamas, Eugenie and Mamie Dupuch, who were to commence studies in May 1885. By the following January Eugenie had been appointed assistant teacher of music. It is unknown how long she held that position, but the *Almafilian* noted in 1912 that Mrs Mamie Dupuch-Bone had died after having served many years as a principal of the Girls' Model School at Nassau.[54]

Public perception of the college's image was important because Alma depended on contributions and on the resources generated by student fees. Parents needed reassurance that their daughters were adequately supervised and were taught the essential social graces and academic subjects. Any discrepancy between parental expectations and the students' experience at the school provoked emotional responses. One parent, who was informed by his daughter that girls at the school regularly danced in the halls, wrote to the principal: "Have we as Methodists come to this, – that we cannot send our daughters to a Methodist school without contamination with this curse and spirit of worldliness ... when in our own Methodist Ladies' College our daughters are encouraged to disrespect and violate the very rules of our church, and are allowed to give themselves over to this soul-destroying pleasure, to sap the vital spark of spirituality should they happen to possess any."[55] The student's father believed that if students were organized into praying circles, this activity would soon destroy the "insatiable" desire to dance. He had paid the college for the "sacred safeguard" of his daughter and was outraged at the perceived failure of the college to fulfil this part of its mandate. So major a part of the college's task was safeguarding its patrons that this type of incident was potentially harmful to the image of the school and ultimately to its financial basis. The purpose of the ladies' college was undoubtedly patriarchal in nature. Fathers, who paid the bills, demanded not only an education but also an environment that would protect and develop their daughters' womanly graces. Femininity, ever fragile, required constant vigilance and protection by those who were wiser and stronger.

THE ONTARIO LADIES' COLLEGE

The early years of Alma and Wesleyan Ladies' colleges described in the previous sections suggest that there were numerous unseen problems which beset the schools after the initial euphoria of their opening. By the early 1900s the WLC had closed, and Alma College had achieved financial stability only temporarily. The Ontario Ladies' College reached a second stage of establishment, which will be studied in closer detail. Although the school had ambitions to become the basis for a women's university, it concentrated on a program that covered a range of secondary school subjects to junior and senior matriculation. One can only imagine what the Hamilton college might have become if it had survived into the twentieth century, but the Ontario Ladies' College provides a concrete example of the transformations, as well as the continuities, that existed in Methodist women's education.

The OLC entered the early 1900s in a thriving state according to the press, which mentioned that the income for 1900 was over $32,000, the largest in its history. With 132 students in attendance, the college was reported to be reaching out "after higher things."[56] The conversazione in February 1900 captured this feeling of well-being, as "hundreds of sweet girl students in their pretty gowns," along with their escorts, "promenaded the halls, examined the curios in the museum, or rested in the handsome drawing rooms."[57] Such events allowed the public to admire the students, who were a picture of the feminine ideal in their white gowns, adorned and accomplished. Education, as Joan Burstyn indicates, was intended to enhance not diminish a girl's femininity and, in turn, increase her marriage prospects, not render her unsuitable for married life.[58] The college events were important spectacles which reassured parents that the female students remained marriageable. The press describes them as "sweet girl graduates" to remind the public that these girls, despite their education, graduated with both their femininity and, by implication, their virtue.

The college's curriculum claimed to extend from the work of the collegiate institutes up to the third year of the University of Toronto, with a musical department, known as the Ontario Conservatory of Music, affiliated with the Toronto Conservatory of Music for examination purposes. In reality, the Ontario Ladies' College students with an MLA or MEL received one to two years' standing at the university. The staff in 1901 represented a well-educated group and included Professor Greenwood (BA, Victoria), Miss Burkholder (BA, Victoria), Miss Horning (BA, Victoria), Miss Paisley (BA, Mount Allison),

Professor Thompson (MA, Queen's), and Miss Teskey (Emerson School of Oratory, Boston). Together, faculty and students created a refined family: "The home-like atmosphere is very apparent everywhere. One might imagine the young ladies all members of one immense family, so prominent is the feeling of genial good-will. Teachers and students are one, sitting down to the same tables, and enjoying the same social life. Can a student filled with the love of the beautiful live under the inspiration of the great masters, and then relapse into ignorant indifference?"[59]

The stress on a homelike atmosphere reassured parents that all the good features of home and family would be re-created in the school structure. The stress on home values implied as well that students would learn their proper place in a patriarchal order that imposed discipline from the father-principal down to the students. The Victorian family ideal headed by father and managed on the domestic front by mother was the primary image replicated in the ideal school structure. The domestic realm was free of the immorality of the market-place and therefore allowed women to carry the pure values and spirituality that would counteract the destructive tendencies of the market.[60] The recurrent stress on the home as a model for schooling reveals the power of this image as an ideal for the middle class. The middle-class family structure imposed a great deal of restraint on a girl's behaviour, her social life, her reading, and her aspirations. Carol Dyhouse has explored the social tensions inherent in the English middle-class family.[61] Daughters' resentment of the constraints imposed daily by mothers is only hinted at in the advertisements of the boarding-school. Yet one school paper suggested that the school could help girls "over that crisis so trying to many mothers and to many girls, namely the transition between childhood and womanhood."[62] Various limitations imposed on a girl's life by her parents were transposed to the ladies' college. The watchful eyes of parents were merely replaced by those of the principal and women teachers at the college. Lessons of obedience, subservience, and propriety were clearly being taught to the college students.

Why were these lessons so important that the college architecture, curricula, and religious instruction combined to project this message to students? Although new commercial values challenged male behaviour to greater competition and individualism, how did a increasingly materialistic culture adapt its vision of ideal female behaviour? The aspect of submission lent a certain consistency to cultural expectations. Wives of middle-class men needed self-discipline and industriousness to manage the domestic front while the husbands engaged in wage labour. The home was to be shaped into a haven of peace and aesthetic harmony by the talents of the educated woman. This refuge would also help create a positive atmosphere for the upbringing of children. In a young girl's life, the college created an interim or extended adolescence that had not been available previously. The momentary pause between her place as a child in her parents' home and as a wife in her own home was a period that was vulnerable in a girl's life. Supporters of ladies' colleges presumably believed that in the correct environment, this pause would help to prepare a young woman for her role in the future. Fears about sloth and indolence, as well as indulgence in sentimentality and novel-reading, reflected a general sense that, in her role as a middle-class wife she would require habits of discipline and industriousness which were clearly part of an industrial society. The home was, therefore, a haven for men to rest from their private labours, and this haven was to be ruled by harmony. Both the home and its mistress were idealized to the extent that she was to achieve perfect control over the domestic details without revealing the effort required.[63] Such control obviously required years of training in the virtues of restraint and self-discipline, as well as in the graces of good conversation and in social skills.

The Ontario Ladies' College was influenced by the late-nineteenth-century rise of home economics as an appropriate subject for women's education. The discipline fit perfectly with the agenda for women's education, which supported the wifely, domestic functions. Although home economics opened up professional opportunities in hospitals and settlement houses and in teaching the discipline, ultimately, the study "as an academic and professional alternative for women was strewn with pitfalls and often led women, not into the larger world, but back to the home."[64] The department of domestic science, which had been established in 1898, was renamed the college of domestic science in 1901. According to the calendar of 1901, "the industrial progress of society made it imperative that practical work be recognized in the educational system."[65] Lillian Massey Treble, the daughter of manufacturer Hart Massey, was a force behind the establishment of this program. She provided dining furniture, desks, stoves, dishes, and silver, as well as a teacher from her school in Toronto every Saturday until 1903, when a permanent teacher was hired.[66]

One notable graduate of the home economics course was Emma R. Kaufman. She was, in fact, a ladies' college student for whom the diploma opened the door to both postgraduate study and international work. After graduating from the OLC, Kaufman studied theology at Victoria University and graduated from the United Church

Training School. She studied at Teachers' College in New York for one year. After a trip to Japan in 1909 and a short-term teaching assignment at Tsuda College, she returned to Japan in 1913 and was appointed to the Tokyo YWCA staff as a volunteer secretary. She eventually became the general secretary of the Tokyo YWCA. After she returned to Canada in 1940, she was appointed a World YWCA executive member. Kaufman also helped to organize a branch of the YWCA in the Caribbean.[67]

In addition to the many options in the curriculum, a wide range of extracurricular activities were available at OLC. Sports such as tennis, basketball, hockey, bowling, and riding gave students a chance to exercise. Physical culture was a required subject unless the student obtained a medical exemption. The program used two systems: the Emersonian, which encouraged exercises for poise, grace, and respiration, and the Swedish system, which employed free-standing and apparatus movements, gymnastic games, and marching.[68] Valued activities included those that would enhance a girl's poise and counter the effects of studying. Medical experts sanctioned different types of exercise for boys and for girls. According to Wendy Mitchinson, they cautioned girls to walk, skip, and play lawn tennis, whereas boys could run, leap, and row.[69] Competition, associated with public life and the market-place, was not considered healthy for girls either in sports or in intellectual activities. From being concerned merely with students' health, the program in 1912 expanded to a course of training leading to a certificate or diploma that would qualify students to become physical education directors at high schools and colleges or managers of playgrounds and outdoor sports.[70] The concern with employment characterized the description of the commercial college as well; the calendar stated, "We make the course thoroughly practical, so that those who obtain a certificate are qualified to take a position at once as accountant, operator or reporter." Similarly, the college of domestic science and art offered a normal course of two years' length that would provide a foundation for "the professional life of a teacher." It awarded all graduates having a junior leaving or matriculation standing a provincial teacher's certificate, with the expectation in 1912 that "some arrangement will be made with the Education Department of Ontario for the recognition of our work for the coming year, but at present no announcement can be made."[71]

Advertisements stressed the OLC's unique abilities, in contrast with cheaper options such as day schools, and warned parents that collegiate institutes and high schools made no provision for the proper oversight and training of students outside school hours or "for the promotion of that social culture which is so highly prized to-day."[72] The school family created and reinforced good taste and refinement, of which the outer appearance was a crucial reflection. The wardrobe requirements therefore called for simplicity and neatness since "all extremes and extravagance are in bad taste." Students wore a navy blue serge dress for winter and a linen dress for spring and fall. The list of requisite clothing continued as follows: two middy blouses, a warm winter coat, a tailor-made suit for street and church, two simple house frocks for after-school wear, stout walking shoes with low heels, and house shoes with rubber heels. Among the forbidden clothes were sleeveless and low-necked gowns, jewellery during school hours, and low outdoor shoes during the fall and winter. Finally, plain underwear was required, and the matron warned that extra charges would be levied for anything "elaborate" that would take up too much of the laundresses' time.[73]

The 1907 calendar revealed that a May Queen was to be chosen yearly, that is, a student who best represented the moral and spiritual values of the college. At the ceremony a guest would read an address entitled "The Ideal Woman." The choice of May Queen was tied to monthly assessments of students' behaviour and a vote taken from among students.[74] All students were thereby invited to participate in celebrating the queenly values, which they would eventually be able to transfer to their own homes and families.

A construction project symbolized the optimism of these years, when a new wing was built that would house a modern gymnasium, indoor swimming-pool, hospital infirmary, and library. In 1915, when Dr Hare retired after forty-one years as principal, he was replaced by the Reverend F. Farewell, whose first task was to try to control the growing crisis in the finances of the school. Two years later the papers recorded that the college might be forced to close. By appealing to the town and to individuals, it was able to raise enough money to keep functioning. The war years and subsequent depression were felt by college authorities, and financial caution remained part of the school's policy. During the early 1920s the classes were divided into senior, sophomore, junior, and elementary. According to Brian Winter, the author of the school's centenary history, the OLC, "rather than being a girls' finishing school as it had been up to the First World War," adopted the curriculum of a private secondary school.[75] This description is at odds with the determination of the school's leadership to provide courses up to the second year of college. The highest level taught at Whitby seems to have been first- or second-year university, with students receiving approximately two years' credit at Victoria College for the ladies' college degree after affiliation in

1884. Hopes of making the college into a Methodist women's university were never realized. The attempt to bring the school in line with Ontario regulations had begun after 1912, when the domestic science department hoped to gain the approval of the authorities, and the issue was raised again in 1915 when Principal Farewell requested provincial inspection of the school. On the recommendation of the inspector, two of the OLC teachers qualified for teaching "under Provincial regulation by taking Summer Courses in Toronto."[76] The school had apparently decided to comply with inspection and provincial regulations, sacrificing autonomy for coexistence within the provincial structure.

THE COLLEGES AND THE PROVINCE

A common feature of the survival into the twentieth century of both the Ontario Ladies' College and Alma College was accommodation with the provincial Department of Education. Alma College's second principal, R.I. Warner, who succeeded B.F. Austin in 1898, gradually realized that a certain amount of compliance with state regulation was necessary for the college to survive. His pragmatic approach included adjusting to the Department of Education's demands. The reasons why the private colleges decided that such a policy was necessary can only be pieced together from the few surviving items of correspondence and minutes of meetings. There is no doubt that the state intentionally extended its authority to include the private schools. When the School Act of 1843 established the position of superintendents, the state gave inspectors the power to define legitimate educational practice.[77] Bruce Curtis argues that school inspectors used the rhetoric of moral improvement to extend political hegemony over all classes. The tasks of superintendents grew to include the licensing, examining, and paying of teachers, in addition to inspecting the schools and writing annual reports. The work of inspectors in investigating and reporting on schools helped to clarify and to centralize the bureaucratic power of the state, to the extent that by the 1880s, education became completely identified with the state.[78] The fact that ladies' colleges operated somewhat independently for a few decades must be seen as a brief interlude in their existence before they would gradually, but certainly come under state control.

Negotiations between the private schools and the Department of Education are evident in correspondence, for example, between the minister of education and Principal Warner of Alma. Warner requested a temporary certificate for an art teacher named Eva Smith.

In 1915 it had been decided that an elementary certificate in art would be required in all high schools by September 1916. The inspector wrote, "If Alma College is to enjoy certain privileges of the High Schools the same standards must be applied."[79] The minister of education added, "It would be manifestly unfair to exempt from that requirement a Private Institution in which candidates are being prepared for the same examinations as candidates in Provincial Schools."[80] Warner replied that "these are times of extraordinary financial stress to private schools generally, and that the rigid enforcement of the regulations just now might be oppressive indeed and unjust in view of all the facts involved."[81] The department was not moved by his request and stated that, under the circumstances, students prepared at Alma would not be eligible to write the bonus papers in middle school art in 1917. In February that year, Warner was asked to justify why Miss Smith could not take the art class required by the department, and he replied that the care of the home had fallen upon Smith when her mother became ill. The department granted her a temporary certificate to teach art to the class preparing for the lower school examination, on the condition that in September Alma either find a qualified teacher or Smith would have to take a summer course and pass the necessary examinations.[82] She, however, was unable to take the summer course in 1917 because of illness.[83] Principal Warner again wrote to the inspector of high schools asking for special consideration on her behalf: "We are most reluctant to seem in any way indifferent to the regulations of the Department of Education but under existing circumstances we feel we may reasonably request the renewal of permit to Miss Smith to teach High School Art at Alma College for the session 1917–1918."[84] This request was granted for the current school year, but for the following September the school was warned to find a qualified teacher unless Smith could take a summer course at the Ontario College of Art. In March 1918 Warner informed the Department of Education that Smith had been granted a three-month leave to take an art course in New York. His support for this ailing teacher was certainly a defence of his right to make decisions in his school, a sphere in which, by virtue of its private nature, principals had traditionally exercised a latitude that was not as evident in the state schools. Warner was, however, resisting a trend that had commenced in the school reforms of the mid-nineteenth century, which tended to centralize the power of the state over education.

The case demonstrates the type of negotiations that took place between the Department of Education and the private schools. The model of the family, which had functioned as the ideal mode of organization since the college's inception, had somehow to accommodate this impersonal and nosy relative, the provincial department.[85] The autonomy of the private schools decreased proportionately as the power of the Department of Education increased, through the inspection function and the right to assess schools, certify the teachers, and give a stamp of approval to the schools' programs. One can only speculate as to how the private schools could have resisted or postponed the bureacratizing power of the state, but clearly the era of independent ladies' colleges was running out.

The relationship between inspection and the formation of a dominant system of public schooling has been explored by Philip Corrigan and Bruce Curtis. The nineteenth century saw the growing identification of public schooling as "the only possible form" at the expense of earlier and alternative forms of education.[86] The Methodist schools had functioned quite independently of government interference for years, until the state claimed the authority to send inspectors to them. This authority subtly shifted the power relations between private schools and the state. The inspector made the workings of the schools visible and thereby helped to accumulate power at the centre of authority, namely, at the state level. If the Methodist schools had controlled large endowments, they might have effectively organized some resistance to the state's growing interference in their affairs. Their uncertain financial future and the acceptance by parents of public education as a reasonable alternative left them on shaky ground. Although resistance took the form of incomplete compliance with government directives, the official policy was cooperation. Since the Methodist ladies' colleges accepted the necessity of attaining approved status and allowing inspectors into the schools, the power of the state over the private school was established. Parents could not be expected to pay for education that was neither accredited nor approved by the state, and the important function of training teachers would collapse if those teachers were not recognized as qualified by the Department of Education.[87]

It is important to recognize that women played an implicit role in this bureaucratizing process, which essentially increased the powers of the state. Because they comprised the majority of teachers at the ladies' colleges, their jobs and their future careers were threatened by any state intervention. Marjorie Theobald observes that in Australia, women were central, not marginal, to the process of state formation, particularly since the state education system emerged from an earlier, family-based model of schooling. Yet in Ontario, as in Australia, the "bureaucratic invisibility" of women teachers meant that their lives and their struggles can only be deduced from the official records of state negotiations.[88] The impersonal standards of government regulation certainly reduced the adaptability of the system to absorb women's personal circumstances or their lack of official credentials.

Conflicts over bureaucratic matters such as credentials and inspection obscure the larger issues at stake. State education was gradually defined in a secular sense, and the degree of tolerance it was prepared to extend to the religious mission of private schools was extremely limited. The conflict was a far more significant struggle than would at first appear. The relationship of the church and Canadian state was clearly being worked out in the realm of education. Although civil disobedience was not openly discussed as an option, strategies of resistance at least showed the schools' reluctance to part with all jurisdiction.

The teaching of science was another area where private schools were expected to meet provincial standards. The minimum standards required to teach science included suitable accommodations, scientific apparatus, and qualified teachers, with the reminder that "after due notice, schools not provincial will be required to provide teachers trained in the provincial training schools in the teaching of science."[89] The science programs would be inspected and each school would have to prepare a list of the equipment, the names of the pupils with the amount of time they had followed the science course, and any other particulars the inspector required.

The private schools did their best to meet the exigencies of underfunding and state intervention. Alma College in 1916 appointed a special committee to solve the problem of a deficit, and it found that the departments of music and elocution yielded a good profit, while the art and commercial departments broke even, but the domestic science and high school departments were operating at a loss. The committee therefore recommended that the high school work either be eliminated or carried out by one teacher since the class was so small.[90] In order to find ways to combine efficiency with an attractive school program, Principal Warner corresponded with other school heads to discover how their programs were organized. In response to one such request, Principal Wigle of Mount Allison Ladies' Academy described the independent relationship between the college and the New Brunswick government. He wrote, "We find that our independent sphere gives general satisfaction to the public, and to the pupils and we maintain an undisputed prestige without the humiliation of outside supervisors."[91]

By 1920, enrolment at Alma totalled 196 students, of whom 71 were boarding students. The students were registered in various programs and "extras" such as elocution, which claimed 28 students, physical culture 68, collegiate 47, commercial 34, domestic science 19, china 9, painting 9, piano 130, violin 8, vocal 27, theory 20, choral 44, and public school 1.[92] In a shift from Warner's downscaling of the college's curriculum, in 1923 Principal Perry Dobson, who had taken over leadership four years earlier, drew the board's attention to the new regulations regarding university-entrance requirements, including senior matriculation, and he suggested that the college undertake some of the senior matriculation classes. In 1924 a subcommittee of the board recommended the appointment of an additional teacher in the high school department, since the work of the department had recently been approved by the government inspector.[93] The following year an affiliation agreement was signed between Alma College and the University of Western Ontario. Under this agreement, students would write the same examinations as the university candidates. The college would be represented on the Senate of the university by the principal.[94] The last MLA degree at Alma was awarded to Irene Hillesheim in 1918 and the last MEL degrees were given to seven students in 1925; by that year the term "matriculation" had been adopted.[95] Alma had successfully accommodated itself to both the tertiary and secondary levels of education as those were defined in the first two decades of the twentieth century. As a junior college approved by educational authorities and affiliated with the University of Western Ontario, it could benefit by association yet continue to offer "private" advantages to parents desiring this accommodation for their daughters. New problems would emerge, but Alma had successfully adapted to the provincial requirements for education and had managed to continue with the features its sponsors believed were central to their mission as a Christian college for young women.

THE MASSEY FOUNDATION COMMISSION ON SECONDARY SCHOOLS AND COLLEGES

Some time before 1921, the leadership not only of the schools but also of the Methodist church sought to define the role of the private schools by means of a commission on secondary education. One memo that summarized the findings of the commission observed: "While a large number of young women are now seeking a course that will prepare them for a livelihood as teachers, nurses, medical practitioners, or business employments and so choose one or other of the courses prescribed, none of these constitutes the highest aim of a woman's life, and there will always be a number who will seek an education which will fit them more perfectly to take their place in the home and in the life of the nation which from the home reaches out into all the phases of the common life of humanity."[96] The commission believed that the School of Household Science, established at the University of Toronto through Lillian Massey Treble, was an ideal education for a woman since it offered the potential for wage earning and at the same time fitted her for her ultimate goal in life. Practical household skills, as well as the importance of "appearance, deportment, and family relations," would give girls "competence in interpersonal relations and correct attitudes towards motherhood and marriage."[97] Of the graduates of the school between 1911 and 1931, one-third found employment as dieticians or food-service experts. Thus the domestic agenda for household science was subverted by those who found employment in hospitals and cafeterias. The fact that it took only a decade to establish domestic science throughout Ontario's school system, including the ladies' colleges, demonstrates the easy fit between the agenda of household science and the assumption "that preparation for one's life work had to be gender-specific."[98]

The commission's report also studied the question of coeducation from the social and educational aspects. Socially, coeducation had some benefits, since it closely approximated a family, while all interaction between the sexes was closely supervised. Educationally, specialized instruction for either boys or girls at an early age should be avoided, and instead a solid secondary education should be given to all. There was, however, a special education geared to each sex, which had its own standards of character; "otherwise we could not speak of a womanly woman and a manly man as ideals, or of a mannish woman or a womanish man as abnormal and almost despicable." Education of this sort would approach the ideal type, strengthen the "defective," and remove excesses. Mitchinson argues that medical experts helped to create these understandings of sex roles because "they provided a scientific rationale for the gender division between the sexes."[99] The differences in roles were required for procreation. The concern with abnormality presumably reflected the influence of sexologists. Jeffrey Weeks claims that this zeal in defining and categorizing sexuality reflected a wider trend in the social sciences to classify by means of scientific description. Issues of sexual and racial hygiene fuelled research in sexology.[100] Sexual difference was understood in a post-Darwinian sense to be rooted in the basic difference of cells. Maleness was characterized by the dissipation of energy and femaleness by the conservation of energy. Males, guided by inherent rationality, could therefore afford to compete and discharge energy, whereas females, who were ruled by the intuitive realm, had to be prevented from becoming overexcited.

The ordination of sexual difference in creation was gradually combined with a post-Darwinian view of the different functions of the sexes.[101] The necessity of maintaining sexual difference was further fuelled by a desire to return to a simpler social organization with clearer sex roles. Perhaps the Methodist school organizers felt that the promise of a clear standard for sex roles in their school curriculum would appeal to supporters of the colleges. Presumably social changes inspired a degree of reflection about women's role. The birth rate in Canada had continued to decline, particularly among the middle classes and in urban centres, until in 1921 the fertility rate of urban couples was 20 per cent lower that for rural couples.[102] Women's age at marriage had increased from twenty-three in the 1850s to twenty-six by 1871. Various legal changes during the years 1872 to 1907 gave married women the right to own property. The visibility of women in wartime work encouraged "reformers to press their more comprehensive demands."[103] In 1918 the Women's Franchise Act gave the vote to every woman over twenty-one who was a British subject. Education had played an important role in these social changes, and the members of the Methodist commission may have felt that it was time reassert the proper social order, namely, patriarchy.

How, then, would women's education serve to protect the necessary difference between the sexes? Ideally, it should not only give woman a choice of subjects useful to her in life, but also provide full development to her womanly character, while not "weakening her mentally with an overweight of subjects for which she may not be adapted." Several decades of female academic achievement had apparently not eradicated the notion that women would be weakened by excess study. The real goal of education was soul development. The agents of this ideal education should be chiefly women, since motherly insight and sympathy were needed, especially during the formative period from fourteen to twenty, when some attempt to correct the "defects" of young women would be required. These defects presumably included such uncontrolled behaviour as sloth, excess independence, and disobedience or any behaviour that was in defiance of authority. With these considerations in mind, the report discouraged coeducation at the secondary level. Interestingly, the problems of young women, which previously had been merely troublesome, were now associated with pathology. The report thus supported the idea of separate education for women, but argued its necessity from the perspective of the special needs of woman's character. The development of femininity and the prerequisites for motherhood were the ultimate ideals of such an educational program. As we shall see in the next chapter, when compared to B.F. Austin's somewhat more radical vocational goals for women, which in effect gave them options other than marriage, or Webster's call for equal opportunities in education and professions, these early-twentieth-century Methodist educators seem not to have made a break with the past. Their ideology bears a closer resemblance to the nineteenth-century cult of "true womanhood" and the ideology of separate spheres than to the pursuit of serious academic preparation.

This report was a precursor to the church's Massey Foundation Commission on Secondary Schools and Colleges, which released its findings in 1921.[104] The main thrust of the Massey report was to determine the church's future relationship to its schools, both in matters of supervision and in financial support. Because the courses of study for students preparing for teachers' examinations or university matriculation were well defined, the report particularly criticized the vocational programs and suggested that rearrangement of these courses could aim to serve three categories of students: boys preparing to work on the farm, girls fitting themselves for home life, and boys or girls preparing themselves for a business career. In addition to the specific preparation required for these vocations, each student should have access to general culture through the study of literature, history, social ethics, and civics. Furthermore, in church schools, religious education needed to be recognized in the curriculum and taught by a qualified instructor. The report was most harsh in its criticism of what it considered as "auxiliary" subjects such as music, art, and bookkeeping, which were taught as self-contained units to students eager to obtain salaried positions. This practice needed to be replaced by a more balanced scheme of education that would prepare students to become members of a community and presumably prepare girls to be housewives only. Since boys going into farming or business were acceptable, this criticism seems specifically directed against vocational training for girls. Thus it too represented a backward step in Methodist education.

The question of coeducation was discussed in a manner that was reminiscent of the earlier report. Coeducation in the "plastic age" between puberty and university was undesirable, particularly because different aspects of personality were being developed: "the femininity which is admirable in girls is contemptible in boys." One of the most desirable qualities to be developed in boys was held to be "masculinity," and in the adolescent age association with girls was liable to produce effeminacy. Part of this "manly" development required the presence of heroes who would inspire boys by leadership and example in study and sport in a way that women teachers could not.[105] The report regretted that there was not one (Methodist) school in Ontario or the west that was a boarding-school for boys only, and it concluded by suggesting that Albert College revert to being a residential boys' school. (This recommendation would be implemented in 1922 with near-disastrous effects on the enrolment and finances of the college).

In the report's evaluation of individual colleges, it was suggested that Albert College should *not* duplicate the work of the provincial secondary schools. In university preparation work, the only class that should be encouraged was for special cases, such as "over-age men." Work at the secondary level should be directed towards three categories of students: boys who would be farmers, girls who were prospective housewives, and girls or boys who were training for careers in secretarial work, stenography, and bookkeeping. This plan for secondary work was based on the presumption that the school would remain coeducational. The contradictory proposals may reflect some difference of opinion within the commission about the necessity of single-sex instruction or coeducation. First-year university work, the commission felt, should be avoided.

The report was very critical of the state of the building and grounds at Alma College. The preparatory department, which attempted to do pre–high school work, should be closed. The seven schools that composed Alma were too self-contained and uncorrelated. Students were allowed to pursue one course such as music, without any complementary studies in history or literature. Instead of permitting such a narrow focus in the student's program, the school ought to restore more balance to fit "a young woman more completely for the manifold interests and activities of her after life in the home, the church and the community."[106]

The OLC gained approval in the Massey report for the homogeneity of its community, in that the school's population was composed of only a few day pupils, thus making the influence of the school life more complete. At the time of its inspection, OLC was offering a high school preparatory class, secondary school subjects, music, household science, and religious education. The college also provided students with preparation for the first-year examinations of the provincial university both in the general course and in honour moderns. Those preparing for matriculation or teachers' certificates were pursuing a broader path, and the report recommended that such students take courses in Bible study and physical culture. One point of criticism was directed at the pretentious titles used by the ladies' colleges, such as college of fine arts, school of expression, or college of domestic science and art. These titles represented a practice that was also prevalent in secondary schools of magnifying "subjects into schools or colleges, teaching staffs into faculties, and diplomas into degrees." The "colleges" were really subjects or, at best, departments.

Although the Whitby college was evaluated as being in a healthy condition, it was reminded that the salaries paid to resident staff should not be allowed to fall too far below the standard in provincial high schools and collegiate institutes, "with which it is in a sense competing." The report also referred to the rule whereby teachers who had just completed their training in the Faculty of Education were required to teach for two years in a provincial school, and as long as private institutions were not recognized under this rule, the college would be at a disadvantage in securing efficient teachers.

MEETING THE CHALLENGES

The initial optimism that had characterized the ladies' colleges was tempered by the numerous financial difficulties they encountered. None of the colleges seems to have received grants either from the church directly or from the state. Revenues raised from tuition were insufficient to finance programs and also meet the accumulated debt and interest payments. Both Alma and the OLC undertook extensive additions to their facilities. These expansions were partly in response to demand and partly in the hope of adding to their income by increasing the student body. In the face of pressures to meet financial objectives, the school authorities tried to plan course offerings that would meet parents' ideals and fit a gradually changing notion of the purpose of female education. From the few written accounts available, it seems that there were those who regarded the ideal female education as equal to the male and another group who supported separate and distinct female education. Provisions were made for students who needed practical and vocationally oriented diplomas, and these included music, art, elocution, domestic science, and business. Teachers' certificates were awarded at both OLC and Alma.

As Sylvanus Duvall indicates in his history of Methodist education in the United States, many colleges offered a degree, but how does one evaluate the school's claim to be a college, as well as the content of the degree? A variety of degrees and diplomas were available, among them the AB, MEL (mistress of English literature), BL (bachelor of literature), or, in the case of the Elizabeth Academy in Mississippi, the *domina scientiarum*. All three Ontario ladies' colleges offered the mistress of English literature and mistress of liberal arts degrees, as well as a variety of diplomas in art, music, domestic science, and elocution. The colleges attempted to be closely associated with university privileges or university-level courses, in addition to the university preparation that was part of the curriculum. They needed to be perceived as offering something more than the public grammar schools or the high schools and collegiate institutes, and association with higher education was one aspect of that "something more." After the colleges affiliated with Victoria University, their graduates were generally given one or two years' credit for their degrees and did extra courses if they were judged deficient in an area.

The increased intervention of the Department of Education had an important effect on Methodist education. The provincial department had final authority over a teacher's qualifications, and if a school continued to employ a teacher who lacked appropriate papers, it could lose its approved status. This process introduced a bureaucratic and impersonal standard that allowed little room for the personal arrangements and individual considerations that had previously characterized the schools.

The actual goal of female education continued to be the subject of debate by church leaders and the students themselves in their school papers. In the *Alma* of 1903, the lady principal, M. Louise Bollert, remarked that "avenues are now flung wide to admit women, their entrance to which was undreamt of, a few years ago."[107] Among the professions she mentioned were medicine and nursing, both at home and in the missionary fields, the Christian ministry, journalism, and law. Bollert reminded women that their service in these professions should be characterized by the desire to serve their day and generation.

Despite this enthusiastic and optimistic view of woman's potential, an editorial in the *Almafilian* of 1909, in its report of a baccalaureate sermon by a Reverend Jas. E. Hughson of Ingersoll, described the fears that this open vision of women's potential aroused. Hughson spoke in terms that were later echoed in the 1921 report of the Massey Commission when he described the aversion one felt for a "manly woman and the effeminate man."[108] By creating such a strong dichotomy, he exploited fears about how education would transform individuals. Ideally, in Hughson's view, it should maintain gender roles. If education blurred or exchanged male for female virtues, the very nature and future of the family would be threatened. The nineteenth-century model of the family and the role of the woman as mother in that family were considered normative for all time. Only the effeminate man really approved of the "strong-minded public woman, who is more at home on the platform or at a convention than she is in the precincts of her nursery or kitchen."[109] Hughson believed that women's disaffection with their lot at home led to unrest and divorce. The glory of man, he explained, was his strength, whereas the glory of woman "is the home, for life begins in the home, and has made man what he is."[110] Hughson's fears of the gender confusion and social disintegration that would result from education were expressed again, at even greater length, in the two reports on education sponsored by the Methodist church.

Contradictions and confusions coexisted, but allowed some women who were inclined to do so to pursue postgraduate studies, vocations, and professions, while others who were differently inclined could perhaps choose the home life or, rarely, a combination of the two. In addition, alumnae organizations such as Alma Daughters gave graduates a lasting contact with their school days and the occasion to continue in an educational milieu. The strength of this bond is demonstrated by the fact that the Wesleyan Ladies' College alumnae still held meetings until 1962, when dwindling numbers were compensated for by the attendance of daughters and granddaughters. The longevity of the association is a strong testimonial to the commitment of its members. The alumnae kept a lively interest in literary matters, as is evidenced by their lecture series in 1890–91 on the writings of Spenser, Browning, J.S. Mill, Keats, and Shelley. A literary club of alumnae organized a lecture series in 1933 as well. Daughters of alumnae were invited to continue the traditions, and apparently they did so.

Teachers or lady principals also experienced a community that was more than the daily round of teaching duties at the colleges. Martha Vicinus has explored the community and intellectual life available to women through the residential women's colleges in England.[111] From the fragments of letters, autograph albums, and alumnae reports that remain, it is clear that similar community life was experienced to some degree in the Methodist ladies' colleges in Ontario,[112] although frequent turnover of teachers and perpetual financial difficulties made this possibility somewhat more remote than seems to have been the case in Britain or the United States. Ultimately, the realities of the times helped to create several definitions of consecrated womanhood, and the education acquired in the ladies' colleges contributed to the achievement of a broader notion. This plurality of ideals was not an intentional creation but resulted from the various options inherent in higher education. The conservatives were correct in believing that nothing would be exactly the same as it had been, but neither the family nor society was threatened to the degree they imagined. Many graduates chose family life, married, and had children.

Not only did the Department of Education directives change the nature of education at the Methodist ladies' colleges, but changes in the tertiary level of education in the province had an effect as well.

The ideal of Methodist education for women underwent a transformation when they were finally allowed to take courses and obtain degrees at the male university. The academic possibilities of a BA for women had been advocated for years by several supporters of women's education within the church. Yet for those who were uncertain or ambivalent about this bold move of allowing women into the university, Methodist education offered other options that were expressions of the more conservative gender ideology present in Methodist education since its beginning.

6 Personalities and Potential Problems in Methodist Education

While Providence may call one woman to the public platform as lecturer or preacher, another to teaching, another to outside professional work there can be no doubt that for woman the sphere is home, and woman's mission home making, as sister, wife or mother. And if her place is in the home, she needs the highest development to make this home an ideal one.[1]

As we have seen, the optimism with which the ladies' colleges had been launched presumed that the public would be convinced the colleges were worthwhile and would express this conviction by giving them large endowments. When these endowments were not forthcoming, the colleges had to search for solutions to their debt-plagued budgets and recurring financial crises. Money problems were not the only threats that faced the schools. A confusion about the purpose of women's education, created by the outspoken advocates of equal education for girls and the conservative rhetoric of those opposed, clouded the issue. The rhetoric of the ideal education for women, whether liberal or conservative, was closely tied to a middle-class concept of woman's role in the home. Moreover, the state was demonstrating increasing interest in controlling the quality of education in private schools, without being willing to assist them financially. The exact relationship between the private school and the state needed redefinition.

The closure of the Wesleyan Ladies' College in 1898 illustrates how a failure to make the necessary accommodations in order to survive into the twentieth century can reveal relationships between the church and its educational mission, the way in which it funded projects, and how it formulated priorities. Was the church, like the state, willing to claim the schools, but unwilling to provide funding? Its priorities shifted with the cultural climate and the growth of the social-gospel movement. Education is thus one indicator of changes in a denomination's priorities. Yet it is also important to account for the actions of individuals within these corporate bodies, particularly when their views might be characterized as extremist or radical. According to Ramsay Cook, Canadian Methodists clung to their doctrines of inerrancy and biblical inspiration because the church had never developed a theology as systematic as that of Calvinism.[2] This need to defend the boundaries of religion led to the heresy trials of two of the Methodists examined here, Alexander Burns and Benjamin Fish Austin. The actions of Burns of the WLC will be examined in the context of that school's demise.

Austin and another clergyman, Thomas Webster, had strong opinions about women's education. It is interesting to note that Austin had three daughters and Webster five, a fact that no doubt added a personal aspect to their views on the subject. A fourth advocate of women's education, Alma College principal R.I. Warner, who held that position from 1898 until 1919, had more conservative views, but these too deserve closer attention. His principalship led the school into the twentieth century, with a shift away from the academic in the direction of female accomplishments and education for the home. The examination of the views of these four Methodist clergymen reveal the diverse attitudes within the denomination towards women's education and help to clarify how difficult it was for the ladies' colleges to present a unified front to the encroaching powers of the state. Women's education was initially viewed as a sign of the progress of civilization, but early in the twentieth century, conservatives saw it as a liberal movement that needed to be controlled and restrained.

ALEXANDER BURNS AND THE WESLEYAN LADIES' COLLEGE

The world around Hamilton's Wesleyan Ladies' College in the latter part of the nineteenth century was changing and challenging the very nature of female college education. Social and economic factors had contributed to the rise of a middle class that had different aspirations for the education of its daughters from the élite schooling offered by the WLC. Without government grants or denominational support, the college had to raise funds through tuition, making college education an expensive option. Moreover, Hamilton's class structure was shifting in response to increased industrialization, urbanization, and transportation. An influx of European immigrants transformed the composition of the city's population, and as a result, the college represented an increasingly remote choice in a local world that was rapidly becoming more and more middle and working class.[3] The unending debate about the merits and disadvantages of coeducation continued in the popular press throughout the eighties. The ideal of the ladies' college student adorned in a white tea dress, absorbing arts and graces as well as academic subjects, was beginning to lose its hold as a cultural symbol. Some families found that it was equally attractive, and much cheaper, to send girls with their brothers to the public secondary schools. Music lessons could be arranged privately, and Sunday schools could provide biblical training.

Furthermore, since the college had opened in 1861, several other colleges had appeared and offered competition for students and resources.[4] Alma College, Alexandra College, and the Ontario Ladies' College all offered similar types of education. Other denominations also provided girls' and young women's education in a variety of settings, such as Toronto, Ottawa, London, and St Catharines.

Denominational politics affected all of the Methodist colleges. The union of Canadian Methodist churches in 1884 directly influenced the educational work of the church. Albert College surrendered its university status and became a feeder secondary school affiliated with Victoria College. The act of 1884 increased the powers of Victoria and led to similar affiliations with Stanstead Wesleyan College, Columbian College, Wesleyan Ladies' College, Ontario Ladies' College, and Alma College.[5] It is ironic that the opening up of a point of access to the university contained the seeds of destruction for the WLC. The affiliation must nevertheless have been greeted initially with enthusiasm by students and staff because it offered recognition of the work of the college and increased its status through the association with Victoria. The process of recognizing students' work required negotiations as the two institutions worked out how much university credit the ladies' college graduates had earned. In so doing, President Burns described fourteen graduates of the WLC in the following statement: "Those ladies have all taken a good stiff course in Psychology, Apologetics, Biblical History, Science and several of them have spent years on Music and Art – some of them graduates in these departments."[6]

Alexander Burns had been born in 1834 in Ireland and had immigrated with his family to British North America while he was in his teens. The family initially settled in Quebec City, but in 1850 it moved to Toronto. Although he had been raised as a Presbyterian, Burns converted to Methodism after attending revival services led by James Caughey. He studied at Victoria College, where he won the Prince of Wales gold medal. Burns entered the Methodist ministry in 1861 and was placed on probation for Stratford and Drayton. Two years later he married Sarah Andrews, the daughter of a Cobourg miller, and in 1864 he was ordained.

Burns's reputation as an academician led to an invitation to become the vice-president of Mount Allison Wesleyan College in New Brunswick, which he declined in favour of a similar position, that of teaching mathematics and astronomy at Iowa Wesleyan College. From 1868 to 1878, he served as president of Simpson College in Iowa. In the latter year Burns became president of the Wesleyan Ladies' College in Hamilton, as well as professor of mental and moral science, logic, evidences, and higher English literature. His academic awards included an honorary DD from Indiana University and an honorary LLD from Victoria College. He was elected senator of the University of Toronto and served as a member of the Board of Trustees and Senate of Victoria.

Alexander Burns held liberal views and believed in the supremacy of reason. His beliefs soon landed him in trouble with the Methodist Church of Canada. Accused of heresy, he was tried but acquitted. Burns was an outspoken advocate of free trade, public schools, and home rule for Ireland. His political career included an unsuccessful bid to become liberal candidate for Hamilton in 1887. An ardent supporter of women's education, he tried various strategies to preserve the life of the WLC in Hamilton.[7]

The absence of college business records or minutes make the precise circumstances affecting the WLC difficult to trace. In 1894 the board of the college reported to the conference of the Methodist Church that the previous quadrennium had been a great success educationally, but some strains were also recorded.

> It has, to some extent, been a trying period. The financial depression so generally felt in all of business has been felt in educational work also. The [private] institutions naturally feel the pressure most, depending as they do on fees alone. As this institution has never either asked or received financial aid from the Church, although it permits the Church to appoint several of its governing Board and gives to the Church every advantage furnished by its institutions owned entirely by the Church. The College has always considered itself an ally of the Church in extending Christian education and its concomitant civilization. The curriculum lays stress on Biblical Literature,

Christian Evidences, and Moral Science, while furnishing to its pupils the practical advantage of a Christian home of refinement and culture.[8]

In 1897 the Hamilton Conference expressed its gratification that the college was functioning efficiently and "that the people may send their daughters to receive instruction from Dr Burns and his staff, feeling assured that they will receive the highest culture and most liberal education."[9] The same unconditional confidence was expressed by the chairman of the board at the convocation that year, when he announced that the college would reopen the following September, "better equipped than ever for the education of women."[10] Such optimism seems unwarranted considering that the college closed its doors in 1898. The exact relationship of the board to Burns, now apparently the owner of the school, is not known. In the church minutes, he is noted in 1898 and 1899 as having been "left without a station" at his own request. He moved to Toronto and died suddenly in 1900 after an illness of one week's duration.[11]

Burns's role in the eventual closure of Wesleyan Ladies' College remains unclear. According to one source, he had worked tirelessly on its behalf.[12] Yet a former student wrote, "I think if Edward Jackson and more of the members of his board had been alive in 1897 Dr Burns would not have been able to get hold of all the college stock and turn the old school into a hotel."[13] This intriguing allegation has thus far proven impossible to substantiate. The ownership of the college at a certain point evidently shifted from the corporate body that had originally been established to ensure the college's survival beyond dependence on one individual. Hints of trouble are evident in an article in the *Hamilton Spectator* on 17 October 1891, which claimed that some of the shareholders of the Dominion Building and Loan Association were causing writs to be issued against Burns and several directors of the association for alleged misappropriation of funds. The other accused directors included the G.W. Ross, Liberal Party member and minster of education, J.R. Stratton, MLA, J.B. McWilliams, T.B. Darling, and Thos. Birkett, mayor of Ottawa. No further information is available about any such financial scheme. However, in May 1895 Burns assumed title of the WLC with the backing of the Edinburgh Life Insurance Company and the Bank of Montreal. The amount of money involved in the transaction was $30,000. In 1898 various liens were placed on the property between February and August. Almost $17,000 worth of liens are recorded in the next three years. On 31 May 1898 Burns sold the property to his wife, Sarah, for $15,000. In July that year a lease agreement was signed between Sarah Burns and Robert Gilkinson. The lease required payment of $2,500 per year for the first two years, gradually increasing to $4,000 in the eighth, ninth, and tenth years. It was effective from 3 September 1898. The following year the school was no longer in operation, but Sarah and Alexander Burns were listed with the Bank of Hamilton for a mortgage of $9,587 and also for a mortgage with the Manufacturers' Life Insurance Company worth $35,000. Perhaps they still hoped to finance and restart the college. By 1900, however, Alexander Burns had died, and Sarah faced the prospect of carrying the financial burden of the institution-cum-hotel. The Burns family had moved to Toronto, and so they were not in Hamilton anymore to oversee the building directly.

In 1905 Sarah Burns and Robert Gilkinson signed a new lease agreement for the sum payment of $1. This lease was discontinued and a new one signed in May that year with Robert Gardener of the Waldorf Hotel, who leased the property from Sarah Burns for $5,000 per year for six years. Mrs Burns continued to be named in transactions concerning the property until 1914, when she died and her son Charles was named as sole executor. The Hamilton Hotel Corporation took over the property for $1, and in August 1914 Metropolitan Life bought the old college building with an accumulated debt of $350,000.

The acquisition of the college by Burns in the mid-1890s had caused some friction between him and the Conference. A motion was passed at the Hamilton Conference in June 1898 that "we as a district meeting regret that Dr Burns has rented the Ladies' College property in the city of Hamilton for hotel purposes, which we believe to be against the whole teaching and practice of our church."[14] In his defence, Dr Burns produced a letter from a lawyer certifying that he had disposed of the property and had executed a registered deed. This letter caused the assembly to propose that the "character of Dr Burns do now pass."[15] In other words, he had cleared his name.

Without additional records, it is impossible to determine whether Burns was desperately trying to save the college against all odds or whether he predicted and assisted in its closing. There is no indication as to how the school undid the conditions set out in the act of incorporation, namely, the presence of shareholders and the composition of the board. The silence concerning the college's closure contrasts strangely with the amount of attention the opening of the school had attracted or the pride that the church and the city of Hamilton had taken in its presence. It is unclear whether this silence results from a loss of sources or was due to embarrassment at the hint of scandal or a sense of betrayal by those who had invested in the college. Had Burns miscalculated, gambled personally on the future of the school, and lost? Did his family suffer financially from the school's indebtedness? Both of his daughters were listed as teachers at the WLC, but there is no evidence that they continued their teaching careers elsewhere. Until financial records, letters, or diaries can be found that reveal the inner story of the college's finances, the final years of the WLC story will remain somewhat of a mystery, as difficult to imagine as the college's past on the grounds where a modern hotel now operates.

Burns and his supporters had actively campaigned for a ladies' university in Hamilton, built on the basis of an expanded college. The campaign led some to fear that the work of the college would be interrupted. Burns, however, wrote to the *Christian Guardian* in 1893, reassuring everyone that the work at the ladies' college would go on. "That a university for ladies should be suggested in a city of 50,000 having no other college, is not to be wondered at. But we would assure our graduates, who now number nearly 400, that there will be no break in the work of their alma mater, however it may be extended and elevated."[16] Previously, in 1883, Burns had actively promoted the possibility of moving Victoria College to Hamilton.[17] He and Burwash of Victoria discussed the location of "our university in Hamilton."[18] This dialogue arose out of Burwash's opposition to federation with the University of Toronto.[19] Despite Burns's active promotion of the idea, neither a Methodist university in Hamilton nor a ladies' university ever came about.

What was the nature of the education offered at the WLC and how did it affect students' lives? In baccalaureate sermons preached at the college, prominent ministers lauded the infinite potential of educated women, but usually concluded with a reminder of the intended results of their education. In 1881 Burns told the crowd gathered in Centenary Church, Hamilton, that the duty of graduates was clearly "Not to take the rostrum or the pulpit, although prejudice alone might protest, but with quiet, queenly, womanly dignity and earnest Christian common sense, to speak and live the truth so as to make it attractive and influential."[20] Woman's ultimate role was thus to refine society by her special qualities; one of the goals of her education was to prepare her to be a social purifier.[21] Only the religious, educated woman could make home and society what they ought to be. Yet social reform was secondary in importance to her role as the "tutelary spirit of the family," where she could exert her greatest influence, not in the wrestling crowd or struggling at the "reeking polls," nor, in fact, anywhere "where man's domain extends, but in her home [which] is woman's sphere."[22]

Some advocates of women's education at the WLC nevertheless phrased their support in terms that were unmistakably progressive. The Reverend Hugh Johnston advised the college graduates in 1892 that their education had placed them on a path which led to equality with men. In the same address he argued that woman should be allowed to practise any profession, receive equal pay, and remain single if she felt called to do so. He urged women to follow opportunities in science, arts, or letters, but he reminded them that the home should continue to claim "the greater part of a woman's attention and her training should be such as to enable her to make her home-life better and more attractive for it."[23] On the subject of enfranchisement, Johnston felt that women had more power without the vote, but he conceded that they should perhaps be allowed to vote on issues affecting the "fireside, such as the abolition of liquor traffic."[24] Messages such as these clearly legitimized the temperance issue as a necessary field for women's action. The rhetoric of equality assumed very clear limits to the sphere of women's activity. Similar mixed messages about the goal of women's education and the acceptability of their involvement in certain political causes were expressed by other Methodist clergymen such as Thomas Webster, B.F. Austin, and R.I. Warner at Alma College.

THOMAS WEBSTER

Thomas Webster was born in Ireland in 1809 and died at Newbury, Ontario, in 1901. His parents immigrated to New York State during the War of 1812. Their strong attachment to the British crown caused them to move again in 1819 to London Township. The Webster home served as a place of worship for local Episcopal Methodist members for seven years. Thomas was converted at seventeen and became an early advocate of temperance. In 1833 he married Mary Bailey, the daughter of the Reverend John Bailey, who had been a student at Cazenovia Seminary. At the conference of the Methodist Episcopal Church in 1838, Webster was received as a probationer; he was ordained deacon two years later, and in 1842 Elder Webster served the London, Belleville, Brighton, and other circuits. His unfinished memoirs paint a graphic picture of the physical demands of the circuit rider's life. Meetings were held once or twice a day and three or four times on Sunday. His circuit in 1838 had extended from Dundas to Toronto and from Lake Ontario to Eramosa, Erin, and Caledon. The roads were rough and the people they served poor. For a year's work, Webster received $80.[25] He and his wife had five children, all girls, a fact that no doubt contributed to his advocacy of the cause of women's education and equality. He was a founder of the *Canada Christian Advocate* and served as its editor for six years. Webster was honoured by his election as presiding elder, senator of Albert College, and member of the General Conference until the union of 1884, and he was twice chosen as delegate to the General Conference in the United States. Wesleyan University in Bloomington, Illinois, awarded him an honorary doctorate.[26] He wrote many editorials, pamplets, and historical sketches, but one of his major publications was *Woman Man's Equal*, published in 1873.[27]

The book is divided into ten chapters, which combined theology ("The Sexes Equal at Creation") with history ("Women in Antiquity") and legal theory ("Woman before the Law" and "Woman and Legislation"). In the last-mentioned chapter, Webster systematically refuted some of the arguments commonly used against women having a vote. He urged that they be educated to realize that they had the same God-given responsibility as men to develop and to use their mental powers. He did not believe that women's active role in the church or politics would undermine the family, particularly because the "responsibility of regulating and ordering a household properly, devolves equally upon both the husband and wife."[28] He urged that unmarried women be allowed to enter the public realm to do good and countered the assertion that women were unfit for public life because they were supposedly unable to speak fluently or reason logically. They, according to Webster, had not been allowed sufficient opportunities to develop their talents. The churches were partly responsible for preventing them from doing so. He referred to the Society of Friends as one example of a religious group that had granted equality to men and women in the exercise of religious services. Even the Methodist Church had strayed from its early beginnings, when it had permitted women to speak in public. Given the opportunity to speak publicly in church and political contexts and prepared for this opportunity by a liberal education, women would show that they were mentally equal. In other words, they had been disadvantaged by a lack of education or opportunity, but this lack did not prove their inferiority of ability. On the contrary, Webster wrote: "The cramping of the mental powers of women, or the attempting to cramp them, lest they might claim equal advantages with the other half of the race, will be classed – and justly so – with the cramping of women's feet by the Chinese."[29]

Women who had entered the study of medicine had been subjected to "opposition and insult" by male medical students, but they had persisted and distinguished themselves in the profession. Presumably Webster, writing in 1873, was reflecting on developments in the

United States, because it was not until 1883 that Augusta Stowe graduated from the Victoria College Medical School, the first woman to receive a medical degree in Canada. The opening of universities to women had brought about no calamities, even in the eyes of those who opposed such a move. Not all universities were open, however, and Webster blamed this situation on men who could not come down from their lofty pedestal to let their sisters or daughters mount it, "lest they should reach their side." Despite the fact that some schools were slow to change, he remained optimistic that better days would dawn and that women would soon occupy the position to which they were entitled "as man's compeer – the position of equality with him in all the relations of life – and enjoy the full rights and privileges of civilized and Christianized citizenship."[30]

There is no doubt that Webster's views were more radical than those of his neighbours in Newbury. Unfortunately, no record survives of what influences may have shaped them. He presumably read the leading journals of the time, which would have exposed him to developments in women's education outside Canada. The presence of Christian feminism was evident, as we have seen, in student newspapers such as the *Calliopean* of the Burlington Ladies' Academy and the *Portfolio* of the Wesleyan Ladies' College in Hamilton. Webster was clearly in touch with the general currents affecting women's position in North America and Britain. In America, Catharine Beecher in the 1840s had advanced her cause to educate middle-class women to be teachers. Already in the 1850s a group of English feminists dedicated to women's education, including Emily Davies and Barbara Leigh Smith, met to discuss strategies for opening up the universities to women. Their work led to the rise of women's halls and colleges at Oxford and Cambridge in the 1860s and 1870s. The rate of women entering institutions of higher education in the United States increased from 11,000 to 85,000 between 1870 and 1900. Women doctors were still few, but Dr Elizabeth Blackwell, for example, influenced many when she lectured in England in 1859. Dr Elizabeth Garret graduated with her MD from the university of Paris in 1869. The opening of Vassar in 1865 and Smith in 1871 gave further prominence to the issue of women's higher education.[31] These early advocates embraced a Christian feminism, which argued that women should maintain their womanliness and their role in the family, but that access to education was their right. Advocates of women's education in the United States and Britain viewed the suffrage issue with some ambivalence because they felt that it could threaten their gains on the educational front. Webster's call for Christian equality should be interpreted within the limitations that were still assumed to apply to women's active participation in society, politics, and the workplace. A call for the full development of women's capabilities did not assume that they would pursue the same goals as men. Indeed, Webster's ideal clearly left men in charge of the leadership of church and state.

He nevertheless believed that women were called to the prophetic office just as men had been, and they had a claim to all the rights and privileges of the church. Women of the New Testament church, such as Anna the prophetess, Priscilla, and Phebe, had been active as fellow labourers with the apostles. He congratulated women of the church who continued Christian work in the present age and used the illustration of the Pastors' and Ladies' Christian Union, originally organized in Philadelphia in 1868, as exemplary of the type of organization that would benefit the church and use women's talents. The object of the union was to assist pastors to visit the sick and encourage people to attend church. The pastor was president of the society, and the church's territory was subdivided into smaller parishes, with two or more women appointed to visit the houses in their parish to assess physical and spiritual needs. The society succeeded because it harnessed the moral and religious power of two-thirds of the church, namely, its women members. The efforts of the Woman's Union Missionary Society, organized in 1861 in New York, highlighted another field of endeavour for women, the mission field. Since the gospel was to be preached to women, the most effective instruments were "lady" missionaries.[32] Webster also referred to the Women's Foreign Missionary Society of the Methodist Episcopal Church as another worthwhile agency made use of the energies and talents of women in the church.

Education was central to his advocacy of women's responsibilities. He was confident that education would make the difference, particularly because he was convinced that women were intellectually equal to men. Were there no limits to what a woman could achieve in Webster's scheme? As the example of the Pastors' and Ladies' Christian Union shows, the ideal organization was ultimately headed by a man. The equality of opportunity that he advocated was still channelled into a version of separate spheres, but one that offered women many more choices than they had previously enjoyed.

Burns and Webster were outspoken advocates of women's education. In their positions as, in Burns's case, principal of the WLC or, in Webster's, editor of the *Canada Christian Advocate* and church historian, both men had the respectability and the platforms from which to speak. Because women rarely spoke publicly or had authority over the administration of education, it was particularly important that the cause of women's education had supporters such as these two. Yet it must be emphasized that their support of women's rights and education was within a framework of Christian feminism, which tied women's opportunities to clear responsibilities within the family, church, and society. Their vision was largely restricted to an ideal middle-class woman whose education gave her some degree of choice in her life course, but who would likely use her education in the family and church and to a limited degree in social concerns.

BENJAMIN FISH AUSTIN

Benjamin Fish Austin was also a supporter of women's education. For the principal of Alma College, every diploma needed to be like a baptism: an "outward and visible sign of an inward and invisible grace."[33] Austin had been born in Brighton, Canada West, in 1850 and had graduated from Albert College with a BA in 1877 and a bachelor of divinity in 1881. He married Frances Connell of Prescott the same year. After several years in the Episcopal Methodist ministry, he was appointed principal of Alma College, a position he held from 1881 to 1897. His achievements in that role were celebrated by the conferral of an honorary doctorate by Victoria College in 1892.[34]

Principal Austin was well respected within Methodist circles for his preaching ability and his work for women's higher education. Despite this respect, by 1897 relations between the Alma College board and the principal had become tense. The board felt that Austin was not devoting enough of his time to the school. He, for his part, wrote to the board revealing mixed feelings about his commitment to the college: "Finding a reprieve of at least a year necessary for straightening my financial affairs, I am undecided whether it is better in the school interests and my own to ask for a year's furlough or to tender my resignation. While the above reasons seem to me of weight, I must confess that family affliction and much anxiety of mind over various matters have rendered me somewhat distrustful of my own judgement."[35] Austin's personal confusion may have been due to the death of his youngest daughter a year earlier.[36] He did resign his position in 1897;[37] two years later he was to be tried for heresy. According to an account of the trial published in a pamphlet,[38] Austin publicly announced himself to be a spiritualist, with a belief in spirit return and communication, at the London Conference of the Methodist Church held at Windsor in June 1899. The same day he was unanimously expelled from the ministry. He apparently spoke for three hours in his own defence, using scientific and biblical arguments to support the idea of spirit return.[39] In his "heresy sermon" Austin argued for a continuous revelation to every people and age, enabling individuals in every age to look for new truth outside the teachings of the fathers. Most ages did not welcome this new truth, and Austin cited the crucifixion of Jesus and the hostility of the authorities towards Luther and Wesley as examples of how people throughout time had been threatened by new revelation. He then accused the church leaders of misunderstanding new discoveries, such as those in astronomy. He argued: "New truths in science are often condemned, and 25 years ago, it was very common and very popular for preachers to sneer at the evolution theory, but today it is no longer sneered at, for there is arising in all intelligent minds ... the conviction that this was the method of creation, and no scientist of note to-day denies it."[40]

Austin's sermon at the Conference roused some to derision and anger and others to counsel him to refrain from taking an open stand about his beliefs. He felt that he had to be honest with the Conference and that if he continued to be a Methodist minister, "I would not do so in shackles."[41] He left Alma College with an unpaid debt and a commitment to follow his interests in publishing and his belief in spiritualism.[42]

Austin's interest in spiritualism placed him outside the mainstream of Methodist thinking. Spiritualism had gained support in Canada already by the 1850s. Ramsay Cook explains its attraction as follows: "In the post-Darwinian age the only acceptable fashion of combating materialistic science was to provide 'proof positive' of a credible alternative."[43] Spiritualism provided that alternative for people such as Austin. His contact with the belief had presumably been made already in the 1870s at Albert College in Belleville, where he met a brilliant student, Mary Merrill, "with hints of psychic powers."[44] His liberal tendencies were becoming more apparent in the 1890s as he turned his attention to social questions. Like many other spiritualists, Austin saw no contradiction between spiritualism and Christian beliefs.[45] Historian Ann Braude supports the notion of congruity between the two, since spiritualism offered a means to remain religious for those who were disillusioned by Calvinism and evangelicalism in the mid-nineteenth century and those disaffected by Darwinism, biblical criticism, and the rise of science. Because the "individual was the ultimate vehicle of truth," spiritualism allowed women to reject the headship of men in religion, politics, and society.[46] It concurred with the Arminian rejection of the Calvinist notion of predestination, but parted "with all evangelicals by rejecting the existence of hell altogether." The renunciation of sin, hell, and judgment was followed by the rejection of a saviour, allowing the individual to be inherently good and able to witness God in the harmony of nature.[47] Spiritualism, for Austin, provided consolation over the death of his daughter and furnished a world-view that encompassed his liberal theology and social ideas.

The official histories of Alma College deal only briefly with Austin's principalship. Edwards claimed that his adventures outside his immediate duties as principal were for the most part "unfortunate." Austin's publishing ventures were costly, and according to Edwards, financial problems precipitated his resignation or dismissal.[48] Riddell mentions Austin's resignation only briefly, claiming that he moved to California to edit a magazine on spiritualism, "a subject in which he had been deeply interested for some time."[49] He was succeeded as principal by Professor R.I. Warner, who had previously taught modern languages and literature. The college minutes do not discuss Austin further, and it is thus impossible to conclude whether he had a following among students or staff.

Yet a quite interesting figure emerges from sources other than those of the college. Indeed, Austin held distinct views on the education of women. These are summarized in a volume of essays that he edited and published in 1890 entitled *Woman: Her Character, Culture and Calling*.[50] In a chapter called "What Christ Has Done for Woman, and What Woman Has Done for Christ," he argued that Christianity conferred a special honour on woman and that the birth of Christ rendered motherhood forever glorious.[51] Woman was exalted to a position wherein she partook in the "blessings, responsibilities, and duties of Christian life," but in addition, she had the "signal glory of womanhood."[52] The "queen of the home" had been lifted up by Christ's birth, not only to equality, but also to a distinctive calling. Austin wrote that any biblical passages which appeared to endorse the submission of women could be explained – and ignored – by placing them in the context of the culture for which they were written.

Women were exalted not only for the function of motherhood, but also for special qualities that they possessed, including such passive virtues as gentleness, meekness, patience, self-denial, and obedience.[53] These virtues were not indigenous to a man's heart, but they bloomed naturally in a woman's. Austin explained that women used their talents to serve others, evangelize, support missions, and fight the battle for social and moral reform.[54] These patriarchal and family ideologies contained class-specific ideals of womanhood, "where the 'ideals' referred not to descriptions of real women, but to normative constructs against which women of different social classes could be judged."[55]

Austin's exaltation of women as mothers was not inconsistent with his educational mission at Alma. Indeed, he proclaimed the necessity of educating women and argued that they should be educated in a way that would give them a specialty or a useful art by which they could earn a living, rather than being forced to marry to escape poverty. It is clear, however, that he referred to the needs of white, middle-class women in his recommendations for women's employment and education. The "ornamental" education dispensed by many ladies' seminaries needed to be replaced with the teaching of practical arts.[56] Austin urged the employment of women in such professions as outdoor labour, horticulture, telegraphy, the civil service, art, art teaching, house decoration, design, and medicine. By outdoor labour, he meant any light farm work, which would have a more wholesome effect on women's health "than the miserable slave life many women lead in factories, shops and stores where long hours, promiscuous associations and poor pay are the general rule."[57] Austin envisioned that even traditionally female occupations such as domestic service would help women escape from their current slavery. Domestic service was one of the most important sources of paid employment for women in Canada, since approximately 41 per cent of all women were employed in this area. The workers tended to be young girls, often of immigrant origins, who had little or no training. Those in the nineteenth century were often of Irish origin and in the early twentieth century were usually from central European countries.[58] Domestic service would require women who had greater intelligence and culture, thus entitling them to greater recognition in the home as trained, scientific housekeepers or governesses.

The higher remuneration and respect that Austin deemed necessary for domestics was also recommended for another profession in which women were well represented, namely, teaching. The inequality in the salaries of female, as compared to male, teachers was unjust and discriminatory. In addition to these occupations, Austin claimed Christian service as a calling for women. The home, school, and church were spheres in which woman was "all-powerful." Yet there were clear limits to her power if she had to achieve her means by influence. Austin was not calling for women to be ordained. He claimed that their influence on society was crucial since "if society is ever to become thoroughly permeated with the Christian doctrine and spirit ... it must be by the agency of Christian women."[59] Professions that traditionally employed women needed to be revalued in terms of status and remuneration, while those that had previously excluded them should be reconsidered. Although his ideas included some non-traditional professions for women, Austin's vision was not intended to overthrow social roles, either in the church or in society. There are many similarities here between the writings of Catharine Beecher and Austin, and presumably he had been influenced by her. Beecher did not acknowledge racial, class, ethnic, or religious backgrounds other than her own, and in fact, she viewed Catholicism as false. She argued that "women should be able to support themselves and deplored the effects of factory labour on females, [yet] her understanding of working-class life, and of the dynamics of class privilege, remained superficial."[60] Beecher opposed suffrage and argued that women should promote change by using their influence. Ultimately, she accepted the prevailing gender system and attempted to increase women's power within that structure. The disadvantage of her strategy was that it "excluded more women than it included and confined women to a single sphere of action."[61]

Austin rejected the two main arguments commonly used against the higher education of women, which were that women were unable to absorb higher education and that evil resulted from educating them. He believed that women were physically and mentally capable of higher learning. The claim that education produced evil results such as "strong-minded women" and "men in petticoats" was inaccurate because higher Christian education could only foster humility, not conceit. Proper education should provide physical development, intellectual training, and religious culture.[62] In sum, the major goal of education was the development of character, as opposed to "mere skill or accomplishment."[63]

Austin's message was shaped by conservative rhetoric, though tainted with radical connotations, and it is certainly true, as Karlyn Kohrs Campbell points out, "that rhetorical invention is rarely originality of argument, but rather the selection and adaptation of materials to the occasion, the purpose, and the audience."[64] Austin's recognition that not all women were destined to marry and that marriage should never be an alternative to economic necessity or boredom was nevertheless clearly progressive. He also rejected traditional reasons why women should not be educated and advocated their ability to learn and to practise a variety of occupations. His views were particularly innovative on the subject of "practical" education and on vocational goals for women. The suggestion that women could work in non-traditional jobs opened the door for their participation in the public sphere. He sanctioned the public involvement of women by suggesting that society would benefit from their special qualities.

Still, Austin's arguments for equality, higher education, and vocational innovation were couched in a conservative rhetoric that ultimately left the typical woman reigning as queen of the home. Her distinctive qualities prepared her to influence society; "in the Church, in the school, in all moral and social reforms, woman's powerful influence is felt."[65] Without direct power, women would not have a chance to intervene directly in the ways that the home or church were organized. Her power relied still on having a husband or family to influence. The conservative aspect of this kind of rhetoric emerged even more clearly in an article in the same volume by the Reverend Morgan Dix. This piece strongly supported the use of single-sex education to underline God-given differences between the sexes. The harmony between the sexes had to be maintained by education through which "the woman shall be enabled to be to the man all that he needs, while he shall hold her in the honour and devotion which are her due."[66]

The complexity of Austin's own position derived from the fact that his views were neither strictly radical nor conservative; nor did he advocate a completely private or totally public sphere of influence for women. Rather, his position was a combination of all these elements in a form that mirrored the education given at Alma College. Indeed, Austin's views must be seen in the context of nineteenth-century expectations for women. By the latter part of the century, the presence of women in social-reform movements, church life, and professions such as teaching was undeniable. Moreover, advanced education continued to challenge boundaries by offering women options. Support for the ladies' colleges, however, was still derived from parents, individuals, and churches, who believed in the primacy of the domestic sphere. Early reformers and proponents of girls' education worked from inside this model; and borrowed from its language in an attempt to meet their goals.

Recent American studies show how successful this strategy could be. According to Anne Scott, the Troy Female Seminary in Troy, New York, combined "an allegiance to certain well-defined ideas about what was proper for women with subversive attention to women's intellectual development."[67] Emma Willard, the head of the Troy seminary, combined traditional views of woman's role with a commitment to her progress. Willard's success lay in the fact that at Troy "feminist values co-existed with traditional ones but also spread more easily when attached to 'correct' views of women."[68] A similar phenomenon is illustrated by the life of the temperance advocate Frances Willard, who both spoke at Alma and wrote an introduction to Austin's book. A local newspaper enthusiastically described her speech at the school's annual closing lecture in 1891, held at the First Methodist Church in St Thomas. "She speaks simply, as a lady always does and she speaks with charity towards all, as a woman always should."[69] Willard called for "mother-hearted women to be the saviours of the race."[70] Using the rhetoric of "true womanhood" and of "domesticity," she spoke in a language that was immediately accessible to her audience.[71] The language that affirmed Christian values but allowed for the opening up of feminist ideas was carefully constructed.

Austin left Alma College and moved to Rochester to become the pastor of the Plymouth Spiritualist Church and to edit the journal *Reason*.[72] In 1913 he became the pastor of the Central Spiritualist Church in Los Angeles, where he served until his death in 1933. His children shared his interests in spiritualist matters; his daughter Beatrice edited *Reason* for ten years and was a student of metaphysical healing and a follower of Ella Wheeler Wilcox and the New Thought movement.[73] This movement supported the idea of a good human self rooted in a divine spirit and the power of the mind to shape "one's total physical and psychic well-being."[74] Austin's daughter Alma worked with him in Los Angeles and was the only child to survive him. From California, he continued to publish essays and books on spiritualism under the imprint of the Austin Publishing Company.[75] In his essays he answered questions about spiritualism and summarized its future in the following words: "The teachings of Spiritualism ... will go on and on, conquering and to conquest, until the whole world shall know and rejoice in the great truth: 'There is no death' and all God's great family are linked in glad communication and fellowship."[76]

Austin's support of women's rights was facilitated by a liberal theology that allowed him to interpret biblical passages with greater latitude than was customary.[77] Although for him, woman's calling was dependent on a view of her nature as special and different from man's, this special nature was not an impediment to education and vocational training; indeed, Austin helped to establish a curriculum at Alma that allowed girls to pursue diplomas and degrees which could earn them money.

Much mystery surrounds his involvement in spiritualism and his move away from higher education for women. Yet as the involvement of his daughters in spiritualism indicates, there were opportunities open to women for public speaking and leadership in the movement that traditional religions denied them.[78] For Austin, the open doors of education, which he had described in 1890, were consistent with the open doors of spiritualism, to which he devoted the rest of his life. Indeed, spiritualism became a major vehicle for the spread of ideas about woman's rights at the turn of the century in North America. Because it emphasized the role of the individual as the receptor of truth and eliminated the need for mediation by minister,

Bible, or church, it attracted social and political radicals, as well as adherents from among progressive evangelicals such as Charles Beecher and Isabella Beecher Hooker. Three immediate factors that provoked interest in spiritualism were a desire for evidence of the immortality of the soul, attraction to a liberal theology, and an attempt to overcome bereavement through communication with a departed loved one.[79] In Austin's case, one could conceivably add a fourth factor, namely, his impatience with the Methodist denomination and forces within Methodist education that sought to limit women's education to preparation for motherhood and traditional accomplishments, rather than wage labour and the new professions. During the principalship of R.I. Warner, this conservative element resurfaced and threatened to erode the seriousness and academic nature of ladies' college education at Alma College.

ROBERT IRONSIDES WARNER

Robert Ironsides Warner, who succeeded Austin in 1898, is our final example of a strong public exponent of a form of Methodist education for women whose views demand further investigation. Unlike Austin, who openly encouraged the opening of new doors to women, Warner chose to limit the number of doors. To withstand pressures from the provincial educational authorities, the college board needed a clear vision of why Alma was distinct and necessary. A major part of this mandate was its claim to offer Christian education for women. Warner, then professor of modern languages, described his vision for the future of the college to the London Conference in 1891. "Is not our Provincial system of education ample to meet all the necessary demands? I unhesitatingly answer, No! And when I do so please do not misunderstand me. There is no one here who feels a deeper sense of patriotic pride, when viewing our splendid school system, than I feel, yet I most unmistakably declare that this splendid national school system fails to supply all that the country demands in respect to the education of women."[80] Warner believed that only the church could fill the "lack" in public education. According to him, Roman Catholics, those "enterprising propagandists," had seen the need for special girls' education and had successfully started schools in south-western Ontario, which had "captured" more than half of the available Protestant girls. He conceded that the convent model successfully met a need in the education of girls, but he warned the audience of the dangers of allowing education to be controlled by Catholics. "It is claimed by many that the Roman Church has its hand on the Governments at Ottawa and Toronto, and exerts a controlling influence on our politics; that it has its hand on the school system and is destroying the basis of our national education – the public school – through the system of separate schools; and that the convent system is a shrewd effort to get the hand of that church upon the homes of the land by securing the education of the homemakers of the future."[81]

Methodist school supporters were aware of the growth of the Catholic school system. Historian Elizabeth Smyth observes that the motivation for the establishment of Protestant denominational schools for girls was a wish to match what the Roman Catholics had provided for young women's education. The Loretto Sisters had been invited by Bishop Michael Power to open a school for girls in Toronto. Bishop Power wrote to Mother Teresa Ball that he was aware that "for a short time there may exist among the Protestants slight prejudice, but when the parents will find that they can obtain a cheaper and better education for their daughters in the Convent than any other establishment, they will certainly avail themselves of its advantages."[82] In Toronto, the two original convent schools were Loretto Academy (established 1847) and St Joseph Academy (1854). These two schools were "among the first institutions in Toronto to provide successfully for a systematic and sustained secondary education for young women."[83] The fees for Catholic education such as that offered by the Sisters of St Joseph in Toronto doubled between 1866 and 1911; in 1866 the cost was approximately $100 per scholastic year and by 1912 it had increased to $250 per year. The fees did not include extras such as music and art. By comparison, at Alma in 1871 the fees were $45 per quarter for the collegiate course, and extras were added to this base tuition; the college year consisted of four terms of ten weeks each. The pay for a female teacher at the convent school ranged between $220 and $400 per year. It accepted pupils of all denominations, and between 1854 and 1920 the proportion of non-Catholic students varied between 9.3 and 14.2 per cent.[84] Teachers' salaries at Alma in 1904 were from $225 to $450, which included $75–150 for board. A large difference can be seen between the salary of the lady principal, Miss Bollert, who earned $550, and Warner, who earned $1,500. It would seem that the costs and tuition of Catholic and Protestant education were quite similar. Clearly, Warner needed to employ anti-Catholic rhetoric to justify the expense of Alma. The tradition of anti-Catholic thinking had originated with B.F. Austin, whose pamphlet *The Jesuits* argued that the presence of this order was a threat to civil liberty.[85] Warner was quite willing to continue to use this opposition in order to strengthen a somewhat troubled hold on Methodist education at Alma. As other Protestant denominations opened schools, such as Bishop Strachan School (1867), St Clements (1884), Havergal (1894), and Branksome Hall (1903), all in Toronto, the competition for scholars increased.

Warner believed that Methodist schools should be based on Christian benevolence in the same way that convent schools were, that is, the church provided the land and, in the case of the Catholics, the nuns did the work as a labour of love, a system that was as effective as a large endowment. The Protestant colleges had survived by means of joint-stock companies, which often undertook the work at a financial loss. Warner suggested that the church, rather than individuals, should carry this burden. He referred to the Presbyterian Church's sponsorship of Ottawa Ladies' College and Senator McMaster's endowment of Moulton Ladies' College as illustrations of the potential for the church or individual philanthropists in education. For those who were unconvinced about the need to educate girls or the necessity for church-sponsored education for them, the argument was framed in the rhetoric of an eventual takeover by Catholics of both culture and society. Yet the question remains, why did Warner and the board believe that Alma College was needed as a "power for culture, for church, and for Christ in this empire province of Ontario"?[86]

In an appeal to "men of wealth" to donate money to the college, Warner underlined the virtue of giving to the cause of girls' education: "whoever thus gives a thorough Christian education to a young woman is exalting and ennobling a queen of the home and a leader in society, and is thus scattering broadcast the blessings of his benevolence upon the world."[87] The author referred to examples of endowments to ladies' colleges in the United States in order to encourage the Canadian man of wealth to do the same. This investment would "preserve his name in perpetual fragrance in the Christian church, and prove more endurable that any monument of brass or marble."[88]

Despite this appeal, as we have seen in chapter 4, the endowments that in the United States played a major role in establishing women's colleges were not forthcoming to the same extent in Ontario. Alma College was rescued, at least in part, by the Massey estate and by other smaller endowments, as well as by campaigns organized by the alumnae. Principal Warner also undertook a campaign in 1899 and raised $6,000 from a citizen's committee, $2,000 from the Hamilton Conference, and $3,000 from the London Conference.[89] Warner and the management of Alma continued to be aware that the key to their security was tied to the attainment and development of these endowments. By 1902 the management was optimistic not only about the future of the college, but also about continuing university ambitions. "Alma College as the only chartered residential Protestant school in Ontario West of Toronto should with the start it has and with proper encouragement make St. Thomas the educational centre West of Toronto for the higher education of young women. With a Matthew Vassar or a Dr Goucher behind it Alma could easily have an enrolment of 500 Students and be a measureless blessing in the life of our Canadian people."[90] As secretary of the senate and head of the modern languages department, Warner had overseen the affiliation of Alma College with the University of Toronto and Victoria University in 1884.[91] The curriculum at Alma was consciously shaped to adapt to external standards, which in this case were set by the university. This trend towards accommodation was further compounded during Warner's principalship when, in 1909, the government's "approved school" scheme meant that Alma had to meet standards imposed by the Department of Education.

The years of Warner's principalship (1898–1919) were marked by continued financial struggles. Yet he helped Alma survive, setting school policy and goals that he believed would allow it to adapt to the educational needs of girls in the twentieth century. Despite his positive efforts to improve the college's finances, a crisis in 1903 suggests serious problems. A letter from Dr John Potts to the principal refers to the possibility of the college being closed, the purpose of the letter being to swear Warner to silence on the matter. This crisis seems to have been averted because by 1905, as a result of a general fund-raising drive, Alma College actually managed to free itself from debt. It was assisted in this drive by the Massey estate, an individual named Peter Wood, and the city of St Thomas.[92] Warner reassessed the college's programs and tried to eliminate duplication in courses with those available at the universities, and by doing so he clearly restricted Alma's mandate to the secondary school level. The principal felt in 1905 that it did not pay for the college to undertake senior matriculation work: "when young ladies have passed the Junior matriculation and have secured desirable attainments in music and other artistic and practical subjects, they have reached the age when they are very likely to prefer to study at the University, especially since the Universities are providing for their comfort in attractive residences. The plan of Chancellor Burwash in sending his son to College to take a course in Commercial and Fine Art studies after passing matriculation and before entering upon the Arts course, is a plan equally suitable for young ladies."[93] The music department had always been one of the most profitable for the school. It prepared students for the local examinations of the University of Toronto. In order to obtain a college diploma in music, students had to complete all the local examinations and part of the work for a licentiate.[94]

In his assessment of the school's programs, Warner also commented on the department of household science and art. According to the principal, it was in a transition state. The program had for some years covered normal school work, and the Alma diploma was given one year's credit at the Normal School of Domestic Science and Art in Hamilton. The closure of the Hamilton school, together with the opening of the Lillian Massey School at the University of Toronto and the Macdonald Institute in Guelph, made it difficult for Alma to offer the normal course. Mrs Treble urged the school to discontinue normal work in favour of "finishing work," through which the ladies' schools would concentrate on preparing young ladies for the home.[95] Under Warner's leadership, there seems to have been a loss in momentum at Alma in trying to provide university-level courses or even a normal school course in domestic science. In music, he believed that Alma should offer the basics and then send students to the university for the upper-level training. Eliminating the higher levels in domestic science and music would no doubt bring about some savings in teachers' salaries.

This loss of a vision for higher education at Alma was not equalled in the area of religious education, which was, for Principal Warner, a vital aspect of the residential school, in relation to both group teaching and personal piety. Religious education in 1905 involved daily Bible readings, attendance at the college worship services, and systematic Bible study on Sundays. Warner urged students to follow a learning guide called the "Spare Minute Bible Course," which covered three years' study and included examinations three times a year. For successful achievement in this program, students received a credit for the percentage they had earned as a bonus in any other department of study. In addition, the Alma YWCA and the college missionary society encouraged systematic Bible study. Students were urged to become active members of their respective churches and to devote themselves to a life of Christian faith. Principal Warner was apparently committed to keeping the college on track in spiritual matters.

Alma was nevertheless feeling pressure from the multiplication of institutions that duplicated its functions. Warner reported to the board: "The competition that the College has to face is getting increasingly keen. The Macdonald Institute Guelph is attracting great numbers, the Music Schools and systems of music examinations require on our part the greatest possible alertness to hold our ground as a music school, and finally we are face to face with the [provincial] approved school scheme and, in a situation demanding large undertakings whether we try to become an 'approved school' or continue our independence."[96] Competition from other schools was only one pressure the principal had to face. Another source of tension was the occasional complaint from a parent when a student had not been adequately supervised. One parent was concerned that his daughter, Berenice, accompanied by three other girls, had met a young man who was a teacher at the school and the party had proceeded to Port Stanley together without any chaperone. Furthermore, the father had heard that the principal's own son had met one of the girls clandestinely and also invited three girls to his room to show them pictures and music. When discovered by Mrs Warner, the girls were allegedly sent to their rooms, but the son was not reprimanded. This father was also concerned that his daughter had tasted port wine at the college. He wrote that his ambition for his daughter was to have her grow into womanhood as a pure, modest, and high-minded girl and that to accomplish this goal she would need to be surrounded by the very best and most elevating of environments.[97] Warner's attempts to guide the school more clearly in spiritual matters may have been a response to a sense of modernization and secularization at the school.

In 1907 the principal assessed the classes and reported that domestic science was a loss and fine art scarcely profitable since students did not want to specialize in those subjects. The staff felt that it was undesirable to attempt to compete with high schools and collegiate institutes and that "students who attend Alma College come from families whose daughters usually desire an all round education including music and art."[98] Warner decided, with the approval of the board of management, to make university junior matriculation the standard for the general course and to continue with the aim of providing a superior boarding-school for young ladies. He realized in 1908 that it would be useful to have the heads of OLC, Albert, and Alma meet together to discuss questions of mutual interest to the colleges, in order that they act harmoniously together. The board of education of the Methodist Church should host such conferences when necessary.[99] In the face of growing control by the provincial Department of Education, the private colleges felt themselves to be allies. They had passed the stage of relative isolation in which they saw their own interests as opposed to those of other similar schools, particularly when these schools competed for financial resources. Survival now depended on cooperation and consultation, and Principal Warner recognized that some degree of pragmatism was necessary. He corresponded with friends and colleagues in an effort to determine what direction the college should take.

By 1915 the option to remain isolated from directives in the Department of Education was no longer available. As Warner's friend, the

Reverend Chas. R. Flanders, former principal of Stanstead Wesleyan College, observed, "the expansion of academy and collegiate privileges on the one hand and the growing ambition for university training among our young women on the other leads one to wonder if the day of these church schools is not drawing to a close."[100] Flanders felt that if the board decided to continue the college, it should announce a "robust and enthusiastic" policy of expansion as soon as the war finished.

Another concerned individual was the Reverend J.W. Graham, general secretary of the department of education of the Methodist Church, who believed that secondary schools would become more prevalent in both the United States and Canada. He argued that household science should be developed at Alma, in addition to the departments of music, art, elocution, and physical culture that were already in existence, since these subjects were "necessary to a young ladies' finishing school and also were self-sustaining." Furthermore, Graham believed that the collegiate department should prepare students for junior, or even senior, matriculation as well as teachers' certificates, since this work would give dignity and standing to an institution, and he preferred such a program to an "M.L.A. or M.E.L. course which is not recognized as giving the student any standing in the educational world."[101] At a board meeting, Warner and Graham moved that the executive consider the feasibility of a reformed curriculum in which the chief work of the college would be to prepare young women to become homemakers.[102] If the early years at Alma, particularly during Austin's principalship, could be characterized as espousing conservative ideology with liberal implications, under Warner the college had clearly shifted into a more firmly conservative ideology. The sense of optimism and unlimited potential that had characterized the first decades of the school were now replaced by a pragmatic approach. The struggle for identity, tempered by recurrent financial problems, contributed to a somewhat lower degree of aspiration in the school's stated purpose.

THE CHANGING NATURE OF METHODIST EDUCATION FOR WOMEN

The years between Principal Austin's tenure and the Massey Commission report witnessed many changes both in education and in the Methodist Church. Graduates of ladies' colleges were finding their way to various jobs, missionary work, social service, and Sunday school teaching. While the OLC and Alma had worked out an accommodation with the Department of Education, the Wesleyan

Ladies' College had disappeared from existence with barely an obituary. Although the debate on the merits of coeducation continued to reappear at regular intervals, the success of women at ladies' college and university examinations diffused a certain amount of critical comment.

The process of state interference and regulation in private school education was not restricted to Ontario. Ailsa Zainu'ddin observed that for Victoria, Australia, the establishment of a registration board for teachers in 1906 was the culmination of a long process that had begun after the passing of the Elementary Education Act. State control had first exerted been in Australia in 1876, when the private schools had had to submit annual returns to the Ministry of Public Instruction. By 1905 new legislation required registration as a prerequisite for the existence of non-government schools or the remuneration of teachers in them. It resulted in a definition of primary versus secondary education, but the effect was that many women proprietors of small schools were forced to conform to external standards or close. The question of registration was not directed at women who ran public schools, but it did affect assumptions about the level of secondary education for women, because the minister of education assumed that "refinement and the undertaking of matriculation studies by women conflicted."[103] The definition of secondary education that came about as a result of the act tied it closely to the requirements of the university, where "women were a newly admitted minority in a predominantly male world."[104] The registration of teachers inhibited the development of a plurality of schools, forcing schools to conform to the external standards of the matriculation examination. As Zainu'ddin points out, the external standards set by matriculation and by admission to the male university made the small schools adapt to higher education on the basis of standards set by men for men. Like the standards imposed by the Department of Education in Ontario that judged facilities for approved schools, in Victoria, Australia, the act of 1905 required healthy and suitable buildings and increased standards for instruction and registration. The effect of the legislation in Australia was that by 1914 twenty-one schools with secondary registration had closed; two-thirds of these had been administered by women.[105] In Ontario the loss of autonomy in the ladies' colleges was also a gradual process and part of the same ongoing story. Yet ironically, it occurred in part out of a genuine desire to preserve and prolong the life of the colleges and continue their mission to educate young women under Methodist auspices.

The force of personality of men such as Austin, Webster, Burns, Warner, and other supporters of women's education was insufficient to allow Methodists to maintain complete control over their own schools in Ontario. Women debated the issues related to their education in their own publications, alumnae meetings, and student societies, but rarely did their opinions form part of the larger public debate on the subject. The closure of the WLC and the survival of Alma, OLC, and Albert, grew out of compromises made by male boards and male principals eager to maintain what had been built. The increasing control of the state was evident in the certification of schools and teachers. The compliance of ladies' colleges with inspection and government controlled and approved school schemes further consolidated the state's authority over education. But the colleges continued to emphasize their unique mission as a transition between the home and the outside world. The church residential school, as Principal Warner defined it, could give more attention than other schools to the harmonious development of the intellectual, physical, and spiritual powers of the students.[106]

The re-entrance of women into Victoria College and eventually into residence at Annesley Hall meant that there was less need for college-level courses at the ladies' colleges. The upper-level courses were considered expensive to run, since teachers in the higher levels were more specialized and demanded better salaries. At Alma, Warner preferred to have instructors who could teach a number of subjects at the lower levels. Faced with the provision by Victoria of a chaperoned residence and social life for college-age students, the ladies' colleges retreated into providing a thorough secondary education with fine arts options, a Christian environment, and guidance for the development of gracious womanhood.

Although there was general agreement on the Christian and educational aspects of the colleges, it is evident from a survey of the personalities of Webster, Burns, and Austin that a diversity of opinion on the specifics of women's education existed within Methodism. Although the three leaders examined here were not necessarily representative of average Methodist opinion, their views are important to consider. The fact that women's education, originally couched in familial and conservative ideology, became associated with liberal thinkers such as Austin foreshadowed an inevitable reconsideration by the church of the future of this education. The threats to womanliness, which the early advocates of education were careful to avert, would become the target of concerned Methodists, who argued that femininity was undermined by higher education. The question that lingers is, to what extent were the student's own subjectivities shaped in a feminist manner by this education, which by today's standards was conservative? The story of women's higher education, which continues in the next chapters with the opening up of university privileges to women, will further explore this question.

Difficult financial times exerted an additional pressure on the Methodist leadership to define a form of education that fit with their ideals but took into consideration budgetary restraints. Financial problems made a policy of accommodation with the state the choice at Alma, as well as at Albert and Ontario Ladies' College. A combination of factors, by contrast, led to the demise of the Wesleyan Ladies' College. At Alma, Warner charted a careful course between government accommodation and a unique Methodist character for the school. Thomas Webster, who was not burdened with the responsibility of school management, was perhaps freer to theorize on the ideal of an equal education for girls. Austin, whose search for intellectual freedom led him into spiritualism and expulsion from the Methodist Church, shared some of Webster's notions of equality of opportunity and education. The limits to that equality were so clearly understood that these writers felt no need to articulate them.

The opening of Victoria College to women in the 1880s had several effects on the students at the ladies' colleges. For some girls, Victoria offered an educational future. Meanwhile, the increased control of the state over inspection and matriculation standards tied the colleges more closely to the state definitions of appropriate curricula. The eventual success of coeducational higher education and its financial benefits weakened the rationale for expensive separate-sex education in favour of the cheaper option, the secondary school.

7 Women at Victoria: The Coeducational Experience Revived

You, in your co-educational universities, have a real opportunity to solve the problems of this comradeship, and, so to speak, to blaze a trail for the rest of mankind, whereby they may enter on the new inheritance of worthy joy and true happiness.[1]

The beginnings of coeducation at Victoria College were discrete and unobtrusive, much like the lady students themselves.[2] It must be noted that the re-opening of Victoria to women was less a formal decision than a gradual process of allowing in one, then another individual, until the numbers grew into a small group. The process of that entry demonstrates the effects of coeducation on the predominant men's culture, as well as on the culture shared by women undergraduates. As Lynn Gordon observes, for the first generation of college-educated women, the choice between single-sex and coeducational institutions determined the nature of their campus experiences.[3] Many expected that the rules protecting femininity, which were shaped during the early years of women's education in the ladies' colleges, would readily transfer to the university setting. Woman's need for protection and refinement required a family-style residence. Not only was the church changing, but urbanization, industrialization, and the rise of materialism were affecting both the individual and the family. Twentieth-century Victoria students were drawn to the attractions of the city and its entertainments, and they felt that they had a right to sample these. Public perception of this pleasure seeking, combined with fears that women would choose not to marry or who might divorce, led many conservatives to associate higher education with all the modern and evil trends, which would undermine the family as it was idealized in its middle-class Methodist form.[4] The opening up of wage opportunities for women led to a fear of displacement of male workers. Clerical work, which had been a male occupation, was gradually taken over by women, since it offered a temporary refuge for middle-class women on their way to marriage or provided a significant alternative to marriage.[5] The New Woman of the twentieth century expected to make choices concerning her life and work, and the spectre of this independent woman created fear in many hearts.

For a few years, Brookhurst Academy in Cobourg gave women a physical home near to Victoria College and a place from which to challenge their exclusion from its classes. Women at both Brookhurst and Victoria showed that they were capable of handling the male curriculum and that their "special nature," which had been used to justify their education in separate ladies' colleges, did not inhibit their intellectual powers. Coeducation at Victoria College further demonstrated that women could be physically present and not morally compromised on a coeducational campus. From a clear minority of students without any claim to physical or mental space on campus to a numerical majority who were leaders in both academic merit and social contributions, Victoria women made their presence known and claimed their permanent place on the campus.

BROOKHURST ACADEMY AND VICTORIA COLLEGE

Brookhurst, under the administration of Mary Electa Adams, had opened in the early 1870s at the request of some Cobourg citizens who wished to have advanced education available to their daughters. Students at the academy who had passed matriculation examinations were allowed to attend lectures at nearby Victoria College. The exams held at Victoria were open to women, and in 1871 the first woman student passed them.[6]

Victoria College men in the 1870s were accustomed to having women students nearby through the presence of Brookhurst. Socially, the girls were a focus for the men, as *Acta Victoriana* noted, the Victoria student paper, when Adams's school finally closed: "The Sophs are disgusted. Brookhurst is deserted; not even a servant to flirt with."[7] Brookhurst had offered musical evenings that were very popular in Cobourg.[8] The students once gave a lawn party as a fundraising event for the "embellishment of Faraday Hall grounds."[9] In describing one of the end-of-year entertainments, the *Cobourg Sentinel* noted that the success of the institution was due to the well-deserved high reputation enjoyed by the Misses Adams as educators.[10] A literary society at Brookhurst produced a newspaper entitled the *Wax Light*, and excerpts from the paper were read at a public entertainment. Students gave these readings in several modern languages, and the newspaper described the acquisition of a conversational knowledge of modern languages as one of the special objects of the institution. (Mary Electa Adams had already promoted the study of modern languages at the Wesleyan Ladies' College in Hamilton.) At the literary evening, students conducted themselves "with modest grace and self-possession, speaking much for the influence surrounding them."[11] Various comments about students at Brookhurst found their way into the pages of *Acta Victoriana*; for instance, in 1878 the paper observed that the Brookhurst girls were looking well since they had returned from holidays.[12]

Mary Crossen, who in 1877 would be one of the first students to attain an MEL degree jointly from Victoria and Brookhurst, was allowed to attend classes with male students at Victoria.[13] Chancellor Nelles personally conducted her through a "secluded door leading from his private residence into the lecture rooms."[14] Crossen took lectures in moral science and logic from Dr Nelles and in physics and chemistry from Dr Eugene Haanel. She subsequently married the Reverend R.N. Burns, a graduate of Victoria, and she served as president of the Committee of Management of the women's residence at Victoria for many years. As noted earlier, Barbara M. Foote of Elora, Ontario, was the first woman matriculated at Victoria. Five other women enrolled as undergraduates, two of whom took honours matriculation to the end of the second year. In October 1879 the faculty and Senate minutes recorded the acceptance of Adeline Shenick into science and the granting of permission for her to read for a BS without residence. She graduated from Victoria in 1887, having studied while she was on staff at the Ottawa Normal School. Nellie C. Greenwood from Battle High School in Maine was granted matriculation in science in October 1880 and graduated four years later with a BSC degree, the first woman in Ontario and only the second woman in Canada to do so.[15] After graduation, she taught English and mathematics at the Peterborough Collegiate Institute and married Wilbur Andrews, dean of science at Mount Allison and later president of Regina College.

The exact amount of work required for matriculation examinations in the 1870s and 1880s is difficult to establish. Gidney and Millar have indicated that between 1885 and 1891, the fourth form of high school prepared for senior matriculation, which functioned as a second-best alternative to the freshman year at college and attracted only a small number of students. Honours junior matriculation, along with the highest non-professional teacher's examinations, was taken at the end of the third form. On completion of form II, pass matriculation, which led directly into the freshman year, could be taken, as well as the professional matriculation examinations and the second-class teachers' examinations. Gidney and Millar claim that in the 1880s only 5 per cent of all high school enrolments were found in the highest forms, and 18 per cent were enrolled in form II. Students enrolled in form I work generally took two years to finish that work and constituted the vast majority of high school students.[16]

The women students who passed Victoria's examinations while being connected with Brookhurst took the first steps in Mary Adams's plans to make the academy a coordinate college connected with Victoria. "A scheme is set on foot to affiliate this [school] with Victoria etc. etc. – We shall see – If it can be carried out it will be the first in Canada & we should like to have a hand in it."[17] Her dreams were not to be, however. Adams observed in her diary in 1880, "A very decided opposition is manifest among the 'heads of houses' to our plan of a 'University-class' for ladies, of Resident matriculants under protection something like Girton – It would be on a small scale to begin with but in my opinion it might be compassed."[18] The faculty of Victoria had approved the scheme, but Adams was wary of another unidentified group who might withhold their approval and make it difficult to attract students. She believed that the country was ready for such a scheme and any opposition, therefore, would be a grave mistake. She mused that if she had enough money, she would hold on to the Brookhurst building and offer privileges to one or two without expecting the enterprise to pay. Her ideal was to provide a modified university course, with music for those with talent, fine art, or the opportunity to obtain a conversational knowledge of modern languages, surrounded by the refined environment of a well-supervised house. By contrast, Alexander Burns believed that the boarding-house model, which met the needs of young men, could do the same for women students, an idea that for Adams showed how thoroughly he had imbibed American ideas. Hers were so much in conflict with those of Burns that she confided to her diary that she would "never like to live near him."[19] Presumably Adams was no longer able to finance Brookhurst, and with disappointment, she therefore closed the school in 1880. "It costs me no little feeling – I have a growing conviction that the requisite patronage for university purposes will soon be available."[20] The closure of Brookhurst left female students with the option of attending one of the ladies' colleges or the collegiate institutes, but with no guaranteed university privileges.

Victoria College had offered matriculation examinations throughout the province, and although women were allowed to take them, they were not initially permitted to attend classes until Mary Crossen received permission to do so. Matriculation exams were held first at Cobourg and then at Brantford, Ottawa, and other centres, until a movement for provincial matriculation gained acceptance.[21] The administration of matriculation examinations by the Department of Education was one more area, in addition to inspection and teachers' certification, that increased the centralized powers of the department and weakened those of individual schools.[22] The Victoria College calendar for 1893–94 states that students had to pass the junior or senior matriculation examinations to gain admission.[23] A student transferring from an undergraduate course in any of the universities in "Her Majesty's dominions" would be admitted with full credit after application to the Senate. Students transferring into the university's third- or fourth-year levels, as some ladies' college graduates did, had to pass examination subjects prescribed by the Senate.[24] Candidates who took these exams had to present certificates of age and good conduct and pay a five dollar fee. Those with a first-class teacher's certificate were accepted at any senior matriculation exam and those with a second-class certificate were allowed at any junior matriculation exam. Women students desiring admission to Victoria College prepared for examinations by following a course of study in a provincial secondary school up to at least form II. They could study at a ladies' college and on the basis of an MEL or MLA degree, ask for admission to the third or fourth year, taking exams in any areas in which they were "conditioned." Students with teachers' certificates, such as the second-class, could apply to take the junior matriculation exam. These options opened the door to university for many women who had not perhaps planned and prepared for such a step, but could use their previous education, teacher's credentials, or ladies' college degrees as a base from which to pass the matriculation examinations.

EARLY WOMEN STUDENTS AT VICTORIA

The closure of Brookhurst did not in fact stop the trend towards allowing women to study at Victoria College. Indeed, according to a note made by Margaret Addison, in the fourteen years that elapsed between the first enrolment of women and the year 1892, sixty-six women entered arts at Victoria. The number of graduates in the first decade was very small, however, with only fourteen obtaining the BA or BSC degree.[25] A gradual increase in the proportions of those earning degrees occurred in the latter part of the 1880s and the early 1890s.

One of the notable graduates from the 1880s was the daughter of suffragist Emily Stowe. Augusta Stowe received her MD degree in 1883. At her convocation, Dr Ogden, dean of the School of Medicine, commented that Stowe had won her degree honourably and that during all the years of her studies, her presence had not created any trouble.[26] It is difficult to imagine what kind of trouble such reserved and highly motivated students were expected to make. Among the students who came with advanced standing from the ladies' colleges was Nettie Burkholder of the WLC, who was admitted as a specialist to the third-year lectures, after she had passed an exam in Latin and mathematics.[27]

What was the nature of the college world these early undergraduates faced? There were several student societies already in existence that were composed exclusively of males. Among these were the Literary Association, the Jackson Society, the Science Association, and the Philosophical Society. Intercollegiate sport included football contests between schools such as the Toronto Medical College, Knox College, University College, and Trinity Medical School.[28] The early female students noticed their exclusion from these activities. As Nellie Greenwood reflected, "I know now that I was never in a position to fully savour the spirit of Victoria. I belonged to no undergraduate societies, I knew nothing of college sports. It never occurred to me to present myself at a class meeting. I never even looked through a window at a Bob party but nevertheless Victoria is my college."[29]

The early women students at Victoria were an exceptional group, well aware that their presence at college was a privilege. Greenwood described her "lonesome feeling," which she lost in 1886 when the number of female undergrads reached seven, and "it was felt that women had a definite and permanent place in the undergraduate life of Victoria."[30] The realization of the women's permanent presence on the campus led to their demand for a physical space that would belong to them. As *Acta Victoriana* recorded in February 1888, the nine ladies who attended college asked the faculty to find them a room where they could go during their spare hours. The male columnist recorded this request with considerable sarcasm: "Of course it is necessary that our lady friends should have a department where they can gossip or make taffy, when not occupied with the arduous duties of college life, and so a room was carpeted, papered, etc., for these bashful mortals, who could not bear the thought of waiting in Alumni Hall, when no lectures were being given."[31] The writer recalled an incident the previous year, when male students had banded together to form a Science Society and had requested a room, a petition that was passed over in silent contempt. He felt that giving in to the ladies' request and ignoring the earlier one was not likely to kindle in the minds of Victoria's men students "those feelings of profound respect and love for the members of the Senate which their position demands."[32] The paper noted the same year that two female students attended their class meetings and in doing so "surpassed all precedents."[33]

There are few sources that give insight into the early women students' perceptions of their life at Victoria or their views on the significance of their attainments, but there is some evidence that they thought themselves quite ordinary. Nellie Greenwood at least noted that not one of the early women students thought she was doing anything unusual, partly because many of them had relatives among the students or teachers of Victoria.[34] This view contrasts with that of the early women students in the United States, who apparently thought themselves very special. For the first generation of American college students, the higher education experience had meant a great deal. They, in turn, "served as mentors to the young women who succeeded them on the college campuses of the Progressive era."[35]

Despite the sarcasm of its comments in 1888, the student paper at Victoria generally appeared to welcome the practice of coeducation. In an 1881 article discussing the idea, one author noted that the woman in search of higher education really *had* to attend the university "if she is to meet her male friends on equal terms."[36] The ladies' colleges, the author contended, were engaged in teaching the same material covered by the university, but their offerings nevertheless remained a very "defective education with a thin layer of accomplishments."[37] He believed that coeducation would not be injurious to young men; in fact, the presence of women in the classroom would improve their morals and manners. The sight of women agitating in political demonstrations created some fear that coeducation had brought about equalization too rapidly, but he still believed that it was the only answer to the demand for the higher education of women.[38] In 1883 another writer in *Acta Victoriana* claimed that coeducation had been a success, and he hoped that the number of lady students would increase.[39]

The arguments in favour of higher education for women were generally based on the assumption that a woman needed training for her profession, which was generally understood to be as a companion to her husband and a teacher in the home. For this reason, woman needed time not only to learn culinary arts and domestic duties, but also to "take her place beside her brothers in the halls of learning, to drink at the same fountain of intellectual joy, and to be inspired by the same lofty enthusiasm."[40] It would be a proud day for the land when young ladies would flock to the universities as earnest students because it would herald "advancement in every sphere of life."[41] Such advancement did not mean a structural change in class, gender, or power relations, but merely an improvement of women's abilities within their sphere.

In the 1890s women remained a small minority within the larger community of male scholars; by 1892, when the move was made to Toronto, there were still only 14 in a student body comprising 226 men.[42] This small group of women had a growing consciousness of the necessity to form associations to meet their social needs. In December 1889 some of them had organized the Ladies' (later Women's) Literary Society, and in February 1891 a Ladies' Missionary Society was founded at Victoria. These organizations were followed by the Ladies' Glee Club in 1892. At the same time, student clubs that had been exclusively male began to allow women in their ranks. The Modern Language Club had a mixed membership by 1893, and the Student Voluntary Missionary Society (SVMS), an interdenominational society affiliated with the YMCA, also admitted women at some point, although when is not clear.[43] Missions provided a common ground for the meeting of the sexes, particularly at conferences such as the Intercollegiate Missionary Alliance, where a woman speaker addressed women's role in missions.[44] The women's literary society provided Sunday afternoon visitors at the Fred Victor Mission, a men's hostel in Toronto. By 1895 the volunteer work was absorbed by the new YWCA.[45] In January 1892 Miss Hazel Burwash was appointed vice-president of the missionary society and Clara Horning the corresponding secretary. The SVMS elected Miss Orpha McCullough as its vice-president in 1893. Such elections reflected practice in the American student mission organizations[46] and demonstrated the acceptance of women in the larger university community, as did the selection of Miss Gertrude Kenny as valedictorian for the year 1893.

The appointment of Mary Sutherland as literary editor of *Acta Victoriana* in November 1894 represented further accommodation of women in the life of the university.[47] Already in 1891 the *Acta* had noted that the ladies' activities had not received enough coverage in the paper. By 1895 the Women's Literary Society felt able to send a "modest and unassuming communication" to the *Acta* requesting that sophomores refrain from "bobbing" the freshettes. The WLS had discussed the previous year's "bob," which had featured some caricatures of the women students, and this discussion had resulted in the following resolution: "Whereas the women do not wish to help in doing anything unkind or inconsiderate towards each other, or anything that might cause the system of co-education to be in the slightest degree condemned; be it resolved that the women of Victoria College refrain from taking any part in the Bob, and that they request the men to show that consideration and chivalrous spirit towards the new woman which was accorded to the old."[48] The male students replied through the *Acta* that if women would not subject themselves to this ridicule, then men should not have to endure it in the presence of female classmates and might reasonably request that women not be admitted.[49] At a meeting of the WLS in 1897, members discussed the question of the senior dinner and whether the ladies would prefer to sit at a table with the guests, at a separate table by themselves, at a separate table with an equal number of gentlemen, or at the ends of the tables of their respective years.[50] Questions of propriety and preference were worked out by the society as the women students carved their place in the male traditions of Victoria.

Despite women's increasing involvement, officially the purpose of education at Victoria continued to be discussed in this period, though it was often described in a way that made it clear the focus was chiefly men who were being educated. In an address to convocation in 1896, Burwash described the fundamental idea of the college as the development of the individual man. The best influence on college students, he noted, was the presence of professors, whose model reflected the highest type of manhood.[51] Ada Pascoe, writing to Victoria from Alma College, still felt it necessary to argue that the higher education of women was "not an influence that would make women pedants, prudes, prigs, or blue-stockings, shrews, amazons, or hard, cold, semi-masculine monstrosities."[52]

The fact that Pascoe felt it necessary to defend women students against such undesirable stereotypes suggests that their education continued to evoke anxiety as well as hostility. The blurring of the normative sexual differences was clearly a charge that haunted women students. Overdevelopment of the intellect could only be accompanied by a loss of femininity. It is unclear whether Pascoe was a student or a teacher at the time she wrote her letter, which was published in the *Acta*, but she was presumably the daughter of the Reverend W.S. Pascoe, who served on the Alma College board from 1886 to 1890. Her argument for higher education was based on the development of broad-mindedness, which would help a woman to expand the life of her family. In another article in the *Acta*, the question of whether marriage rates were lower among college women was debated, with a conclusion that contradicted Pascoe's family orientation. Lady graduates could do much better as teachers and instructors or by engaging in literary work, this article averred, than "by burying in the kitchen or pantry, the education and culture they have acquired at the expense of so much time and money."[53] The anonymous author concluded that there were many examples available of what the college woman could do when she was not burdened with a partner. The weakest argument ever given against college education for women, therefore, was that it unfit or disinclined them for married life. This argument struck at the heart of the middle-class ideal that for many supporters justified women's education.

How did the college graduates of these years use their education? A high level of achievement meant that women increasingly took honours and medals for academic merit. Clara Horning won a gold medal in modern languages, and Miss A.E. Le Rossignol took the Nelles scholarship in 1895.[54] Another outstanding scholar was Mary E. Highet, who received a BA from Victoria in 1891 and an MA the following year. She completed her PHD on a scholarship at Cornell in 1895 and taught modern languages at the State Normal School in New Paltz, New York. Dr Highet then studied for a year in Berlin and in 1902 was appointed professor of modern languages at Elmira College, a position she held until she retired in 1930. After her retirement, she returned to Canada and her home town of Barrie, where, as a member of the United Church she was active in the Women's Missionary Society.[55] Emma S. Baker, of the class of 1899, had received her preparatory education at the Newmarket High School, attended Albert College for two years, and then taught for a short time at a Presbyterian ladies' college in Toronto before going abroad to study for a year at the Sorbonne and for a further year at Newnham College, Cambridge. She came to Victoria to do the honour philosophy course. By 1902 Baker was carring out experiments and doing postgraduate work in pyschology and had earned a PHD from the University of Toronto. Despite this achievement, very little information is available locally about Baker. In 1902 she left Ontario to become the lady principal of Mount Allison; eleven years later she was no longer in Canada, having accepted an appointment as professor of pyschology, ethics, and economics at the Women's College of Maryland.[56]

Many Victoria women, in fact, went into teaching, although most of those who remained in Canada taught at the secondary level.

Nellie Greenwood taught at Peterborough Collegiate Institute, M. Donley at Dundas High School, H.E. Potts at Port Hope High School, E.O. Woods at Perth Collegiate, May Sutherland at Fergus High School, and H.S. Albarus at Morrisburg; Clara Horning became head of moderns at the OLC. Of these seven, at least two eventually married and left teaching, but the records are not complete. The School of Pedagogy in Toronto attracted a fair number of Victoria graduates who then moved to positions in the ladies' colleges, among them E. Moore and Mary C. Rowell at Alma, as well as in the collegiate institutes and high schools.

THE VICTORIA WOMEN'S ASSOCIATION

The presence of women undergraduates at Victoria required a women's organizational structure that would promote their needs. The relationship of such an organization would, of necessity, fall outside management structures such as the Senate that oversaw Victoria College. The formation of a new structure, its relationship to the powers that controlled Victoria, and the methods used by the women to attain their ends are the basis for the following discussion of the Barbara Heck Association (1897–1901), later renamed the Victoria Women's Residence and Educational Association (1901–12) and finally the Victoria Women's Association (1912–present).

The story of the Barbara Heck Association is an exciting example of a movement by women for women's education, with the dominant concern being for the social well-being of women students and their residence life. The association was organized by a group of Methodist women in Toronto, including Margaret Burwash, Margaret Hopkins (Mrs George) Cox, Lillian Massey Treble, and Mrs Chester D. Massey. These women formed a powerful group because they had either close connections to those in power at Victoria College or a certain amount of personal wealth to invest in the cause of women's education. The determination of this group of women and the effectiveness of their organization has left a lasting imprint on the education of women at Victoria. Margaret Burwash believed that their education should be largely in the hands of women; as she wrote to Margaret Addison in 1895: "I believe in men and women standing together in intellectual work, but there is a side of our nature which is exclusively feminine, which cannot be developed or moulded by men. It is a great misfortune for any young woman to be dwarfed or warped in this 'quality' ... In time I hope to see women instructors in university work. But if we could now have a cultured woman of strong personality, who had the gift or grace of keeping in touch with young people, at the head of college home life it would be a great step in advance."[57]

A call to all Methodist women was communicated through the *Christian Guardian* in March 1897 to celebrate Queen Victoria's diamond jubilee and to honour the founder of Canadian Methodism, Barbara Heck, by erecting a residence for the women students at Victoria. For the students who were "absent from home and its protecting influence," its author argued, "there must not be neglected the religious safeguards, the domestic influences and the social nature, and in college relationships these invaluable considerations can be obtained only by a college residence under proper direction and control."[58]

Women students at Victoria were obliged to rent rooms in boarding-houses, and as a result they lost the main benefit of life at the university. According to Margaret Burwash, who wrote again on the subject in April 1897, college life had a greater influence on a student than her studies. Students in boarding-houses, she commented, experienced numerous problems. "Domestic habits are wholly broken up. It cannot be expected that the student boarder will share the family life, in some cases she lodges in one house and boards in another: in others the lodging is changed as often as three times in one year. Thus it is seen that the life our women students are obliged to live is totally subversive of one fundamental principle of womanly character."[59] The contact with refinement in a residence would give students "knowledge of social usages and customs and the grace and charm which come from refined manners ... differentiating the cultured man or woman from the boor."[60] Male students also boarded, but the effects were not perceived to be threatening to their manhood in the way that the womanhood of female students was jeopardized. Since morals and manners were so closely tied to the proper development of a woman's nature, her behaviour required constant supervision and limitation. Rowdiness and unsupervised behaviour would not effect permanent damage on a man since his future required him to live in the world. Masculinity could withstand the rigours of a rougher life. Femininity, alas, could not. A list of boarding-houses assembled for the year 1896–97 indicates that rooms were available in the area surrounding the university. Some landladies specified males only or females only, and some offered only rooms, while others provided room and board. Mrs Thompson on Cumberland Street, for example, offered room and board for $3.50, whereas Miss Wilcox on Alexander Street provided rooms to ladies for $2.75–3.00 per week. The list contained sixty-one addresses in all.[61]

The need for a women's residence was presented by alumnae to the Montreal Conference in the spring of 1897. Students who lived in boarding-houses were not only freed from the restraints of home life but were also strangers to the church. These students without a common abode "ran the great risk of developing into blue-stockings or Bohemians, both equally objectionable types of young womanhood."[62] These negative stereotypes were very familiar to women students, and their behaviour was consciously shaped to avoid just such charges. Marjorie Theobald has traced the history of the term "bluestocking" to the eighteenth century, when it referred to an informal sisterhood of intellectual women. Only in the nineteenth century was the term employed to mock educated women. The implication was that the acquisition of knowledge by educated women was inappropriate. The bluestocking appropriated masculine knowledge in order to gain self-esteem and the option to be economically self-sufficient. This acquisition took place in a manner "which went beyond the proper bounds of women's sphere and offended the canons of patriarchal society."[63] The proper use of women's intellect was the acquisition of accomplishments that could be used "discretely in the private sphere."[64]

Bessie Scott was a student at University College in Toronto between 1888 and 1891. In an article written early in the 1900s, she reflected on her college experience that only fifty years before, a woman who desired an education higher than a finishing school was seen as "unnatural, phenomenal and was likely to be misunderstood by her own sex and avoided by the opposite one as that obnoxious, spectacled monstrosity, a 'blue-stocking.'" Scott felt that honour was due "to those brave women who were willing to bear that sobriquet and to have a slur cast upon their very womanhood."[65] She saw herself and her colleagues as humble followers in the footsteps of those early pioneers who were subject to a lesser degree to adverse criticism. Scott still felt the need to defend herself against the charge that college life unfit a woman for home life and made her unwilling to marry. She believed that intellectual studies could be mixed with preparation for domestic life, and women could choose to combine the study of domestic science with political science if they desired. But to prepare women only for domestic life could lead to disappointment. Life, she wrote, "is not a failure even if the true knight does not come to his fair lady … What more pitiable than a poor girl whose one hope of earthly salvation is this knight."[66] Questions of the suitability of college life and its effect on women students were clearly tied to the future role of the college graduate. Neither female nor male supporters of women's education intended a radical change to the status quo of gender relations. The need for manners and morals was just as pressing as it had been at the ladies' colleges, but now the moral guardians of women students had the increased threat of city life, as well as somewhat rebellious students, to deal with.

Part of the dialogue on the necessity of a residence for women was strengthened by the reports of students such as Emma Baker who had studied abroad and heaped praises on the residences for women at the English universities, or alumnae such as Mary Highet who was familiar with the American scene.[67] Highet, in an article in the *Christian Guardian*, referred to the example of residences at Bryn Mawr, Wellesley, and Vassar, where girls could enjoy athletics and social, as well as spiritual, activities. She reminded readers, however, that "the residence is not a boarding school where almost every act of the student is regulated by certain fixed laws ... nor is it a mere boarding-house." The ideal residence would be a "true home, where each is interested in the other's welfare and where the selfishness which college life so often engenders is replaced by self-sacrificing consideration for the rights and feelings of all."[68] The ideal residence for college women would thus recreate the atmosphere of a home away from home.

Other women alumnae who were interested in promoting a residence for Victoria women were featured at public events, such as a meeting in 1897 of the newly formed Barbara Heck Association at the Dominion Methodist Church in Toronto. On the platform in their academic robes on this occasion were Miss Kenney, BA, Miss Cluff, BA, Miss Schenick, BA, and Miss Bessie Scott.[69] Scott and Cluff spoke from experience about "the trials, temptations, and hardships that were the lot of a young girl during the four most important years of her life."[70] Their experience, the *Evening Journal*'s reporter on the event implied, was a strong argument for the residential idea. Loneliness, homesickness, and unfriendly landladies could make a student feel cut off from her family. Some boarding-houses were so cold that residents had to wear overshoes and mittens to stay warm enough to be able to study. The lack of imposed structure could presumably cause a student to drift academically, or even spiritually. University College's Bessie Scott looked "longingly at our sisters at Cornell ... with their beautiful home on University Campus and wish some rich friend of Varsity would die and leave (or leave without dying) a bequest to enable us to make at least a beginning of such a thing in Toronto."[71]

Alumnae of Victoria were not the only people interested in the campaign for a women's residence at the college, for the idea was also attractive to parents of prospective students. One mother responded to solicitation by the Barbara Heck Association by stating that the object of the fund appealed very deeply to her heart and it caused her great sorrow that she could not contribute more generously. She hoped that the residence would be complete by the time her own daughter attended college and that her daughter would develop a "strong type of womanhood."[72] This type of womanhood did not mean a woman who rejected all traditional expectations, such as marriage and children, but one who would fulfil those roles with a clearer sense of her spiritual and intellectual depth.

The organization was substantially aided by a $50,000 donation from Hart Massey, which allowed its organizers to begin the search for land on which to build a residence. This search provoked one angry letter to the editor of *Acta Victoriana* concerning the acquisition of 400 feet frontage, of which 200 feet would be used for the ladies' residence and 200 remain for the athletic ground. The writer angrily suggested that 170 feet would be sufficient for the ladies' residence. Men were losing ground in more ways than one; "if the male students are to have this scant courtesy shown them, how long will it be before Victoria will be turned into a ladies' seminary and a theological institute?" this writer demanded.[73] There were those who felt a distinct physical and moral threat from the presence of women students.

The Barbara Heck Association organized more than one meeting with speakers to promote the cause of a women's residence. An April 1897 meeting was addressed by Emma Baker, recently returned from Cambridge, and Margaret Addison, another graduate. According to Baker, life in residence was "society in miniature – one acquired a *savoir faire* from the continual contact with people in the different societies."[74] The contact allowed for the organization of sports and clubs such as the debating club, which at Cambridge, for example, met during the hour after dinner.

The women students in 1896 who might have been interested in the Heck Association's goals included 37 in regular degree programs and a further 9 who were listed as specialists in arts, presumably special students not pursuing a degree. Out of a total of 253 students, 46, or 16 per cent, were women.[75] By December 1897 the association could report the formation of a central executive committee, which was supplemented by local committees in the various towns and cities of Ontario. The organization appealed to its members and friends for $25,000 to pay for the site and furnishings of the residence, a sum that would supplement the money provided by the Massey gift. The committee continued fund-raising, undaunted by the fact that by the end of 1897 only $2,000 had been raised.[76]

The following April, women students took a new initiative. A group of women graduates met at Victoria to form an alumnae society. Those present at this time included Adeline Shenick, Margaret Addison, Nettie Burkholder, L.E. Horning, May Sutherland, and Misses Howson and Livingstone. The meeting elected the following officers: honorary president, Margaret Burwash; president, Margaret Addison; vice-president, Nettie Burkholder; secretary-treasurer, Louise Nelles; and corresponding secretary, Miss Kerr. The close connections between this group and other women's social groups associated with Victoria were evident by the fact that at the end of this particular meeting the members joined the committee of the Barbara Heck Association and the wives of faculty for tea.[77] Women at Victoria realized that they needed to work together to fulfil their purpose, and these early social gatherings provided the common ground for the articulation of their shared goals.

Such organization of women's presence on campus was not unobserved by male students. When the class of 1898 graduated, one student commented that "when '98 came to College the men students trembled; it almost looked as if they were going to be shoved to the wall. Even the faculty looked grave and talked of limiting the number of women students. The building, they said, was not planned with a view to being used as a ladies' college."[78] The men increasingly felt the intellectual competition as women students such as E.G. Swanzey of that year's class took prizes. In 1901, for example, H.E. Wigg won the governor-general's silver medal, and Clara Woodsworth was awarded the Jones silver medal and Mercy Powell the McLaren gold medal.[79]

College life in this period was increasingly marked by an emphasis on moral and social reform, and the YWCA was one society that exposed college women to possible roles in this work. One student described the YWCA meetings in 1908, in which the girls were talking about "city missions and it made your heart burn within you to hear their call for volunteers."[80] But, wrote Kathleen Cowan, she did not want to give up Sunday evenings nor did she claim to be a singer. Yet for many, moral fervour seemed a particularly feminine trait. College women, on account of their superior advantages, were to be leaders in the moral reforms that would lead to the uplifting of the race. The interest in reform also brought representatives from the Toronto Methodist Deaconess Home to address students at Victoria.

Although not all students were equally interested in the reforms, it was hoped that by cultivating a general interest, students attending YWCA meetings could "discover the particular work to which we are called."[81] The YWCA organized Bible study in its weekly meetings, and the fourth meeting of the month, devoted to missionary work, was held in Jackson Hall in union with the missionary society of the college.[82] In October 1899 Alice Chown, herself a alumnae of both the Wesleyan Ladies' College and Queen's University, wrote an article in *Acta Victoriana* explaining the social settlement movement and calling for a movement in Canada to establish people's institutes where all social classes could gain physical and mental culture.[83]

Student voluntary associations were increasingly preoccupied with social questions, a trend that reflected the direction of the Methodist Church in general. In the 1890s churchmen were becoming conscious that Canadian society was increasingly pluralistic and secular. External forces were affecting the life of the church and personal piety. Industrialization gave more people a regular wage to spend on recreation and consumer goods at stores such as Eaton's. Church membership, which had increased by 36,399 members between 1888 and 1892, grew by only 27,584 between 1892 and 1896 and by 19,584 between 1896 and 1900. This slow-down in growth was accompanied by a general sense that a change in the church was required; there was less agreement on its specific form. Some believed that the church needed to preach "traditional evangelical theology," while others felt that it should become more liberal and more active in society.[84]

A liberal emphasis on the ethics of Jesus and concern for fellow human beings was evident on university campuses in the United States as well as in Canada during this period. As George Marsden explains, "Christians still inspired by millenial dreams of moral and material progress going hand in hand, hoped to temper social strife with an ethic of love."[85] Thus during the rise of the social sciences as an academic discipline, many Christians assumed that science would be an ally of faith. This ethic of care, based on the application of the social gospel, contained a call for women that was not inconsistent with the previous generation's social-reform direction, which had been based on woman's moral sense. The depth to which women responded to this call can be seen in their involvement in the Student Volunteer Moment, later the Student Christian Movement, and other domestic, as well as international, missions.[86]

In the fall of 1899 the class entering Victoria College contained eleven women. Any available information concerning the lives of these students and their influence on college life must be gleaned from such sources as the graduates' column in *Acta Victoriana*. The graduating class of 1900, for example, included the future dean of women at the University of British Columbia, M. Louise Bollert, who served as assistant literary editor of *Acta* during 1898–99 and president of the Women's Literary Society in 1899–1900. Mabel Chown, future social activist and writer, acted as literary editor of *Acta* during her final year and was also a member of the Women's Literary Society. The graduates' column lauded Chown's "womanly nature, uniting the spirit of the new woman, claiming for her sex greater enlightenment and usefulness, with the charm and dignity of the older type," which would undoubtedly find its place in the world.[87] The column also noted that Etta May Graham had served as president of Victoria's YWCA and was holder of the senior stick, a recognition of excellence in student achievement traditionally held only by the male students, but which had now become part of the women's tradition as well.

In 1901 the name of the Barbara Heck Association was changed to the Victoria Women's Residence and Educational Association. The turning-point in the fund-raising program came that year when Margaret Hopkins Cox proposed to give $20,000 to the educational fund, provided that one half of it be used to purchase a block of land north of Czar (now Charles) Street.[88] The plans of the architect, George M. Miller, were adopted the same year. By April 1902 the cornerstone of the women's residence was laid, and the Board of Regents of Victoria resolved that a group of ladies be organized to act as a Committee of Management for the residence.[89] Finally, in October 1903, Annesley Hall opened its doors to students. The constitution of the Committee of Management gave its members charge of the regulations for students, the direction of finances, and the appointment of staff. The standing committees appointed were four and overlooked the "house," finance, the gymnasium, and the infirmary.

Early in 1900 the Heck Association had also aspired to do something for the physical culture and social life of women students. Concern for the womanliness, as well as for the health, of students was no doubt a motivating factor. Mrs Emma Scott-Raff was engaged as an instructor in physical culture for one year, to continue the work that had been done the previous year by a Mrs Cutter from the Conservatory of Music. The work was extended in 1901 to included voice culture and expression. The following year Dr Leila Davis was appointed medical adviser for students in physical culture. By 1903 the work of both Scott-Raff and Davis was placed under the control of the Committee of Management. Miss Helen Scott of Ottawa was nominated matron of the residence, and in October 1903 Margaret Addison became dean of residence.

The years between 1880 and 1910 thus were vital to the presence and acceptance of women students on campus. The re-entry of women to Victoria in the mid-1880s, after their expulsion in 1842, was a victory for supporters of equal education for women. Students arrived from secondary schools, collegiate institutes, ladies' colleges, teaching jobs, or normal school programs. Once they had successfully achieved matriculation, they were allowed to begin university studies. Those who had deficiencies in certain areas had the opportunity to do extra work and take examinations. The standardization of the entrance process helped to eliminate any sense of special privileges to women students and gave their presence a seriousness. Their success at the university level proved that women were mentally and physically able to handle the challenge of university studies.

About the women students' private lives in these early years at Victoria we have little information. Some lived at home or with relatives while attending Victoria and others in boarding-houses. As we have seen, Nellie Greenwood completed her baccalaureate as an external student, managing to study for exams in addition to a full-time career as a teacher. The excessive care taken by the chancellor to preserve the modesty of the first woman student, Mary Crossen, became unnecessary as male and female students proved that propriety could be maintained in a coeducational setting. Yet women students were very conscious that their behaviour at the university was constantly monitored by the public and especially by male students. Although women reassured their colleagues that nothing had changed, men obviously felt that things had. Many women won awards and honours at the university, and some chose not to marry after they finished. The model of a stronger womanhood, which women students felt could combine scholastic goals with domestic ideals, did not appeal to some males. Although at Victoria, relations between the sexes seemed cordial, a glance at student publications at the University of Toronto reveals demeaning cartoons and humour. The woman student is pictured as a vamp who uses her college days to hunt for a marriage victim. The bluestocking sterotype had expanded to include the brain women, jazz-mad, or the old-fashioned type to whom college is not "an educational centre. It is a marriage market." The author of one poem concludes: "I hate women. They endanger my career."[90] This caricature of the traditional goal of women's lives cast woman as predator and ultimately as a threat to a man's well-being.

Nevertheless, women students discovered a realm of pure delight in their friendships, academic achievements, and social life at university. They mingled with male students in classes and on campus and found that men "were not their intellectual superiors."[91] University women believed that they had a right to knowledge and assumed that if they behaved, their presence on campus would be tolerated and perhaps even appreciated.

They excelled in a variety of courses at Victoria. Jo La Pierre has studied the curricula of various Canadian universities during this period and observes that women students took advantage of the increased number of modern language and English language courses. The introduction in the late nineteenth century of the honours BA as a minimum standard for admission to a specialist teacher's certificate meant that many women flocked to this program. After Victoria College moved to Toronto in 1892, it continued to offer women an arts program, but now in conjuction with the University of Toronto.[92]

The early women students found companionship despite their small numbers. They began to organize social clubs to meet their needs in the 1890s. The gradual acceptance of their presence did not, however, end the debates about the purpose of women's education or the effects of coeducation. The presence of women students at Universities continued to be debated into the twentieth century. A fear of feminization was not only confined to university campuses. In the United States, the research of G. Stanley Hall from 1873 on focused renewed attention on the nature of masculinity. Hall's interpretation of the "plasticity of sex" during adolescence implied that boys could become feminized. Women teachers were a threat to boys since they were too docile, on the one hand, to be a model for masculinity, and on the other hand, they were susceptible to losing their femininity by competing with men on equal terms. The "women peril" was the expression of fears of the consequences of women's advance towards the vote and towards previously male professions.[93] Susan Gelman describes how a teacher shortage in the first two decades of the twentieth century in Ontario caused concern among educators that boards had been forced to hire increasing numbers of women teachers. They argued that if any secondary school was staffed by more than one-third women teachers, the quality of education received by the older boys would be compromised.[94]

The first generation of women graduates from Victoria moved into a variety of teaching, social-service, and family careers. Once there was a significant group of alumnae, they worked towards the improvement of conditions on campus for women students, particularly in relation to housing. The Barbara Heck Association provided such a focus for both alumnae and other interested Methodists. Because some of the latter were able to donate part of their wealth towards the cause of Methodist women's education, the Heck Association and later the Victoria Women's Association was a group to be reckoned with. Although their work gave financial and moral support to women's education, these women did not challenge male control of education or question the middle-class norms that excluded many.

The association placed a great deal of emphasis on the presence of a strong woman with academic credentials and leadership experience to administer Annesley Hall. Margaret Addison, a Methodist clergyman's daughter and a graduate of Victoria, was such a candidate. She was intensely interested in international women's higher education and would attempt to bring her insights, gathered from travels and research, to the development of women's academic culture at Victoria. Addison would lead Victoria women for over three decades, a period to which the following chapter is devoted.

8 Margaret Addison and Annesley Hall

Our household is running pleasantly. I think there is a trifle less gaiety than in October, but late hours and high excitement are telling seriously on our young women.[1]

Margaret Addison was born in 1868 in Horning's Mills, Ontario. She attended schools in Trenton, Newcastle, and Richmond Hill and graduated from Victoria College in 1889 with a BA. There is no record of where she lived during her studies at Victoria, but presumably it was in boarding-houses since Brookhurst had closed in 1880. She took first-class honours in modern languages and won the silver medal. After graduation, Addison taught in high schools in Stratford and Lindsay and at the Ontario Ladies' College in Whitby. In 1900 she travelled to Germany and France to study educational methods, and she also visited the women's residences of Oxford and Cambridge.[2] That year, Addison confided a dream to her diary that Victoria would start a residence even before the proposed building was ready, in the same way as Girton College, Cambridge, which began in a rented house in Hitchin with six students, or Newnham College, Cambridge, which began with five. At this time in Toronto, the Barbara Heck Association was pursuing its goal of raising money to buy a site and furnishings for the proposed residence. As she toured the buildings at Newnham, Addison asked Anne Jemima Clough about the origins of the college and whether she thought the same could be accomplished in Toronto. Clough replied that "you could begin as we did."[3]

Several other features of Addison's trip left a lasting impression on her and helped her formulate ideals for Canadian women's higher education. She visited Toynbee Hall, a settlement house in London, and noted periodicals of interest on physical education. At Oxford she reacted positively to the sense of college life. "Every body is in earnest about something, & there is a college spirit, an esprit de corps, which is delightful. As I look at these, I am forced to the opinion, that if there is a falling off of girls in our universities at home it is partly due to the absence of the college spirit."[4]

The ideal college life that Addison sampled in England must have contrasted sharply with that of Victoria's women as she had experienced it in the 1880s, a minority with no claim on a physical or spiritual space on campus and accommodated largely in rooming-houses. The humility that Nellie Greenwood claimed characterized the first graduates was no doubt tied to this sense of marginality on the early campus at Cobourg, as well as during the years 1892–1903 on the Toronto campus, before Annesley Hall opened. The early graduates of Wellesley, Smith, and Vassar, or even of the Ontario ladies' colleges, were surrounded by architecture that affirmed their ambitions and future accomplishments, college societies of which they were the leaders, and social events in which they were the focus of attention.

Addison saw in England that women students had emotional ties to their colleges, and she believed that this sense of belonging could combine students' educational goals with their spiritual needs. This perception was not new, for Mary Electa Adams had travelled to England during the 1870s and had attempted to reconstruct a spiritual and educational ideal for women's education in her own school, Brookhurst. Addison had in turn been influenced by Adams and would carry her vision forward. While at Girton, she met a Miss Welsh, who, she observed, resembled Adams. Girton, she concluded in her diary, was finer than Newnham,[5] particularly because each girl had two rooms, a bedroom and a study, with folding doors between. The classrooms were cozy and homelike and the carpets soft, and if the reception room was pretentious, the library was beautiful. Girton was more expensive than Newnham by $130 per year. The buildings had been erected through gifts and legacies, and the institution more than paid its way. Addison noted wryly that it should be solvent since it charged $525 per year. The students at Girton seemed to her "rather more of the gay society class" with less of the spirit of earnestness. After dinner Addison attended the Political Club of the college, where the students carried on a parliamentary debate. They were arranged on each side as Liberal or Conservative, while the middle seats held the Independents and Liberal Unionists. The speaking, she observed, was very good indeed.[6]

One of the goals that Addison articulated in her diary during this visit to Girton was the desire to establish a journal of education, with sections corresponding to those of the Ontario Teachers Association, which would discuss all the "knotty questions of education."[7] She decided that if she had the money, she would send people abroad each year and establish scholarships for those who were not part of the university, but who had made contributions to education. Addison's desire to do something for education in Canada was tempered by a humble appraisal of her abilities. "How I should like to do something for the education of my own country, but when I look around, & see the advantages others have had, which I have not, my hopes grow rather small. However, God never holds us responsible for talents we have not, and if I do my own little corner well, surely He will provide many more able persons than I to do the work which I think should be done, and am not gifted enough to do."[8]

Another goal was to make the residence for women at Victoria a reality. Addison felt that the costs to the student could not exceed $9 per week, yet this fee would not cover the living expenses, a servant, rent, and the salary of a woman vice-principal. However, with a grant of $1,000 from outside sources, she believed that the scheme would work. Another dream that was inspired by her visit to Girton was a Methodist girls' school "conducted on ideal principles," with a connected training school for servants.[9]

Addison also visited St Hugh's Hall, Oxford, which aspired to degree work and had begun with four students in a hired cottage, but by 1900 had twenty-four students, a principal, and a vice-principal. The college contained a few tiny single rooms with no study space and two double rooms with separate sofa beds, which cost £70 per year. The dining-room was a large homelike room with two long tables, which accommodated all the students.[10] The lawn had two tennis courts, and a hockey facility was located some distance from the hall. Addison had a long conversation with the principal of St Hugh's, Miss Moberly, who commented that not many of the girls took the full BA course because they did not have good high school preparation for Greek and Latin and could not catch up to the required standard. Moberly believed that girls should learn Greek and Latin early in life, concentrate on Greek from age seventeen to nineteen, and then add German or other languages later. Because so much religious discussion was in the air and because "women were naturally theologians," the principal believed that women should at least be able to read their Greek New Testaments. The advantage of having a residence in a hall, according to Moberly, was to convey a home feeling, to teach girls to give and take, and to rub their rough corners smooth. The purpose of college education was as much preparation for the home as for teaching, "but mothers are sometimes lacking in sympathy and relegate their daughters to a sphere practically that of an upper servant, without appreciating the need of a mental life."[11]

At St Hilda's, Oxford, Addison noted that the college was more aristocratic in its furnishings than any other residence. The dining-room was a fine large room set with small tables, which made the setting more homelike and easier to serve.[12] A few days later she travelled to Somerville College, Oxford, where she met the principal, Agnes Maitland. Addison noted that the principal was "tall and commanding ... strong in her opinions, and a woman of much originality in carrying out what she desires." Despite this strength, she did not think that Maitland was "particularly philosophical ... and not in the least given to sentiment."[13] Somerville College had celebrated its twenty-first birthday and had grown to two buildings, with two or three cottages, which accommodated eighty-two students. Maitland advised Addison to avoid close buildings and build quadrangles with windows opening out into fresh air. The girls' rooms were better furnished at Somerville than at any of the other colleges. It issued its own diploma, offered its own tutoring, and supplied many of its own dons. Addison used her free time between visits to do research. At the Bodleian Library she read books by Dorothea Beale, the lady principal of the Cheltenham Ladies' College, and other studies of women's education. The stimulating effects of her visits and readings were noted in the observation in her diary that she dreamed all night of visiting colleges and schools.[14] Addison was obviously quite fascinated by the women principals of the colleges, and their appearance, personality, and conversations are described in the diary. She was perhaps already comparing herself and wondering whether she could fill such a role in Canada if the need arose.

THE NEW DEAN OF RESIDENCE

Margaret Addison's opportunity to serve the cause of higher education came in 1902 in the form of a request from Margaret Burwash to stand for appointment as dean of Annesley Hall. Mrs Burwash was representing the Victoria Women's Residence and Educational Association. As historian Lynn Gordon explains, "The interest of older women in seeing the next generation go to college is a highly significant feature in the history of women's access to coeducational institutions."[15] Older Methodist women certainly took an active role in the development of women's education at Victoria. They had concerns that higher education could potentially alter women's role in a negative way. Their involvement was motivated by a desire to preserve the womanliness of students. The association nominated members to serve on the Committee of Management, which oversaw all aspects of Annesley Hall. With mixed feelings, Addison agreed to accept the position at Annesley. She was glad to move closer to her aging parents but sad to give up teaching. Yet, she wrote, "If I had in any way sought the position, or done anything to procure it … I should be overcome with fear & trembling."[16] She felt, however, that God had sent her, and there was nothing left but to say yes to his bidding. In June 1903 Addison packed her books and furniture and left Lindsay. In her first week in Toronto, she made sixty-five calls and went out to tea every evening. The pace must have been overwhelming, since she recorded in her diary: "How I regret leaving Lindsay."[17] This regret was echoed in 1906 when she had to ask for a salary increase, since she was $800 poorer as Dean than she would have been had she stayed in teaching.

Among Addison's duties was corresponding with prospective students and arranging their room assignments and room-mates. She described one of the rooms to a student as pale green with oak furniture. The walls had moulding so that pictures might be hung. Students were responsible for the first instalment of the rent in October and the second in February. She expressed a certainty that God would make the residence a blessing not only to the church and nation, but to the students as well. It was important, she felt, that students entered the college with a spirit of helpfulness and thoughtfulness, especially since the first year set the tone for the succeeding years.[18]

Addison took her leadership role seriously and tried to get to know her students. Her responsibilities weighed heavily; she confided in her diary, "I was so weary, & miserable, and depressed after three days of headache & pain, & poor nights of sleep, and the prospect looked so gloomy, I felt unequal to the duties of this evening."[19] She dreaded the reading of the rules to the new students. They, to her relief, responded positively to the regulations and agreed to follow them. Among the rules were that lights were to be out at 10 PM, that the telephone was private and messages could be given to the dean, and that messages received would be recorded and delivered by the parlour maid. Numerous restrictions pertained to visitors in the rooms. Students could take girl friends to their rooms to study in the mornings or in the afternoon, but any visitors had to be personally escorted. Gentlemen were allowed to call on the second or fourth Friday between 7 and 10 PM. Strict rules governed dining hours, the only excusable absence from table being illness.[20] Students in Annesley Hall were not allowed to attend public entertainments other than those in their own college, unless accompanied by the dean or an escort formally approved by parents or guardians. First- and second-year students were not allowed to go to evening church with gentlemen, and no student was permitted to go out walking or driving with gentlemen in the evening.[21]

In May 1905 Addison had to deal with a student who had broken one of these rules. On a holiday two women students had left the hall after 10 PM in the company of two males to go a nearby ice-cream store. Addison spoke with the students and consulted with Dr and Mrs Burwash. Finally, she also wrote the parents of one student and explained that if the student did not promise to obey the rules in the future, her room would not be reserved for her the following year. Addison wrote to the student's mother, "In a large city like Toronto, such conduct is sufficient to cause much unpleasant comment about the young lady, and to bring reproach upon Annesley Hall, both of which you would deplore as would we."[22] She justified these rules by saying that regulations were necessary in a large city because it contained temptations undreamed of by those living in smaller towns, where young women had the benefit of direct guidance by parents. One new student confessed that she was not sure it was right to leave her home, and the dean responded that God had sent her to school in order that she would eventually become a more useful member of society. Addison felt that her students were all good, and although some were going to be trying, they were still lovable.[23]

In her report to the Committee of Management in 1903, Addison gave a detailed description of her work. The residence during that year had sixty-three inhabitants, of whom thirty-five were undergraduates at Victoria, thirteen at the University of Toronto, eight special students registered at Victoria, and seven music or other students. Thirteen Victoria students held special scholarships, which were offered to women who either had been teachers or were daughters of Methodist ministers. The rooms cost between $160 and $200 per year for a single and $132 for a double. The duties of the dean included setting the Christian and moral tone of the hall, maintaining its government, and disciplining its residents. In addition, she needed to be "conversant with University politics, and as wise as the Registrar concerning the curriculum."[24] She conducted prayers, nursed the sick, chaperoned students, allocated rooms, transacted business, kept the correspondence, and mediated disputes.

After a year as head of the residence, Addison had serious reservations about the structure of university life for women. She reported in 1904 to the Committee of Management: "There is something wrong about university or student life which brings our young women to their final year, and sends them out as nearly physical wrecks as they are. My observation leads me to believe that the fault lies not in too heavy a curriculum, nor in too severe studies, but in the excess of social life in the fall term which causes students to postpone all earnest effort until the New Year or later."[25] Furthermore, Addison believed that there were too many student societies and committee meetings, which resulted in hasty preparation and superficial study. The social life, she believed, was not of a high order, and "as long as students are so bound up in themselves and in each other, that their elders occupy little place in either their esteem or their plans, as long as they neglect what some one called the 'beautiful convention of manners' their spirit is not such as will serve to best develop their highest character."[26] The earnestness that Addison had observed at Oxford had not taken root in the student population at Victoria. Residence life had obviously not produced the serious and spiritual ideals its promoters had anticipated.

Physical culture occupied a serious place in Annesley Hall life. This emphasis was shared by advocates of women's education in the United States, who felt that a healthy balance of exercise, diet, sleep, and dress would solve any health problems related to higher education. American high schools offered calisthenics and supervised exercises for girls, which were similar to those given at the Ontario Ladies' College in Whitby.[27] Students were required to tidy and dust their rooms and make their own beds. Visitors were allowed in Annesley Hall between 3 and 6 PM, and formal calling days were set aside. Students were requested to conduct themselves as "Christians" and "ladies," with self-control and courtesy.[28] Dinner was the most formal meal; it started with grace and ended with Scripture reading. Two French and two German tables were part of the seating arrangements at dinner. There was usually one maid present at each table, who waited on the diners as at a formal meal.[29]

Some of the ambiguity of the dean's role was revealed in connection with Addison's teaching of a course at Victoria. According to Professor Burwash, Addison had been appointed to this responsibility at her own request because she thought it would give her more authority to be recognized as a member of the faculty. He stated that this appointment was not intended "to give her any serious work and if salary were proposed I doubt if the appointment could be carried."[30] Earlier, when Professor L.E. Horning had left for a year in Europe, he had engaged Addison to take over his work, and in this case, Burwash had argued, any salary would have to come from Horning.[31] In the end, Addison never received a faculty appointment, and no woman was in fact named to the Victoria faculty until Mary Rowell was hired in 1919 as a lecturer in French.[32]

Addison's view of these matters differed from Burwash's. In 1908 she wrote in her diary that the year before, the chancellor had told her that she was appointed lecturer in German. She taught pass German for first- and second-year students in 1907, and part of that work included relieving Dr Horning in his absence. She wrote further that she had not requested to be put on the faculty since she would not have been so presumptuous. By 1908 a Mr Owen had been hired to assist in the teaching of German, and when Addison asked the chancellor if the appointment meant that she was to do no more teaching, he replied yes. When she asked if it meant dropping her name from the staff, he said no, because having her name there gave her a certain standing.[33] Addison received no financial compensation for her brief contribution to Victoria's teaching and was not consulted about her desire to either teach or have her name used in the calendar. Her symbolic role as a member of faculty illustrated her limited powers in relation to those of the chancellor.

It might have seemed that more power was possible when, in 1908, the Wrong Report, proposing a separate college for women at the University of Toronto, drew the university women together to prepare a response.[34] Addison consulted on the issue with Mabel Cartwright, principal of St Hilda's, the women's residence at Trinity College.[35] Some of the university women initially saw a separate college as an opportunity for them to have control over the education of women, employ more women teachers, and develop a positive college experience similar to that found in England or the United States. The realists, however, predicted that with limited finances, women would receive neither the facilities nor the quality of teaching that was hoped for, and they felt that the university should deal directly with the problems of overcrowding and too few women faculty members, and not waste resources on a plan such as that proposed by the Wrong Report. The issue of the report was important in that it mobilized university women to work together across college and denominational lines and to demand representation in university decision-making bodies. The students organized such an interuniversity body when in 1916 they formed a Women's Student Council for the university.[36]

Table 1
Fathers's occupation of Victoria women students, 1915–16

	Number	*Percentage*
Merchants	17	16
Ministers	15	14
Farmers	11	10
Doctors	11	10
Teachers	11	10
Manufacturers	5	5
Lawyers	2	2
Other	10	10
Retired	5	5
Unknown	17	18
Total	104	100

Source: Annual Report for the Senate, March 1916, Margaret Addison Papers, box 2, file 12, UCA.

YEARS OF GROWTH AND CHANGE

The Annesley Hall residence was soon inadequate to meet the needs of the growing numbers of women students, and in 1905 a building known as the Drynan property was purchased to provide additional rooms. South Hall, as the new residence was called, was located at 75 Queen's Park Crescent and had Mrs Sheffield as head.[37] In 1909–10 the population of South Hall included twenty-seven women, of whom one was a teacher of physical culture, six were students from the Faculty of Education, eight undergraduates of Victoria College, two transfers from Annesley (university department not given), seven in domestic science, two in art, and one in music. Of the sixty-four women undergraduates at Victoria that year, the religious backgrounds included fifty-seven Methodists (89 per cent), five Presbyterians (8 per cent), one Baptist (1.5 per cent), and one whose denomination was undesignated (1.5 per cent).[38] This distribution of religious affiliation remained constant for 1915–16, when students included ninety-six Methodists (91 per cent), six Presbyterians (6 per cent), two Anglicans (2 per cent), and one Baptist (1 per cent). As table 1 shows, the occupations of the fathers of Victoria's women students were various. The largest percentages were merchants (16 per cent) and ministers (14 per cent), with the remaining 70 per cent from other occupations. Women students came therefore from relatively prosperous backgrounds, and the majority appear to have been from the urban middle class. Women students' registration that year, as shown in table 2, was concentrated in the general course with

Table 2
Women undergraduate registration at Victoria, 1915–16

	Number	*Percentage*
Science	1	1
Honours household science	13	14
Mathematics and physics	3	3
Moderns	22	23
Classics	4	4
Household science general	16	17
General course	36	30
Total	95	100

Source: Annual Report for the Senate, March 1916, Margaret Addison Papers, box 2, file 12, UCA.

38 per cent (thirty-six students); the second highest registration was in moderns with 23 per cent (twenty-two students).

Addison attributed the increased academic success of students by 1910 to the existence of Annesley Hall and the Annesley Student Government Association, which had been functioning since 1906. Student government had the advantage that it "satisfied the desire for representative government, is in accord with the growing democracy of the age, offers exceptional opportunity to learn the value of self-control for themselves and others, develops *esprit de corps*, creates contentment and a sense of personal responsibility for the honour of the institution."[39] For Addison what would bind the student government, residence life, and the concerns of all Victoria's women students together further would be the presence of a dean of women, as opposed to a dean merely of Annesley Hall. She believed that an enlarged role for the dean would serve the interests of women at Victoria, particularly those who were not in residence. Her request in 1909 for such a change was supported by a recommendation by women graduates of Victoria, who felt that there was an growing separation between resident and non-resident students. These graduates believed that there should be a dean of women, such as in American colleges, who could advise women and do some teaching as well.[40]

Earlier, in 1907, Addison had requested that she be recognized as an ex-officio member of the Board of Regents of Victoria and be present at all board meetings, in the same way that the heads of the women's residences at Oxford, Cambridge, and St Andrew's attended all meetings of their boards.[41] She felt that student government gave students responsibility for each other and also provided the opportunity for student leaders to meet with the dean to discuss problems. But the representative government model would only continue to work if the dean had the authority to make decisions over the whole of women's student life at Victoria. No doubt Addison had been influenced by her meetings in 1900 with the independent women principals of Somerville, St Hilda's, and Newnham during her travels in England. In 1912 she would claim that the model of student government at Victoria was based on a similar system at Wellesley College, but modified to suit Victoria's conditions.[42]

Presumably, by 1909 Addison had reached a point where she felt that she needed more power over the growing numbers of women students at Victoria, only some of whom lived in residence while others lived in boarding-houses or with parents or relatives. In reality she had little autonomy. She was responsible not only to the women's Committee of Management, whose powers concerned the finances, social life, and management of the residence, but also to the male authorities at Victoria. It was inevitable that her sense of vision would eventually come into conflict with both. Addison's diary is restrained about the tensions involved in being accountable to these different groups. Her ideal of a dean of women might have been bolder than the power structures or perhaps even the women's Committee of Management at Victoria were willing to countenance. Having seen similar models work in both the United States and England, where women had successfully taken charge of their colleges, she believed that even within the coeducational setting of Victoria, women students both in and outside residence required a strong head. The single residence model, with a dean of residence who had limited powers, no longer fitted the situation at Victoria, where students lived in a variety of settings and needed a central point for both student life and leadership. The increase in women students at the college, combined with those taking courses elsewhere who needed residence, meant that Annesley Hall, even with the addition of South Hall, had become inadequate.

Reporting in 1909 on her first years at Annesley, Addison felt that she had failed to convey to the Committee of Management the importance of the work of dean and "its mighty potentiality." As a result, the committee did not give her the sympathetic understanding that she needed and without which she "felt her power of service limited."[43] In the same report she recommended that the committee find a way to put Annesley Hall on a more business-like basis and have the officers of the hall work together in unity, which they had never been able to do before, since there were three or more persons whose positions were completely independent from one another. One can infer from her remarks that there had been conflict between the dean, the housekeeper, and Emma Scott-Raff, and Addison wanted recognition that she had authority over these women. Part of the problem was that the Barbara Heck Association had hired Mrs Scott-Raff in 1900 for the work of physical culture, and two years later it had also hired Dr Leila Davis as medical adviser for students in physical culture. When the Committee of Management was constituted, these previous appointments were made accountable to the committee and not to the dean. The duties of these officers had not been defined, nor was their relation to each other clearly stated. In 1903 the same committee had appointed Margaret Addison as dean to succeed the matron, Helen Scott.[44] Addison might have preferred that any appointments which predated her arrival at Annesley be put directly under her authority, but such was not the case. This ambiguity concerning who was actually in charge contributed considerably to tensions between the officers of the residence.

An incident in 1911 brought conflict between Addison, Burwash, and the Annesley Committee of Management into the open. Burwash showed by his actions that he was eager to discredit student government, a fact that Addison no doubt perceived as a lack of confidence in her management. Burwash wrote to Addison that year expressing concern that students allegedly had the habit of visiting until midnight in their rooms and that they went out every night of the week and attended dances without chaperons. These matters, according to Burwash, could "destroy the value of our residence for young women in the eyes of our Methodist people." Part of the reason for his concern was the fact that "we are on the eve of trying a new experiment in residence matters as soon as the new residence for men is opened."[45] A committee of the Senate was formed to investigate the whole matter.[46] The question was reviewed during the following year, and a majority of the Committee of Management expressed confidence in Addison and the workings of student government.[47] The Alumnae Association also sent a statement unanimously supporting the principle of student government.[48] A minority of members of the Committee of Management, however, were not satisfied with this decision, and they demanded tighter rules.

The crisis reflected a lack of confidence in the management of the residence, with one faction supporting stricter supervision while Addison and her supporters upheld the principle of student government and responsibility. The minority dissenters from the committee complained to the Board of Regents about Victoria women students' attendance at theatres, which included Shakespearean drama as well as a local establishment called the Bluebird.[49] Students, they believed, should attend the theatre only when properly chaperoned by the dean, and not by young men who called for the students, paid for their tickets, and served as their escorts. At dances no proper chaperons were allegedly provided, and students returned from such entertainments at 2:30 AM. The letter of complaint was signed by Mrs Wood, Margaret Burwash, Lillian Massey Treble, Susie D. Massey, Margaret P. Massey, and Mrs Timothy Eaton.[50] The eight members who refused to sign were Louise Starr, Florence Lang, E.J. Kerr, Mary E. Carty, Mary Carman (wife of Bishop Carman), M.F. Gurney, N.L. Rowell, and Hannah Fudger.[51] Addison believed that the ideal held by the Burwashes and the president of the Committee of Management was one of strong central authority where the dean commanded the obedience of the students, as opposed to a cooperative model of student government. Burwash and his wife were unwilling to sign an agreement with the women students which was approved by the Senate, and in 1912 he resigned his position as chancellor and president.[52] Mrs Burwash had been one of the original founders of the Barbara Heck Association, and this dispute must have struck a sad note in the history of women's residence life at Victoria. There are hints of other points of conflict in Addison's correspondence and diary, but her restraint makes it difficult to glean the details. She struggled with headaches and depression, which were no doubt exacerbated by these conflicts as well as by the limits to her power in the management structure.

That Margaret Addison was not universally liked is evident from a letter Mrs Burwash received in 1913 from her niece, Margaret Proctor, a graduate of the School of Household Science, who was currently working at Bryn Mawr College. Proctor emphatically expressed her dislike of Addison, of Annesley Hall, and also of Annie Laird of domestic science. "You know I never was either an Annesley Hall or a Lillian Massey favorite. If the D——d DEAN wants to run the poor housekeeper and have her under her direction, Let her by all means … She'll hang her self. The big mistakes are being made by keeping both Miss Addison and Miss Laird, they are not Big women, they know absolutely nothing of human nature and the departments they order will be worse than mediocre."[53]

In 1911 Mrs Sheffield, presumably to gain more recognition and power, requested that her position of mistress of South Hall be renamed dean. The by-laws of the Committee of Management for Annesley and South halls in 1910 had ensured that the head of South Hall was accountable to the committee, but had not increased Addison's powers. The revised by-laws in 1914 stated that the dean was responsible to the Committee of Management for "the general direction of the residences, and for the discipline and management of Annesley Hall."[54] Thus the mistress of South Hall continued to be directly responsible to the Committee of Management rather than to Addison. The new chancellor, R.P. Bowles, who had taken office in 1913, amended the constitution in 1914 so that instead the Committee of Management being allowed to make regulations for the government of the students, it was to "confer with the President and Senate of the College with regard to regulations for the government of the students."[55] The committee only had a nominal say in student government after this revision to the constitution. By 1915–16, sixty-six students resided in Annesley Hall, twenty-three in South Hall, and sixteen in the Annex, a house on Charles Street that was rented for the purpose.[56] Students in the first and second years were organized into groups of eight with a leader, and these groups were hosted by faculty wives, who entertained the students in their homes.[57] In 1916 financial pressures demanded the reorganization of South Hall as an adjunct of Annesley, with the latter in control of all financial matters. The salary of the mistress was reduced, and eventually, partly because of ill health, Mrs Sheffield resigned. This resignation, combined with that of Burwash, was to some extent a victory for Addison.

Various conflicts affected Margaret Addison's health until she finally took a leave during the year 1917. The complexity of her job can be inferred from the fact that two replacements were hired during her leave, Marjorie Curlette of the Westbourne School and Mary Hurd Skinner, with a BA Victoria in 1898. Prior to Addison's leave of absence, the death of Lillian Massey Treble in 1916 had prompted a report from the dean that both returned to some of Addison's old dreams and suggested her continuing discomfort at Victoria. She still hoped for the establishment of a Methodist girls' school with both residential and day options and an academic standard as high as any collegiate institute or high school. Perhaps she saw a more useful role for herself in such an institution than was possible at Victoria. Another need in women's education, noted Addison, was a women's college such a Wellesley, Vassar, or Royal Holloway in England.[58]

A student union was opened in 1917 for the social needs of women students under the supervision of Mary Skinner, who reported to Addison. The union was organized to meet a need in the life of Victoria College women and provide a meeting ground for all undergraduate women who lived in residence, boarding-houses, or at home, as well as for members of the Alumnae Association. The purpose of the space was thus to provide a centre for social activities. The union offered a common room, committee rooms, a library, and a large dining-room, where three meals a day were served.[59]

In reporting to the Committee of Management in 1917, Addison had some criticisms of current student life. The college was facing some of the problems that had already been experienced by American colleges, including a withdrawal among students from involvement in the church and less dependence upon faith or the influence of the Holy Spirit. She blamed the changes on the students' having grown up in a materialistic world, where they had never developed a spirit of self-denial or self-sacrifice as the past generation had.[60] Addison expressed the hope that in the future there would be a more vigorous mental life for women in the college and that comradeship between women and men would be based on common intellectual interests, as opposed to mere social or sports interests. It is interesting that in 1917 she cautioned that thought should be given to the planning of new buildings so that they would be an expression of the needs of women students, "rather than to have the needs controlled by the buildings."[61]

Women students continued to increase yearly; in 1913 there had been 135 undergraduates and in 1917 there were 179. Of the 79 students who lived outside the residence, 22 were in boarding-houses. The accommodations changed frequently as appendix 2 illustrates. During the years 1917–20 South Hall was discontinued as a residence, which left three halls, Annesley, the Annex, and 113 Bloor Street West, the latter headed by Mary Rowell. In her report, Addison questioned how the head of a college could best serve the interests of the students who were bristling with questions about missions, social service, city welfare, vocations, and employment. On the other hand, many girls came to Canadian universities from small towns, where they had been accustomed to greater freedom. In order to meet the concrete needs within the residence related to meals and questions of privileges, as well as to represent the larger world to students, Addison concluded that the residence should house women who had outside occupations and who would answer students' questions. Each residence would thus be presided over by a head who was a recent graduate, and together with the dean they would form a council.

During these years the impact of the First World War was felt in student life at Victoria. Students knitted for the war effort and worked in services such as picking fruit and other farm labour. The Women's Literary Society undertook to run a patriotic tea room in addition to a discussion program on the war. Profits raised by the tea room were donated to the Red Cross. Addison described the mood among the students: "I think that the continual sense of the national tragedy wears upon one more than one knows, and I am sure it is so with these young girls."[62] In a letter to her sister, Addison described her involvement in a committee of five appointed by the Women's Emergency Corps. Their job was to draw up an application form to be used by women who would be willing to take the place of men who enlisted. Opposition was raised by the Trades and Labor Council, and the committee approached the head of the council. The women assured it that they did not intend to replace men with women, but to have a list of women in reserve, "ready and capable to take the place of those men who might be needed to finish the war."[63] The council preferred that such positions be offered first to returned soldiers, then to men who were overage or unfit, and only when these options failed, to a woman. Working-class men feared that these middle-class women would volunteer their labour for far less than a man's wage. Other student activities included involvement at the Fred Victor Mission and at one of the settlement houses in the city. Margaret Addison was a representative of the YWCA at a conference on social problems held in New York in 1914, which included speakers such as the theologian Walter Rauschenbusch, Professor Harry Ward from Boston, Vida Scudder from Wellesley College, and the Reverend J.S. Woodsworth from Winnipeg. The Victoria YWCA reached the largest membership in its history during these years, with 147 members in 1916 out of a student enrolment of 167.

The intensity of student social life continued to be a concern. Addison wrote in 1919 that the women of the university had urged again and again that social life at the university be taken into "careful consideration and that public opinion be established in favour of greater quiet, earlier hours, more study, a saner life, but men do not look at life as women do. It is not given to them, apparently, to see individual lives and they cannot see our point of view." She predicted that otherwise young lives would be wrecked.[64] After Mary Skinner resigned because of illness and Mary Rowell found it impossible to both teach and supervise a residence, Addison had to reconsider how to administer the growing population of women students.[65]

A DEAN OF WOMEN STUDENTS

Not until 1920 did the Committee of Management agree to a trial year for the plan that Addison had been proposing for a decade, namely, to unify the different aspects of college life by appointing a dean of women students with authority over all women students and status as a faculty member. The Women's Student Union moved in 1920 from South Hall (which had been used for union purposes for three years) to the south end of Annesley Hall. The common room and library, together with the gymnasium, were separated from the rest of the building and became the union for all women students. Five heads of houses were chosen to be in charge of second-floor Annesley, third-floor Annesley, Oaklawn, the Annex, and South Hall, and these women, together with the dean of women, formed the new dean's council. The five heads were appointed by the dean of women, the dean of arts, and the college president. In Addison's words, "Everything is to be united under one woman, who is to have the position of Dean of Women, and today I was appointed to that position, at a salary of $2,500."[66] Dr Bowles suggested, however, that, effective 1921, the dean would not live in any of the residences.[67] Hazel Cleaver, a graduate of 1918, was appointed head of the Annex and Cornelia Harcum head of Oaklawn, as the residence at 113 Bloor Street West was now called. Harcum was well qualified for the position since she had graduated from Goucher College in Maryland, taught at Wellesley and Vassar, and served as dean of women at Rockford in Illinois, and was now an assistant to Professor C.T. Currelly of the Royal Ontario Museum. The head of Upper Annesley was Winnifred Barnstead, a graduate of Dalhousie and one of the senior librarians at the Toronto Public Library. Lillian Smith, who the head of Lower Annesley, was in charge of the children's work at the public library.[68]

The revised powers of the Committee of the Management were described as advisory on matters such as the furnishing of dormitories, in contrast with the early years, when it had controlled virtually all aspects of the residence life.[69] It was the turn of the Committee of Management in 1921 to complain that its powers had been cut and to question whether there was any point in its continuing to exist. To mollify the committee, the president of Victoria College gave it hiring powers over positions such as the dietitian, janitor, and household director. It did not regain power, however, to appoint the dean of women and the heads of houses. The Committee of Management finally agreed with the chancellor's proposal to appoint Addison as dean of the residences in addition to her position as dean of women. Her sketch of the history of the committee concluded that during the first ten years, and also at a later period (1918–26), outside forces had entered too much into the internal organization, but that in the end "things right themselves."[70]

Things did not right themselves very quickly, however, and in 1921, after continued conflict about her role, Margaret Addison considered offering her resignation. She made it clear to the chancellor that she was not trying to get back into residence. This statement would confirm that she had actually moved out of the residence which had been her home for almost two decades, a move that must have caused her some distress. To be reduced to having an office at Victoria was in complete opposition to the ideal that Addison held of a dean as mentor and model to the students. The role, as she defined it, required women who were single and devoted to the college life. To be accountable to parents, Victoria authorities, and the community at large for the well-being of college women was a task that required a devotion which could not be defined within the limits of "office hours." The standards of bureaucratic efficiency that had shaped the structures of male education were now being applied to the dean. This male model was in direct opposition to Addison's own conception of her task as mentor and mother, as well as spiritual guide, to her women students. Her struggle with the authorities at Victoria was not just about power but also about a different conception of leadership and student needs. In a letter to a friend in 1920, she described the small office she had at the college, which had previously served as Dr Blewett's classroom and later as a ladies' study. The girls now studied either in the library or at Annesley Hall. Addison's office contained "my own furniture, books, tables, couch, pictures, etc. What time I do not live in the office or at Annesley Hall, I spend at Miss Coleman's – which means that I sleep and breakfast there."[71] Coleman, a niece of Mary Electa Adams, had been a favorite of Addison's since the early days when they taught together at the Ontario Ladies' College.

Some of the misunderstandings between the dean and the college were apparently due to the interference of "Mr and Mrs M [Massey?]," who had given large sums of money to the college and had strong views on how it should be organized. They preferred to see a committee composed of men and women deal collectively with the problems of both residences. Addison, in contrast, fought strongly to keep the women's matters under control of women and the dean of women. She described the discussion in her diary as "a protest against the autocracy of men in the affairs of the women."[72] The Masseys, if that is who was meant, apparently thought that there was too much emphasis on home life and domestic matters, and these had to be left behind when women went to college. Addison interpreted this view as opposition to her authority in Annesley Hall. The chancellor reminded Addison that the amount of money Mrs M—— had given for a union gave her a "certain claim upon the affairs of the union."[73]

The men in 1913 had obtained a residence, which had 113 students in the first year. The dean of residence was Vincent Massey, who had recently returned from Oxford. Interestingly enough, he was immediately appointed to a post as lecturer in modern history, in addition to his responsibilities in residence.[74] This appointment and other changes showed the greater claim that male students were allowed to make on the facilties and resources at Victoria. The Annex and the Charles Street boarding-houses were taken over for the use of male students. Not only had the numbers of women increased, but they were housed in a variety of settings both on and off campus. In 1914–15 there were 81 students in residence, 21 in boarding-houses, and 33 elsewhere in Toronto, presumably with family or friends. By contrast, in 1921 there were 146 women students in residence, 20 boarded, and 75 lived elsewhere in Toronto. Women were given the option of living off-campus at the United Church Training School on St Clair Avenue West. The numbers continued to increase so that in 1925 there were 313 women and in 1928, 454. That year there were 100 more women registered than men, with 356 men in arts and 404 women in arts and 54 in household science. From the early years of residence, when in 1906, 57 women had been accommodated, the growth had continued until in 1926, when 186 women were in residence.[75] New arrangements needed to be made for them.

The questions of social life, dancing, attendance at theatres, and secret societies had been debated from the early years among the leadership of Victoria College. Already in the first decade of Annesley Hall, student social life had posed a concern. Margaret Burwash had been particularly disturbed in 1905 to read in the *Globe* of the installation of a chapter of the Kappa Alpha Theta society among the women of the University of Toronto. A meeting of the sorority in Philadelphia had apparently been attended by several University College women who had lived in Annesley Hall the previous year. Burwash had heard that six months of fraternity life often ruined a student's career, and thus she viewed the growth of these organizations with anxiety.[76] Apparently, in 1907 Chancellor Burwash had agreed to the formation of a sorority at the college, and four years later this group was formally constituted as a chapter of Kappa Kappa Gamma.[77] In 1923 the agitation surfaced again as a new group requested a sorority, and a committee decided two years later that it was essential to the well-being of the students that no sorority exist. The application for a new sorority was withdrawn, and the existing one agreed not to accept new members. Yet the college could not hold back the tide of social change indefinitely. In 1927, after years of debate, dancing was allowed in the three residences, but not in the college building. Addison described the college's adaptation to this trend.

When the war ended, dancing came in like a mighty tidal wave, before which we were powerless. We occupied the equivocal position of seeming, to the public, to stand out against it, while we knew very well our students were dancing. We approved chaperones etc., and they were dancing in places where we had no control. Now, all College dances are to be held in our *own* buildings, we are present at them, we exercise supervision over them, we advise concerning them. Our students are safer than they were, and they have not abused their privileges. Incidentally, we (the authorities) feel less like hypocrites, and the students feel the same way, I fancy.[78]

OTHER ENTERPRISES FOR WOMEN

Two other enterprises were directly sponsored by members of the Victoria Women's Residence and Educational Association: the School of Expression and the School of Household Science. Several members of the association had sufficient personal wealth to provide substantial assistance to these schools. Yet the projects sowed considerable conflict in the previously harmonious atmosphere for women at Victoria. Both programs represented new interpretations of what women should study, or what women's studies consisted of, an interpretation not shared by the academically minded alumnae of Victoria.

The School of Expression evolved out of a perceived need to offer physical culture to students. Emma Scott-Raff was hired to serve as principal and provide classes in physical culture, voice culture, and English literature.[79] The program grew and was financed by donations from wealthy Methodists such as Mrs Cox. Its graduates were qualified to teach physical culture in colleges or collegiate institutes, thus adding at least $300 per year to their earning ability. Mrs Scott-Raff's enthusiasm for the enterprise was not shared by all university women. Chancellor Burwash, who was a friend of hers, had hoped to give Scott-Raff more work either at Annesley Hall or in teaching theological students how to preach, but neither the Board of Regents nor the Senate was inclined to permit this expansion of her position.[80] In 1901 Alice Chown wrote to Mrs Burwash that she was concerned about the recommendation of the Victoria women's association for the establishment of a school of expression. She believed that colleges should only offer courses that afforded the highest mental training and also that the proposed department of expression should not be connected to the residence. Further, she objected to Scott-Raff's "superficiality, her constant desire to train for poses & effects, her utter lack of comprehension of what true culture means."[81] The students petitioned the board to protest strongly against the department of expression on the grounds that there was a nominal qualification for entrance, which allowed students of no academic standing to rank with undergraduates and encouraged diploma graduates of the school to be considered graduates of Victoria. The students felt that the course was substandard and that it was not planned by university authorities but by the instructress. Finally, they protested that Scott-Raff, although she had no university standing, was ranked with the faculty as head of a "so-called Department."[82]

The school was supported by an endowment from Mrs Timothy Eaton, and in 1907 it was renamed after her the Margaret Eaton School of Literature and Expression.[83] The directors met the following year at the house of Mrs Eaton and appointed Chancellor Burwash president.[84] Thus, although funded by the philanthropy of wealthy Methodists, the school maintained an informal affiliation with Victoria through the presence of the chancellor on its board. This affiliation presumably irritated those who did not want Victoria to be associated with the Margaret Eaton School at all. Yet for others the school had an appealing program: by 1911 the enrolment totalled 260 students.

The School of Domestic Science was another enterprise with direct links to the Victoria women's association.[85] The main organizer of the school was Lillian Massey Treble. Her father had founded the Fred Victor Mission in memory of his deceased son, Frederick Victor, and Lillian took a deep interest in the mission. She became convinced that better home conditions were a fundamental requisite for the poor, and consequently in 1896 she opened a small cooking school in the mission building at the corner of Jarvis and Queen streets. The minister of education, George W. Ross, and the Senate of the University of Toronto were presented with a proposal for a curriculum and a degree that would qualify teachers to teach the subject in provincial high schools. Apparently, some "conservative" members of the Senate opposed the proposal, but nevertheless in the spring of 1902 a curriculum was established leading to the degree of bachelor of household science, and in October the following year the first small class was enrolled. That some university women had reservations about this development was evident in a discussion at the alumnae association of University College in 1902; questions were asked as to whether the proposed introduction of domestic science into the university might be against the interests of higher education for women.[86] The debate among university women reflected a broader discussion in North America about the place of home economics in women's education. Yet Mrs Treble began making plans for a suitable building to house the program, and in January 1913 it was formally opened.[87]

Mrs Treble was concerned in 1909 that the debates regarding a separate college for women should not interfere with the establishment of her school, and she insisted that it be clearly understood that "the object of the building is the promotion of the study of Household Science as a part of the University curriculum, and that no plan should be made with reference to other matters which would interfere with the convenience and success of that work."[88] Mrs Treble had apparently wanted to give the school to Victoria College, but Chancellor Burwash advised her that since the sciences were taught by the University of Toronto, it should be given to the university. The agreement between the university and the donor in 1907 had specified that if the school ceased to exist, Victoria would receive payment for the value of the land and the building.[89]

Alumnae and students at Victoria did not feel that either the household science courses or the program in expression exemplified their ideal of women's studies at the university. Women had been allowed into the male curriculum, and for many that was an achievement they wanted to protect. Jo La Pierre, in her study of the curriculum of women students at the University of Toronto, notes its similarity to that offered by Queen's and McGill. The BA was based on a four-year program after junior matriculation "involving four years of Latin, English, and one modern language, plus at least one course in mathematics, physics, chemistry, history, or philosophy in the first two years."[90] As table 2 indicates, the majority of undergraduate women at Victoria were registered in the general course (38 per cent) and moderns (23 per cent) and the smallest numbers in science (1 per cent), mathematics and physics (3 per cent), and classics (4 per cent). With this curriculum, women felt that their degrees would have to be considered on a par with men's. The pursuit of separate education in the form of special subjects such as domestic science or elocution was a threat to the progress that had been achieved for women in higher education.

Many women students and alumnae felt that by thus achieving equality in the curriculum, their education would be taken seriously. Yet women students still sought protection of those aspects of their student life on campus that recognized their difference. Did they hope to achieve a perfect equality and sameness with the male students, or did they have traditions that were unique, vital, and requiring protection? For Margaret Addison, it was clearly necessary to separate certain aspects of women's student life and keep them under women's control. She observed in 1920 that there were some at the university who "realizing the new freedom that women enjoy and having made no study of the Women's Movement are caught by the fallacy long ago outworn and outlived viz., that women must be like men and do the same things; that equality signifies uniformity."

These advocates of equality wanted to make Annesley Hall like Burwash Hall, the men's residence, but they did not see that Annesley had long ago surpassed Burwash, and they had forgotten that women wish to "develop their own personalities in their own way, and according to their own genius."[91] Despite these arguments, Addison had heard that male students at Burwash admitted with envy that Annesley Hall had a spirit which the men's residence did not. Yet by 1920 she also felt that men and women were cooperating better than ever before and that both were recognizing that there could be union and cooperation without uniformity and that men could do some things and women others, but with shared intellectual and spiritual standards. A frequent criticism against coeducation was that women followed men's leadership and did not exercise enough initiative, but Addison believed that "our women" were guarding against this danger.[92]

ADDISON'S LAST YEARS AT VICTORIA

The plan to have five different heads with no one person over Annesley Hall had been declared in 1921 a failure after one year. In the new structure, Gertrude Rutherford was appointed head of Annesley, while the dean of women still supervised the dining-room, housekeeping, nursing, and the residences through the dean's council.[93] A renewed discussion about the future of coeducation took place in 1923 when the Alumnae Association reviewed the advisability of a separate college for women.[94] Victoria faculty members also registered some concern about the predominance of women students at the college. Debates on the subject of coeducation focused on the advantages of separate colleges such as at Oxford and Cambridge and some institutions in the eastern United States.[95] The fact that women represented a numerical majority at Victoria called their presence into question in a way that had not been the case when they were a small minority. Historian Lynn Gordon suggests that the very success of the social separatism practised by college women themselves led male administrators and faculty members to use it as a precedent for academic separatism. She notes that the growing number of women students and their success alarmed males and inspired their call for a separate college to protect men from the effects of effeminization.[96] This attitude is evident in a proposal suggested by the faculty, but not effected, which would have denied admission to first-year women with junior matriculation if they came from schools that offered senior matriculation. Walter T. Brown, writing from Yale in 1929, described how Brown University had separate colleges for men and women. The women's college, he stated, was four blocks away on a different campus, and the courses were taught separately except for science laboratories.[97]

It would appear that the experiment of allowing women into Victoria was almost a victim of its own success. For some, the number of women students at Victoria was beginning to seem a threat to the more important mission of the college, which was to educate men. This unease represents a continuity going back to the early days of the Upper Canada Academy and Victoria College, and it was clearly present in the history of coeducational secondary and higher education in the United States as well. By the early twentieth century in that country, many critics of coeducation had shifted their focus from the potential danger to girls of masculinized high schools to the threat of the feminization of boys in coeducational classrooms taught by women.[98] At the university, the increasing numbers of women posed a threat to the masculine culture.

One student, who was later a university faculty member, recalled that Margaret Addison felt herself to be *in loco parentis* and believed that she had to safeguard the students in the big city, with the result that they lived under strict rules. Yet this recollection contradicts an impression that, in the early days at least, students went out every night and rarely studied until the winter term. The student, who was at Victoria in the 1920s, remembered that restaurants were out of bounds, as were dancehalls, unless one had written permission from one's parents. Social events were quite unsophisticated, and there were university tea dances and a ball that was the big event of the year. At promenades one chose a partner and walked up and down conversing. In addition, there were class parties, hikes, and dinners. According to Dorothy Forward, one made very good friends at the college, and that was where some of her lifetime friendships began.[99] Another excellent glimpse of life from the student's perspective is provided in the diary of Kathleen Cowan, kept in 1907–10. She described an occasion when the students were entertained by the dean in her room, an event they found far too respectable. As Cowan reported, "we nearly 'busted' because it was so proper."[100] Addison's concern for her students included not only deportment, but a check on their physical well-being, which in 1925 evidently revealed that 63 out of 161 girls were suffering from goitre. She felt that her students were not as healthy as they could be. "It is astonishing how few there are in that large number whose hearts are rugged and perfect. Surely, surely, we must learn to live more simply and quietly if the next generation is not to suffer."[101]

In 1925 Mrs George Herbert Wood gave her residence to Victoria College to be used for women students, on condition that it retain the name Wymilwood.[102] The house had been purchased before the war for $150,000 and contained eleven fireplaces and ten bathrooms. Mrs Joseph Flavelle offered to furnish Wymilwood and to finance the changes required to convert the house into a residence. Her offer of $50,000 was made on condition that a matching amount be raised. Miss Kilpatrick was hired as head of Wymilwood, an arrangement that proved satisfactory. Supporters of a women's residence at Victoria worked together with one single aim: "to try to make the Kingdom of God prevail right here at home."[103] A campaign was launched in 1925 to raise $250,000 for another new residence for women students. Addison concluded in 1926 that the ideal organization would be to have one person responsible for the residences who had some teaching duties, a second person who would be the head of the union and dean of women, and a third who would serve as dietitian in the union with administrative duties. She felt that the decentralization of residence and society life made it difficult for one person to stay in touch with students and their needs. The result was that "we are crushing out the thing which is most beautiful of all, that is, the personal contact."[104]

Events after church union in 1925 created new priorities and pressures for education at Victoria. Although women made up two-thirds of the student population after the war, their needs were not necessarily considered first. Victoria historian C.B. Sissons claims that fund-raising under the Centenary Fund went primarily towards building the theological college, Emmanuel, leaving little for the needs of women.[105] Emmanuel was officially opened in 1931, and the Board of Regents determined to build five houses for its students at a cost of $250,000. Addison sent a letter to the next board meeting requesting a similar sum for a women's residence. The board considered and rejected a proposal to reduce the number of Emmanuel houses to three in order that the rest of the money be spent on the needs of women students. Women, however, received only $50,000 for the renovation of residences along Bloor Street.[106] It seems that the Methodist tendency to subordinate women's education to that of males, particularly theologues, still prevailed. The long-awaited Addison Hall would not be opened until September 1959.

In her final report to the Committee of Management in 1931, Margaret Addison had noted that when she read the first rules of Annesley Hall aloud to present-day students, they would rock with laughter and disbelief that such rules could ever have existed. "One rejoices greatly in the increased freedom of women," she noted. Yet she observed that the new generation was increasingly "set loose" from any faith in God or reliance on prayer.[107]

Addison had spent almost three decades involved in the higher education of women at Victoria. During her career she had met some of the major figures in the field in both England and the United States, as well as in Canada. She had served with the International YWCA, the Student Christian Movement, and the University Women's Club, and had attended numerous international conferences of these organizations. She remained convinced that it was a privilege to spend her time around young people, despite the heavy responsibilities her position must have carried. She counselled her niece to travel abroad and see life because "what we need most in Canada are women of vision, even more, I think, than men of vision, for too many women are circumscribed by the walls of their homes."[108]

The organization of women's student life at Victoria had certain continuities with the early movement for women's education that had been initiated by Mary Electa Adams at Brookhurst. Adams's experiment came to a premature end, but gains were won for women at Victoria as they eventually claimed a place in male classrooms. The numbers of women students grew very slowly during the first two decades after their admission to the college, and consequently they did not pose a great threat to established male traditions. They won a degree of toleration, and perhaps even appreciation, as younger sisters in the Victoria family, which in some cases they literally were. The move to Toronto allowed for new traditions to be established, and the building of Annesley Hall and the purchase of other buildings provided a permanent home for women students on the campus. Despite this home, the debate concerning coeducation versus a separate college for women re-emerged with great regularity. The creation of a home for women students had been facilitated by the work of the Committee of Management and the alumnae. Yet relations between the management, the benefactors, and the university required regular review and were subject to some serious tensions. Margaret Addison's career, devoted to higher education for women in Canada, was built in the midst of these tensions. Her ideals were shaped by contact with leaders in higher education in several countries and were not always shared by either the women's Committee of Management or the male authorities at Victoria. The relationships of money and power, as well as prestige, directly influenced decisions about education at the college. The same ambivalence about girls' education that had been evident at the ladies' colleges continued to trouble Methodist higher education, even when the numbers of women involved attested to its importance.

9 Conclusion

This study of Methodist education for women ends in 1925, the year of church union, when the Methodists joined with two other Protestant denominations to form the United Church of Canada. Many changes in public and private education had taken place between the founding of the Upper Canada Academy in 1832 and the federation of Victoria University with the University of Toronto sixty years later. The Methodist vision for education, strongly rooted in the desire to provide a Christian environment for students, was guided by uniquely talented individuals and funded by the gifts of both those with much to give and those with little. Methodist higher education for women was in one sense not unique. The travels of some of the leaders of the educational movement, such as Mary Electa Adams and Margaret Addison, and their contacts with educational developments in England and United States, as well as in other parts of Canada, ensured that different influences were embedded within the ongoing experiment. Professors who came to teach in Methodist educational institutions had experienced higher education in colleges in Europe, the United States, and Canada, and they eagerly shared what they had seen in those places. The recurrent debate about the merits of coeducation was fuelled by opinions from individuals who had observed education at Yale, Harvard, Brown, Wellesley, Oxford, Smith, Vassar, Mount Allison, and numerous other schools. Relations between church and state and between the provincial university and the denominational colleges, as well as the forces of industrialization, immigration, and urbanization in Ontario, contributed to the fact that

Methodist education developed as a hybrid which had influences from various sources, but was neither exclusively British nor American. Although there were a multitude of influences on Methodist education for women, it is inaccurate to apply historical models purely from British or American literature to the Canadian case. The distinctions between academy and seminary that Horowitz described for the United States do not apply to the Upper Canadian Methodist academies and seminaries. It seems that in the Canadian case, Latin was taught at some seminaries and that names depended on the desire of the school's owners to be associated with a higher level of learning. As Anna Sonser's work on the Wesleyan Ladies' College of Hamilton shows, careful study of the curriculum, based on comparison with other schools of the time, gives a better sense of the innovative and traditional elements of women's education. Similarly, James McLachlan's model for American boys' schools and their preferred location in rural settings does not apply to Ontario Methodist education. Methodists in the province largely sought the culture and civilization represented by towns such as Cobourg, St Thomas, and Hamilton, as well as Toronto. The towns that were chosen for colleges were healthy and pleasant, but close to railway lines and well able to offer that contact with good society which the larger centres boasted. The fear remained for Methodists that they would be thought uncivilized and uneducated, and so the search for culture and respectability was as important or more so than the quest for moral protection.

As Alison MacKinnon argues, the story of women's exclusion from and admission to the male university in the last quarter of the nineteenth century contains themes common to Australia, Canada, the United States, and Britain, themes that have been documented in recent years by historians of education in those countries.[1] Her work challenges researchers to explore the meaning of women's higher education by examining educational outcomes and the effect of the experiences on individual students. In Methodist women's education, glimpses of student and faculty life from surviving diaries and letters show the exhilaration of learning, the spiritual devotion to the educational ideal, and the difficulty of working under a male hierarchy. Mary Electa Adams's frustration with Principal Hare at the Ontario Ladies' College, Margaret Addison's interactions with the chancellor and board at Victoria, and Jane Van Norman's comments about her brother, the principal of the Burlington Ladies' Academy, reveal both the frustration and the strategies that women used to try to work within the management models which were allowed. Without permission to speak publicly or the chance to influence policy in their respective schools, these women educators were unrecognized experts in their field. Mrs Hurlburt of the Cobourg school apparently intended to write a monograph on women's education, but there is no evidence that such a work was ever published. Margaret Addison's personal papers are filled with historical notations on the history of women at Victoria, which perhaps were part of an unrealized goal to document that history in a monograph.

The women heads of colleges and residences were not entirely powerless in the face of male principals and administration; the very confidence acquired from years of teaching and first-hand experience gave them strength to resist policies they disagreed with or to institute changes they believed in. In many cases, they were far more experienced in the field of women's education than the board members or even the principals of the ladies' colleges. Adams, for example, worked out the curriculum for the Wesleyan Ladies' College in cooperation with leaders from the community. Margaret Addison stubbornly persisted with her ideal of a dean of women for Victoria until both the Committee of Management and the chancellor were brought around to her concept. Mrs Van Norman moved to New York and was a founding member of the Women's Educational Association, which studied the questions of women's education and raised money for colleges. The available records, though scant, do reveal that these women had a strong spiritual commitment to the cause of women's education, which gave them the strength to overcome frustrations caused by uncooperative male boards or authorities.

This study of Methodist education for women reveals changes as well as continuities in that education. Both the social life and the academic content, from the ladies' colleges to the dances finally allowed at Victoria in the 1920s, reveal the changing cultural context within which propriety and womanhood were defined. Major and minor rebellions, such as stealing the college bell, hiding in a closet, smoking, or attending public theatres or dances, pitted the will of college students against those who attempted to define morality and behaviour for them. As the rate of social change accelerated on campus in the twentieth century after the devastation of war and depression, the gap between college and university authority and student demands widened. Yet Victoria students were profoundly influenced by movements such as the Student Christian Movement that allowed coeducational socialization and often provided marriage partners in the process, as well as life work. Addison expressed concerns about the frantic social life and the lack of spiritual quiet in students' lives, but she did not lose her optimism that a spiritual and intellectual college life could be achieved for women students at Victoria.

One of the difficulties in assessing the difference between a college's claims and the actual schooling it offered is reflected in the different levels of education as a whole in both men's and women's colleges of the nineteenth century. Although the claims of colleges were at times inflated, the relatively low levels at both the men's and women's colleges make the precise definition of educational standards difficult to pinpoint. The mandate of some of the early colleges was broadly defined, as witnessed by the wide range in the ages of students at some schools. Many male and female schools had preparatory programs connected with them to help bring deficient students up to the college standard. Vassar found that its early students were not adequately prepared for college-level work, and the new college was forced to carry out preparatory work to bring students to the necessary levels.[2] L. Clark Seelye, former professor at Amherst, who became the president of Smith College in 1873, insisted that Smith have requirements similar to Amherst's, and he opposed the establishment of preparatory departments, such as those at Vassar and Wellesley, which he believed degraded the collegiate programs. Gidney and Millar observe that the University of Toronto in the 1850s lowered matriculation standards in classics to allow boys to make the transition from grammar schools to university.[3] The preparatory function was in most cases a transitional arrangement and was generally discontinued when students arrived at college with the necessary prerequisites. Victoria College discontinued the preparatory department for males in the 1860s, but in the previous decade this department had entirely overshadowed undergraduate work.[4]

Not only did the levels of academic preparation shift during the nineteenth century, but the classical liberal curriculum itself was redefined in some schools, with a resulting decline in classics and an increase in options. Yet in the United States, some women's colleges were reluctant to give up the classical curriculum.[5] Education at Victoria College and the University of Toronto by the 1880s offered the basics of a liberal education with the possibility of options, combining the goal of mental culture with vocationalism. In the province's secondary schools, Ryerson had balanced the traditional study of classics with the introduction of sciences and modern languages.[6] The calendar for Victoria University in 1893 shows that for most programs, students had to take pass Latin in at least their first year, and for some programs they had to take between two to four years of Latin. Greek was required for students in Oriental languages, but in other departments such as political science, they could substitute Greek with either French or German. In the departments of mathematics and sciences, students were advised to take either Latin or

Greek in their first year.[7] Women students at the University of Toronto received no special curricular accommodations and had the choice, as male students did, to concentrate more heavily on their honours subject in their third and fourth years.[8] As the Victoria University calendar of 1896–97 indicates, instruction was divided between the University of Toronto and the arts faculty of Victoria, a division that had been worked out in the process of federation in the 1880s. Victoria gave instruction in such subjects as Latin, Greek, ancient history, English, French, German, Oriental literature, ethics, and theology. The University of Toronto provided lectures in the sciences, modern history, mathematics, Italian, and Spanish.[9]

The exact level of nineteenth-century women's education prior to its standardization at the college level is thus difficult to evaluate. Yet the aspirations of women students and the nature of their studies and accomplishments, which were so practical for women, provide fruitful areas of investigation. The seriousness of higher education and the academic options, as well as the attempts to keep girls in school for entire school years or programs, rather than interrupt their education, and their contact with academic women and other students were all important features of advanced female education for the period. The liberal arts curriculum for many students offered opportunities to excel, as demonstrated by the women students who increasingly took prizes in languages and literature. Degrees in home economics from the School of Household Science and diplomas from the Margaret Eaton School continued a tradition of women's studies that had originated in the domestic science and elocution programs at the ladies' colleges. Creative endeavours in fine arts and music attracted many ladies' college and university students and formed another vital field within women's studies in the nineteenth and early twentieth centuries. Science, mathematics, and medicine were available at the University of Toronto to the small minority of women who pursued them. For students who attained diplomas and degrees, the possibilities for further education or employment opened new doors, providing them with options other than marrying or allowing them to find community with like-minded women. For those who followed more traditional paths, life after college offered opportunities for other types of work, volunteerism, club affiliation, or social reform. Despite the fragmented evidence, the difficulty of tracing students who changed their names, and the loss of records, glimpses of female accomplishments, friendships, and active alumnae organizations emerge.

The quest for female communities in educational settings, which has been so eloquently described by Martha Vicinus, Helen Horowitz, and Patricia Palmieri, applies in a lesser degree to Methodist women's education.[10] Although community was one aspect of the narrative, the full story was punctuated by loneliness and spiritual struggle. A frequent turnover of teaching staff at the colleges meant that friendships were difficult to maintain. For those who made a long-term career in education, such as Margaret Addison, Mary Electa Adams, or Ella Gardiner, struggles with health problems and loneliness filled their years. Their exemplary role as lady principals or deans did not necessarily leave them free to make friends with either students or faculty. Gardiner noted in her diary that she had attended John Street Presbyterian Church three times on one Sunday to hear a Dr Parsons preach.[11] The life of the spirit provided essential nourishment in an otherwise bleak situation.[12] School principals such as B.F. Austin, J.J. Hare, and Nathanael Burwash had family lives in addition to their college work, as well as public roles acknowledged by such rewards as honorary degrees; the lady principals, by contrast, lived much more restricted and unacknowledged lives. Adams was fortunate that her sister often taught at the same school as she did, allowing the sisters to establish a household of sorts, as well as many shared interests. But at the Ontario Ladies' College in 1880 she felt somewhat desolate, as she confided to her niece Helena Coleman. "I wish I could see your little room but more still, the occupants. I have such a hungering for some associations that are personal to myself, that it is almost painful at times. Whitby is truly for the most part, strangely incongenial. There is a dreadful lack of inspiration somehow – perhaps it is my own fault, still not altogether I am sure – if any body would say a pleasantly stimulating thing to me. I wish you and Arthur could be here: it would help mightily."[13]

The lady principals did not earn a great deal of money, nor were they independently wealthy. In 1886 Adams wrote to Helena that she needed to borrow money from Arthur Coleman to repay a debt of $250 plus half a year's interest. Later, in 1893, when she had retired to homestead in Alberta, she was very worried about money owed to her by the Ontario Ladies' College, and the following year she hired a lawyer to plead her case, since the Adams-Coleman ranch was experiencing financial difficulties.[14] Margaret Addison corresponded regularly with her sister Charlotte and also developed a friendship with Helena Coleman, with whom she had taught at the Ontario Ladies' College. Surrounded as these lady principals and deans were by women students and other faculty, there nevertheless was loneliness and despair, which each one struggled with in her own way. Community and fellowship no doubt flowered in the colleges and residences, but the very real pressures on the colleges for their very existence, the financial worries, the conflict and competition, and the lack of access to real power certainly undermined some of the positive aspects of college life.

The curriculum in the colleges mirrored changes in the expectations of a woman's life. The earliest academies took girls who might typically have had some advanced tutoring in the home but who would have stayed with their parents until they married and established their own households. Daughters of clergymen, farmers, mayors, and businessmen found their way to the various ladies' colleges or to Victoria because their parents had decided that their daughters' education was worth pursuing. Part of the motivation was undoubtedly a deeply felt desire to provide daughters with a Christian training. In many cases, sacrifices were necessary to send them to school, but sometimes farmers could pay in commodities instead of cash, or students such as Letitia Youmans could work as pupil-teachers to pay back their tuition. Even for those students who were fortunate to go to an academy or college, as well as for their teachers, family life could interrupt their studies and claim them back to help at home or to nurse relatives. Mary Electa Adams left a job to care for a sick mother. Margaret Addison, on the other hand, helped to care for her aged father while working full-time at Victoria. A strictly pragmatic interpretation of why parents educated their daughters – for their role in the family, for the accomplishments, or for wage labour possibilities – does not account for the parents' concern about the spiritual welfare of daughters and the sacrifices that they made to that end.[15]

One consistent theme that runs through the history of the ladies' colleges is the interference of the state in Methodist women's education. From casual comments by the inspector advising the Alma Ladies' College to restrict its teaching to the accomplishments to the gradual increase of power by provincial authorities through certification of teachers, matriculation examinations, and approved school programs, the state took the upper hand. As the ladies' colleges competed in an educational market against much cheaper options such as the public schools, they became more vulnerable to external controls. Without a wealthy clientele or the security of large endowments, the colleges increasingly had to heed directives from the government. The state intended to make women's education fit within the three-tier model that had been imposed with seeming success on men's education. With efficiency as its goal, the Ontario Department of Education gradually but relentlessly eliminated the diverse structures that had existed for women's education and in the process made employment impossible for teachers who did not meet provincial standards, regardless of their experience or ability.[16] Although debates on the merits of coeducation continued well into the twentieth century, many parents simply chose to send girls to school with their brothers. This choice too was linked to greater efficiency and economy. At the university level, many women saw the opening up of the curriculum to women in coeducational settings as a great achievement. However, the proposal of a separate college for women at the University of Toronto in 1909 shows that for men the presence of women on campus was still unsettling. For university women, a separate college was initially appealing because they hoped that it might allow women to have autonomy over their own education, but the reality of scarce resources quickly made them realize that their education would likely be marginalized and considered second-class.

When Victoria College readmitted women in the 1880s, they followed a curriculum that offered an education equal to that of the male students. Yet the establishment of the schools of domestic science and expression and the debate over Wrong Report for a separate college reflected the continuing ambivalence about the place of women in a common and equal curriculum with men. The academic, and later the residence, life at Victoria gave women a space that for some was a "realm of pure delight" in which they could have social contacts with each other as well as with college alumnae. The residence hosted speakers from many different countries and organizations, bringing the larger world into the small sphere of Annesley Hall. Yet the coexistence at Victoria of male and female students was at times uneasy, partly because of the increased numbers of women students and their academic success.

Today, the women's residences of Annesley Hall and Addison Hall remain as tributes to the work of the Victoria Women's Educational and Residence Association, but Wymilwood, the gracious mansion donated for the use of women students, is almost unrecognizable in its present guise as a centre for all students. The Lillian Massey School of Household Science, which was a creative attempt to offer education to women largely administered and taught by women, has been appropriated for government purposes, and the financial consequences, as well as the human costs of the closure, have yet to be critically examined. Similarly, the Margaret Eaton School of Literature and Expression, another experiment in education largely directed by women for women, did not fit within the tertiary model imposed by state bureaucracy and it too eventually closed.[17]

Although some of the ladies' college organizers thought that endowments would be the key to their success, the struggles of

Margaret Addison to make changes in her position show that money or even a well-organized women's Committee of Management did not always make a difference when the balance of power was ultimately in the hands of male boards and chancellors. Within these dominant structures, Addison did not pursue an academic career, nor did she acquire a doctorate, with the consequence that in the academic hierarchy, her qualifications would never be considered equal to the professors at Victoria, and her teaching was not worth remuneration. Although her conception of a more powerful dean of women was likely inspired by some of the principals she had met, such as those of Wellesley College or St Hugh's, Oxford, her position remained that of a mother responsible for her children, but waiting patiently to be given household money by a capricious husband.

The definition of a girl, young woman, and woman underwent changes during the years between the 1830s and 1925. The change in terminology from females to ladies to women reflected evolution in the roles that women were to play. As the interval between the girl's life as a daughter in her parents' home and a wife in her own was extended by the experience at school, new terms were needed to describe this phase. David Allmendinger's study of Mount Holyoke students reveals that the college experience altered the life cycles of students by inserting several years of education between maturity and marriage.[18] Although more study is needed, one can infer that Canadian women who studied for a year or more also extended the time between leaving their parents' home and marriage, just as Letitia Youmans did by attending the Burlington Ladies' Academy and then teaching for two years before she married. The college years also prepared some women to fulfil their lives outside marriage.

Historian Lynn Gordon notes that the nineteenth-century academies proved women's intellectual abilities, maintained the "rhetorical connections between domesticity and schooling, and trained some young women to support themselves."[19] From the female seminaries to the college woman, shifts and transformations in the ideology and rhetoric derived from the "cult of true womanhood." The ideology of separate spheres continued to influence the debate concerning the purpose of women's education, the advisability of coeducation, the special nature of women, and their place in the divine design. These shifts in ideology found expression in the residential arrangements for women, the clothes they were expected to wear, the organization of meals, study hours, and social life, the pursuit of sport, clubs, and college leadership, the amount of vocational counselling, the types of female principals or deans, the diet, and the medical care. Additional information about women's education and health has recently been provided by Wendy Mitchinson, who demonstrates how physicians argued against higher education exactly at the time when increasing numbers of Canadian women were entering the university.[20] Medical arguments against higher education claimed that it would unsex women. Supporters of women's education tended to employ the ideology of women's physical or even mental weakness, occasionally as a strategy to disarm critics, but also in some cases because they believed in the weakness of women. Whether the supporters of women's education believed in this argument or just used it for their own purposes, the fact remains that the health of college students was vitally important and required constant vigilance and appropriate programs of rest and exercise.[21] The residence movement at Victoria was clearly concerned not only with a pure moral and spiritual community, but also with a healthier environment for young women. The presence of a professional dietitian, gymnastics, curfews, and prescribed sports can be viewed as part of this healthful environment.

In the United States, conservatives argued that higher education would destroy women's desire to stay in the home, and liberals claimed that colleges would produce better wives and mothers. Despite this rhetoric, Gordon notes that women "made the decision for higher education independently, often in opposition to the rhetoric around them, and many did not define their purposes in terms of domesticity."[22] In Ontario there were a variety of opinions concerning the proper form of education for women. One school of thought supported separate education for males and females, with clearly separate goals in mind. Another group argued for the same education for males and females but with ultimately separate goals. Finally, the most radical vision and most rare was of the same or equal education with similar goals, a view that meant a complete rejection of separate spheres. These three characterizations can be seen throughout this study as informing the rhetoric about women's education. Even in the case of Thomas Webster, the argument for equality of education still assumed the gendered nature of its final goal.

From the domestic orientation of the cult of true womanhood to the reform- and society-minded consciousness of the woman's movement of the mid to late nineteenth and the early twentieth centuries, this book has explored the role of ideology in shaping women's education. It has used the example of Methodist education for women in Ontario as an expression of an ideal Christian girl, who, with the help of education, would develop into Christian womanhood. The emphasis on refinement and on a chaperoned and cultured environment in the colleges made "ladies" an appropriate descriptor.

"Female" and "ladies" were used interchangeably in the early to mid-nineteenth century for respectable middle-class women. When women attended university and had new freedoms, "ladies" no longer seemed appropriate. The change in terminology from "females" to "ladies" to "women" reflected changes in the roles that women were to play. As one writer in a University of Toronto student publication argued, the terms "boy" and "girl" connote a state in which the concerns of the individual are regulated for him or her. Even at a private school or high school, the writer claimed, a girl has her lessons mapped out, and her home life is supervised by a governess. By contrast, an undergraduate has to plan her study and her life in an unsupervised boarding-house. University life, the writer concluded, would not fully benefit an individual who was denied status as a man or a woman.[23]

A family provided the ideal environment for a young woman. The early academies, seminaries, and ladies' colleges were organized on a familial model with power concentrated in a father-principal supported by women teachers and a governess who provided a motherly influence. Education, it was suggested, was sometimes better left to the experts, who would provide the daughter with a family setting but with increased options for other experiences and exposures. Rarely did the college brochures explain why the school could do a better job of raising a child than the nuclear family, but it was understood that the school could administer a more even discipline in a solid Christian environment. Implied in these suggestions was the idea that the relationship between daughters and mothers could become problematic. As Miss Moberly, the principal of St Hugh's College, commented to Margaret Addison in 1900, mothers sometimes treated their daughters like servants. The experience in the adopted family of the ladies' college would return the girl better prepared to take up her duties in the home, using her education to exert a beneficial influence on the other children. One writer in the *Canada Christian Advocate* in 1852 asked, "How often has the education of an elder daughter educated all the younger children, sent a brother to college, and raised the whole household from obscurity to the highest position in society?"[24] With an education, the daughter could take wings and fly away because as an accomplished instructor, she could "retrieve all her losses."[25]

It is difficult to estimate how many parents made the educational choice for their daughters on the basis of pragmatic hopes that they would be qualified wage earners, but the evidence of graduates shows that different vocations in teaching, business, domestic science, elocution, commercial arts, and music were pursued through

Methodist education for women. Helena Coleman studied music at the Ontario Ladies' College with "a view to earn something as a music teacher," a vocation her family considered particularly appropriate in her case because she had been afflicted with polio at the age of eleven.[26] The colleges must be considered, not only in relation to the curriculum and the student life, but also for their functions in teacher training and employment. An early study of the role of the academies, seminaries, and women's colleges in the United States pointed out the schools' important role in offering this training to women of various class backgrounds at a time when women's abilities as teachers were gaining acceptance.[27]

The family model that functioned in the ladies' seminaries and colleges did not apply as readily once women were admitted to Victoria College. Still, the defenders of women's university privileges argued that there should be no opposition between university life and home life. Women were not made unfit for the domestic sphere by university life, and their health and morals were not undermined by the experience. Principal Hutton of University College was quoted in the *Christian Guardian* in support of a residence for Methodist students. Where is the parent, he argued, "who has not scruples manifold in launching his daughter on the tender mercies of the casual boarding house?" The university was not responsible for the "deadly follies of fashion, the deadly tyranny of society, the craze about so-called social duties and dress." The home and the university fought together as allies against these social trends.[28] The residence was intended at least to duplicate family supervision for women students. Even the women supporters of the residence were somewhat divided about the amount of liberty students should have. Clearly, the question of supervision was only partly related to propriety, with a more implicit agenda being the curbing of the autonomy of women students. Despite restraints, the image of the educated woman became associated with liberal thinking and with a breakdown in social norms. No longer the moral authority of the nineteenth century, this New Woman was a threat to men, the family, and the continuance of the human race. A conservative backlash that combined appeals to the weak biology of women and their recast sinful nature would gradually undermine many of the gains their education had effected.

Once the university residence for women was established at Victoria, students were supervised by the dean of residence. College women ultimately no longer felt the need for the family model that had governed relations at the ladies' colleges. The greater maturity of college students required self-government and influence by example.

The first years of Annesley Hall were thus marked by frequent interaction and involvement of alumnae and other older women in the activities of students. By the 1920s, however, a women students' council and the residences council would provide a form of self-government, at least for the women's residences at Victoria, although struggles for genuine autonomy continued, particularly in the face of a persistent patriarchal authority structure.

The creation of a women's culture at Victoria required the attainment of scholastic excellence, as well as the development of extracurricular activities, such as clubs, that would contribute to a greater sense of belonging and the forging of an identity as college women. Part of the resulting culture was separate from male activity on campus, and part became a shared college life, as men allowed women to take part in their societies or new clubs were created. The residence movement at Victoria was a key factor in the creation of mental and physical space for women at the university. Although the residence operated under the eye of the chancellor and Senate, nevertheless it was initiated, sponsored, and administered on a daily basis by the women members of the Victoria Women's Residence and Educational Association.

The story of Methodist women's education in Ontario has a continuity that until now has not been fully recognized. The degree of cohesion can only be seen in a study that surveys almost one hundred years of education and includes both ladies' college students and university women. The traditions established by pioneers such as Mrs Van Norman, Mrs Hurlburt, and Mary Electa Adams were continued by such women as Margaret Proctor Burwash and Margaret Addison, both of whom were students or teachers at the ladies' colleges and later took leadership roles in the university. Schools that might be considered failures because of their brief existence, such as the Dundas Female College or the Burlington Ladies' Academy, contributed enormously to shaping the notion of education for women in parents' and students' minds. Often as one school closed, some of its teachers and former students would move on to teach in other schools or open new ones. The ideal of women's education, which was discussed in the church and secular press and no doubt found its way into formal and informal discussions at church meetings and around supper tables, caught the popular imagination. It created a desire among parents that their daughters might be instructed in a Christian manner, in order that they would prove worthy of their role in the Christian family and at the same time gain an education that might enable them to earn a living if necessary.

In the examination of almost ninety years of women's education, several features of the Methodist educational mission emerge. The female seminaries and ladies' colleges offered a tremendous flowering of creativity in education, an experiment that drew many dedicated individuals to them. The fact that these schools were often more expensive to run than anticipated does not diminish the accomplishments of those who fought for their recognition and funding. In the case of Alma College and the Ontario Ladies' College, the buildings stand as reminders of the Victorian ideals of graciousness and grandeur, anachronisms in an age in which other values would gradually replace the moral sweetness of a woman dedicated to the family and its needs alone. Part of the mission of Methodist education was to provide a broadly Christian environment for women. Religious activity and revivals at these colleges were frequent, especially in these early years. Various clubs, such as missionary and temperance societies, flourished as a result of this spiritual fervour. One minister claimed in 1901 that the best way to keep female members bright and cheery was to put them diligently to work in the church.[29] Ladies' college education prepared women for this work by teaching them how to organize in clubs, speak publicly, produce a magazine, and write opinion columns. However, although one aspect of Methodist education was a tremendous enthusiasm to innovate, create new schools, and to develop programs, there was a tension as well. The Methodist educational organizers were ambivalent about the ends of this education. Once the girls were educated, the denomination and society did not allow them the freedom to exercise what they had learned. There was no attempt to make room at the top, and the frustrations of women educators such as Adams and Addison reveal the limitations placed on their power. The ultimate power in the family, school, and church remained male, and education did not change this fact.

The belief that womanly nature could be adorned by education gained acceptance. In a sermon preached at Alma College, Albert Carman reminded the audience that "our daughters may be as cornerstones, polished after the similitude of a palace," and he argued, to have this effect, education had to be thorough and sound.[30] Although some claimed that this educational polishing required a study of exactly the same subjects as male students studied, others argued for a separate curriculum. Special methods and training were required to help women achieve a Christian and womanly maturity. Woman's nature and training placed her in a unique relationship to the transcendent, a connection that was potentially empowering. This relationship to the transcendent, which had initially justified women's removal from the public sphere, resulted in women's action in the public realm by the end of the nineteenth century and the beginning of twentieth.

The extent to which women challenged the gender roles that had traditionally limited their sphere of action can be studied through the lens of education. The major assumptions about their nature that were questioned in the nineteenth century were the ideas that there were "natural" feminine and masculine values which had been ordained in creation and that God had ordained that men would rule and women would submit. Part of the freedom to challenge the male hierarchy and superiority derived from a shift in the nineteenth century from received authority to individual experience, which allowed many women to claim their own experience as an authoritative base for social critique. This included their educational experiences. Women graduates – as teachers, novelists, journalists, and social activists – spoke from a small platform that their own authority gave them, and these were voices that had been previously marginalized from any public realm. Their knowledge and their authority were derived from their education, as well as from the concrete conditions of the real world and of human needs. Thus women challenged religion from the perspective of the concrete and practical, as opposed to the theological and abstract.[31]

Women were assured of an important place in the kingdom of God, and their earthly life and education were intended to prepare them for that place. The emphasis on the need for usefulness in education, as opposed to ornamentals and shallow accomplishments, was tied to this perception of preparing women for the kingdom of God. The attainment of mental discipline, or thoroughness in study, was intended to help women to think. As Leonard Sweet has argued for the United States, the female seminaries and ladies' colleges increasingly fostered a notion of femininity that stood independent of the separate spheres underlining it and led to a gradual acceptance of the intellectual equality that would result from a good education.[32]

Although participants and graduates of ladies' colleges had options that led to wage labour opportunities, persistent structural inequalities meant that their education would be considered special, that is, not equal. But even though inequalities persisted, the world into which the ladies' college graduate moved offered new opportunities. A shift connected with the social-gospel movement meant that many Christians came to view the kingdom of God as something that could be realized by working towards improvements on earth.[33] Women, whose special qualities and education had prepared them for a place in the heavenly kingdom, were now in a prime position to lead the front lines in the reclaiming of the earth as the Lord's. This movement would require a woman with the vehemence of a mother lion and the refinement of a well-bred lady, who could speak and act in the public sphere and not offend propriety.

One model for this contradictory ideal was Frances Willard, who dazzled audiences throughout North America in her temperance advocacy.[34] Another may have been Mary Electa Adams or, in the twentieth century, Margaret Addison. Addison reveals the delicate balance that was needed in a letter in which she observed that women were in a transition stage "of the woman question, waging war against the very old notions, yet with a certain conservatism in our hearts, finding it difficult not to be aggressive and still to be aggressive enough, not to offend, and also to be brave enough to step out of the beaten track because it is to the interest of the world we should."[35]

In addition to teaching, both missionary work overseas and activity in organizations such as the Student Volunteer Movement, the Student Christian Movement, and the YWCA were fields in which the college graduate could use all her skills for social improvement. Graduates of Victoria College, among them Rose Cullen, Maud Edgar, and Mabel Jamieson, attained national leadership positions in these voluntary organizations. The involvement of Margaret Addison in student conferences and international student organizations no doubt created a climate in which students were encouraged to do the same, just as the presence of Ella Gardiner at Albert College encouraged numerous graduates to undertake mission work. Addison kept tract of women graduates of Victoria College up to the class of 1921, and out of a total of 568 graduates, 268 had married, 134 were employed in education, and 35 had entered business. Thirty-five were single women at home, and there were 12 in libraries, 7 dietitians, 5 nurses, 4 lawyers, 3 farmers, 2 doctors, 2 in literature, 2 in research, 1 in settlement work, 1 doing camp work, 1 in the Student Christian Movement, and 2 in industrial work. Finally, there were 28 whose occupations were unknown, and 26 had died.[36] The diversity of occupations, as well as the number who chose marriage, reveals that graduates followed both traditional and non-traditional career paths. Although Addison does not list missionary work as a separate category, a significant number of women went overseas as missionaries or as the wives of missionaries.

Ladies' college students, as well as the first two generations of women at Victoria University, were no doubt marked by their experience of the grand halls, the fervent religious atmosphere, and the encouragement to discipline their minds and spirits. Although many of the founders of this educational movement may have visualized a controlled and consecrated womanhood, working from within the family and casting an influence in subtle ways, a small poem in the Alma College school paper revealed a somewhat more radical view of women's reality:

They talk about a woman's sphere
As though it had a limit …
There's not a place in earth or heaven,
There's not a task to mankind given,
That has a feather's weight of worth
Without a woman in it.[37]

Appendix One

SOME VICTORIA WOMEN STUDENTS ENROLLED IN 1899

BAKER, EMMA S. Studied abroad before joining the class of 1899 in the honours philosophy course and served as president of the YWCA and vice-president of the Philosophical Society.

CHOWN, SUSIE Completed her preparatory training at Whitby, took her first year at Queen's, and later completed the general course at Victoria.

DUCKETT, EDITH Of American origin, she attended the Ontario Ladies' College and graduated in honours moderns.

GOULD, ETHEL Matriculated from Colborne High School and entered Victoria with the class of 1898. She interrupted her education for a year and graduated from the general course with theological options and honours English.

HENWOOD, ALICE Graduated from Port Hope High School and entered Victoria in 1895 in the general course. She later attended the Normal School in Hamilton.

KYLE, MARGARET Attended Harbord Collegiate Institute in Toronto and completed the general course at Victoria. She was in the Tennis Club and served as president of the Women's Literary Society.

McKEE, KATHARINE Took the general course.

REYNAR, MARIANNE Daughter of Professor A.H. Reynar of Victoria. Graduated from Cobourg Collegiate Institute and took honours moderns at Victoria. She then attended the Normal School in Hamilton.

TAYLOR, LILY Graduated from Moulton College, entered University College, and dropped out after two years because of ill health. Subsequently she transferred to Victoria College and graduated from the general course. She later attended the Normal School in Hamilton.

Appendix Two

WOMEN'S RESIDENCES AT VICTORIA, 1903–1925

1903–present	Annesley Hall, Queen's Park Crescent
1906–17	South Hall, 75 Queen's Park Crescent
1917–20	South Hall, converted into student union
1920–21	South Hall reverted to a residence
1912–14	97 Bloor Street West
1914–27	The Annex, 81 Charles Street West
1918–?	Oaklawn, 113 Bloor Street West
1922–27	The Annex, 79 Charles Street West
1926–present	Wymilwood, Charles Street
1959–present	Addison Hall, Charles Street

Notes

ABBREVIATIONS

AO Archives of Ontario
AV *Acta Victoriana*
CCA *Canada Christian Advocate*
CG *Christian Guardian*
HPL Hamilton Public Library
UCA United Church Archives, Toronto
UTA University of Toronto Archives
VULA Victoria University Library Archives
WHSA Whitby Historical Society Archives

INTRODUCTION

1 Although the modern term "women" is used here, this study will attempt to follow the usage of the times. The early schools in Upper Canada frequently referred to young adolescent women as females, an expression later replaced by "young ladies"; they would eventually become ladies, a combination of physical maturation and emotional development.

2 McKillop, *Matters of Mind*, 84–5. For an excellent survey of the relationship between higher education and Christianity, see Marsden and Longfield, *The Secularization of the Academy.* On American higher education, see Marsden, *The Soul of the American University.*

3 Marshall, *Secularizing the Faith*, 10.

4 Tyack and Hansot, *Learning Together*, 143.
5 See Noll et al., *Evangelicalism.*
6 Westfall, *Two Worlds*, 80.
7 On the relationship between Romanticism and the conscience, see Cranston, *The Romantic Movement*; Reardon, *Religion in the Age of Romanticism*; Welch, *Protestant Thought in the Nineteenth Century*, 1: 52–5.
8 Marshall, *Secularizing the Faith*, 69.
9 Allen, *The Social Passion*, 4.
10 Valverde, *The Age of Light, Soap, and Water*, 17–18.
11 Bordin, *Women and Temperance*, notes that the temperance movement was ecumenical from the beginning.
12 Hewitt, *Women's Activism and Social Class.*
13 Davidoff and Hall, *Family Fortunes.*
14 A.F. Scott, *Natural Allies.*
15 Bendroth, *Fundamentalism and Gender.* See also Hill, *The World Their Household*, for a discussion of how the twentieth-century merger of women's missionary societies with denominational boards effectively reduced women's power as well as their visibility in management positions in mission administration. The opening up of women's ordination in several Protestant denominations seems to allow a minority of exceptional women to gain access to the profession of the ministry, but one may question to what extent this opening up is accompanied by a more conservative gender- and family-oriented ideology for the majority. See, for example, Prelinger, *Episcopal Women*, for a critical examination of women's changing involvement in the Episcopal Church. Although women had flocked to religious training schools and often outnumbered male students, by 1930 schools such as Massachusetts's Gordon Bible College voted to restrict women to one-third of the student body. In this regard, see Brereton, *Training God's Army.* This policy, argues Bendroth, was a clear reversal and effectively reduced women students to the extent that in the 1950s, the Gordon campus was entirely male. The post – World War II idealization of the private realm and women's call to serve it exclusively undermined the achievements of earlier decades. See Bendroth, *Fundamentalism and Gender*, especially chapter 5. I plan to examine the contradictions of twentieth-century gender ideology in the religious context in a forthcoming study of the World's Student Christian Federation and the Student Christian Movement of Canada.
16 McKillop, *Matters of Mind*, 96.
17 For an analysis of women's economic opportunities, see Strong-Boag, *The New Day Recalled*, 41–71.
18 Prentice et al., *Canadian Women*, 141.

19 Hill, *The World Their Household*, 14.

20 The history of women at the University of Toronto is documented in Ford, *A Path Not Strewn with Roses.*

21 McKillop, *Matters of Mind*, 128.

22 Sonser, "'A Respectable English Education,'" 88.

23 Strong-Boag notes that in 1920, 81.62 per cent of Canada women enrolled in arts and sciences, compared to 48.84 per cent of males. Traditional fields such as education, nursing, and household science claimed women university students. There was a significant decline in the percentage of women in male-dominated fields such as medicine and law, as well as in religion and theology, between 1920 and 1940. See *The New Day Recalled*, 21–2.

24 Curtis, *True Government by Choice Men?* 175.

25 Prentice, *The School Promoters*.

26 Purvis, *Hard Lessons*, 48–62. Purvis defines a woman as a female over fourteen years of age.

27 Prentice, *The School Promoters*, 68.

28 Smith-Rosenberg, *Disorderly Conduct.*

29 Lerner, *The Creation of Feminist Consciousness.*

30 Ibid., 216.

31 School histories provide a useful starting-point for further analysis. Two histories of Alma College were used, one by the Reverend Wesley Edwards, *The History of Alma College*, and the other edited by Katharine Riddell, *Alma College Centennial Book, 1877–1977*. Albert College's history has been written by Waldo Smith in *Albert College, 1857–1957*, and is currently being rewritten by Arie Kortrijk of Albert College. The history of the Ontario Ladies' College has been described by Brian Winter in *Vox Collegii Centennial, 1874–1974*. Marion V. Royce provided the groundwork on the Methodist education for women, especially the Wesleyan Ladies' College, in her article "Methodism and the Education of Women in Nineteenth Century Ontario."

32 See Victoria University Dean of Women Records, 87.073V, UCA, which contain information on women who graduated from Victoria between 1884 and 1964 whose surnames begin with the letters A–M. The rest is lost.

33 Conversation with archivist Ruth Dyck Wilson, United Church Archives, June 1991.

34 The fragment of the diary that remains is held at the archives of Mount Allison University, Sackville, NB.

CHAPTER ONE

1 "Obituary, Rebecca Hurlburt," CG, 11 June 1890.

2 Student Register # 2, 1837–42 (Names of Female Students Boarding in Upper Canada Academy), Victoria University Registrar's Office, 87.143, UCA. A total of thirty-one women were registered in 1839–40, but not all their ages were noted. Hurlburt's classmates came from Cobourg, Cramhe, Amherstburg, Kingston, Pickering, Trafalgar, Indiana, St Thomas, Brockville, Ontonibee, Hallowell (Picton), Humber, Longueil, Ottawa, Niagara, Rice Lake, and Hope.

3 "Upper Canada Academy," CG, 29 June 1836.

4 Ibid., 1 June 1836.

5 Maria Boulter's salary in 1839 was £62 10s. per annum, and the assistant female teacher received £50. See Minutes, Committee of Management, 17 July 1839, Upper Canada Academy, 87.040, UCA. In 1840 the case of Boulter's sister was considered, and it was decided that she be charged the usual fee for board, but no charge was levied for tuition since she did not receive her lessons in school hours. Her case was an exception, "she being a sickly sister." See Committee of Management, 17 Aug. 1840, Upper Canada Academy, UCA.

6 Burwash, *History of Victoria College*, 56. He noted that two of the most pre-eminent students of the female department of the Upper Canada Academy were Mary Electa Adams and Letitia Youmans. Houston and Prentice found a different total: of 62 female students in 1840 out of a total of 134. See Houston and Prentice, *Schooling and Scholars*, 323.

7 See, for example, Masters, *Protestant Church Colleges in Canada*; Hodgins, *The Establishment of Schools and Colleges in Ontario, 1792–1920*; Sissons, *A History of Victoria University*; Johnston, *McMaster University, vol. 1*.

8 Some notable exceptions include the pioneering work of Marion V. Royce in "Methodism and the Education of Women in Nineteenth Century Ontario" and "Education for Girls in Quaker Schools in Ontario." See also Bennett, "Little Worlds"; Davey, "Trends in Female School Attendance in Mid-Nineteenth Century Ontario"; Houston and Prentice, *Schooling and Scholars in Nineteenth-Century Ontario*; Moorcroft, "Character Builders: Women and Education in Whitby, Ontario, 1900–1920"; Prentice, "Scholarly Passion and Two Persons Who Caught It"; Rousmaniere, "To Prepare the Ideal Woman." A significant contribution to the history of Catholic women's education was made by Elizabeth M. Smyth in "The Lessons of Religion and Science." For Catholic education in Quebec, see Danylewycz, *Taking the Veil*; Dumont and Fahmy-Eid, *Les Couventines*.

9 Houston and Prentice, *Schooling and Scholars*, 41. See also La Pierre, "The Academic Life of Canadian Coeds, 1880–1900."

10 For the Atlantic provinces, see Reid, "The Education of Women at Mount Allison, 1854–1914." On grammar schools, see Royce,

"Arguments over the Education of Girls." On secondary schools, see Ketchum, "The Most Perfect System"; Gidney and Millar, *Inventing Secondary Education*; Gray, "Continuity in Change." On university education, see Ronish, "Sweet Girl Graduates"; Gillett and Sibbald, *A Fair Shake*; Marks and Gaffield, "Women at Queen's University, 1895–1905"; Stewart, *"It's Up to You."* For a study of the Methodist Women's Missionary Society, see Gagan, *A Sensitive Independence.*

11 Gauvreau, *The Evangelical Century*, and Van Die, *An Evangelical Mind*, have begun this analysis. See also Airhart, *Serving the Present Age.*

12 Van Die, *An Evangelical Mind*, 8.

13 Gauvreau, *The Evangelical Century*, 7–8.

14 Marshall, *Secularizing the Faith*, 25–30.

15 Ibid., 33.

16 McKillop, *Matters of Mind*, 89–90.

17 CG, 11 May 1836.

18 See, for example, Nathanael Burwash, who claimed that when "in the far future the developed history of our land and of other lands has rendered its impartial verdict, we believe that it will be seen then that in taking her present place she [Victoria College] did not miss the greatest things in the work of human progress." *History of Victoria College*, 441.

19 On the relationship between power, gender, and history, see J.W. Scott, *Gender and the Politics of History.* On the reproduction of élites, see Delamont, *Knowledgeable Women.*

20 Francis and Smith, *Readings in Canadian History Pre-Confederation*, 256; Prentice et al, *Canadian Women*, 21–2; French, *Parsons and Politics*, 39–43; Grant, *The Church in the Canadian Era*, vol. 3, chapter 1.

21 Jean Burnet, "Occupational Differences and the Class Structure," in *Readings in Canadian History*, ed. Francis and Smith, 257–67.

22 Ibid., 259.

23 Jacques Monet, "The 1840's," in *Readings in Canadian History*, ed. Francis and Smith, 287–305.

24 John McCallum, "Urban and Commercial Development until 1850," in *Readings in Canadian History*, ed. Francis and smith, 365–83.

25 Masters, *Protestant Church Colleges in Canada*, 36.

26 Grant, *The Church in the Canadian Era*, 6.

27 Sissons, *A History of Victoria University*, 9.

28 French, *Parsons and Politics*, chapter 6.

29 Ibid.

30 Burwash, *History of Victoria College*, 187.

31 Grant, *The Church in the Canadian Era*, 40–1.

32 Muir, "Methodist Women Preachers," and *Petticoats in the Pulpit.*

33 Krommenhoek, "The Church Should Have Championed the Woman's Cause," 152.

34 MacFarlane, "Educating, Sanctifying, and Regulating Motherhood."
35 Smith, *Albert College, 1857–1957*, chapter 2.
36 "The Seminary Board," CCA, 15 Aug. 1855.
37 Minutes, Building Committee, 1831, Upper Canada Academy/ Victoria College, Cobourg, 87.040, UCA.
38 Mrs Smith was hired at a salary of £75 per annum plus the tuition of her children and residence in the academy, with the understanding that she provide her own furniture, wood, and provisions. See Minutes, Building Committee, 20 June 1836, Upper Canada Academy, UCA.
39 CG, 27 Dec. 1837.
40 Minutes, Management Committee, Oct. 1837, Upper Canada Academy, UCA.
41 CG, 27 April 1842.
42 Tyack and Hansot, *Learning Together*, 121.
43 Houston and Prentice, *Schooling and Scholars*, 78.
44 CG, 26 Dec. 1849.
45 Theobald, "Women's Studies in Colonial Victoria."
46 Theobald, "The Sin of Laura."
47 Grumet, *Bitter Milk*, 43.
48 Theobald, "The Sin of Laura," 268.
49 See Houston and Prentice, *Schooling and Scholars*, 42–3.
50 Gidney and Millar, *Inventing Secondary Schools*, 31.
51 Gauvreau, *The Evangelical Century*, 8.
52 Gidney and Millar, *Inventing Secondary Education*, 199.
53 Taylor, *Before Vassar Opened*, 279. The first class at Vassar contained seven girls from British North America.
54 Gidney and Millar, *Inventing Secondary Education*, 270.
55 See Curtis, *True Government by Choice Men?*
56 See, for example, Gidney and Millar, *Inventing Secondary Education*, 163, on Ryerson's attempt to establish high English and classical schools in the 1860s that would have excluded girls from classics and in effect become male preserves. See also Prentice, *The School Promoters*, 111. Parents were not moved by the decrees of the education department and had no intention of taking their daughters out of the local grammar school. See Houston and Prentice, *Schooling and Scholars*, 322.
57 Gidney and Millar, *Inventing Secondary Education*, 271–2.
58 Ibronyi, *Early Voices*.
59 Ibid., 4.
60 Nellie Greenwood, "Victoria Is My College," Typescript, Nellie Greenwood Personal Papers, box 1, UCA.
61 Ford, *A Path Not Strewn with Roses*, 27.
62 Ibronyi, *Early Voices*, 7.

CHAPTER TWO

1 *CG*, 5 June 1830.
2 See Cazenovia Seminary, *First Fifty Years*. See also a list compiled by J.W. Lamb, "Lady Students at Cazenovia Seminary from Upper Canada," 1983, UCA.
3 See Webster, *Woman Man's Equal*.
4 I am grateful to Mary O'Brien of Syracuse University Archives for providing this information. Apparently, the first female student from British North America at the college was Martha L. Allison of Saint John, New Brunswick. As John Reid indicates in "The Education of Women," she played an important role at Mount Allison as preceptress. She was also the first woman to become a professor at that institution and eventually held the position of professor of natural sciences and ancient and modern Languages.
5 *CCA*, 30 June 1852. The school was under the patronage and control of the Methodist Episcopal Church. In 1852 there were 131 male students and 92 female students. Two years later the school was renamed the Baldwin Institute.
6 *CCA*, 16 Feb. 1853.
7 Houston and Prentice, *Schooling and Scholars*, 42.
8 Genesee Wesleyan Seminary, *Catalogue of the Officers and Students*, Syracuse University Archives. See also Theobald, "'Mere Accomplishments?'"
9 Costs for the education per quarter were $5 for tuition, $5 for music, $1.50 for drawing and painting, $1.50 for board, washing, light, and fuel per week, and $1.50 for room rent per quarter.
10 Genesee Wesleyan Seminary, *Catalogue of the Officers and Students*.
11 Houston and Prentice, *Schooling and Scholars*, 34.
12 Ibid., 41. See also Davey, "Trends in Female School Attendance."
13 Houston and Prentice, *Schooling and Scholars*, 42. The other distinguishing features of academies and seminaries was their organization with one or more teachers and the possibility of financial assistance from church, state, or educational corporation.
14 Reid, "The Education of Women," 6. See also Moody, "Breadth of Vision," 3–31.
15 Masters, *Protestant Church Colleges in Canada*, 5. This interpretation is supported by Gidney and Millar, *Inventing Secondary Schools*, 31. See also French, *Parsons and Politics*, 211.
16 Egerton Ryerson to Lord Glenelg, Colonial Department, 13 Feb. 1836, Ryerson Papers, box 1, 17, UCA.
17 Ibid.
18 During the first decade of Cazenovia Seminary, five Native men from Upper Canada attended the college. They came from Grape Island, River Credit, and Lake Simcoe.

19 Ryerson to Lord Glenelg, 13 Feb. 1836, Ryerson Papers, box 1, 17, UCA.
20 See also Prentice, *School Promoters*, 71.
21 Masters, *Protestant Church Colleges in Canada*, 13–14.
22 Ibid., 11.
23 Prentice, *School Promoters*, 54.
24 CG, 25 Sept. 1830.
25 Building Committee, 20 June 1836, Upper Canada Academy, UCA.
26 Sissons, *A History of Victoria University*, 17. Ryerson saved the day by convincing the colonial secretary to instruct the lieutenant-governor, Sir Francis Bond Head, to advance £4,100 to the academy.
27 See Burwash, *History of Victoria College*, chapter 3, and Sissons, *A History of Victoria University*, chapter 1.
28 Burwash, *History of Victoria College*, 29.
29 Sissons names the Sturgis family as among these wealthy Quakers, but it is not clear if a member of this family is the person named by Burwash as Joseph Sturge. The appeals on behalf of Natives may have been a fruitful way to raise funds, but in reality only ten Natives were enrolled in the six years of the academy. See Sissons, *A History of Victoria University*, 33.
30 CG, 3 April 1831.
31 Ibid.
32 Ibid.; emphasis in original. See also Prentice, *School Promoters*, 50, for a discussion of how ignorance began to be associated with crime.
33 CG, 23 April 1831.
34 Masters, *Protestant Church Colleges in Canada*, 102; Van Die, *An Evangelical Mind*, 70.
35 Westfall, *Two Worlds*, especially chapter 3.
36 Ibid., 77.
37 Ibid., 78.
38 Cochrane, "The True Beauty of Womanhood," in *The Church and the Commonwealth*, 311–20. Cochrane (1831–98) was a Presbyterian minister who founded the Brantford Presbyterian Ladies' College in 1874 and served as its governor and lecturer in philosophy. For further information on him, see Grant, *Life of William Cochrane*.
39 Managing Committee, 20 June 1836, Upper Canada Academy, UCA.
40 According to Burwash, Ryerson's duties connected with the dissolution of Methodist union in 1840 made it impossible for him to fulfil his responsibilities at the academy.
41 Burwash, *History of Victoria College*, chapter 3.
42 Sissons, *A History of Victoria University*, 22–37.
43 Committee of Management, 3 Feb. 1841, Upper Canada Academy, UCA.
44 Van Norman apparently had an unusual relationship with the Conference. He did not want to take a circuit because his wife was opposed to itinerancy, and consequently the Conference accepted his member-

ship as a teacher in a connectional institution. See Sissons, *History of Victoria University*, 29.

45 Burwash, *History of Victoria College*, 58–63.

46 Burwash, *History of Victoria College*, 63; Sissons, *A History of Victoria University*, 30. Johann Heinrich Pestalozzi was born in Zurich in 1746 and became an influential educator. He applied Rousseau's ideas on education to groups of students and emphasized the importance of the home as an educational environment. The natural goodness of the world needed to be imprinted on the child in order that he or she also become naturally good. Another influential European educator was Emmanuel von Fellenberg, whose school, Hofwyl, in Switzerland was visited by numerous observers and was tremendously influential. One aspect of Hofwyl that was transposed to some North American schools was the emphasis on the cultivation of physical faculties through gymnastics, fencing, and swimming, as well as of the intellectual faculties. See McLachlan, *American Boarding Schools*, chapter 2.

47 Sissons, *A History of Victoria University*, 30.

48 Committee of Management, 3 Feb. 1841, Upper Canada Academy, 87.040, UCA.

49 *CG*, 16 Feb. 1842. Sissons, *A History of Victoria University*, 30.

50 Sissons, *A History of Victoria University*, 30.

51 J. Hurlburt, D. Van Norman, and Wm Kingston to E. Ryerson, 15 Nov. 1841, Ryerson Papers, box 2, 49, UCA.

52 *CG*, 16 Feb. 1842.

53 Sissons, *A History of Victoria University*, 30.

54 Sully Cow was a young Native girl who had been sent to the academy. Little is known about her experience there. Sissons states that "she found it difficult to adapt herself to the amenities of boarding school life: she, or rather her sponsor, stands charged with five shillings for breakages – 1/6 for a pane of glass, 1/6 for a looking glass, and 2/ for a pitcher." Another Native girl who came from the same mission was named Susan Sundy, and about her school experience nothing is recorded. Sissons, *A History of Victoria University*, 33.

55 Student Register #2, 1837–42, Victoria University Registrar's Office, 87.143, UCA.

56 J. Hurlburt to Ryerson, 24 Oct. 1840, Ryerson Papers, box 2, 43, UCA.

57 *CG*, 3 Nov. 1841.

58 Alison Prentice, "Education and the Metaphor of the Family: The Upper Canadian Example," in *Education and Social Change*, ed. Katz and Mattingly, 110–32.

59 *CG*, 27 April 1842.

60 J. Hurlburt to E. Ryerson, 11 Oct. 1841, Ryerson Papers, box 2, 47, UCA.

61 Ibid.

62 Ibid.
63 See Bryant, *The Unexpected Revolution*. On women in higher education, see Potts, "New England's Chilly Climate for Coeducation."
64 Potts, "New England's Chilly Climate for Coeducation," 4.
65 A clear description of Ryerson's ideal of college education can be found in his inaugural address, Burwash, *History of Victoria College*, appendix 2, 495–506. For the level of education in these early years at Victoria, see Gidney and Millar, *Inventing Secondary Schools*, 12.
66 "Cobourg Ladies' Academy," CCA, 23 Oct. 1845. Clergymen Thomas Alexander taught ecclesiastical history and evidences, Joseph Harris history and philosophy, and J. Hurlburt chemistry and natural philosophy.
67 CG, 30 Nov. 1842.
68 CG, 24 Aug. 1842.
69 Meeting of Financial Committee, 20 Jan. 1845, Victoria College, 87.040, UCA.
70 D.C. Van Norman and W. Kingston to E. Ryerson, 31 March 1841, Ryerson Papers, box 2, 45, UCA.
71 D.C. Van Norman to E. Ryerson, 2 May 1845, Ryerson Papers, box 3, 70, UCA.
72 Ibid.
73 Minutes, Board of Victoria College, 21 April 1842, UCA.
74 W. Kingston to Ryerson, n.d., Ryerson Papers, box 2, 52, UCA.
75 Sissons, *A History of Victoria University*, 47.
76 CG, 24 Aug. 1842.
77 CCA, 20 April 1847.
78 CCA, 23 Oct. 1845; CCA, 16 June 1846.
79 CCA, 20 April 1847.
80 CG, 30 Nov. 1842.
81 Ibid.
82 Cobourg Ladies' Seminary, *Annual Circular, 1845*, Higher Education for Women in Canadian Journals 70 (1869), Periodical DC, I, AO.
83 Sissons, *A History of Victoria University*, 63.
84 Cobourg Ladies' Seminary, *Annual Circular, 1845*.
85 Ibid.
86 *Van Norman Institute*, 26–7.
87 Ibid.
88 Ibid.
89 Ibid.; emphasis in the original.
90 Burwash, *History of Victoria College*, 121; CG, 11 June 1845.
91 CG, 11 June 1845.
92 Houston and Prentice, *Schooling and Scholars*, 250.
93 Ibid., 78.

94 McKillop, *Matters of Mind*, 98.
95 Cobourg Ladies' Seminary, *Annual Circular*, 1845.
96 "Ryerson's Inaugural," 21 Oct. 1841, in Burwash, *History of Victoria College*, 495–507.
97 Ibid., 498.
98 Taylor, *Before Vassar Opened*, 267.
99 Solomon, "The Oberlin Model and Its Impact on Other Colleges," 83.
100 Burwash, *History of Victoria College*, 507.
101 Burlington Ladies' Academy, *Catalogue of the Officers and Students*.
102 Ibid. The academic content of the curriculum was organized in a way that was similar to the Cobourg seminary. The first course, called the useful, covered subjects such as spelling, reading, botany, history, natural philosophy, chemistry, geology, astronomy, and rhetoric. The second course, entitled the ornamental, included French, music, perspective, drawing and painting, embroidery, and principles of etiquette and manners. In addition, students could take Spanish, Italian, Greek, German, Latin, bookkeeping, and mathematics. Completion of the first course resulted in graduation with a diploma of the first degree, and if a student completed both courses of study, the diploma would be called the first and second degree.
103 Davey, "Trends in Female School Attendance."
104 See also Prentice, *The School Promoters*, 55.
105 Dorcas, "Home Culture," *Calliopean* 1, no. 3 (23 Dec. 1847).
106 "The Condition of Woman," *Calliopean* 1, no. 3 (23 Dec. 1847), 24.
107 Youmans, *Campaign Echoes*.
108 Jane Van Norman, Correspondence, [1844?]-1857, with A. Dunham Emory, Trafalgar, UCA.
109 A.D. Emory to Jane Van Norman, n.d., UCA.
110 The *Calliopean* was instituted as a literary paper aimed at the improvement of the participants. In conjunction with this aim, the paper had as its special object the elevation of the standard of female education in Canada, in order to promote domestic happiness and social virtue (CCA, 31 Aug. 1847). The paper carried poetry, literary works, and discussions about the nature of female education. One article, entitled "Superficial Attainments," criticized the type of female education that left women with a few "gaudy accomplishments." The author claimed that the reign of Victoria would bring about changes which would "emancipate her own sex from the thralldom of ignorance and superstition." See *Calliopean* 3, no. 1 (23 Dec. 1847): 38.
111 Jane Van Norman to A.D. Emory, n.d., UCA.
112 Ibid.
113 Ibid.
114 Ibid.

115 Youmans, *Campaign Echoes*, 60.
116 *See Catharine Bell Van Norman: Her Diary.*
117 Jane Van Norman to A.D. Emory, n.d., UCA.
118 Ibid.
119 *CG*, 30 July 1851.
120 MacLear, *The History of the Education of Girls in New York*, 20. According to MacLear, the group aimed to create professions for women, such as teaching, nursing, and work as family assistants. In 1869 it underlined the importance of domestic economy and the need for all women to have training so that they could earn their living in case of poverty. Also, according to MacLear, the group wanted to divert the large number of women who were already working in factories by trying to make work in the home more respected and more remunerative. The group donated $20,000 towards two schools for women in Iowa and Wisconsin. The original plan was to open a professional school in conjunction with these schools, but not enough financial support was forthcoming.
121 Pujol and Van Norman, *The Complete French Class-book*. See also Van Norman Institute, Prospectus, 1857–67, New York Public Library, New York City.
122 *AV* 26 (Jan. 1903): 4.
123 Little remains of these short-lived schools. The list of courses advertised indicates that the curriculum was very similar to that of the Cobourg Ladies' Academy. The obituary of one of the students, Janet Forbes, provides the only student's name that I have been able to find. Forbes was a member of the Methodist Episcopal Church and had attended the Adelaide Academy for nearly a year, "principally supporting herself by her own exertions." She died of cholera in 1851. *CCA*, 26 July 1851.
124 Jesse Hurlburt obtained a civil post in Ottawa and wrote several publications there; he died in 1891. *Macmillan Dictionary of Canadian Biography*, 335.
125 "Report of the Committee of Picton Ladies' Academy," *CG*, 25 Oct. 1848.
126 *CG*, 25 Oct. 1848, 10 April 1850.
127 "Report of the Committee of Picton Ladies' Academy," *CG*, 27 June 1849. See also "Mr. McMullen's Academies," *CG*, 10 April 1850; and Picton Academies for Ladies and Gentlemen, Prospectus, 22 May 1850, MSS Misc. Coll., 1, 5, AO.
128 Theobald, "The Sin of Laura."
129 Dr Charles West, quoted in Taylor, *Before Vassar Opened*, 102.
130 Taylor, *Before Vassar Opened*, 102.
131 *CG*, 16 Jan. 1844.
132 *CCA*, 7 Aug. 1845. Emphasis in the original.

CHAPTER THREE

1 Albert Carman to P. Carman, 13 July 1857, Carman Papers, box 1, UCA.
2 *CCA*, 15 Sept. 1852.
3 *CCA*, 17 Aug. 1853, 12 July 1852.
4 Smith, *Albert College*, 1.
5 Ibid., 2.
6 Belleville College, *General Catalogue of the Officers and Students*, 22.
7 Duvall, *The Methodist Episcopal Church and Education up to 1869*, 68.
8 Masters, *Protestant Church Colleges in Canada*, 107. The University Act of 1849 completely secularized King's College and changed its name to the University of Toronto. Strachan eventually succeeded in obtaining another charter in 1853 for Trinity College, an Anglican college with both arts and divinity curricula.
9 Moir, *Church and State in Canada West*, 117.
10 Ibid., 128.
11 *CCA*, 2 May 1855.
12 Smith, *Albert College*, 3.
13 *CCA*, 17 March 1858.
14 Teaching staff included the Reverend J.H. Johnson as professor of ethics, belles-lettres, and mental philosophy; J.N. Maring, who taught classics and natural sciences; and G. Goldsmith, English; Eliza Deaver acted both as preceptress and teacher of French, Italian, Spanish, drawing, and embroidery; Eveline Masury taught music. See Belleville Seminary, *Announcement*, 14 Oct. 1858, Albert College Papers, UCA.
15 Smith, *Albert College*, 13.
16 Cochrane, ed., *Men of Canada*, 1: 12.
17 "Belleville Seminary," *CCA*, 28 July 1858.
18 A. Carman to P. Carman, 19 June 1858, Carman Papers, box 1, file 1b, UCA.
19 Ibid.
20 A. Carman to P. Carman, 19 Nov. 1858, Carman Papers, box 1, file 1b, UCA.
21 Ibid.
22 A. Carman to P. Carman, 13 Sept. 1858, Carman Papers, box 1, file 1b, UCA.
23 *CCA*, 16 Feb. 1859.
24 Smith, *Albert College*, 10. See also Moir, *Church and State in Canada West*.
25 Smith, *Albert College*, 12.
26 R. Burns to A. Carman, 7 Aug. 1860, Carman Papers, box 1, file 22, UCA.

27 Smith, *Albert College*, 14.
28 Metty Carman to her mother, 28 July 1858, Carman Papers, box 1, file 1b, UCA.
29 Ibid.
30 A. Carman to P. Carman, 28 Jan. 1858, Carman Papers, box 1, file 1, UCA.
31 Ibid.
32 A. Carman to P. Carman, 6 Jan. 1858, Carman Papers, box 1, file 1b, UCA.
33 Ibid.
34 A. Carman to P. Carman, 30 Dec. 1858, Carman Papers, box 1, file 1b, UCA.
35 "Albert University," *CCA*, 24 April 1867.
36 A. Carman to P. Carman, 4 Dec. 1858, Carman Papers, box 1, file 1c, UCA.
37 A. Carman to P. Carman, 21 Dec. 1859, Carman Papers, box 1, UCA.
38 A letter written by Ada indicates that by some point in the 1860s she was working as a teacher in Omemee. She wrote, "Our school here beats Iroquois – we have three teachers. Its very pleasant for me now, I do not get so tired as I did when I had to keep order, I was hardly able to keep 47 little urchins quiet every day." Ada Carman to Metty Carman, 30 Jan. 186?, Carman Papers, box 1, file 2a, UCA.
39 Report to the Board, 1862, Financial Records, Albert College, box 2, UCA.
40 Belleville College, *General Catalogue of the Officers and Students.*
41 A. Carman to J.J. Passmore, 24 Oct. 1861, Carman Papers, box 1a, file 1a, UCA.
42 Ibid.
43 A. Carman to J.J. Passmore, 4 Nov. 1861, Carman Papers, box 1, file 2a, UCA.
44 Petition to Miss Passmore from students, 22 Nov. 1861, Carman Papers, box 1, file 2a, UCA.
45 The references included in the circular advertising the American School Institute indicate connections with major educational institutions in the area, such as Rutgers, Yale, and Brown, as well as with the Female Academy of Albany, the Troy Female Seminary, and the Ontario Female Seminary of Canandaigua, NY. One of the testimonials for the institute was written by D.C. Van Norman of the Van Norman Institute, New York, commending the agency's competence.
46 Anna Green to A. Carman, 23 Sept. 1863, Carman Papers, box 1, file 2b, UCA.
47 J.E. de Wolfe to A. Carman, 15 Aug. 1864, Carman Papers, box 1, file 2c, UCA.

48 Clara Brown to A. Carman, 5 Sept. 1868, Carman Papers, box 1, file 2b, UCA.
49 Graham to Rev. Shepard, 9 Oct. 1863, Carman Papers, box 1, file 2b, UCA.
50 Mary Jane Masson to A. Carman, 21 Jan. 1864, Carman Papers, box 1, file 2c, UCA.
51 E.A. Hurd to A. Carman, 5 Nov. 1864, Carman Papers, box 1, file 2c, UCA.
52 Ibid. Emphasis in original.
53 Smith, *Albert College*, 23; *CG*, 22 June 1892; *CCA*, 5 May 1880.
54 I have not been able to determine where this school was located.
55 After the Belleville Seminary affiliated with the University of Toronto, it obtained a charter in 1866 to grant degrees in arts, amended in 1870 with enlarged powers to confer degrees in arts and other faculties. The seminary in 1863 had three female teachers and in an advertisement described itself as the Belleville Seminary and Methodist Female College (*CCA*, 22 July 1863). In 1867 the *CCA* referred to a ladies' college senate and called the institution the Belleville Ladies' College, but by 1869 the calendar mentioned a course of study at Alexandra College (*CCA*, 13 Nov. 1867, 17 March 1869).
56 Alexandra College, *Calendar*, 1872, box "Albert College," UCA.
57 The register for 1865 reveals that there were seventeen girls of Episcopal Methodist affiliation, one Congregationalist, one Presbyterian, and one Church of England. In the winter of 1866 there were twenty-three Episcopal Methodist girls, one Congregationalist, four Wesleyan Methodists, and one Presbyterian. See Records of Students Registered [1865–71], Albert College, 88.116v-5, UCA.
58 A. Carman to E. Ryerson, 9 Dec. 1875, Ryerson Papers, box 6, 191, UCA.
59 Ibid.
60 *CCA*, 2 Aug. 1876.
61 *CCA*, 23 Aug. 1876.
62 Rev. W. Graham, "The Co-education of the Sexes," *CCA*, 19 July 1876.
63 *CCA*, 25 June 1873.
64 Thomas Webster, "The Education of Women," *CCA*, 22 April 1874.
65 Ibid.
66 Ibid.
67 *CCA*, 1 July 1874.
68 "Convocation at Albert University," Carman Papers, box 3, file 10b, UCA.
69 A. Carman to editor of *Toronto Globe*, n.d. [1880s?], Carman Papers, box 24, file 57, UCA.
70 Ibid.

71 Smith, *Albert College*, 31.
72 Albert College, *Collegiate Course*.
73 Belleville Business College, *Annual Circular and Catalogue, 1884–5*, Albert College Archives, Belleville.
74 Ibid.
75 Ibid.
76 Ibid.
77 Albert College, Announcement, 1891/92, Albert College Archives.
78 Ella Gardiner was the daughter of the Reverend James Gardiner, who had served as editor of the CCA, and missionary secretary to the church. See Smith, *Albert College*, 27.
79 Smith, *Albert College*, 27.
80 Ella Gardiner diary, quoted in Smith, *Albert College*, 26.
81 Ella Gardiner, "The Missionary Movement in Albert College," CG, 4 July 1900; "Missionary Conference of Albert College," CG, 23 May 1900.
82 Albert College, Announcement, 1897/98, Albert College Archives.
83 Smith, *Albert College*, 28.
84 Ibid., 40.
85 Theobald, "Women's Studies in Colonial Victoria," and "The Sin of Laura."
86 W.P. Dyer to A. Carman, 26 March 1903, Carman Papers, box 11, file 56, UCA.
87 "Albert College" (anonymous report), 1906, Carman Papers, box 12, file 71, UCA.

CHAPTER FOUR

1 Austin, *Woman; Her Character, Culture and Calling*, 382.
2 Davey, "Trends in Female School Attendance," 239–40.
3 Gidney, "Elementary Education in Upper Canada."
4 Gidney and Millar, *Inventing Secondary Education*, 126–49.
5 Ibid., 187.
6 Women graduates could work as music teachers but not as concert performers or composers of music.
7 McKillop, *Matters of Mind*, 105.
8 On the subject of depressions in Ontario, see Morton, *A Short History of Canada*, 89–120.
9 See Reid, "The Education of Women at Mount Allison." See also Reid, *Mount Allison University*.
10 The CG expressed this lack as follows: "For years there had been a very earnest enquiry on the part of a large class of our people for a place of education, first in its intellectual advantages and secure in its

moral influences. When the crash of 1856–7 came, it appeared as though it would take a score of years to recover such an amount of independence as would give the hope that an institution for female education could be secured" (9 Oct. 1861).

11 CG, 8 Aug. 1860. The school also experimented with a juvenile department, which was intended as a nursery for the higher departments, but was discontinued because of the crowded state of the building. Hester Ann Horner, a student at the Dundas school was awarded a baccalaureate of science in 1858, according to her diploma, which is in Special Collections, HPL.

12 Royce, "Methodism and the Education of Women."

13 CG, 12 Dec. 1860.

14 Prentice, "Scholarly Passion," 262.

15 T.R. Woodhouse, quoted in Royce, *Landmarks*, 5. The date of 1866 for the Dundas school's closure given in that source seems late when compared to other accounts, which claim that it closed in 1861. Dr Samuel Rice was involved in the Dundas school, but as the text states, he initiated the move to start a larger school in Hamilton. The Dundas school had a capacity of approximately fifty-five boarders and twenty-five day students, whereas the Hamilton school hoped to educate over a hundred. The building in Dundas may have been considered inadequate for the larger goal, and the relocation of the school in Hamilton may have also been connected to both the grandeur of an available hotel building and Hamilton's more prominent position.

16 Royce, *Landmarks*, 12.

17 Margaret Proctor Burwash to Ned Burwash, 4 Jan. 1898, M.P. Burwash Personal Papers, box 1, 6, UCA.

18 See *Dictionary of Hamilton Biography*, 1: 170, and Sissons, *A History of Victoria University*, 99–101.

19 Royce, *Landmarks*, 6.

20 CG, 31 July 1861.

21 Edward Jackson, president of the board in 1870, proprietor of the Hamilton Tin Factory, and director of the Gore Bank, Lake Erie Railway Company, and the Bank of Hamilton, was a lifelong supporter of Methodist education. His wife, Lydia, was associated with the Hamilton Ladies' Orphan Asylum and the Benevolent Society. Edward Jackson organized a fund for the Centenary Church and later endowed a chair in theology at Victoria College. See "Edward and Lydia Jackson," *Canadian Methodist Magazine* 3, no. 2 (Feb. 1876): 97–104.

22 Royce, *Landmarks*, 7. The CG notes that "these gentlemen took the initiative by taking shares of from five thousand dollars to one thousand, the noble-minded Vice President, a Presbyterian, taking four

thousand dollars, indicating his sympathy with the undertaking" (9 Oct. 1861).

23 Royce, *Landmarks*, 10.

24 Davey, "Trends in Female School Attendance," 252.

25 This information was given to me by Miss Murchie, archivist at Centenary United Church, Hamilton.

26 Charles McCullough, "The Old College," *Hamilton Spectator*, 18 March 1937.

27 Wesleyan Ladies' College, *Catalogue*, 1861, Special Collections, HPL.

28 Pomeroy, "Mary Electa Adams," 108.

29 Horowitz, *Alma Mater*, 5.

30 Ibid., 12. On the ideal of the family as a model for schooling, see Prentice, "Education and the Metaphor," 110–32.

31 Wesleyan Ladies' College, Catalogue, 1866/67. On American schools, see Solomon, *In the Company of Educated Women*.

32 Horowitz, *Alma Mater*, 74–5; McLachlin, *American Boarding Schools*.

33 *CG*, 9 Oct. 1861.

34 *CG*, 2 Oct. 1861.

35 Ibid.

36 S.D. Rice to the editor, *CG*, 14 Dec. 1864.

37 Heslegrave, "The Cult of True Womanhood."

38 *CG*, 30 Aug. 1865.

39 G. Roberts to A. Carman, 4 July 1863, Carman Papers, box 1, file 2c, UCA.

40 Wesleyan Ladies' College, Catalogue, 1881/82, UCA.

41 WLC, Catalogue, 1887/88.

42 WLC, Catalogue, 1891/92.

43 Winter, *Vox Collegii*.

44 Ibid., 17.

45 The members of the first board were all from Whitby and included James Holden, Nelson Reynolds, Henry Taylor, G. Young Smith, John Rice, Hazard Wilcox, Walter Coulthard, Joshua Richardson, John L. Smith, James Powell, Richard Hatch, Thomas McClung, W.D. Matthews, Mr Holden, director of the Port Perry Railroad, and Mr Coulthard, vice-director of the railroad.

46 The new board of directors included men from the Whitby and Oshawa area, as well as ministers from elsewhere in Ontario. See Ontario Ladies' College, Calendar, 1875/76, Trafalgar Castle School Archives, Whitby.

47 Ontario Ladies' College, Calendar, 1878, RG 2 G-4, 1, 5, AO.

48 Ibid.

49 Judge Burnham quoted in *Whitby Chronicle*, 10 Sept. 1874.

50 *CCA*, 11 Sept. 1872.

51 Ibid.
52 Ontario Ladies' College, Calendar, 1874/75, RG 2, 1, 5, AO.
53 Ibid.
54 OLC, Calendar, 1875/76, RG 2 G-4, AO.
55 Ibid.
56 Minnie to Jenny, 2 Nov. 1878, Trafalgar Castle School Archives, Whitby.
57 Ibid.
58 Ibid.
59 *Whitby Chronicle*, 4 July 1878.
60 *CG*, 17 Dec. 1879.
61 *CG*, 23 May 1877.
62 Winter, *Vox Collegii*, 22.
63 John G. Reid, "Adams, Mary Electa," in *Dictionary of Canadian Biography*, vol. 12.
64 Ontario Ladies' College, Calendar, 1880/81, RG 2, G-4, 1, 5, AO.
65 Mary Electa Adams diary, 5 Aug. and 4 Oct. 1880, Elsie Pomeroy Papers, 5001/11, Mount Allison University Archives.
66 Ibid., 20 Sept. 1880.
67 Ibid., 10 Oct. 1880.
68 Ibid., 12 Sept. 1881.
69 Ibid., 13 Oct. 1882. Adams further described Hare as weak, self-indulgent, not very manly, and underhanded.
70 M. Addison to Arthur Addison, 15 Oct. 1889, Margaret Addison Personal Papers, box 1, "Correspondence to Family 1889–1913," UCA.
71 Winter, *Vox Collegii*, 25.
72 "The College in 1889," *Toronto Saturday Globe*, 26 Oct. 1869.
73 See Moorcroft, "The Woman's Missionary Society of Tabernacle Methodist Church, Whitby."
74 Ontario Ladies' College, Calendar, 1891/2, RG 2, G-4, box 1, env. 5, AO.
75 *Whitby Chronicle*, 24 June 1892; Winter, *Vox Collegii*, 26.
76 *CG*, 17 Aug. 1881.
77 Letters from an OLC student, Sept. and Oct. 1882, 230000-134, WHSA.
78 Ibid.
79 *Whitby Chronicle*, 21 June 1895. On Chown, see Gauvreau, *The Evangelical Century*, 195; Van Die, *An Evangelical Mind*, 145.
80 *CG*, 28 June 1899.
81 Dyhouse, *Girls Growing Up in Late Victorian and Edwardian England*, 87.
82 "Address to the Students of the O.L.C.," *Sunbeam*, March 1899, 4–6.
83 Ibid.
84 Riddell, *Alma College*, and Edwards, *The History of Alma College*. Dr Katharine Dobson Riddell, recipient of an honorary LLD from the University of Toronto, was the daughter of Alma's president, the

Reverend Perry Silas Dobson. After graduating from Alma, she taught at the school for several years.

85 Edwards, *The History of Alma College*, 1.

86 Minutes of meeting, 3 April 1877, Board of Management, Alma College, box 1, 1, UCA.

87 Minutes of meeting of Board of Management, May 1878, Alma College, box 1, 1, UCA.

88 Webster, *Woman Man's Equal*. For an account of Thomas Webster's career, see chapter 6 and "Obituary of Thomas Webster," *Minutes of the London Methodist Conference 1901*.

89 Executive Committee, 2 July 1878, Alma College, box 4, 1, UCA.

90 Riddell, *Alma College*, 8–9.

91 Ibid., 9.

92 Executive Committee, 14 Oct. 1881, Alma College, box 4, 1, UCA.

93 Ibid.

94 Ibid.

95 Ibid. For their services, the steward and stewardess were paid $300 each per annum. The school also appointed an engineer to look after the plumbing, gas, and heating and to be "generally useful" for a salary of $225 per year.

96 Executive Committee, 9 Jan. 1881, Alma College, box 4, 1, UCA.

97 A. McLachlin to A. Carman, 24 Aug. 1882, Carman Papers, box 2, file 8b, UCA.

98 Ibid.

99 Edwards, *The History of Alma College*, 17.

100 Principal's report, 22 Dec. 1881, Alma College, box 12, 19, UCA.

101 Riddell, *Alma College*, 17.

102 The college tried to free itself from this debt and hired the Reverend Mr Clement as financial agent and, in 1892, the Reverend J.P. Rice, who after three years also resigned. See Edwards, *The History of Alma College*, 19.

103 Edwards, *The History of Alma College*, 18.

104 Alma College, Calendar, 1889/90, box 18, UCA.

105 See Report to the President and Board of Management [undated, but from the late 1880s], Committee on Agency, Alma College, box 12, 17, UCA. The Presbyterian school was located at the corner of Bloor and Jarvis streets.

106 Gidney and Millar, *Inventing Secondary Education*, 244.

107 Special report to the Board of Management, Minutes, n.d., Alma College, box 13, 22, UCA.

108 Prentice, *The School Promoters*, 75.

109 Smyth, "'A Noble Proof of Excellence.'"

110 Alma College, Calendar, 1889/90, box 18, UCA.

111 Ibid.

112 Ibid.

113 Bell-Smith, a graduate of an English art school as well as the Ontario College of Art in Toronto, was a professor of art from 1881 to 1908. His influence on the school's art program is evident in the fact that in 1893 Alma College's exhibit at the Chicago World's Fair won "a coveted diploma and medal as well as half the awards given to private schools in Ontario." See Riddell, *Alma College*, 13.

114 Board of Management Minutes, 16 Nov. 1887, Alma College, box 1, 1, UCA.

115 Duvall, *The Methodist Episcopal Church*, 73.

116 "The Ladies' College Convention," *Whitby Chronicle*, 12 Feb. 1874.

117 See Executive Committee, 14 Oct. 1881, Alma College, box 4, 1, UCA.

118 Ontario Ladies' College, Calendar, 1894/96, RG 2 G-4, 1, 5, ao.

119 "Alma College," *CG*, 19 Dec. 1900.

120 Executive Committee, 3 April 1882, Alma College, box 4, 1, UCA.

121 Davey, "Trends in Female School Attendance," 241–3.

122 B.F. Austin to A. Carman, n.d., Carman Papers, box 4, file 16a, UCA.

CHAPTER FIVE

1 *CCA*, 6 Dec. 1876.

2 Green, "The Wesleyan Ladies' College of Hamilton."

3 The colleges seem to have carried some debt. In 1902, for example, Alma Ladies' College was assessed to be worth $83,376 while carrying a debt of $38,054, whereas Mount Allison Ladies' College was worth $125,000 and carried a debt of $8,000 and Ontario Ladies' College was worth $115,706 with a debt of $10,550. See *Cyclopedia of Methodism in Canada*, 3: 330.

4 Gidney and Millar, *Inventing Secondary Education*, 317.

5 Ibid.

6 See also Curtis, *Building the Educational State*, 274–5.

7 Prentice, "Education and the Metaphor," 110–32.

8 Smith-Rosenberg, "The Female World of Love and Ritual," 64.

9 Wesleyan Ladies' College, *Act of Incorporation*, 1861, Special Collections, HPL. The college began as the Wesleyan Female College, was later called the Wesleyan Ladies' College, and was then renamed the Hamilton Ladies' College in approximately 1890.

10 Wesleyan Female College, Catalogue, 1862/63, Wesleyan Ladies' College, Collection, UCA. The subjects were further divided into algebra, geometry, trigonometry, natural philosophy, rhetoric, logic, sacred history, chemistry, zoology, botany, astronomy, geology, natural theology, mental philosophy, and moral philosophy.

11 Wesleyan Ladies' College, Catalogue, 1891/92.
12 Burlington Ladies' Academy, *Catalogue of the Officers and Students*. By contrast, Horowitz claims that the American female seminaries never offered Greek or Latin. See Horowitz, *Alma Mater*, 11. Some of the descriptions of the female seminaries in Taylor's *Before Vassar Opened* contradict this claim by Horowitz.
13 *Van Norman Institute*, 24–26.
14 Wesleyan Ladies College, Catalogue, 1891/92. For a discussion of the role of accomplishments, see Theobald, "Mere Accomplishments?"
15 Sonser, "'A Respectable English Education.'"
16 Wesleyan Ladies' College, Catalogue, 1891/92.
17 Ibid.
18 Dundas Wesleyan Institute, Calendar, 1876, UCA.
19 Woodhouse. *The History of the Town of Dundas*, 57–8.
20 Burwash, *History of Victoria College*, 134.
21 Wesleyan Ladies' College, Catalogue, 1862/63.
22 Sonser, "A Respectable English Education," 100.
23 Wesleyan Ladies' College, Catalogue, 1881/82, UCA.
24 Ibid.
25 Ibid.
26 "Wesleyan Female College," CG, 17 Dec. 1862.
27 "Wesleyan Ladies' College," *Portfolio* 9, no. 7 (May 1889): 126.
28 "Hamilton Ladies' College, Annual Commencement Exercises," CG, 29 June 1892.
29 Not everyone agreed with the non-sectarian perspective, as a letter to the CG indicates: "I stand for no coquetry with Presbyterians, Episcopalians, or anybody else." R.H. of London to the editor, CG, 9 Sept. 1896.
30 "Hamilton Ladies' College," CG, 28 June 1893.
31 Wesleyan Ladies' College, Calendar, 1865.
32 Wesleyan Ladies' College, Calendar, 1874, "Educational Institutions," UCA. The collegiate department was headed by Rice as principal, with the Reverend Mr Wright, MA, in natural sciences, and the Reverend W.H. Withrow, MA, in metaphysics, evidences, and classics. In addition to these male teachers, the school had Miss M. Allen, MEL, teaching literary criticism, Miss L. O'Loane, MEL, mathematics, and Miss Anna Duncan, MEL, rhetoric and moral science.
33 *Wesleyan Ladies' College, 1890*.
34 Arthur P. Coleman diary, 1867, box 1, VULA.
35 Ibid., 22 Sept. 1867, 16 June 1874.
36 Ibid., 16 June 1874.
37 Chown, *The Stairway*. See Introduction by Diana Chown in the second edition.

38 Valverde, *The Age of Light*, chapter 7.
39 Socknat, *Witness Against War*, 57–9.
40 Lerner, *The Creation of Feminist Consciousness*.
41 Lucy Lister, "Woman in Her Relation to Moral and Social Reform," *Portfolio* 8, no. 10 (June 1888): 152–4. Lister's father, Joseph Lister, was on the board of the King Street Methodist Church for many years. Of his thirteen children, five attended the WLC. See *Dictionary of Hamilton Biography*, 1: 127.
42 Nettie Burkholder, "After Graduation, What?" *Portfolio* 8, no. 10 (June 1888): 154–6.
43 Nettie Burkholder, "The Financial Capabilities of Woman," *Portfolio* 10, no. 8 (June 1890).
44 Margaret Brent, "The Study of Law for Women," *Portfolio* 15, no. 5 (Feb. 1895): 3–6.
45 "Editorials," *Portfolio* 8, no. 4 (Dec. 1887).
46 Minutes, Board, 25 June 1887, Alma College, UCA.
47 "Music as a Bread Winner for Girls," *Almafilian* 5, no. 1 (July 1891).
48 "Mrs. Maurice Sharon," *Almafilian* 7, no. 1 (Thanksgiving 1910): 6. The same issue also carried an obituary of Nettie Bainbridge-Powell, MLA in 1886, identified as a doctor who had resided in Marion, Ind.
49 *Almafilian*, 6, no. 1 (July 1892), 24, 2.
50 Minutes, Executive Council, Sept. 1883, Alma College, box 15, 1, UCA.
51 Ibid.
52 Ibid., Jan. 1891.
53 Ibid.
54 Minutes, Council, Jan. 1891, Alma College, box 15, 1, UCA; CG, 23 Jan. 1884; *Almafilian* 8, no. 4 (April 1912). Much later, in 1929, the admission of Jewish girls was debated and no motion was passed, but the recommendation was made that the principal should register no more than four or five Jewish girls at any one time. See Minutes, Board of Management, 17 Sept. 1929, Alma College, box 5, 4, UCA.
55 Parent to Dr Warner, Feb. 1910, Alma College, box 13, UCA.
56 "Ontario Ladies' College," CG, 3 Jan. 1900, 14 Nov. 1900.
57 "Whitby College Converzazione," CG, 21 Feb. 1900.
58 Burstyn, *Victorian Education and the Ideal of Womanhood*, 36.
59 Mabel Burkholder, "Inside the Walls, A Sketch of Daily Life at the Ontario Ladies' College, Whitby," *Canadian Methodist Monthly* 58, no. 2 (1903): 506–15.
60 Ariès and Duby, *A History of Private Life*, 4: 74.
61 Dyhouse, *Feminism and the Family in England, 1880–1939*. On the relationship between reading and femininity, see Gorham, "The Ideology of Femininity and Reading for Girls, 1850–1914," 39–59.

62 "The Boarding School for Girls and Its Advantages," *Alma* 1, no. 1 (July 1903).
63 Martin-Fugier, "Bourgeois Rituals," 261–338.
64 Eschbach, *The Higher Education of Women in England and America, 1865–1920*, 169.
65 Ontario Ladies' College, Calendar, 1901/03, RG 2, G-4, box 1, 5, AO.
66 Winter, *Vox Collegii*, 33. The department was affiliated in the early years with the Lillian Massey School in Toronto. The WLC did not appear to have a domestic science department, but a series of cookery classes, sponsored by the alumnae association, were given at the school by a Mrs Ewing.
67 Emma R. Kaufman Personal Papers, Microfilm, 1881–1979, UCA.
68 Ontario Ladies' College, Calendar, 1912/14, Trafalgar Castle School Archives, Whitby.
69 Mitchinson, *The Nature of Their Bodies*, 40.
70 Ontario Ladies' College, Calendar, 1912/14.
71 Ibid.
72 Ibid.
73 Ibid.
74 Winter, *Vox Collegii*, 34.
75 Ibid, 46.
76 Principal Farewell to A.H. Colquhoun, deputy minister of education, 27 Sept. 1916, OLC, code I-270, 1916: Private Schools, RG 2, P-3, box 18, AO.
77 Curtis, *True Government by Choice Men?* 62.
78 Curtis, *Building the Educational State*, 369.
79 J. Wetherell to Principal Warner, 5 Oct. 1916, code 1–270/1917: Private Schools, RG 2, P-3, 32–5/74.
80 A.H. Colquhoun, deputy minister of education, to Rev. Warner, 11 Oct. 1916, ibid.
81 R.I. Warner to A.H. Colquhoun, 16 Oct. 1916, ibid.
82 A.H. Colquhoun to Rev. Warner, 3 March 1917, ibid.
83 A.H. Colquhoun to Rev. Warner, 24 Sept. 1917, ibid.
84 A.H. Colquhoun, to Rev. Warner, 24 Sept. 1917, ibid.
85 See McLachlin, *The American Boarding School Experience*, 257–60. According to McLachlin, public schools tended to be modelled on factories, while private schools continued to call up the family as their prototype.
86 Corrigan and Curtis, "Education, Inspection and State Formation."
87 See also Smyth, "The Lessons of Religion," which describes the same bureaucratization process and its effect on St Joseph's Academy; also Smyth, "'A Noble Proof of Excellence.'"

88 Theobald and Selleck, *Family, School and State in Australian History,* 25–44.

89 Copy of Memorandum Sent to Private Schools in 1915, Board of Management Correspondence, Alma College, box 10, 11, UCA.

90 Minutes, Board of Management, 7 July 1916, Alma College, box 5, 4, UCA.

91 H. Wigle to Rev. Warner, 21 Jan. 1918, Alma College, box 11, 14, UCA.

92 Minutes, Board of Management, 13 Jan. 1920, Alma College, box 5, 4, UCA.

93 Ibid., 20 May 1924.

94 Copy of Agreement of Affiliation, Board of Management, 14 May 1925, Alma College, box 5, 4, UCA.

95 See Register of Graduates, Alma College. I am grateful to Heather Meier, former administrator of the college, for this information.

96 Commission on Secondary Education, Report to the Board of the Educational Society of the Methodist Church [1916?], Alma College, box 12, 23, UCA.

97 Marta Danylewycz, "Domestic Science Education in Ontario: 1900–1940," in *Gender and Education in Ontario*, ed. Heap and Prentice, 129–48.

98 Ibid., 139.

99 Mitchinson, *The Nature of Their Bodies*, 40.

100 Weeks, *Sex, Politics and Society,* 144.

101 Michael Gauvreau explores how leading Presbyterian and Methodist clergymen tried to combine evolutionary naturalism with historical criticism of the Bible in the late nineteenth century; see Gauvreau, *The Evangelical Century.* See also McKillop, *A Disciplined Intelligence*. Marlene Shore has traced the influences of science on social research in Canada in *The Science of Social Redemption*.

102 Prentice et al., *Canadian Women*, 166.

103 Ibid., 204.

104 *Report of the Massey Foundation Commission.*

105 Ibid.

106 Ibid.

107 M. Louise Bollert, "Opportunities for Young Women In Professional Life," *Alma* 1, no. 2 (Nov. 1903): 2.

108 "The Home for Woman," *Almafilian* 5, no. 7 (June 1909): 1–2.

109 Ibid.

110 Ibid.

111 Vicinus, *Independent Women*, especially chapter 4.

112 See, for example, Pauline Fearman, autograph album, Special Collections, HPL.

CHAPTER SIX

1 Margaret Addison, "Higher Education for Women," CG, 30 May 1894.
2 R. Cook, *The Regenerators*, 20.
3 Temple, "The Development of Higher Education for Women in Ontario," chapter 2. See also Katz, *Family and Class in a Canadian City.*
4 In 1888 the number of ladies' colleges had multiplied to the extent that the "competition for patronage is as keen as in any commercial calling." See Report of the Wesleyan Ladies' College, Niagara Conference, June 1888, UCA.
5 Burwash, *History of Victoria College*. See also Masters, *Protestant Church Colleges in Canada.*
6 Rev. A. Burns to Nathanael Burwash, 24 May 1893, unaccessioned records from Victoria College Vault, UCA.
7 A.B. McKillop, "Burns, Alexander," *Dictionary of Canadian Biography,* 12: 142–3.
8 Report of the Wesleyan Ladies' College, Hamilton, *Journal of the Methodist General Conference*, 1894, 179, UCA.
9 *Minutes of the Hamilton Methodist Conference*, 1897, 100, UCA.
10 "Hamilton Ladies' College," CG, 30 June 1897.
11 Hamilton Methodist Conference, *Minutes*, 1899, 22, and *Minutes*, 1899, 167. See also "Obituary: Alexander Burns," *Minutes of the Hamilton Methodist Conference*, 1900, 133–5.
12 Hamilton Methodist Conference, *Minutes*, 1900, 133–5.
13 Louise Wright Griffiths, "Unpublished Report to the Alumnae," 1933, Wesleyan Ladies' College Archives, HPL.
14 *Journal of the Hamilton Annual Conference*, June 1898.
15 Ibid.
16 A. Burns, "The Wesleyan Ladies' College – A Correction," CG, 30 Aug. 1893.
17 "Does Hamilton Want Victoria University?" *Hamilton Spectator*, 7 Dec. 1883.
18 N. Burwash to N.H. Pillard, president of the Board of Trade, Hamilton, 31 July 1886, Nathanael Burwash Papers, box A, UCA.
19 Masters, *Protestant Church Colleges in Canada*, 115.
20 "Baccalaureate Sermon," *Portfolio* 3, no. 2 (June 1881): 83.
21 The extent to which ladies' college education influenced women to become active participants in social reform and clubs in Canada requires further research. For studies of women in American institutions such as the Sunday school, see Boylan, *Sunday School*; for the temperance movement, see Bordin, *Women and Temperance.*
22 Rev. Dr Tiffany, "W.F. College," 13 June 1879, Historic Hamilton 6, 64–6, Clipping file, HPL. Concerning spheres, Lynn Gordon comments,

"In practice, then, the lives of Victorian men and women resembled overlapping circles more than separate realms." See *Gender and Higher Education*, 14.

23 "Rev. Dr. Johnston Preached," *Hamilton Times*, 3 June 1892, in Victorian Hamilton Scrapbook, 10, 5, 77–8, HPL.

24 Ibid.

25 Rev. Thomas Webster, "My Memoirs. A Story of Pioneer Life in Canada West," apparently written in 1871, typescript with an introduction by William Webster Carter, 1934, Thomas Webster Personal Papers, UCA.

26 "Rev. Thomas Webster, D.D," excerpts from *Minutes of the London Methodist Conference*, 1901, biography file, UCA.

27 Webster, *Woman Man's Equal*, 177.

28 Ibid.

29 Ibid.

30 Ibid., 187.

31 Eschbach, *The Higher Education of Women*, 32–135.

32 Webster, *Woman Man's Equal*, 311.

33 Austin, "What Christ Has Done for Woman," in *Woman; Her Character*, 380.

34 During his principalship, Austin made and patented a model of the Holy Land.

35 B.F. Austin to the Board, 21 May 1897, Alma College, box 10, UCA.

36 R. Cook, *The Regenerators*, 69–78. See also Family Scrapbook, B.F. Austin Personal Papers, UCA, for an obituary of his daughter Kathleen, who died of pneumonia in 1896 at the age of two.

37 Secretary of the Board to B.F. Austin, 1897, Alma College, box 10, UCA.

38 *The Heresy Trial of Rev. B.F. Austin.*

39 Ibid.

40 Ibid.

41 Ibid. Subsequent writings and addresses show how Austin attempted to fuse his spiritualist beliefs with the teachings of the Bible. In a chapter called "The Spiritual Phenomena of the Bible," he used various texts from the Bible to prove the existence of independent spirit voices, spirit levitation, spirit communication in dreams, healing, trance, and spirit writing. See Austin, "The Spiritual Phenomena of the Bible."

42 The family scrapbook contains a clipping which states that Austin had left Alma to be on the editorial board of Linscott Publishing.

43 R. Cook, *The Regenerators*, 67.

44 Ibid., 71. Austin's company published Mary Merrill's biography, and Austin wrote the preface.

45 Ibid., 73.

46 Braude, *Radical Spirits.*

47 Ibid., 38–41.

48 Edwards, *The History of Alma College*, 32. According to Morgan, *Canadian Men and Women of the Time*, Austin became president of the William Smith College for Women, Geneva, NY, in 1903. This is the only reference to this appointment and may be inaccurate.

49 Riddell, *Alma College*, 20.

50 Austin, *Woman: Her Character*, 199–209.

51 Ibid., 200.

52 Ibid.

53 Ibid., 206.

54 Ibid.

55 Purvis, *Hard Lessons*, 59.

56 Austin, *Woman; Her Character*, 34.

57 Ibid., 36.

58 Prentice et al., *Canadian Women*, 123. Domestic science courses were advocated partly for these untrained domestic workers to elevate an unregulated and highly exploited occupation. If such education were made more attractive and professional, then young girls would be drawn to the jobs.

59 Austin, *Woman; Her Character*, 38.

60 Boydston, Kelley, and Margolis, *The Limits of Sisterhood*, 226.

61 Ibid., 232.

62 Austin, ed., *Woman; Her Character*, 376.

63 Ibid., 382.

64 Campbell, *Man Cannot Speak for Her*, 380.

65 Ibid.

66 Morgan Dix, "The Education of Woman for Her Work," in *Woman; Her Character*, ed. Austin, 451.

67 Scott, "The Troy Female Seminary," in *Making the Invisible Woman Visible*, 83.

68 Ibid.

69 Quoted in the *Almafilian* 5, no. 1 (July 1891): 24.

70 Quoted in Gifford, "For God and Home and Native Land," 315.

71 Hardesty, *Women Called to Witness*, 152. For the cult of true womanhood, see Welter, "The Cult of True Womanhood, 1820–1960," and Cott, *The Bonds of Womanhood*. See also Ryan, *Cradle of the Middle Class*, and Gordon, *Gender and Higher Education*.

72 Austin is first listed in the Rochester city directory in 1905 as a publisher living at 10 Arlington Street. In 1908–09 he was described as the pastor of the First Spiritualist Church. I am grateful to the Rochester Public Library for this information.

73 Ruether and Keller, *Women and Religion in America*, 3: 38–40.

74 Ibid.

75 See, for example, Austin, *The A.B.C. of Spiritualism*. Austin published his poems in a collection entitled *Rifts in the Cloud* (Rochester, NY: The Austin Publishing Co., 1907). His other publications include *The Temperance Union, Popular Sins of the Times* (1878), a collection of sermons, *The Methodist Episcopal Pulpit* (Toronto: Hunter Rose and Co., 1879), *Rational Memory Training, The History of the Jesuits*, and *Glimpses of the Unseen*. These publications are listed in "Sketch of Dr. Austin's Life," in *The Heresy Trial of Rev. B.F. Austin*.
76 Austin, *The A.B.C. of Spiritualism*.
77 On the subject of Austin's liberal theology, see R. Cook, *The Regenerators*, 69–78.
78 See Skultans, "Mediums, Controls and Eminent Men."
79 Braude, *Radical Spirits*, 33–4.
80 Quoted in the *Almafilian*, 5, no. 1 (July 1891): 1.
81 Ibid.
82 Quoted in Smyth, "The Lessons of Religion," 123.
83 Ibid.
84 Ibid., 202. See also Smyth, "'A Noble Proof of Excellence.'"
85 R. Cook, *The Regenerators*, 70.
86 *Almafilian*, 5, no. 1 (July 1891): 2.
87 Ibid.
88 Ibid.
89 Board of Management Correspondence, 9 Jan. 1899, Alma College, box 10, 4, UCA.
90 Report to the Board of Alma College, 20 Nov. 1902, box 12, 20, UCA.
91 Alma had also affiliated in 1884 "for examination purposes" with the Ontario School of Art. This meant that students who passed the examination were given a licence to teach drawing and painting in the public schools and collegiate institutes of the province. See Report by B.F. Austin to the Board of Management, 17 April 1884, Alma College, box 12, 19, UCA. See also Riddell, *Alma College*, 7.
92 R.I. Warner to Dr Carman, 26 April 1904, Carman Papers, box 12, file 63, UCA.
93 Report to the Board from Principal Warner, 10 Nov. 1905, Alma College, box 12, 20, UCA.
94 Ibid.
95 Ibid.
96 Principal Warner's Report to the Board, 24 Nov. 1908, Alma College, box 12, 20, UCA.
97 C.H. Goddard to R. McConnell, 26 Nov. 1906, Board of Management, Alma College, 10, 7, UCA.
98 Minutes, Board of Management, 13 April 1909, Alma College, box 4, 3, UCA.
99 Ibid., 16 Nov. 1908.

100 C.R. Flanders to Principal Warner, 5 Dec. 1916, Alma College, box 10, 12, UCA. Flanders had graduated from Victoria in 1881, and he received an honorary DD from Wesleyan Theological College in Montreal in 1896. He served as principal of Stanstead from 1893 to 1902 and in various churches until he died in Winnipeg in 1920.

101 Rev. J.W. Graham to Rev. C.R. Flanders, 9 March 1917, Alma College, box 11, 13, UCA.

102 Minutes of the Board, 14 Jan. 1915, Alma College, box 1, 2, UCA.

103 Zainu'ddin, "'The Poor Widow, the Ignoramus and the Humbug.'"

104 Ibid., 34.

105 Marjorie Theobald has observed that the ladies' colleges in Melbourne, Australia, tended to reproduce the dominant culture in terms of relationships of class and gender. Yet the notion of the accomplished women was compatible with educational excellence, pushing at the borders of female professionalism and learning. See Theobald, "'Mere Accomplishments?'"

106 "Principal Warner's Decennial," *Alma*, June 1907, Alma College, box 24, UCA.

CHAPTER SEVEN

1 A.H. Gray, *The Relations of Men and Women*, 4–5.

2 La Pierre, "The Academic Life of Canadian Coeds."

3 Gordon, *Gender and Higher Education*, 21.

4 Tyack and Hansot, *Learning Together*, 204.

5 Ibid., 213.

6 La Pierre, "The Academic Life of Canadian Coeds."

7 *AV* 3, no. 1 (Oct. 1880). The building had belonged to Judge Boswell before it was purchased by Mary Electa Adams for her school.

8 See *Cobourg Sentinel*, 31 March 1877, in which the musical performances of Misses Wilgress, Dumble, McEvers, and Mabley were described.

9 Ibid., 15 June 1878.

10 Ibid., 3 July 1878.

11 Ibid.

12 *AV* 1, no. 2 (Nov. 1878).

13 Ibronyi, *Early Voices*.

14 "The Admission of Women to Victoria College," Typescript by Maude Stapleford, Victoria 1907, 90.146V, 1, 19, UCA.

15 Ford, *A Path Not Strewn with Roses*.

16 Gidney and Millar, *Inventing Secondary Education*, 311.

17 Mary Electa Adams diary, 22 March 1880, Elsie Pomeroy Papers, Mount Allison University Archives.

18 Ibid., 22 March 1880.

19 Ibid.

20 Ibid., 25 May 1880.

21 Stapleford, "The Admission of Women to Victoria College," 4, UCA.

22 Curtis, *True Government by Choice Men?*

23 For the junior matriculation, the candidate had to be fifteen years of age and pass exams in Latin, mathematics, English, history, and geography and in one of the groups that included Greek, French, or German; French and either physics or chemistry; or German and either physics or chemistry. Candidates taking the senior matriculation had to take pass subjects in Latin; English; history; mathematics; Greek, French, or German; and one of the two sciences, such as biology or physics.

24 *Victoria University, Calendar, 1893–94*, 17–18.

25 Margaret Addison Personal Papers, General Material, box 2, UCA.

26 "Victoria University Convocation," *Canadian Methodist Magazine*, 17, no. 1 (1883): 567–8.

27 Senate Minutes, 30 Nov. 1888, Victoria University, 1855–1908, box 1, UCA.

28 *AV*, 2 (Nov. 1879): 2.

29 Nellie Greenwood, quoted in Ibronyi, *Early Voices*, 11.

30 Ibid.

31 *AV* 2, no. 5 (Feb. 1888).

32 Ibid.

33 *AV* 2, no. 5 (Feb. 1888).

34 Ibronyi, *Early Voices*, 14.

35 Gordon, *Gender and Higher Education*, 33.

36 J.H. Campbell, "Co-education in Universities," *AV* 3 (April 1881): 7.

37 Ibid.

38 Ibid.

39 *AV* 6, no. 5 (Feb. 1883).

40 *AV* 9, no. 3 (Dec. 1885).

41 Ibid.

42 The fourteen students were J.G. Kenney, A. McDonell, H. Albarus, A. Campbell, M.E. Henwood, L.F. Nelles, M.Sutherland, S.J. McAllister, O. McCullough, A. McCullough, M. Langford, B. Morrow, A. Percival, and O. Totten. See Victoria University, Registrar's Office 1892–93, 4, UCA.

43 *AV* 14 (Dec. 1891): 3.

44 Rosemary Gagan indicates that the SVMS was patronized by wealthy Methodists such as Chester Massey, J.W. Flavelle, and Timothy Eaton. See Gagan, *A Sensitive Independence*, 119.

45 La Pierre, "The Academic Life of Canadian Coeds," 182.

46 The Student Volunteer Movement for Foreign Missions, founded in 1888 by John R. Mott, a Methodist layman and YMCA secretary, in twenty-five years had sent 4,784 lay missionaries overseas, of whom one quarter were women. See Boyd, *Emissaries*, 28.
47 Ibronyi, *Early Voices*, 18.
48 Minutes, Women's Literary Society, Victoria College, 1891–96, Dean of Women, 90.134, 2, UCA.
49 *AV* 19, no. 2 (Nov. 1895).
50 Minutes, WLS, Victoria College, 25 Feb. 1897, Dean of Women, 90.134, 2, UCA.
51 N. Burwash, "Address at Convocation by Chancellor Burwash, *AV* 20, no. 2 (Nov. 1896).
52 Ada Pascoe, "The Higher Education of Young Women," *AV* 17, no. 2 (Nov. 1893).
53 *AV* 19, no. 2 (Nov. 1895).
54 *AV* 18 (April 1895).
55 "Mary E. Highet," A73–0026/150(45), UTA.
56 *AV* 38, no. 1 (Oct. 1913).
57 M. Burwash to M. Addison, 25 Feb. 1895, 90.141, 1, 1, UCA.
58 "To the Women of Methodism," *CG*, 31 March 1897.
59 M. Burwash, "An Appeal to the Methodist Women of Canada," *CG*, 7 April 1897.
60 Ibid.
61 "Victoria University Boarding House List, 1896–97," M.P. Burwash Papers, 10, 147, UCA.
62 M.E. Highet, "Women's Residence at Victoria," *CG*, 16 June 1897.
63 Theobald, "The Sin of Laura."
64 Ibid., 269.
65 Bessie Scott, "College Women," handwritten manuscript, n.d., B80–0033/001(06), UTA.
66 Ibid.
67 E.S. Baker, "English Residential Colleges," *CG*, 16 June 1897; M.E. Highet, "Residence Life in American Colleges," *CG*, 23 Feb. 1898.
68 Highet, "Residence Life."
69 It has been impossible to determine if this Bessie Scott is the same one who attended University College for two years before she interrupted her studies to become a teacher in Ottawa. See LaPierre, "The Academic Life of Canadian Coeds."
70 Clipping from the *Evening Journal*, 28 May 1897, M.P. Burwash Papers, 10, 14, UCA.
71 Bessie Scott, "College Women," B80–0033/001(06), 11, UTA.
72 "A Letter to The Barbara Heck Committee," *CG*, 1 June 1898.
73 Letter to the editor, *AV* 20, 6 (April 1897).

74 "Locals," *AV* 20, 6 (April 1897).

75 The calendar in 1896–97 lists the following women students: Miss Wilson from Toronto (postgraduate), and fourth-year students Miss E. Ackerman, Picton; Miss N. Langford, Orangeville; Miss E.M. Perrin, Lindsay; and Miss A.E. Le Rossignol. Third-year students were Miss Rose Barker, Toronto; Miss E.B. Howson, Toronto; Miss N.E. Livingstone, Toronto; Miss L.F.C. Nelles, Toronto; Miss M. Smith, Whitby. In the second year were Miss F. Barhite, Toronto; Miss Mary Clarke, Brockville; Miss M. Cooper, Melbourne; Miss Fausta Danard, Allenford; Miss A.J.C. Dawson, London; Miss F. Deacon, Milton; Miss M. Fife, Peterborough, Miss Martha Harvey, London; Miss M. Hawkins, Toronto; Miss I.M. Kerr, Toronto; Miss E. Moore, Islington; Miss Mary Rowell, London; Miss May Hurd Skinner, Toronto; Miss Grace Swanzey, Toronto; and Miss W. Wilson, Toronto. In the first year were Miss Lena Burr, Albert College; Miss D. Davison, London; Miss E. Duckett, Whitby; Miss E.W. Gould, Colborne; Miss L. Grenfell, Carleton Place; Miss A.F. Henwood, Welcome; Miss M. Kyle, Toronto; Miss V.A. Lackner, Berlin; Miss K. McKee, Toronto; Miss C.B. Proctor, Sarnia, Miss M.A. Reynar, Cobourg; and Miss E. Taylor, London.

76 *AV* 21, no. 3 (Dec. 1897).

77 *AV* 21, no. 7 (April 1898).

78 *AV* 21, no. 8 (May 1898).

79 "Victoria University Medals, Scholarships, and Prizes," *CG*, 20 Nov. 1901.

80 Cowan, *It's Late, and All the Girls Have Gone*, 1907–10, 83.

81 *AV* 21, no. 8 (May 1898).

82 *AV* 23, no. 1 (Oct. 1899).

83 Ibid.

84 Marshall, *Secularizing the Faith*.

85 Marsden, *The Soul of the American University*, 175. See also Shore, *The Science of Social Redemption*.

86 The question of women's place in these new social sciences remains. One might ask whether the increasing emphasis on quantitative research gradually excluded women from the social sciences. Women anthropologists such as Ruth Benedict and Margaret Mead were fortunate to found both sympathetic mentors and room to build a career.

87 *AV* 23, no. 8 (May 1900). Mabel Chown was a sister of Susannah Amelia and Alice Chown, and their father was the Reverend Edwin Anning Chown. I am grateful to Diana Chown for this information.

88 Margaret Hopkins Cox was born in Peterborough and married George Cox in 1862. They moved in 1887 to Toronto, where she was involved in many charities. See N. Burwash, *Margaret Hopkins Cox*.

89 The committee consisted of Mrs Cox, Mrs Lillian Massey Treble, Mrs C.D. Massey, Mrs W. Massey, Mrs Gurney, Mrs G. Kerr, Lady Flavelle, Mrs H.H. Fudger, Mrs A. Kemp, Margaret Eaton, Mrs Carman, Mrs Bain, Mrs Sutherland, Mrs Starr, Margaret Burwash, and Miss LeRossignol. Of the married women, Carman, Bain, Sutherland, and Burwash were faculty wives or wives of Methodist clergy, and the remainder were wives of successful businessmen. Lady Flavelle died in 1932, having served as a member of the committee from 1902 to 1932. Another long-standing member was Mrs Carman, who served from 1902 to 21.

90 "A Him of Hate," *Goblin* 2, no. 6 (April 1922), UTA.

91 Bessie Scott, "College Women," B80–0033/001(06), 11, UTA.

92 La Pierre, "The Academic Life of Canadian Coeds."

93 Tyack and Hanot, *Learning Together*, 157–8.

94 Gelman, "The 'Feminization' of the High Schools?" 98.

CHAPTER EIGHT

1 M. Addison to friends, 13 Dec. 1919, Addison Papers, box 1, UCA.

2 "Canadian Women in the Public Eye, Miss M.E.T. Addison," *Saturday Night*, 4 April 1925.

3 M. Addison, Diary, 2 Nov. 1900, Addison Papers, UCA.

4 Ibid., 8 Dec. 1900.

5 The acceptance of the higher local examination in Britain meant that women taking the local exams needed a hostel to stay in; the result was Newnham College. Two halls at Oxford, the non-denominational Somerville and the Anglican Lady Margaret Hall, had been founded between 1878 and 1879. Students were taught by dons from the men's colleges and took a special women's exam. In 1884 they took the degree examinations, but only in the 1890s did the movement for degrees begin. At Girton, Emily Davies obtained privileges for her students through favours extended by examiners, who marked the students papers unofficially. Women attended lectures with the men. In 1881 Professor Sidgwick was instrumental in securing for Newnham College women the permission to sit the Tripos (final) exam, but the Senate did not let women graduate with degrees. See Bryant, *The Unexpected Revolution*. Despite these achievements, at Oxford women were not admitted to formal membership until 1919 and at Cambridge until 1948. See Perry Williams, "Pioneer Women Students at Cambridge, 1869–81," in *Lessons for Life*, ed. Hunt, 171–91. The relative sizes of the women's colleges in 1897 varied significantly from 109 students at Girton and 166 at Newnham. At Oxford, Lady Margaret Hall had 48, St Hugh's Hall 24, and St Hilda's Hall 17. In London,

men's colleges and took a special women's exam. In 1884 they took the degree examinations, but only in the 1890s did the movement for degrees begin. At Girton, Emily Davies obtained privileges for her students through favours extended by examiners, who marked the students papers unofficially. Women attended lectures with the men. In 1881 Professor Sidgwick was instrumental in securing for Newnham College women the permission to sit the Tripos (final) exam, but the Senate did not let women graduate with degrees. See Bryant, *The Unexpected Revolution*. Despite these achievements, at Oxford women were not admitted to formal membership until 1919 and at Cambridge until 1948. See Perry Williams, "Pioneer Women Students at Cambridge, 1869–81," in *Lessons for Life*, ed. Hunt, 171–91. The relative sizes of the women's colleges in 1897 varied significantly from 109 students at Girton and 166 at Newnham. At Oxford, Lady Margaret Hall had 48, St Hugh's Hall 24, and St Hilda's Hall 17. In London, Bedford College had 192 women students, Westfield College 44, and Royal Holloway 111. See Vicinus, *Independent Women*, 127.

6 M. Addison, Diary, 2 Nov. 1900, Addison Papers, UCA.

7 Ibid., 4 Nov. 1900.

8 Ibid., 8 Dec. 1900.

9 Ibid.

10 This contrasted to the arrangement instituted by Emily Davies at Girton, which imitated the men's colleges by having a high table with the first mistress and her assistant seated above the students. Vicinus comments that neither the male model nor the family-style model proved suitable for the women's colleges, but that many years were spent looking for the appropriate style of corporate life. See Vicinus, *Independent Women*, 129.

11 M. Addison, Diary, 4 Dec. 1900, Addison Papers, UCA. Addison's impressions of St Hugh's are somewhat in contrast to those of a former student there who wrote, "our Principal had no conception of either comfort or beauty .our rooms were deplorably furnished, and our food ordered without intelligence and cooked without care or supervision." Joan Evans quoted in Vicinus, *Independent Women*, 131.

12 Addison was obviously impressed with the women's colleges. By contrast, Virginia Woolf's description of the established men's colleges, as compared to the newer women's ones, reveals that the women drank water while the men drank wine. The men had access to libraries, dining halls, and chapels, which had been established by centuries of wealth and tradition. The women lived with plain meals, plain architecture, and little access to tradition, whereas the men had "smoke and drink and the deep arm-chairs and the pleasant carpets." See Woolf, *A Room of One's Own*, 25.

13 M. Addison Diary, 8 Dec. 1900, Addison Papers, UCA. According to Vicinus, Agnes Maitland had been hired in 1889 and in the following fifteen years she doubled the enrolment of Somerville, built a library and housing, and hired a full staff. The hall was named Somerville College in 1894. See Vicinus, *Independent Women*, 132.
14 M. Addison, Diary, 9 Dec. 1900, Addison Papers, UCA.
15 Gordon, *Gender and Higher Education*, 24.
16 M. Addison, Diary, 8 June 1903, Addison Papers, UCA.
17 Ibid., 23 June 1903.
18 M. Addison to Miss A.E. Weekes, 14 Sept. 1903, Addison Papers, UCA.
19 M. Addison, Diary, undated, Addison Papers, box 1, UCA.
20 "Home Rules for Annesley Hall, 1903," 2–23, 90.141V, UCA.
21 "Regulations of the Committee of Management," n.d., Annesley Hall Student Government, 2–23, 90.141V, UCA.
22 M. Addison to parent, 25 May 1906, box 2, 87.168V, UCA.
23 M. Addison, Diary, undated, Addison Papers, box 1, UCA.
24 M. Addison's Report to the Committee of Management, May 1904, box 2, file 3, 90.064V, UCA.
25 Ibid.
26 Ibid.
27 Tyack and Hansot, *Learning Together*, 152.
28 Dean's Report to the Victoria Women's Residence and Educational Association, 1904, M.P. Burwash Papers, 6, 96, UCA.
29 M. Addison to Rev. Wallace, 12 Jan. 1912, 2, 14, 90.141, UCA.
30 Statement by N. Burwash, n.d. [1907?], M.P. Burwash Papers, 6, 96, UCA.
31 Ibid.
32 In 1918 Rowell, with a BA from Victoria in 1898, was serving as head of the third house for Victoria's students at 113 Bloor Street West. In his official history of Victoria, Sissons described her as a "graduate of twenty years, quiet, dignified, large in sympathy, feminine but not a feminist, she played a useful and unobtrusive part in the College until her retirement in 1935." Sissons, *A History of Victoria University*, 279.
33 M. Addison, Diary, 17 Jan. 1908, Addison Papers, UCA.
34 In March 1909, in response to fears about overcrowding at the University of Toronto, a senate subcommittee chaired by Professor George Wrong submitted a proposal that called for the establishment of a separate college for women.
35 Mabel Cartwright to M. Addison, 27 Feb. 1908; 90.141, 1, 8; 90.141, 2, 12, UCA. Although Cartwright had been educated in England and was an Anglican, the two women shared a lifelong devotion to the higher education for women and an agreement that college life should be rooted in Christian faith.

36 Minutes, Committee of Management, 13 Jan. 1916, vol. 3, 1914–18, 1, 3, UCA.

37 Burwash, *History of Victoria College*, 454. See appendix 2 in this book for a summary of the different residences used for women.

38 Deans' Report of Annesley and South Halls, 1909–10, to the Committee of Management, 90.064, 2, 6, UCA.

39 Ibid.

40 Recommendation of the women graduates of Victoria at a special meeting of the Alumnae Association, 14 Nov. 1909, 90.064, 1, 2, UCA.

41 Annual Report of the Dean of Annesley Hall to the Committee of Management, 1906/7, M.P. Burwash Papers, 6, 98, UCA.

42 M. Addison to Rev. G.M. Campbell, Mount Allison Ladies' College, 12 Jan. 1912, 90.141, 2, 14, UCA.

43 M. Addison, "Report to the Committee of Management," 14 Oct. 1909, M.P. Burwash Papers, box 6, 99, UCA.

44 "Statement prepared at the request of the Committee of the Joint Commission by the Chairman of the Ladies' Committee of Management on the Organization, Methods of Administration and Division of Duties obtaining in Annesley Hall," n.d., in "Documents for Use of Commission on Annesley Hall," Victoria University Women's Residence, 90.141, box 1, 8, UCA.

45 N. Burwash to M. Addison, 30 Jan. 1911, 90.141, 1, 12, UCA.

46 See "Documents for Use of Commission on Annesley Hall," Victoria University Women's Residence, 90.141, box 1, 8, UCA.

47 Sissons, *A History of Victoria University*, 243.

48 Resolution by the Alumnae Association to the Senate, n.d., M.P. Burwash Papers, 6, 99, UCA. A motion by Dr Bell, seconded by Dr Burwash, to reconsider the rules concerning dances, theatre, and chaperonage was tabled.

49 Margaret P. Massey and H.A. Sutherland to the Board of Regents of Victoria University, 19 April 1912, 90.064V, box 1–4, UCA.

50 Letter to the Board of Regents from Certain Members of the Ladies' Committee of Management [1912], in "Documents for Use of Commission on Annesley Hall," Victoria University Women's Residence, 90.141, box 1, 8, UCA.

51 From an undated memo, M.P. Burwash Papers, 6, 99, UCA.

52 Sissons, *A History of Victoria University*, 244. Chancellor Burwash's scepticism about the usefulness of student government is evident in the following comments: "My experience is that while the enlisting of students to maintain proper order in the residence on their own responsibility may be all right, still some very definite principles or rules for the government of the residence are necessary .and they should not be left entirely to make such rules for themselves. Quite a little difficulty has arisen in connection with Annesley Hall in that

respect." See N. Burwash to C.V. Massey, 29 Feb. 1912, N. Burwash Papers, 10, 14, UCA.

53 M. Proctor to M.P. Burwash, 25 Nov. 1913, 4, 70, M.P. Burwash Papers, UCA.

54 By-laws of the Committee of Management of Annesley and South Halls, 8 Jan. 1914, Addison Papers, 2, UCA.

55 M. Addison, "Sketch of the History of the Committee of Management of Annesley Hall," typescript, 14 May 1914, Addison Papers, 2, UCA.

56 Appendix 2 contains a list of the houses used as residences.

57 M. Addison to Charlotte Addison, 7 Nov. 1914, Addison Papers, box 1, UCA.

58 Dean's Report to the Committee of Management, 13 Jan. 1916, 90.064, 2, 12, UCA.

59 Announcement of the Women's Student Union of Victoria College, 1917, 90.146V, 1, 27, UCA.

60 Report to the Committee of Management, 8 March 1917, Annesley Hall, 90.064, 2, 13, UCA.

61 Ibid.

62 M. Addison to Charlotte Addison, 5 Dec. 1914, Addison Papers, box 1, UCA.

63 M. Addison to Charlotte Addison, 12 Feb. 1916, Addison Papers, box 1, UCA.

64 M. Addison to "friends," 13 Dec. 1919, Addison Papers, box 1, UCA.

65 Sissons, *A History of Victoria University*, 281.

66 M. Addison to "my very dear friends," 5 May 1920, Correspondence to family, Addison Papers, box 1, UCA.

67 Minutes of the Committee of Management, 15 April 1920, 90.064, 2, 12, UCA.

68 M. Addison to friends, 7 June 1920, Addison Papers, box 1, UCA.

69 By the constitution of the Committee of Management, 1903, the eighteen members were responsible for hiring the dean, the director of the household, and the servants, fixing the salaries, and making regulations concerning student behaviour.

70 M. Addison, "Sketch of the History of the Committee of Management," n.d., Addison Papers, box 2, file "generalized," UCA.

71 M. Addison to a friend, 20 Dec. 1920, Addison Papers, box 1, UCA.

72 Ibid.

73 Ibid.

74 Sissons, *A History of Victoria University*, 259.

75 Notes concerning women's statistics, n.d., Addison Papers, 2, UCA.

76 M. Burwash to M. Addison, 17 July 1905, 90.141, 1, 6, UCA.

77 Sissons, *A History of Victoria University*, 282–3.

78 M. Addison to Charlotte Addison, 2 April 1927, Addison Papers, box 1, UCA.

79 Scott-Raff was born in Waterdown and raised in Owen Sound, the daughter of a Methodist minister. She studied art and drama in Ontario and in England. For more details on her, see Murray, "Making the Modern."

80 Sissons, *A History of Victoria University*, 242.

81 A. Chown to M.P. Burwash, 1 Aug. 1901, M.P. Burwash Papers, 9, 135, UCA.

82 Petition to the Board of Regents by women undergraduates of Victoria University, n.d., M.P. Burwash Papers, 9, 135, UCA.

83 See Margaret Eaton School of Literature and Dramatic Art, Calendar, 1925/26, Margaret Eaton Reading Room, Benson Building, University of Toronto. Connections with Victoria were maintained by, for example, the presence on faculty of Pelham Edgar of Victoria and with the university by Mossie Mae Kirkwood, then dean of women at University College. Presumably, the bachelor of physical and health education degree at the University of Toronto eventually undermined the mandate of the school. I would like to thank Elizabeth Osborne, Secretary at the Benson Building, for her assistance. Information on the school is scattered and deserves to be collected and placed in the University of Toronto Archives.

84 The faculty in 1908 included Scott-Raff, Charlotte Ross, N.T. Thomas, F. Withrow, C. Wreyford, Nothnagel, Goudis, and Thrall.

85 A full study of the history of household, or domestic, science is unfortunately beyond the scope of this book. Such a study would need to trace the origins of the teaching of domestic science as it developed within the ladies' colleges, the high schools, and finally the university. The supporters of these courses saw domestic science as a perfect combination of the ideal role of women with a modern, scientific training. Its development was influenced by domestic science innovators in the United States, who met at conferences in Lake Placid in the early 1900s. There was a tension between the nineteenth-century domestic science advocates such as Adelaide Hoodless and twentieth-century educated women such as Alice Chown, who found Hoodless's activities embarrassing. Chown, as field secretary of the Canadian Household Economic Association, wrote to the minister of education, Richard Harcourt, that the Americans saw the Canadian domestic science programs as a bit of a freak, and she felt, "Domestic Science was just emerging from a personal subject into the control of the Educational Department & our educational work in general was not to be judged by the narrow & insufficient training of one person." See A. Chown to R. Harcourt, 7 July

1901, RG 2 D-7, 3, Education Dept. Records, File: 1902–05, AO. In another letter Chown bluntly stated that not only Mrs Hoodless's lack of science but "also her lack of mental training" made her incapable of doing really first-class academic work. See A. Chown to R. Harcourt, 2 July 190?, ibid.

86 Minutes, Alumnae Association, University College 1902, series III, Annual Meetings, 1898–1928, A69–0011/013, box 13, UTA.

87 The school, located at Bloor Street and Queen's Park, contained a gymnasium, swimming-pool, faculty room, library, museum, lecture hall, household art room, reading room, and household science and food chemistry classrooms.

88 N. Burwash to President Falconer, 28 April 1909, M.P. Burwash Papers, 9, 133, UCA.

89 Ibid. See Agreement between Lillian Massey and the University of Toronto, B80–0024, UTA.

90 La Pierre, "The Academic Life of Canadian Coeds." The Victoria College calendar for 1896–97 confirms this description of the requirements for a BA.

91 M. Addison to friends, 28 Oct. 1920, Addison Papers, box 1, UCA.

92 M. Addison to a friend, 20 Dec. 1920, Addison Papers, box 1, UCA.

93 M. Addison to friends, 22 Dec. 1921, Addison Papers, box 1, UCA.

94 M. Addison to friends, 10 Nov. 1923, Addison Papers, box 1, UCA.

95 Sissons, *A History of Victoria University*, 282.

96 Gordon, *Gender and Higher Education*, 43.

97 Walter T. Brown to the chancellor; quoted in Sissons, *A History of Victoria University*, 282.

98 Tyack and Hansot, *Learning Together*, 146.

99 Interview with Dorothy Forward, 26 April 1974, Oral History Project, B78–0003, cassette 1, UTA.

100 Cowan, *It's Late, and All the Girls Have Gone*, 94.

101 M. Addison to Charlotte Addison, 5 Nov. 1925, Addison Papers, box 1, UCA.

102 Mrs Wood was born the daughter of John Stavely in Montreal and married George Herbert Wood, chairman of Wood, Gundy and Co. She served on the board of the Deaconness Society and the Women's Missionary Society, and was an active member of Central Methodist Church.

103 M. Addison to friends, 7 Dec. 1925, Addison Papers, box 1, UCA.

104 M. Addison to friends, 29 Nov. 1926, Addison Papers, box 1, UCA.

105 Sissons, *A History of Victoria University*, 294.

106 Ibid.

107 M. Addison's final report to the Committee of Management, 4 June 1931, 90.064, 2, 2, UCA.

108 M. Addison to Louise Addison, 24 March 1926, Addison Papers, box 1, UCA.

CONCLUSION

1 Mackinnon, "Male Heads on Female Shoulders?"
2 Horowitz, *Alma Mater*, 41.
3 Gidney and Millar, *Inventing Secondary Education*, 242.
4 Ibid., 271.
5 Solomon, *In the Company of Educated Women*, 79.
6 Gidney and Millar, *Inventing Secondary Education*, 240.
7 Victoria University, Calendar, 1893–94.
8 La Pierre, "The Academic Life of Canadian Coeds," 234.
9 Victoria University, Calendar, 1896, 21. Students could follow pass or honours courses.
10 Palmieri, "Here Was Fellowship."
11 Ella Gardiner diary, 7 Dec. 1891, quoted in Smith, *Albert College*, 27.
12 Ibid.
13 M.E. Adams to Helena Coleman, 15 Feb. 1880, Helena Coleman Manuscript Collection, box 5, 134, VULA.
14 M.E. Adams to Helena Coleman, 24 June 1894, VULA.
15 In his article, Allmendinger argues from the pragmatic, which underestimates the desire that parents had to provide daughters with a Christian education as an expression of their faith. See Allmendinger, "Mount Holyoke Students."
16 External standards imposed on schools in Victoria, Australia, had similarly devastating effects on the careers of women teachers and administrators. See Zainu'ddin, "'The Poor Widow, the Ignoramus and Humbug.'"
17 Recent work by Heather Murray on the Margaret Eaton School and the dissertation in progress by Anna Conese will help to expand our knowledge of this fascinating institution. The demise of the domestic science program at the University of Toronto will be examined in a thesis by Jennifer Walsh.
18 Allmendinger, "Mount Holyoke Students."
19 Gordon, *Gender and Higher Education*, 16.
20 Mitchinson, *The Nature of Their Bodies*, 82–7.
21 Ibid.
22 Gordon, *Gender and Higher Education*, 16.
23 Macdonald, "Women or Girls?"
24 "Reasons for Educating Our Daughters," CCA, 13 Oct. 1858.
25 Ibid.

26 Francis Colemen to H. Colemen, 3 Sept. 1884, Helena Coleman Papers, box 5, 138, VULA.

27 MacLear, *The History of the Education of Girls*, especially chapter 6. For teacher history in Ontario see also Gelman, "The 'Feminization' of the High School," and Danylewycz and Prentice, "Teacher's Work."

28 Professor Hutton, quoted in "Home Life and College Life," CG, 20 Nov. 1901.

29 Rev. Thomas Pate, quoted in ibid.

30 Carman, "Strength and Beauty in a Woman's Character." The scriptural reference is from Psalm 144:12.

31 Say, *Evidence on Her Own Behalf*.

32 Sweet, "The Female Seminary Movement." See also A.F. Scott, *Making the Invisible Woman Visible*.

33 See McKillop, *A Disciplined Intelligence*, 216–28.

34 Willard may have dazzled her temperance audiences, but she failed to support the anti-lynching campaign of the African-American woman journalist Ida B. Wells and sought to undermine her credibility. See Giddings, *When and Where I Enter, and Ware, Beyond the Pale*.

35 Margaret Addison to a friend, n.d. [1904?], Dean of Women Papers, 2–19, 90.141V, UCA.

36 Notes from 25 March 1927, Addison Papers, box 28, UCA.

37 *Almafilian* 8, 3 (Feb. 1912), in Alma College, box 24, UCA.

Bibliography

MANUSCRIPT SOURCES

ALBERT COLLEGE ARCHIVES

ALMA COLLEGE ARCHIVES

ARCHIVES OF ONTARIO
Education Department Records, 1902–05

HAMILTON PUBLIC LIBRARY SPECIAL COLLECTIONS
Louise Wright Griffiths, "Unpublished Report to the Alumnae," 1933.
Victorian Hamilton Scrapbook, Clipping file.
Wesleyan Ladies' College Archives File
Wesleyan Female College, Act of Incorporation

MOUNT ALLISON UNIVERSITY ARCHIVES, SACKVILLE, NB
Mary Electa Adams Diary

TRAFALGAR CASTLE SCHOOL ARCHIVES, WHITBY
Letters from Minnie to Jenny, 1878

UNITED CHURCH OF CANADA ARCHIVES, TORONTO
Minutes of the Methodist General Conference, 1876–1914
Margaret Addison Papers
Benjamin Fish Austin Papers
Margaret Proctor Burwash Papers

Nathanael Burwash Papers
Albert Carman Papers
Samuel Dwight Chown Papers
William Cochrane Papers
Nellie Greenwood Papers
Emma R. Kaufman Papers
Samuel Sobrieski Nelles Papers
Jane Van Norman, Correspondence with A. Dunham Emory, microfilm.
Thomas Webster Papers
Wesleyan Ladies' College

UNIVERSITY OF TORONTO ARCHIVES
School of Household Science Papers
Minutes, Alumnae Association, University College, 1898–1928
Margaret Addison Student File
Dorothy Forward, Oral History Interview, 1974
The Goblin
Mary E. Highet Student File

VICTORIA COLLEGE PAPERS, UNITED CHURCH ARCHIVES
Annesley Hall Committee of Management, 1903–32
Barbara Heck Memorial Association, 1897–1901
Student Register #2, 1837–42 [Female Students Boarding in the Upper Canada Academy]
Victoria Women's Association, 1912–
Victoria Women's Residence and Educational Association, 1901–12
Women's Literary Society, 1891–
Women's Student Union Advisory Committee, 1917–25
Wymilwood Committee of the Annesley Hall Committee of Management, 1925–32

VICTORIA UNIVERSITY, DEAN OF WOMEN
Dean of Annesley Hall, 1903–20; Dean of Women, 1920–90
Collection Relating to Annesley Hall, Women at Victoria University, Outside Women's Organizations, and Women in Education

WHITBY HISTORICAL SOCIETY ARCHIVES
Letters from an Ontario Ladies' College student, September and October 1882
Ontario Ladies' College, Clipping file

SCHOOL AND COLLEGE CATALOGUES

Albert College (Belleville Seminary), Belleville, Announcement of Belleville Seminary, Belleville, October 1858.

– Announcement, 1891/92, 1897/98.
– *Collegiate Course*. Belleville: Daily Intelligencer Office, 1885.
– *General Catalogue of the Officers and Students of the Belleville College, Belleville, Canada West, 1857–66*. Belleville: Intelligencer Office, 1866.
Alexandra College. Calendar, 1872.
Alma Ladies' College. Calendar, 1889/90.
– Register of Graduates.
Belleville Business College. *Annual Circular and Catalogue ... 1884–5*. Belleville: Daily Intelligencer, 1884.
Burlington Ladies' Academy, Hamilton. *Catalogue of the Officers and Students* ... Hamilton, Canada West, 1847.
Cazenovia Seminary, New York. *First Fifty Years of Cazenovia Seminary, 1825–1875: Proceedings of the Semi-Centennial Jubilee, General Catalogue*. Cazenovia, NY, 1877.
Cobourg Ladies' Seminary. *Annual Circular ... 1845*. Cobourg: Canada Christian Advocate Office, 1845.
Dundas Wesleyan Institute. Calendar, 1876.
Genesee Wesleyan Seminary (later College). *Catalogue of the Officers and Students* ... Lima, NY: Livingston Co., 1833.
– *Catalogue of the Officers and Students* ... Lima, Rochester, NY: Gem Press, 1834.
Margaret Eaton School of Literature and Dramatic Art, Toronto. Calendar, 1925/26.
Ontario Ladies' College, Whitby. Calendar, 1874/75, 1875/76, 1878, 1880/81, 1891/92, 1894/96, 1912/14.
Picton Academies for Ladies and Gentlemen. Prospectus, 1850.
Van Norman Institute, New York. Prospectus, 1857–67.
– *Van Norman Institute for the Education of Young Ladies*. New York: Charles Shields, 1860.
Victoria University. Calendar, 1893/94, 1896.
Wesleyan Ladies' College (Hamilton Ladies' College). *Act of Incorporation*. 1861.
– Calendar, 1865, 1874, 1881/82, 1887/88, 1891/92.
– Catalogue, 1861, 1862/63, 1866/67.
– *Wesleyan Ladies' College, 1890*. Hamilton: Times, 1890.

JOURNALS AND NEWSPAPERS

Acta Victoriana, 1878–1925
British American Presbyterian (Toronto, 1872–77
Canada Christian Advocate
Canadian Methodist Magazine, 1874–96
Christian Guardian, 1829–1925
Globe (Toronto), 1867–1918
Hamilton Spectator

BOOKS AND PAMPHLETS

Addison, Margaret. "Higher Education for Women." *Christian Guardian*, 30 May 1894.

Airhart, Phyllis D. *Serving the Present Age: Revivalism, Progressivism, and the Methodist Tradition in Canada*. Kingston, Montreal: McGill-Queen's University Press, 1992.

Allen, Judith. "Contextualizing Late-Nineteenth-Century Feminism: Problems and Comparisons." *Journal of the Canadian Historical Association*, 1990, 17–35.

Allen, Richard. *The Social Passion: Religion and Social Reform in Canada, 1914–28*. Toronto: University of Toronto Press, 1971.

Allmendinger, David F., Jr. "Mount Holyoke Students Encounter the Need for Life-Planning, 1837–1850." *History of Education Quarterly* 19, no. 1 (Spring 1979): 27–46.

Anderson, Cora. "Shall Women Preach? Principles and Practices in the Salvation Army and in the Methodist Church in Ontario 1882–1900." *Conrad Grebel Review* 8, no. 3 (Fall 1990): 275–88.

Antler, Joyce. *Lucy Sprague Mitchell: The Making of a Modern Woman*. New Haven, Conn.: Yale University Press, 1987.

Ariès, Phillippe, and George Duby, eds. *A History of Private Life*. Vol. 4, *From the Fires of Revolution to the Great War*. Ed. Michelle Perrot. Trans. Arthur Goldhammer. Cambridge, Mass.: Harvard University Press, 1990.

Austin, Benjamin Fish. *The A.B.C. of Spiritualism*. Los Angeles: The Austin Publishing Co., 1920.

– "The Spiritual Phenomena of the Bible." In *100 Conundrums for the Clergy, also an Open Letter to Orthodox Clergy: The Spiritual Phenomena of the Bible*. Rochester, NY: Austin Publishing Co., 1906.

– , ed. *What Converted Me to Spiritualism*. Toronto: B.F. Austin Publishing Co., 1901.

– *Woman; Her Character, Culture and Calling*. Brantford, Ont.: Brantford Book and Bible House, 1890.

Baker, E.S. "English Residential Colleges." *Christian Guardian*, 16 June 1897.

Bendroth, Margaret Lamberts. *Fundamentalism and Gender. 1875 to the Present*. New Haven, Conn.: Yale University Press, 1993.

Bennet, Paul. "Little Worlds: The Forging of Identities in Ontario Protestant Denominational Schools and Special Institutions, 1850–1930." EdD thesis, University of Toronto, 1990.

Bliss, Michael. *A Canadian Millionaire: The Life and Business Times of Sir Joseph Flavelle, Bart., 1858–1939*. Toronto: University of Toronto Press, 1992.

Bordin, Ruth. *Woman and Temperance: The Quest for Power and Liberty, 1873-1900*. Philadelphia: Temple University Press, 1981.

Boyd, Nancy. *Emissaries: The Overseas Work of the American YMCA, 1895–1970*. New York: The Woman's Press, 1986.

Boydston, Jeanne, Mary Kelley, and Anne Margolis. *The Limits of Sisterhood: The Beecher Sisters and Women's Rights and Women's Sphere*. Chapel Hill, NC: University of North Carolina Press, 1988.

Boylan, Anne M. *Sunday School: The Formation of An American Institution*. New Haven, Conn.: Yale University Press, 1988.

Braude, Ann. *Radical Spirits: Spiritualism and Women's Rights in Nineteenth-Century America*. Boston: Beacon Press, 1989.

Brereton, Virginia Lieson. *Training God's Army: The American Bible School, 1880–1940*. Bloomington, Ind.: Indiana University Press, 1990.

Brouwer, Ruth Compton. "The 'Between-Age' Christianity of Agnes Machar." *Canadian Historical Review* 65, no. 3 (Sept. 1984): 347–70.

– *New Women for God: Canadian Presbyterian and India Missions, 1876–1914*. Toronto: University of Toronto Press, 1990.

Brown, Jennifer. "'A Disposition to Bear the Ills…': Rejection of a Separate College by University of Toronto Women." Canadian Women's History Series, no. 7. Toronto: History and Philosophy of Education Department, Ontario Institute for Studies in Education, 1977.

Bryant, Margaret. *The Unexpected Revolution: A Study in the History of the Education of Women and Girls in the Nineteenth Century*. London: University of London Institute of Education, 1979.

Burkholder, Mabel. "Inside the Walls, A Sketch of Daily Life at the Ontario Ladies' College, Whitby." *Canadian Methodist Monthly* 58, no. 2 (1903): 506–15.

Burkholder, Nettie. "After Graduation, What?" *Portfolio* 8, no. 20 (June 1888): 156–6.

– "The Financial Capabilities of Women." *Portfolio* 10, no. 8 (June n.d.).

Burnet, Jean. "Occupational Differences and the Class Structure." In *Readings in Canadian History*. Toronto: Holt, Rhinehart, and Winston, 1986.

Burnside, Albert. "The Contribution of the Rev. Albert Carman to Albert College, Belleville, and to the Methodist Episcopal Church in Canada, 1857–1884." MA thesis, Toronto Graduate School of Theology, 1982.

Burstyn, Joan N. "Narrative versus Theoretical Approaches: A Dilemma for Historians of Women." *History of Education Review* 19, no. 2 (1990): 1–7.

– *Victorian Education and the Ideal of Womanhood*. New Brunswick, NJ: Rutgers University Press, 1984.

Burwash, Margaret. "An Appeal To The Methodist Women of Canada." *Christian Guardian*, 7 April 1897.

Burwash, Nathanael. *History of Victoria College*. Toronto: Victoria College Press, 1927.

– *Margaret Hopkins Cox*. n.p., n.d.

Campbell, J.H. "Co-education in Universities." *Acta Victoriana* 3, no. 7 (April 1881).

Campbell, Karlyn Kohrs. *Man Cannot Speak for Her*. New York: Praeger, 1989.

"Canadian Women in the Public Eye, Miss M.E.T. Addison." *Saturday Night*, 4 April 1925.

Carman, Albert. "Strength and Beauty in a Woman's Character." In Woman; Her Character, Culture and Calling, ed. B.F. Austin. Brantford, Ont.: Brantford, Book and Bible House, 1890.

Catharine Bell Van Norman: Her Diary: 1850. Burlington, Ont.: Burlington Historical Society, 1981.

Chown, Alice. *The Stairway.* Toronto: University of Toronto Press, 1988; repr., Boston: Cornhill Co., 1921.

Cleverdon, Catharine. *The Woman Suffrage Movement in Canada*. Toronto: University of Toronto Press, 1974 [1950].

Clifford, Geraldine Joncich, ed. *Lone Voyageurs: Academic Women in Coeducational Institutions 1870–1937*. New York: Feminist Press at the City University of New York, 1989.

Cochrane, William. *The Church and the Commonwealth*. Brantford, Ont.; Melbourne and Port Adelaide, Australia: Bradley and Garretson, 1887.

– *Men of Canada; or Success By Example*. Vol. 1. Brantford, Ont.: Bradley, Garretson and Co., 1891.

Cook, Ramsay. *The Regenerators*. Toronto: University of Toronto Press, 1985.

Cook, Sharon Anne. "'Continued and Persevering Combat': The Ontario Woman's Christian Temperance Union, Evangelicalism and Social Reform 1874–1916." PHD dissertation, Carleton University, 1990.

Corrigan, Philip, and Bruce Curtis. "Education, Inspection and State Formation: A Preliminary Statement." Canadian Historical Association, *Historical Papers*, 1985: 156–71.

Cott, Nancy. *The Bonds of Womanhood: "Woman's Sphere" in New England, 1780–1960*. New Haven, Conn.: Yale University Press, 1975.

Cowan, Kathleen. *It's Late, and All The Girls Have Gone: An Annesley Diary, 1907–10*. Toronto: Childe Thursday, 1984.

Cranston, Maurice. *The Romantic Movement*. Oxford: Blackwell Publishers, 1994.

Curtis, Bruce. *Building the Educational State, Canada West, 1836–1871*. London: Falmer Press, 1988.

– *True Government by Choice Men? Inspection, Education, and State Formation in Canada West*. Toronto: University of Toronto Press, 1992.

Cyclopedia of Methodism in Canada. Vol. 3, *1881–1908*. Toronto: Methodist Book and Publishing House, 1903.

Danylewycz, Marta. *Taking the Veil: An Alternative to Marriage, Motherhood and Spinsterhood in Quebec, 1840–1902*. Toronto: McClelland and Stewart, 1987.

– and Alison Prentice. "Teachers, Gender, and Bureaucratizing School Systems in Nineteenth Century Montreal and Toronto." *History of Education Quarterly* 24, no. 1 (Spring 1984): 75–100.

– "Teacher's Work: Changing Patterns and Perceptions in the Emerging School Systems of Nineteenth- and Early Twentieth-Century Central Canada," in *Women Who Taught. Perspectives on the History of Women and*

Teaching, ed. Alison Prentice and Marjorie Theobald. Toronto: University of Toronto Press, 1991.

Davey, Ian E. "Trends in Female School Attendance in Mid-Nineteenth Century Ontario." *Histoire sociale/Social History* 8 (Nov. 1975): 238–54.

Davidoff, Leonore, and Catherine Hall. *Family Fortunes: Men and Women of the English Middle Class, 1780–1850*. Chicago: University of Chicago Press, 1987.

Delamont, Sara. *Knowledgeable Women: Structuralism and the Reproduction of Elites*. London, New York: Routledge, 1989.

DeSwarte Gifford, Carolyn. "For God and Home and Native Land." In *Women in New Worlds*, ed. Hillah Thomas and Rosemary Skinner Keller. Nashville, Tenn.: Abingdon Press, 1981.

Dickson, Irene and Margaret Webster. *To Keep the Memory Green: A History of Ewart College, 1897–1987*. Toronto: Ewart College, 1986.

Dictionary of Hamilton Biography. Vol. 1. Hamilton: W.L. Griffin, 1981.

Dix, Morgan. "The Education of Woman for her Work." In *Woman; Her Character, Culture and Calling*, ed. B.F. Austin. Brantford, Ont.: Brantford Book House, 1890.

Douglas, Ann. *The Feminization of American Culture*. New York: Knopf, 1977.

Dumont, Micheline, and Nadia Fahmy-Eid. *Les Couventines: L'éducation des filles au Québec dans les congrégations religieuses enseignantes, 1840–1960*. Montréal: Boréal, 1986.

Duvall, Sylvanus Milne. *The Methodist Episcopal Church and Education up to 1869*. New York: Teacher's College, Columbia University Press, 1928.

Dyhouse, Carol. *Feminism and the Family in England, 1880–1939*. Oxford: Basil Blackwell, 1989.

– *Girls Growing Up in Late Victorian and Edwardian England*. London: Routledge & Kegan Paul, 1981.

Edwards, Wesley. *The History of Alma College*. St Thomas, Ont.: Alma College, 1927.

Eschbach, Elizabeth Seymour. *The Higher Education of Women in England and America, 1865–1920*. New York: Garland Publishing, 1993.

Ford, Anne Rochon. *A Path Not Strewn with Roses: One Hundred Years of Women at the University of Toronto*. Toronto: University of Toronto Press, 1985.

Francis, R. Douglas, and Donald Smith. *Readings in Canadian History Pre-Confederation*. Toronto: Harcourt, Brace, Jovanovich, 1988.

Frankfort, Roberta. *Collegiate Women: Domesticity and Career in Turn of the Century America*. New York: New York University Press, 1977.

French, Goldwin. *Parsons and Politics*. Toronto: Ryerson Press, 1962.

Gagan, Rosemary R. *A Sensitive Independence: Canadian Methodist Missionaries in Canada and the Orient, 1881–1925*. Kingston, Montreal: McGill-Queen's University Press, 1992.

Gauvreau, Michael. "The Empire of Evangelicalism." In *Evangelicalism: Comparative Studies of Popular Protestantism in North America, The British Isles, and Beyond, 1700–1990*, ed. Mark A. Noll et al. New York: Oxford University Press, 1994, 219–52.

– *The Evangelical Century*. Kingston, Montreal: McGill-Queen's University Press, 1990.

Gelman, Susan. "The 'Feminization' of the High School: Women Secondary School Teachers in Toronto, 1871–1930." In *Gender and Education in Ontario*, ed. Ruby Heap and Alison Prentice. Toronto: Canadian Scholars' Press, 1991.

Giddings, Paula. *When and Where I Enter: The Impact of Black Women on Race and Sex in America*. New York: William Morrow, 1984.

Gidney, R.D. "Elementary Education in Upper Canada: A Reassessment." *Ontario History* 65, no. 3 (1973): 169–85.

– and W.P.J. Millar. *Inventing Secondary Education: The Rise of the High School in Nineteenth-Century Ontario*. Kingston, Montreal: McGill-Queen's University Press, 1990.

Gifford, Carolyn DeSwarte. "For God and Home and Native Land." In *Women in New Worlds*, eds. Hillah Thomas and Rosemary Skinner Keller. Nashville, Tenn.: Abingdon Press, 1981.

Gillett, Margaret. *We Walked Very Warily: A History of Women at McGill*. Montreal: Eden Press Women's Publications, 1981.

– and K. Sibbald, eds. *A Fair Shake: Autobiographical Essays by McGill Women*. Montreal: Eden Press, 1984.

Glazer, Penina Migdal, and Miriam Slater. *Unequal Colleagues: The Entrance of Women into the Professions, 1890–1940*. New Brunswick, NJ: Rutgers University Press, 1987.

Goodsell, Willystine, ed. *Pioneers of Women's Education in the United States: Emma Willard, Catharine Beecher, Mary Lyon*. New York: McGraw-Hill, 1931.

Gordon, Lynn D. *Gender and Higher Education in the Progressive Era*. New Haven, Conn.: Yale University Press, 1990.

Gorham, Deborah. "The Ideology of Femininity and Reading for Girls." In *Lessons for Life: The Schooling of Girls and Women, 1850–1950*, ed. Felicity Hunt. Oxford: Basil Blackwell, 1987.

– *The Victorian Girl and the Feminine Ideal*. London: Croom Helm, 1982.

Grant, John Webster. *The Church in the Canadian Era*. Vol. 3. Toronto: McGraw-Hill Ryerson, 1972.

– *A Profusion of Spires: Religion in Nineteenth-Century Ontario*. Toronto: University of Toronto Press, 1988.

Grant, R.N. *Life of William Cochrane, D.D.*. Toronto: William Briggs, 1899.

Gray, A. Herbert. *The Relations of Men and Women*. [An Address Before the First National Conference of Canadian Students] Toronto: S.C.M., 1923.

Gray, Ann M. "Continuity in Change: The Effects on Girls of Co-Educational Secondary Schooling In Ontario 1860–1910." MA thesis, University of Toronto, 1984.

Green, Donna. "The Wesleyan Ladies' College of Hamilton: A Unique Chapter in Women's Education." Unpublished paper, Department of History, McMaster University, March 1989.

Griffiths, Louise Wright. "Unpublished report to the Alumnae [of the Wesleyan Ladies' College]." 1933.

Grumet, Madeleine. *Bitter Milk: Women and Teaching*. Amherst: University of Massachusetts Press, 1988.

Hall, Nancy. "The Professionalization of Women Workers in the Methodist, Presbyterian, and United Churches of Canada." In *First Days, Fighting Days: Women in Manitoba History*, ed. Mary Kinnear, 120–33. Regina: Canadian Plains Research Center, University of Regina, 1987.

Hardesty, Nancy. *Women Called to Witness: Evangelical Feminism in the 19th Century*. Nashville, Tenn.: Abingdon, 1984.

Heap, Ruby, and Alison Prentice, eds. *Gender and Education in Ontario*. Toronto: Canadian Scholars' Press, 1991.

The Heresy Trial of B.F. Austin. Toronto: Sermon Publishing Co., n.d. [1899?].

Heslegrave, Linda. "The Cult of True Womanhood and the Development of Ladies' Colleges in Ontario in the Nineteenth Century." Unpublished paper, Department of History, McMaster University, 1976–77.

Hewitt, Nancy A. *Women's Activism and Social Class: Rochester, New York, 1822–1872*. Ithaca, NY: Cornell University Press, 1984.

Highet, M.E. "Residence Life in American Colleges." *Christian Guardian*, 23 Feb. 1898.

– "Women's Residence at Victoria." *Christian Guardian*, 16 June 1897.

Hill, Patricia R. *The World Their Household: The American Woman's Foreign Mission Movement and Cultural Transformation, 1870–1920*. Ann Arbor: University of Michigan Press, 1985.

Hodgins, J. George. *The Establishment of Schools and Colleges in Ontario, 1792–1910*. 3 vols. Toronto: L.D. Cameron, 1910.

Holden, Pat, ed. *Women's Religious Experience*. London: Croom Helm, 1983.

Holland, Dorothy C., and Margaret A. Eisenhart. *Women, Achievement Culture*. Chicago: University of Chicago Press, 1990.

Horowitz, Helen. *Alma Mater*. Boston: Beacon Press, 1984.

Houston, Susan E., and Alison Prentice. *Schooling and Scholars in Nineteenth-Century Ontario*. Toronto: University of Toronto Press, 1988.

Hunt, Felicity, ed. *Lessons for Life: The Schooling of Girls and Women, 1850–1950*. Oxford: Basil Blackwell, 1987.

Iacovetta, Franca, and Mariana Valverde, eds. *Gender Conflicts: New Essays in Women's History*. Toronto: University of Toronto Press, 1992.

Ibronyi, Barbara. *Early Voices: Women at Victoria*. Toronto: Victoria University Press, 1984.

Johnson, Lesley. "The Schooling of Girls in the 1950s: Problems with Writing a History of 'Women's Education.'" *History of Education Review* 19, no. 2 (1990): 8–15.

Johnston, Charles M. *McMaster University.* Vol. 1, *The Early Years*. Toronto: University of Toronto Press, 1975.

Katz, Michael B. *Family and Class in a Canadian City: Mid-Nineteenth Century Hamilton*. Cambridge, Mass.: Harvard University Press, 1975.

– *The People of Hamilton, Canada West: Family and Class in the Mid-Nineteenth Century.* Cambridge, Mass.: Harvard University Press, 1975.

– and Paul Mattingly. *Education and Social Change: Themes from Ontario's Past*. New York: New York University Press, 1975.

Kealey, Linda, ed. *A Not Unreasonable Claim: Women and Reform in Canada, 1880s–1920s*. Toronto: Women's Press, 1979.

Ketchum, Anthony. "The Most Perfect System: Official Policy in the First Century of Ontario's Government Secondary Schools and Its Impact on Students between 1871 and 1910." EDD thesis, University of Toronto, 1979.

Knox, Ellen. *The Girl of the New Day.* Toronto: McClelland and Stewart, 1919.

Krommenhoek, Cora. "'The Church Should Have Championed the Woman's Cause': Women's Liberation and the Methodist Church in Canada, 1874–1925." *Canadian Methodist Historical Society Papers, 1991 and 1992*. Toronto, 1993.

Kyle, Noeline. *Her Natural Destiny: The Education of Women in New South Wales*. Kensington: New South Wales University Press, 1986.

Lagemann, Ellen Condliffe. *A Generation of Women: Education in the Lives of Progressive Reformers*. Cambridge, Mass.: Harvard University Press, 1979.

La Pierre, Paula J.S. "The Academic Life of Canadian Coeds, 1880–1900." *Historical Studies in Education/Revue d'histoire de l'éducation* 2, no. 2 (Fall 1990): 225–47.

– "The First Generation: The Experience of Women University Students in Central Canada." PHD dissertation, University of Toronto, 1992.

Lasser, Carol, ed. *Educating Men and Women Together: Coeducation in a Changing World*. Urbana and Chicago: University of Illinois Press, 1987.

Legendre, Carmelle. "The Baptist Contribution to 19th Century Education for Women: An Examination of Moulton College and McMaster University." MA thesis, McMaster University, 1981.

Lerner, Gerda. *The Creation of Feminist Consciousness*. New York: Oxford University Press, 1993.

Lewis, Jane. *Labour and Love: Women's Experience of Home and Family, 1850–1950*. Oxford: Basil Blackwell, 1987.

McCallum, John. "Urban and Commercial Development until 1850." In *Readings in Canadian History*, ed. R. Douglas Francis and Donald Smith. Toronto: Holt, Rhinehart, and Winston, 1986.

Macdonald, H.S. Grant. "Women or Girls?" *Sesame* 1, no. 3 (Jan. 1899): 1–24.

MacFarlane, Mary Anne. "Educating, Sanctifying, and Regulating Motherhood: The Cradle Roll Department in Methodist Sunday Schools." *Canadian Methodist Historical Society Papers*, 1991–92, 167–91.

– "A Tale of Handmaidens: Deaconesses in the United Church of Canada, 1925–1964." MA thesis, University of Toronto, 1987.

McKillop, A.B. *A Disciplined Intelligence*. Kingston, Montreal: McGill-Queen's University Press, 1979.

– *Matters of Mind: The University in Ontario, 1791–1951*. Toronto: University of Toronto Press, 1994.

MacKinnon, Alison. "Male Heads on Female Shoulders? New Questions for the History of Women's Higher Education." *History of Education Review* 19, no. 2 (1990): 36–47.

– "A New Point of Departure." *History of Education Review* 13, no. 2 (1984): 1–4.

– *One Foot on the Ladder: Origins and Outcomes of Girl's Secondary Schooling in South Australia*. Queensland: University of Queensland, 1984.

– "Women's Education: Linking History and Theory." *History of Education Review* 13, no. 2 (1984): 5–14.

McLachlan, James. *American Boarding Schools: A Historical Study*. New York: Charles Scribner's Sons, 1970.

MacLear, Martha. *The History of the Education of Girls in New York and in New England, 1800–1870*. Washington, DC: Howard University Press, 1926.

Macmillan Dictionary of Canadian Biography. Ed. W. Stewart Wallace. London, Toronto: Macmillan, 1963.

Marks, Lynne and Chad Gaffield. "Women at Queen's University, 1895–1905: A Little 'Sphere' All Their Own?" *Ontario History* 78, no. 4 (Dec. 1986): 331–49.

Marr, Lucille. "Church Hierarchy and Christian Nurture: The Significance of Gender in Religious Education in the Methodist, Presbyterian and United Churches of Canada, 1919–1939." PHD dissertation, McGill University, 1990.

Marsden, George M. *Fundamentalism and American Culture: The Shaping of Twentieth Century Evangelicalism, 1870–1925*. New York: Oxford University Press, 1980.

– *The Soul of the American University*. New York: Oxford University Press, 1994.

– and Bradley J. Longfield, eds. *The Secularization of the Academy*. New York: Oxford University Press, 1992.

Marshall, David B. *Secularizing the Faith: Canadian Protestant Clergy and the Crisis of Belief, 1850–1940*. Toronto: University of Toronto Press, 1992.

Martin-Figier, Anne. "Bourgeois Rituals." In *A History of Private Life*, ed. Michelle Perot. Cambridge, Mass.: Belknap Press, 1990.

Masters, Donald C. *Protestant Church Colleges in Canada*. Toronto: University of Toronto Press, 1966.

Mattingly, Paul H., and Michael Katz. *Education and Social Change: Themes from Ontario's Past*. New York: New York University Press, 1975.

Melder, Keith. "Mask of Oppression: The Female Seminary Movement in the United States." *New York History* 55, no. 3 (July 1974): 261–79.

Mitchinson, Wendy. *The Nature of Their Bodies: Women and Their Doctors in Victorian Canada*. Toronto: University of Toronto Press, 1991.

– "The W.C.T.U.: 'For God, Home and Native Land': A Study in Nineteenth Century Feminism." In *A Not Unreasonable Claim: Women and Reform in Canada, 1880s-1920s*, ed. Linda Kealey, 151–67. Toronto: Women's Educational Press, 1979.

Moir, John S. *Church and State in Canada West: Three Studies in the Relation of Denominationalism and Nationalism, 1841–1867*. Toronto: University of Toronto Press, 1959.

– and C.T. McIntire, eds. *Canadian Protestant and Catholic Missions, 1820s-1960s*. New York: Peter Lang, 1988.

Monet, Jacques. "The 1840s." In *Readings in Canadian History*, ed. R. Douglas Francis and Donald Smith. Toronto: Holt, Rhinehart, and Winston, 1986.

Moody, Barry M. "Breadth of Vision, Breadth of Mind: The Baptists and Acadia College." In *Canadian Baptists and Christian Higher Education*, ed. George Rawlyk. Kingston, Montreal: McGill-Queen's University Press, 1988.

Morgan, Henry, ed. *Canadian Men and Women of the Time*. Toronto: William Briggs, 1912.

Morton, Desmond. *A Short History of Canada*. Edmonton, Alta: Hurtig Publishers, 1983.

Moorcroft, Kathleen. "Character Builders: Women and Education in Whitby, Ontario, 1900–1920." EDD dissertation, University of Toronto, 1979.

– "The Women's Missionary Society of Tabernacle Methodist Church, Whitby, Ontario: The Educational Goals and Achievements of its Members at the Turn of the Century." Unpublished term paper, Ontario Institute for Studies in Education, May 1978.

Muir, Elizabeth Gilan. "Methodist Women Preachers: An Overview." *Canadian Methodist Historical Society Papers* 7 (1987).

– *Petticoats in the Pulpit: The Story of Early Nineteenth-Century Methodist Women Preachers in Upper Canada*. Toronto: United Church Publishing House, 1991.

Murray, Heather. "Making the Modern: Twenty-Five Years of the Margaret Eaton School of Literature and Expression." *Essays in Theatre/Études théâtrales* 10, no. 1 (Nov. 1991): 39–55.

Noll, Mark, et al. *Evangelicalism: Comparative Studies of Popular Protestantism in North America, the British Isles, and Beyond, 1700–1990*. New York: Oxford University Press, 1994.

Noll, William T. "Women as Clergy and Laity in the 19th Century Methodist Protestant Church." *Methodist History* 15 (Jan. 1977): 107–21.

Palmieri, Patricia A. "Here Was Fellowship: A Social Portrait of Academic Women at Wellesley College, 1880–1920." In *Women Who Taught: Perspectives on the History of Women and Teaching*, ed. Alison Prentice and Marjorie Theobald, 258–84. Toronto: University of Toronto Press, 1991.

Parr, Joy. *The Gender of Breadwinners: Women, Men, and Change in Two Industrial Towns, 1880–1950*. Toronto: University of Toronto Press, 1990.

Pascoe, Ada. "The Higher Education of Young Women." *Acta Victoriana* 17, no. 2 (Nov. 1895).

Pederson, Diana. "The Call to Service: The YWCA and the Canadian College Woman, 1886–1921." In *Youth, University and Canadian Society*, ed. Paul Axelrod and John Reid, 187–215. Kingston, Montreal: McGill-Queen's University Press, 1989.

Pomeroy, Elsie. "Mary Electa Adams: A Pioneer Educator." *Ontario History* 41 (1949): 107–17.

Potts, David. "New England's Chilly Climate for Coeducation: Women at Wesleyan University, 1872–1912." Unpublished paper presented at the annual meeting of the History of Education Society, Atlanta, GA, 2 Nov. 1990.

Prang, Margaret. "'The Girl God Would Have Me Be': The Canadian Girls in Training, 1915–39." *Canadian Historical Review* 66, no. 2 (1985): 154–84. Toronto: United Church Publishing House, 1991.

Prelinger, Catherine M. *Episcopal Women*. New York: Oxford University Press, 1992.

Prentice, Alison. "Education and the Metaphor of the Family: The Upper Canadian Example." In *Education and Social Change: Themes from Ontario's Past*, ed. Michael B. Katz and Paul H. Mattingly. New York: New York University Press, 1975.

– "Scholarly Passion and Two Persons Who Caught It." *Historical Studies in Education/Revue d'histoire de l'éducation* 1, no. 1 (Spring 1989): 7–27.

– *The School Promoters*. Toronto: McClelland and Stewart, 1977.

– "Towards A Feminist History of Women and Education." In *Approaches to Educational History*, ed. D.G. Jones et al. Winnipeg: University of Manitoba, 1980.

– et al. *Canadian Women: A History*. Toronto: Harcourt Brace Jovanovich, 1988.

– and Marta Danylewycz. "Teachers, Gender, and Bureaucratizing School Systems in Nineteenth Century Montreal and Toronto." *History of Education Quarterly* 24, no. 1 (Spring 1984): 75–100.

– and Marjorie Theobald, eds. *Women Who Taught: Perspectives on the History of Women and Teaching*. Toronto: University of Toronto Press, 1991.

Pujol, Louis and D.C. Van Norman. *The Complete French Class-book, Embracing Grammar, Conversation, Literature*. New York: A.S. Barnes and Co., 1875.

Purvis, Jane. *Hard Lessons: The Lives and Education of Working-Class Women in Nineteenth-Century England*. Oxford: Basil Blackwell, 1989.

– *A History of Women's Education in England*. Philadelphia: Open University Press, 1991.

Rawlyk, George. *Canadian Baptists and Christian Higher Education*. Kingston, Montreal: McGill-Queen's University Press, 1988.

– *Ravished by the Spirit: Religious Revivals, Baptists, and Henry Alline*. Kingston, Montreal: McGill-Queen's University Press, 1984.

Reardon, M.G. *Religion in the Age of Romanticism*. Cambridge: Cambridge University Press, 1985.

"Reasons for Educating Our Daughters." *Canada Christian Advocate*, 13 Oct. 1858.

Reid, John G. "The Education of Women at Mount Allison, 1854–1914." *Acadiensis* 12, no. 2 (Spring 1983): 3–33.

– *Mount Allison University: A History to 1963*. Toronto: University of Toronto Press, 1984.

Report of the Massey Foundation Commission on the Secondary Schools and Colleges of the Methodist Church of Canada. Toronto: Massey Foundation, 1921.

Richey, Russell E. "The Social Sources of Denominationalism: Methodism." In *Denominationalism*, ed. Russell E. Richey, 163–84. Nashville, Tenn.: Abingdon, 1977.

Riddell, Katharine, ed. *Alma College Centennial Book, 1877–1957*. St Thomas, Ont.: Alma College, 1927.

Ronish, Donna Yavorsky. "Sweet Girl Graduates: The Admission of Women to English-Speaking Universities in Canada in the Nineteenth Century." PHD dissertation, University of Montreal, 1985.

Rosenberg, Rosalind. *Beyond Separate Spheres: Intellectual Roots of Modern Feminism*. New Haven, Conn.: Yale University Press, 1977.

Rousmaniere, Kate. "To Prepare the Ideal Woman: Private Denominational Girl's Schooling in Late Nineteenth Century Ontario." MA thesis, University of Toronto, 1984.

Royce, Marion V. "Arguments over the Education of Girls – Their Admission to the Grammar Schools of this Province." *Ontario History* 68 (March 1975): 1–13.

– "Education for Girls in Quaker Schools in Ontario." *Atlantis* 3, no. 1 (Fall 1977): 181–92.

– *Landmarks in the Victorian Education of 'Young Ladies' under Methodist Church Auspices*. Canadian Women's History Series, 4. Toronto: Ontario Institute for Studies in Education, 1977.

– "Methodism and the Education of Women in Nineteenth Century Ontario." *Atlantis* 3, no. 2, part 1 (Spring 1978): 131–43.

Ruether, Rosemary Radford, and Rosemary Skinner Keller, eds. *Women and Religion in America*. Vol. 3, *1900–1968*. San Francisco: Harper & Row, 1986.

Ryan, Mary P. *Cradle of the Middle Class: The Family in Oneida County, New York, 1790–1865*. Cambridge: Cambridge University Press, 1981.

Say, Elizabeth A. *Evidence on Her Own Behalf: Women's Narrative as Theological Voice*. Savage, Md: Rowman & Littlefield Publishers, 1990.

Scott, Anne Firor. *Making the Invisible Woman Visible*. Urbana and Chicago: University of Illinois Press, 1984.

– *Natural Allies: Women's Associations in American History*. Urbana and Chicago: University of Illinois Press, 1992.

Scott, Joan Wallach. *Gender and the Politics of History*. New York: Columbia University Press, 1989.

Semple, Neil. *The Lord's Dominion: The History of Canadian Methodism*. Kingston & Montreal: McGill-Queen's University Press, 1995.

Shook, Laurence K. *Catholic Post-Secondary Education in English-Speaking Canada: A History*. Toronto: University of Toronto Press, 1971.

Shore, Marlene. *The Science of Social Redemption*. Toronto: University of Toronto Press, 1987.

Sissons, C.B. *A History of Victoria University*. Toronto: University of Toronto Press, 1952.

Sklar, Kathryn Kish. *Catharine Beecher: A Study in American Domesticity*. New Haven, Conn.: Yale University Press, 1973.

Skultans, Vieda. "Mediums, Controls and Eminent Men." In *Women's Religious Experience*, ed. Pat Holden, 15–27. London: Croom Helm, 1983.

Smith, Waldo. *Albert College, 1857–1957*. Belleville: Albert College, 1957.

Smith-Rosenberg, Caroll. "The Female World of Love and Ritual." In *Disorderly Conduct*. New York: Oxford University Press, 1986.

Smyth, Elizabeth M. "The Lessons of Religion and Science: The Congregation of the Sisters of St. Joseph and St. Joseph's Academy Toronto, 1854–1911." EDD dissertation, University of Toronto, 1990.

– "'A Noble Proof of Excellence': The Culture and Curriculum of a Nineteenth Century Ontario Convent Academy." In *Gender and Education in Ontario*, eds. Ruby Heap and Alison Prentice, 273–94. Toronto: Canadian Scholar's Press, 1991.

Socknat, Thomas. *Witness against War: Pacifism in Canada, 1900–1945*. Toronto: University of Toronto Press, 1987.

Solomon, Barbara Miller. *In the Company of Educated Women*. New Haven, Conn.: Yale University Press, 1985.

– "The Oberlin Model and Its Impact on Other Colleges." In *Educating Men and Women Together*, ed. Carol Lasser. Urbana and Chicago: University of Illinois Press, 1987.

Sonser, Anna. "'A Respectable English Education': Innovation and Tradition in Literary Studies at Wesleyan Ladies' College (1861–1897)." *English Studies in Canada* 19, no. 1 (March 1993): 87–103.

Stamp, Robert M. "Teaching Girls Their 'God Given Place in Life': The Introduction of Home Economics in the Schools." *Atlantis* 2, part 2 (Spring 1977): 18–34.

Stapleford, Maude. "The Admission of Women to Victoria College." Unpublished paper, Victoria College, 1907.

Stewart, Lee. *"It's Up to You": Women at UBC in the Early Years*. Vancouver: University of British Columbia Press, 1990.

Strong-Boag, Veronica. "Canada's Women Doctor's: Feminism Constrained." In *A Not Unreasonable Claim: Women and Reform in Canada, 1880s–1920s*, ed. Linda Kealey, 109–29. Toronto: The Women's Press, 1979.

– *The New Day Recalled: Lives of Girls and Women in English Canada, 1919–1939*. Toronto: Copp Clark Pitman, 1988.

– *The Parliament of Women: The National Council of Women of Canada, 1893–1929*. History Division Paper, no. 18. Ottawa: National Museum of Man, National Museums of Canada, 1970.

Sweet, Leonard. "The Female Seminary Movement and Women's Mission in Antebellum America." *Church History* 54, no. 1 (March 1985): 41–55.

Taylor, James Monroe. *Before Vassar Opened*. Boston and New York: Houghton Mifflin Co., 1914.

Temple, Anna. "The Development of Higher Education for Women in Ontario." PHD dissertation, Wayne State University, 1977.

Theobald, Marjorie R. "Julie Vieusseux: The Lady Principal and Her School." In *Double Time: Women in Victoria – 150 Years*, eds. M. Lake and F. Kelly. Ringwood, Victoria: Penguin Books, 1985.

– "'Mere Accomplishments?' Melbourne's Early Ladies' Schools Reconsidered." *History of Education Review* 13, no. 2 (1984): 15–28.

– "Scottish Schoolmistresses in Colonial Australia." *Canadian History of Education Association Bulletin* 5, no. 3 (Oct. 1988): 1–17.

– "The Sin of Laura: The Meaning of Culture in the Education of Nineteenth-Century Women." *Journal of the Canadian Historical Association*, 1990, 257–71.

– "Women's Studies in Colonial Victoria." *Melbourne Studies in Education*, 1989–90, 14–34.

– and R.W.J. Selleck, eds. *Family, School and State in Australian History*. Sydney: Allen & Unwin, 1990.

Thomas, Hillah, and Rosemary Skinner Keller. *Women in New Worlds*. Nashville, Tenn.: Abingdon Press, 1981.

Thompson, Nancy. "The Controversy over the Admission of Women to University College." MA Thesis, University of Toronto, 1974.

Tyack, David, and Elisabeth Hansot. *Learning Together: A History of Coeducation in American Public Schools*. New Haven, Conn.: Yale University Press, 1990.

Valverde, Mariana. *The Age of Light, Soap, and Water: Moral Reform in English Canada, 1885–1925*. Toronto: McClelland & Stewart, 1991.

Van Die, Marguerite. "'The Double Vision': Evangelical Piety as Derivative and Indigenous in Victorian English Canada." In *Evangelicalism*, ed. Mark Noll, 253–72. New York: Oxford University Press, 1994.

– *An Evangelical Mind: Nathanael Burwash and the Methodist Tradition in Canada, 1839–1918*. Kingston, Montreal: McGill-Queen's University Press, 1989.

Vicinus, Martha. *Independent Women: Work & Community for Single Women, 1850–1920*. Chicago: University of Chicago Press, 1985.

Walford, Geoffrey, ed. *The Private Schooling of Girls*. London: Woburn Press, 1993.

Ware, Vron. *Beyond the Pale: White Women, Racism and History*. London: Verso, 1992.

Warne, R.R. *Literature as Pulpit: The Christian Social Activism of Nellie L. McClung*. Waterloo, Ont.: Wilfrid Laurier University Press, 1993.

Webster, Thomas. *Woman Man's Equal*. Cincinnati, Ohio: Hitchcock Walder; New York: Nelson and Philips, 1873.

Weeks, Jeffrey. *Sex, Politics, and Society: The Regulation of Sexuality since 1900*. London and New York: Longman, 1989.

Welch, Claude. *Protestant Thought in the Nineteenth Century*. Vol. 1, *1799–1870*. New Haven, Conn.: Yale University Press, 1972.

Welter, Barbara. "The Cult of True Womanhood, 1820–1960." *American Quarterly* 18 (Summer 1986): 151–74.

Westfall, William. *Two Worlds: The Protestant Culture of Nineteenth Century Ontario*. Kingston, Montreal: McGill-Queen's University Press, 1989.

Whitehead, John S. *The Separation of College and State: Columbia, Dartmouth, Harvard, and Yale, 1776–1876*. New Haven, Conn.: Yale University Press, 1973.

Williams, Perry. "Pioneer Women Students at Cambridge, 1869–81." In *Lessons for Life: The Schooling of Girls and Women, 1850–1950*, ed. Felicity Hunt. Oxford: Basil Blackwell, 1987.

Winter, Brian. *Vox Collegii Centennial, 1874–1974*. Whitby, Ont.: Ontario Ladies' College, 1974.

Woodhouse, T. Roy. *The History of the Town of Dundas*. Dundas, Ont.: Dundas Historical Society, 1968.

Woody, Thomas. *A History of Women's Education in the United States*. 2 vols. New York: Science Press, 1929.

Woolf, Virginia. *A Room of One's Own*. Middlesex, England: Penguin Books, 1928.

Youmans, Letitia. *Campaign Echoes: The Autobiography of Letitia Youmans*. Toronto: William Briggs, 1893.

Zainu'ddin, Ailsa G. Thomson. "'The Poor Widow, the Ignoramus and Humbug': An Examination of Rhetoric and Reality in Victoria's 1905 Act for the

Registration of Teachers and Schools." *History of Education Review* 13, no. 2 (1984): 29–42.

– *They Dreamt of a School: A Centennary History of Methodist Ladies' College Kew, 1882–1982*. Melbourne: Hyland House, 1982.

Zuber, Robert. "Learning, Work and Worship: F.D. Maurice." *Religious Education* 81, no. 4 (Fall 1986): 594–608.

Index